An Invitation to Reflexive Sociology

An Invitation to Reflexive Sociology

Pierre Bourdieu and Loïc J. D. Wacquant

The University of Chicago Press

The University of Chicago Press, Chicago 60637
The University of Chicago Press, Ltd., London
© 1992 by The University of Chicago
All rights reserved. Published 1992
Printed in the United States of America
10 09 08   7 8 9

ISBN (cloth): 0-226-06740-8
ISBN (paper): 0-226-06741-6

Library of Congress Cataloging-in-Publication Data

Bourdieu, Pierre.
    An invitation to reflexive sociology / Pierre Bourdieu
and Loïc J. D. Wacquant.
        p.   cm.
    Includes bibliographical references and index.
    ISBN 0-226-06740-8 (cloth). — ISBN 0-226-06741-6
(pbk.)
    1. Sociology. 2. Bourdieu, Pierre.   I. Wacquant,
Loïc J. D.   II. Title.
HM24.B669   1992
301—dc20   91-43725
                                                   CIP

❂ The paper used in this publication meets the minimum
requirements of the American National Standard for
Information Sciences—Permanence of Paper for Printed
Library Materials, ANSI Z39.48-1992.

Contents

Preface | Pierre Bourdieu

This book originates in my encounter with a group of doctoral students in sociology, anthropology, and political science at the University of Chicago who had organized, under the guidance of Loïc Wacquant, a semester-long seminar on my work. When I came to Chicago in the Spring of 1988, I was given in advance a long list of questions, observations, and objections at once meticulous, precise, and well grounded, and we discussed "toe-to-toe," in an atmosphere of great kindness, what are in my eyes the most fundamental issues of my research. The game of question and answer then continued and expanded in the form of interviews and dialogues held, over several months, in Chicago and Paris, with an always equally demanding and penetrating Loïc Wacquant.

When the idea was initially suggested of bringing together in book form the transcripts of these interviews, a few of which had already been published in part in various journals, I was undecided at first: was there not a certain self-complacency in thus offering in print semi-improvised statements and imperfectly crystallized reflections? At the same time, I had the feeling that, thanks especially to the organization and to the footnotes that Loïc Wacquant had given it, this extended dialogue provided a successful solution to the problem I had confronted for quite some time without finding a way of reconciling contradictory constraints: how to give an overview of the core intentions and results of my research that would be systematic yet accessible. I believe that the mixed genre that was progressively invented as we proceeded through this dialogue, marrying the shorthand formulations and liberties of oral discourse with the rigor of a body of notes linking this discourse to key elements of the written work, allows us to give a synthetic view of my fundamental concepts and of their relations without falling into the academic routinization of thought. Thus, instead of a simplistic and simplifying exposition, it should give interested readers a form of direct access to the generative principles of a work that is quite diverse both in its objects and its methods and, it may be confessed, not always very "pedagogical."

The questions that were put to me raised a whole continent of serious objections and criticisms. Friendly confrontation with the most advanced products of American social science forced me to explicate and to clarify presuppositions that the peculiarities of the French context had hitherto allowed me to leave in the state of implicit assumptions. It gave me an opportunity to display more fully the theoretical goals of my work, goals that I had till then kept somewhat in the background due to a mixture of scientific arrogance and modesty (hauteur et pudeur). The debates, shorn of aggressivity as well as of complacency, yet always candid and informed, I engaged in at various American universities during that stay, and which are now so cruelly lacking in the French university, were for me an extraordinary incitement to reflect upon my own work. Better, they helped me overcome the repugnance that I felt toward so many exercises in theoreticist exhibitionism in fashion in Paris and which inclined me to a quasi-positivist rejection of "grand" theory and "grand" discourse on grand theoretical and epistemological issues.

I must, before closing, ask for the reader's indulgence toward one of the effects, no doubt a very irritating one, of the very genre of the interview: he who is its object is put to the question, that is, *sur la sellette*, as we say in French, constituted as the focus of all gazes, and thus necessarily exposed to the temptation of arrogance and self-complacency. Abrupt statements, peremptory pronouncements, and simplifying assessments are the counterpart, perhaps inevitable, of the freedom granted by the situation of dialogue. The latter will have served its purpose if it has induced me to confess or to betray some of the weaknesses that lay behind many of my scientific choices.

I would like to extend my warm thanks to the students who participated in the initial workshop at the University of Chicago, among them, Daniel Breslau, Josh Breslau, Carla Hess, Steve Hughes, Matthew Lawson, Chin See Ming, Janet Morford, Lori Sparzo, Rebecca Tolen, Daniel Wolk, and Eunhee Kim Ti.

Preface | Loïc J. D. Wacquant

This book will likely disconcert consumers of standardized theoretical products and disappoint harried readers in search of a formulaic and simplified translation of Bourdieu's writings—a "manual in basic Bourdieuese." It does not contain a comprehensive digest of his sociology or a point-by-point exegesis of its conceptual structure; it is neither a primer nor an exercise in (meta)theory-building. It attempts, rather, to provide keys to the internal logic and broader economy of Bourdieu's work by explicating the *principles that undergird his scientific practice.*

The premise of *An Invitation to Reflexive Sociology* is that the enduring significance of Bourdieu's enterprise does not reside in the individual concepts, substantive theories, methodological prescriptions, or empirical observations he offers so much as in the manner in which he produces, uses, and relates them. To borrow an opposition dear to him, it is the *modus operandi* of Bourdieu's sociology, not its *opus operatum*, that most fully defines its originality. The purpose of this book, the rationale behind its peculiar architecture, is to give access to a "mind in action" by exemplifying what Weber (1949: 41) would call "the conventional habits" of Pierre Bourdieu as "investigator and teacher in thinking in a particular way."

The form of the book—an "oral publication"[1] consisting of a thematic dialogue and a spoken programmatic introduction to a research seminar—was tailored to fulfill this purpose. As a medium of scholarly communication, the interview has a number of well-known

---

1. Merton (1980: 3) argues for the cognitive value of "oral publication in the form of lectures, seminars, teaching laboratories, workshops and kindred arrangements."

drawbacks.[2] It runs the risk of granting ephemera the status of print, and of allowing for evasion, sophistry, and for the easy turning of questions. But, provided that a concerted effort is made to avoid these pitfalls, the interview form also has several unique advantages. First, it makes it possible to put forth provisional formulations, to suggest varying angles on an issue, and to essay different uses of a concept that can serve as so many bridges to a more complex and differentiated understanding of their purpose and meaning. Second, it facilitates quick, suggestive and efficient rapprochements, parallels, and counterpositions between object domains and operations that the normal organization of scientific work tends to disjoin and keep separate; this is particularly worthwhile when the thought in question covers empirical topics and draws on intellectual traditions as disparate and dispersed as does Bourdieu's. Third, by breaking with the authoritative or authoritarian, didactic cast of standard academic monologue (the *macros logos* of the Sophist in Plato), the interview permits the actual intervention of otherness, of critique, and thus of dialogics at the very heart of the text: by forcing the thinker to react to the thoughts of others, materialized by the interviewer (with whom the reader may identify when the questions interjected resonate with the ones he or she might want to raise), it compels him to reject self-closure into a historically limited language and intellectual tradition so as to locate himself in a wider semantic space. Fourth, and most importantly, a dialogue gives the reader a sense of the mental process whereby the author arrives at his or her positions; it is well suited to capturing a sociological method *in actu*. To sum up: an analytic interview shakes the author from a position of authority and the reader from a position of passivity by calling attention to the form of inquiry itself and by enabling them to communicate free of the censorship embedded in conventional forms of scholarly intercourse.

2. The interview is more common to the French academic universe, at least in its biographical mode, than it is to the American sociological field, where (positivistic) canons of scientific censorship strongly repress self-interrogation and presumably more "literary" media of scholarly presentation (see Wacquant 1989c). For instance, Raymond Aron (1981), Claude Lévi-Strauss (Lévi-Strauss and Eribon 1991), and Georges Dumézil (1987) have published intellectual self-portraits. In English, Foucault (1977b, 1980, 1988) and Habermas (1986) have discussed their work in the form of interviews. Bourdieu (1980b, 1987a) himself has published two collections of papers that include a number of interviews and oral presentations.

Rather than a summation or a summary, then, the present volume is an *invitation* to (re)think Bourdieu by thinking along with him. This means that it "is intended to be read, not studied," to steal a line from Peter Berger's (1966: 7) opening page to *An Invitation to Sociology.* It "delineates the world to which the reader is being invited, but it will be clear that the latter will have to go beyond this book if he decides to take the invitation seriously." It is a springboard into Bourdieu's work that will serve most profitably as a guide to his other writings and as a "tool box" (Wittgenstein) for posing and solving sociological problems.

An Invitation to Reflexive Sociology is divided into three independent parts that complement each other: the first is exegetical and the second primarily analytical, while the third takes off from the more concrete problems of sociological training.

Part 1 offers keys to the broader economy and inner logic of Bourdieu's work by sketching out the contours of his intellectual landscape and the structure of his theory of knowledge, practice, and society. In it, I dissect Bourdieu's proposed strategy to overcome the antinomy of objectivism and subjectivism—social physics and social phenomenology—and to construct a generative anthropology of (symbolic) power and of its manifold forms and mechanisms. Stressing his rejection of the duality of the individual and society, I explicate the methodological relationalism that informs his conceptualization of the dialectic of social and cognitive structures and also anchors his understanding of the ties between social theory and research. I conclude by stressing the distinctiveness of Bourdieu's conception of "epistemic reflexivity," showing its internal connection to his views on reason, morality, and politics—in short the regulative idea of the intellectual mission that underlies his practice.

Part 2, the Chicago Workshop, consists of a *constructed dialogue* in which Pierre Bourdieu clarifies the overall thrust of his theoretical and research practice, and reflects upon that practice in candid and accessible terms. The various sections review the principal results of his investigations published during the 1980s and highlight a number of *epistemic displacements* effected in his work: among others, from the sociology of academics to the sociology of the sociological eye; from structure to field; from norm and rule to strategy and habitus; from interest and rationality to *illusio* and "practical sense;" from language and culture to symbolic power; and from a transcendental to a historicist conception of scientific reason that aims at putting the instruments of social science to work for a politics of intellectual freedom. Together, they clarify Bourdieu's central concerns, his view of the relations of sociology to philosophy, economics, history, and politics, as well as the distinctive claims and intentions of his intellectual venture.

This interview is based on a series of discussions with Pierre Bourdieu conducted in French and in English over a period of three years in Chicago and Paris. Its nucleus comes from remarks made by Bourdieu in response to the participants to the Graduate Workshop on Pierre Bourdieu, an interdisciplinary group of doctoral students at the University of Chicago who spent the Winter Quarter of 1987/88 studying his work. These initial remarks were methodically expanded and complemented by written exchanges which I edited (and in part rewrote) into a unified text.

In articulating the questions and themes that organize this dialogue, I sought both to disentangle the central conceptual and theoretical nodes of Bourdieu's sociology and to address the recurrent objections and criticisms that the latter has met from its foreign readers. The interview was also designed to situate Bourdieu's key arguments vis-à-vis salient positions and issues in Anglo-American social science. Elaborations, qualifications, illustrations, and key references to his other writings (especially his post-*Distinction* work, much of which is yet untranslated) form the extended subtext of the footnotes, which I wrote.

Part 3, the Paris Workshop, is a slightly edited transcript of the introductory presentation made by Pierre Bourdieu to his graduate research seminar at the Ecole des hautes études en sciences sociales in the Spring of 1988. This annual seminar brings together some twenty to thirty students and researchers from a variety of disciplines (thence, in the particular case, the frequent references to linguistics and history), including a strong contingent of foreign scholars who come to Paris every year to study and work with Bourdieu. Former members of the workshop regularly present their research and act as informal mentors for the younger participants.

In this seminar, Bourdieu seeks to inculcate not a definite theory or a finite set of concepts but a *generalized disposition to sociological invention*. He does so by inverting the accepted order of pedagogy: his teaching proceeds from practice to axiomatics and from application back to principles, illustrating the fundamental epistemological rules that govern the construction of sociological objects in the very movement whereby he discusses them.[3] To counter the intellectualist bias inherent in the situation of academic training (and in keeping with his anti-intellectualist philosophy of practice), it builds incrementally from practical understanding to discursive mastery of the principles of sociological reason. Bourdieu advocates, and adopts, a total and self-referential pedagogy that steadfastly refuses the splintering of theoretical and research operations into isolated activities and territories whose separation serves only to reproduce the accepted—and forced—division of scientific labor of the day.

Whereas my role as interlocutor and editor was a very active one in the second part of the book, in the third part I stayed close to the original to retain the organic connection between the expository style and the substance of Bourdieu's pedagogic practice. Only minor modifications to the French original were made so as to convey the overall scientific posture that Bourdieu seeks to transmit through his own oral (and moral) stance, and to give the reader the vicarious experience of Bourdieu's teaching. Throughout the book, the term *sociologist* is employed to refer generically to practitioners of the various specialized social science disciplines. The use of masculine and feminine pronouns was alternated as much as possible, but potentially sexist language was not avoided altogether so as not to aggravate the burden of translation and the stylistic difficulty of the resulting text.

One of the hallmarks of a genuinely new, that is, *generative* way of thinking is its ability not only to transcend the circumscribed intellectual context and empirical terrain of its initial enunciation and to produce novel propositions, but to think itself and even to *out-think* itself. Bourdieu's work is not free of contradictions, gaps, tensions, puzzlements, and unresolved questions, many of which are openly acknowledged, and perhaps at times accentuated, in the pages that follow. It is free, however, from the urge to *normalize* sociological thinking.

Pierre Bourdieu is viscerally opposed to the dogmatization of

3. This movement is opposite to that effected in *The Craft of Sociology: Epistemological Foundations* (Bourdieu, Chamboredon, and Passeron 1973, trans. 1991), a book which the present volume complements and revises in numerous ways (see Bourdieu's remarks to that effect in the postface to *The Craft of Sociology*).

thought that paves the way for intellectual orthodoxies. A reflexive sociology which seeks to "effect the dissemination of weapons of defense against symbolic domination" (Bourdieu 1980b: 13) cannot, on pain of self-destruction, demand a closure of thought. Therefore an invitation to think with Bourdieu is of necessity an invitation to think beyond Bourdieu, and against him whenever required. This book will have reached its objective, then, if it serves as an *instrument of work* that readers adapt for purposes of their own concrete analyses. Which means that they should not be afraid, as Foucault (1980: 53–54) intimated of Nietzsche's thought, "to use it, to deform it, to make it groan and protest."

I

Toward a Social Praxeology:
The Structure and Logic of Bourdieu's Sociology

Loïc J. D. Wacquant

Getting hold of the difficulty *deep down* is what is hard. Because it is grasped near the surface it simply remains the difficulty it was. It has to be pulled out by the roots; and that involves our beginning to think in a new way. The change is as decisive as, for example, that from the alchemical to the chemical way of thinking. The new way of thinking is what is so hard to establish. Once the new way of thinking has been established, the old problems vanish; indeed, they become hard to recapture. For they go with our way of expressing ourselves and, if we clothe ourselves in a new form of expression, the old problems are discarded along with the old garment.

Ludwig Wittgenstein, Vermischte Bemerkungen

The wide-ranging work produced by Pierre Bourdieu over the past three decades has emerged as one of the most imaginative and fertile bodies of social theory and research of the postwar era. After a protracted period of incubation, its influence has risen steeply and expanded steadily—across disciplines, from anthropology, sociology, and education into history, linguistics, political science, philosophy, aesthetics, and literary studies; and geographically from France's continental neighbors to Eastern Europe, Scandinavia, Asia, Latin America, and the United States.[1] Bourdieu's near-encyclopedic *oeuvre*[2]

1. See appendix 3 for a broad sample of recent discussions of Bourdieu's sociology. Expository or critical books devoted to Bourdieu's work are now available in French (Snyders 1976, Accardo 1983, Collectif 'Révoltes Logiques' 1984, Caillé 1987, and Ansart 1990, among others), German (Eder 1989, Bohn 1990, Gebauer and Wulff, in press), Spanish (Sanchez de Horcájo 1979), Japanese (Yamamoto 1988), Swedish (Broady 1990), and English (Harker, Mahar, and Wilkes 1990; Robbins 1991; Calhoun, LiPuma, and Postone 1992; several more volumes in English are in the making). In the past two years, interdisciplinary conferences on Bourdieu's work have been held in the United States, Japan, Mexico, and Germany. Broady and Persson 1989 give bibliometric evidence of Bourdieu's growing readership in America showing a pronounced inflection around the turn of the 1980s. For illustrations of Bourdieu's impact in the different disciplines, see Ringer 1991, Rébérioux 1988, and Chartier 1988b for intellectual, social, and cultural history respectively; Hanks 1990, Woolard 1985, and Corson 1991 for anthropological linguistics; Ortner 1984, and Rosaldo 1989 for anthropology; Bon and Schemeil 1980, and Dobry 1986 for political science; Schatzki 1987, Derrida 1990, and Dreyfus 1991 for philosophy; Gamboni 1983a and 1989, Shusterman 1989, and Bürger 1990 for aesthetics; Terdiman 1985, and Viala 1988 for literary theory.

2. Bourdieu is author of some 25 books and approximately 260 articles (not including translations and collections in a dozen foreign languages ranging from Hungarian,

throws a manifold challenge at the current divisions and accepted modes of thinking of social science by virtue of its utter disregard for disciplinary boundaries, the unusually broad spectrum of domains of specialized inquiry it traverses (from the study of peasants, art, unemployment, schooling, law, science, and literature to the analysis of kinship, classes, religion, politics, sports, language, housing, intellectuals, and the state), and its ability to blend a variety of sociological styles, from painstaking ethnographic accounts to statistical models, to abstract metatheoretical and philosophical arguments.

More profoundly, though, the unsettling character of Bourdieu's enterprise stems from its persistent attempt to straddle some of the deep-seated antinomies that rend social science asunder, including the seemingly irresolvable antagonism between subjectivist and objectivist modes of knowledge, the separation of the analysis of the symbolic from that of materiality, and the continued divorce of theory from research (Bourdieu 1973c, 1977a, 1990a). In the course of this effort, Bourdieu was led to jettison two other dichotomies that recently claimed center stage in the theoretical forum, those of structure and agency on the one hand, and of micro- and macroanalysis on the other, by honing a set of conceptual and methodological devices capable of dissolving these very distinctions.[3] Oblivious to the vagaries

---

Arabic, and Japanese to Finnish, Dutch, and Serbo-Croatian). The bibliography at the end of this book contains a selection of his major publications with a special emphasis on those available in English.

3. See Giddens 1984, Alexander 1988, Sztompka 1991: 5–27, Sewell 1992, and Brubaker and Wacquant forthcoming, on the structure/agency problem, and Collins 1981b and 1987, and Alexander et al. 1987 on the micro-macro puzzle. For reasons that will become clearer below, it is erroneous to include Bourdieu among the proponents of "structuration theory," as do Münch (1989: 101), and Wiley (1990: 393). Structuration theory, as its progenitor emphasizes (Giddens 1990a: 310), is centrally concerned with issues of social ontology and conceptualization; the impetus behind Bourdieu's theoretical moves has always been a desire to grapple with new empirical objects, and he has evidenced little interest in refining a conceptual scheme. Moreover, Bourdieu's theory of practice predates Giddens' (1979, 1984) theory of structuration by at least a decade, and is rooted in a different set of philosophical questions (though recently Giddens [1986a] has fastened on the opposition of objectivism and subjectivism that forms the epicenter of Bourdieu's project). For a condensed statement of the dialectic of habitus and field, or position and dispositions, by which Bourdieu seeks to efface the micro/macro and agency/structure dilemmas, see Bourdieu 1980d and 1981c. Karp 1986: 132–34, Miller and Branson 1987, Coenen 1989, Harker et al. 1990, and Sewell 1992 discuss some of the differences and similarities between Giddens and Bourdieu.

of intellectual fashion, Bourdieu has steadfastly argued the possibility of a *unified political economy of practice*, and of symbolic power in particular, that effectively welds phenomenological and structural approaches into an integrated, epistemologically coherent, mode of social inquiry of universal applicability—an *Anthropologie* in the Kantian sense of the term, but one highly distinctive in that it explicitly encompasses the activities of the analyst who profers theoretical accounts of the practices of others (Bourdieu 1982a and 1988a).

Yet, paradoxically, this work so catholic and systematic in both scope and intent has typically been apprehended and incorporated in "bits and pieces." Garnham and Williams's (1980: 209) warning that "fragmentary and partial absorption of what is a rich and unified body of theory and related empirical work across a range of fields . . . can lead to a danger of seriously misreading the theory" has turned out prescient. If a selected number of his concepts (such as that of cultural capital) have been extensively, and often quite fruitfully, used by American social scientists working in specific areas of research or theorizing,[4] Bourdieu's work *in globo* is still widely misunderstood, and its overall economy and internal logic remain elusive. The confounding variety of interpretations, the mutually exclusive criticisms, and the contradictory reactions it has elicited testify to this, as does the fragmentation and truncation that has accompanied its transatlantic importation.

Thus, to simplify greatly, the assimilation of Bourdieu's writings in the English-speaking world has so far proceeded around three main nodes, each anchored by one of his major books.[5] Specialists in education gather around *Reproduction in Education, Society and Culture;* anthropologists concentrate on Bourdieu's ethnographies of Algeria and on the exposition of the theory of habitus and symbolic capital contained in *Outline of A Theory of Practice,* while sociologists of culture,

4. Among the most prominent users of the notion of "cultural capital" in America and Great Britain, one can list Alvin Gouldner (1979), Randall Collins (1979 and 1987), Cookson and Persell (1985a), Ivan Szelenyi (1988, also Martin and Szelenyi 1987), Paul DiMaggio (1982), Mike Featherstone (1987a and b), and John Urry (1990). For more recent examples see Eyerman, Svensson and Soderqvist 1987, Lareau 1987, Lamb 1989, Farkas et al. 1990, Katsilis and Rubinson 1990, Beisel 1990, and DiMaggio 1991a; consult Lamont and Lareau 1988 for a partial survey.

5. A more detailed and nuanced survey can be found in "Bourdieu in America: Notes on the Transatlantic Importation of Social Theory" (Wacquant 1992).

aesthetics, and class fasten on *Distinction* (Bourdieu and Passeron 1979; Bourdieu 1977a, 1984a). Each group of interpreters typically ignores the others, so that few have discerned the organic connections, theoretical and substantive, that link Bourdieu's wide-ranging inquiries into these and other domains. As a result, despite the recent flurry of translations and the now-extensive and fast-proliferating secondary literature that has burgeoned around his writings, Bourdieu remains something of an intellectual enigma.

By way of prolegomenon to the main body of the book, then, I propose to sketch in broad brushstrokes the central postulates and purposes that give Bourdieu's undertaking its overarching unity and thrust. To anticipate: based on a non-Cartesian social ontology that refuses to split object and subject, intention and cause, materiality and symbolic representation, Bourdieu seeks to overcome the debilitating reduction of sociology to either an objectivist physics of material structures or a constructivist phenomenology of cognitive forms by means of a genetic structuralism capable of subsuming both. He does this by systematically developing not a theory *stricto censu* so much as a sociological *method* consisting essentially in a manner of posing problems, in a parsimonious set of conceptual tools and procedures for constructing objects and for transfering knowledge gleaned in one area of inquiry into another.[6] "However important, the specific object of [this or that] research counts less indeed . . . than the method which was applied to it and which could be applied to an infinity of different objects" (Bourdieu and de Saint Martin 1982: 50)[7] because it is inscribed in the structures of a durable and transposable scientific habitus.[8]

6. "Sociology is the art of thinking phenomenally different things as similar in their structure and functioning and of transferring that which has been established about a constructed object, say the religious field, to a whole series of new objects, the artistic or political field and so on" (Bourdieu 1982a: 40–41).

7. Mary Douglas (1981: 163) finds that "the great interest of Bourdieu lies in his method." Broady's (1990) massive analysis of Bourdieu's work concludes that it does not offer a general theory of society but should instead be construed primarily as a theory of the formation of sociological knowledge which is homologous, in the space of the social sciences, to the tradition of historical epistemology (associated with the names of Bachelard, Canguilhem and Cavaillès) in the philosophy and history of the natural sciences and mathematics.

8. As Rogers Brubaker (1989a: 23) puts it: "One can most profitably read Bourdieu by treating the concepts, propositions, and theories set forth in his work not, in the

Two caveats are in order here. First, there is something of a contradiction, at minimum a strong tension, between Bourdieu's work and
the "photographic" mode of exposition of it adopted below. The former is one which is ever in progress; Pierre Bourdieu is endlessly re-
vising and revisiting the same Gordian knot of questions, objects, and
sites, as his recursive and spiraling mode of thinking unfolds over
time and across analytic space.[9] The linear technique of exposition
used in the following, on the other hand, tends to "freeze" this movement by artificially synchronizing formulations that correspond to different stages of Bourdieu's intellectual development and therefore
evince varying degrees of theoretical elaboration. Though the main
intentions and fault lines of Bourdieu's thought were firmly laid down
as early as the mid-1960s, there are still significant shifts, turns, and
breaks in his work that will be glossed over here as the internal dynamism of its theoretical structure is underplayed.[10]

Second, suggesting contrasts, parallels, or kinships between Bourdieu and salient positions in the field of British and American social
science may unwittingly encourage the very kind of hasty and reductionist readings that have often marred his importation into the latter
(see Wacquant 1992). The dialectic of familiarization and estrangement involved in the "translation" of intellectual products across the
boundaries of national fields has its risks. There is a fine line between
forced assimilation and illuminating homologies, a sensitive trade-off
between clarity and accessibility on the one hand, and faithfulness
and accuracy in form, content, and genealogy on the other. As a rule,
I have favored the former over the latter, trusting that the reader

---

first instance, as bearers of logical properties and objects of logical operations, but as
designators of particular intellectual habits or sets of habits. The more general and abstract the concept or proposition, the more important it is to read it in this dispositional
manner."

9. Harker et al. 1990 and Vervaeck 1989 point out how Bourdieu's thought progresses
in a spiral-like form.

10. For instance, within the same broad relational framework, anchored by the
pivotal distinction made in 1966 between "Class Condition and Class Position" (Bourdieu 1966), one can detect a notable evolution from earlier to later conceptions of class
as an historical construction rooted in social space (Bourdieu 1984a, 1985a, 1985b, 1987b,
1991d; see Eder 1989 for a discussion). Oftentimes, minute or seemingly cosmetic altera-
tions in vocabulary (from interest to *illusio*, from dominant class to field of power, from
cultural capital to informational capital, or, more recently, from habitus to *conatus*) signal important analytic refinements and changes.

will bear in mind that the significance of Bourdieu lies in the actual *movement* of his scientific practice, more so than in the synchronic account that an exegete, no matter how knowledgeable and skilled, can give of it.

1   Beyond the Antinomy of Social Physics and Social Phenomenology

The task of sociology, according to Pierre Bourdieu (1989a: 7), is "to uncover the most profoundly buried structures of the various social worlds which constitute the social universe, as well as the 'mechanisms' which tend to ensure their reproduction or their transformation." This universe is peculiar in that its structures lead, as it were, a "double life." [11] They exist twice: in the "objectivity of the first order" constituted by the *distribution* of *material* resources and means of appropriation of socially scarce goods and values (species of capital, in Bourdieu's technical language); and in the "objectivity of the second order," in the form of systems of *classification*, the mental and bodily schemata that function as *symbolic* templates for the practical activities—conduct, thoughts, feelings, and judgments—of social agents. Social facts are objects which are also the object of knowledge within reality itself because human beings make meaningful the world which makes them. [12]

A science of society thus understood as a bidimensional "system of relations of power and relations of meaning between groups and classes" [13] must of necessity effect a *double reading*. Or, to be more precise, it must craft a set of double-focus analytic lenses that capitalize on the epistemic virtues of each reading while skirting the vices of both. The first reading treats society in the manner of a *social physics*: as an objective structure, grasped from the outside, whose articula-

11. The notion of the "double objectivity" of society is given its fullest elaboration in Bourdieu 1990a (chapter 9, "The Objectivity of the Subjective"), 1984a (conclusion), and 1978d.

12. "Social science cannot 'treat social facts as things,' in accordance to the Durkheimian precept, without missing everything that they owe to the fact that they are objects of knowledge or recognition (if only of misrecognition) within the very objectivity of social existence" (Bourdieu 1990a: 135, my translation; see also Bourdieu 1989e and 1987b).

13. This is the definition of a "social formation" given in 1970 by Bourdieu and Passeron (1977: 5, my translation) in *Reproduction*.

tions can be materially observed, measured, and mapped out independently of the representations of those who live in it. The strength of this objectivist or "structuralist" point of view (epitomized by the Durkheim of *Suicide* and exemplified in France, at the moment when Bourdieu first delineates the central propositions of his theory, by Saussurian linguistics, Lévi-Straussian structuralism and, secondarily, by Althusserian Marxism) is in undermining the "illusion of the transparency of the social world."[14] Breaking with commonsense perceptions enables it to uncover the "determinate relations" within which men and women necessarily enter to "produce their social existence" (Marx). Thanks to the tools of statistics, ethnographic description, or formal modeling, the external observer can decode the "unwritten musical score according to which the actions of agents, each of whom believes she is improvising her own melody, are organized" (Bourdieu 1980b: 89) and ascertain the objective regularities they obey.

The chief danger of the objectivist point of view is that, lacking a principle of generation of those regularities, it tends to slip from model to reality—to reify the structures it constructs by treating them as autonomous entities endowed with the ability to "act" in the manner of historical agents. Incapable of grasping practice other than negatively, as the mere *execution* of the model built by the analyst, objectivism ends up projecting into the minds of agents a (scholastic) vision of their practice that, paradoxically, it could only uncover because it methodically set aside the experience agents have of it.[15] It thus destroys part of the reality it claims to grasp in the very movement whereby it captures it. Pushed to its limits, objectivism cannot but produce an ersatz subject, and portray individuals or groups as the passive supports of forces that mechanically work out their independent logic.

14. Bourdieu, Chamboredon, and Passeron (1973: 329–34) show that, beyond the differences that separate their theories of the social system, Marx, Durkheim and Weber converge in their theories of sociological knowledge. In particular, they all agree on the "principle of non-consciousness" which posits, against the "illusion of transparency" to which all members of society are spontaneously inclined, that social life is explained by causes irreducible to individual ideas and intentions. "If sociology as an objective science is possible," explains Bourdieu, it is because "subjects are not in possession of the totality of the meaning of their behavior as an immediate datum of consciousness and their actions always encompass more meaning than they know or wish" (Bourdieu et al. 1965: 18, my translation).

15. The "scholastic fallacy" that lies at the heart of the epistemology of structuralism is discussed in Bourdieu 1990a: 30–41, 1990e, and below, part 2, sec. 1.

Lest it fall into this reductionistic trap, a materialist science of society must recognize that the consciousness and interpretations of agents are an essential component of the full reality of the social world. True enough, society has an objective structure; but it is no less true that it is also crucially composed, in Schopenhauer's famed expression, of "representation and will" *(Darstellung und Wille)*. It matters that individuals have a practical knowledge of the world and invest this practical knowledge in their ordinary activity. "Unlike natural science, a total anthropology cannot keep to a construction of objective relations because the experience of meanings is part and parcel of the total meaning of experience" (Bourdieu et al. 1965: 20).[16]

The subjectivist or "constructivist" point of view (expressed in hyperbolic form by the Sartre of *Being and Nothingness* and best represented today by ethnomethodology in its culturalist variant and by certain strands of rational-choice theory in its rationalistic mode) attends to this "objectivity of the second order." In contrast with structuralist objectivism, it asserts that social reality is a "contingent ongoing accomplishment" of competent social actors who continually contruct their social world via "the organized artful practices of everyday life" (Garfinkel 1967: 11). Through the lens of this *social phenomenology*, society appears as the emergent product of the decisions, actions, and cognitions of conscious, alert individuals to whom the world is given as immediately familiar and meaningful. Its value lies in recognizing the part that mundane knowledge, subjective meaning, and practical competency play in the continual production of society; it gives pride of place to agency and to the "socially approved system of typifications and relevances" through which persons endow their "life-world" with sense (Schutz 1970).

But an unreconstructed phenomenology of social life suffers, according to Bourdieu, from at least two major flaws. First, conceiving social structures as the mere aggregate of individual strategies and acts of classification[17] makes it impossible to account for their re-

16. Put differently: "Knowledge of the social world must take into account a practical knowledge of this world which pre-exists it and which it must not fail to include in its object even though, as a first stage, it must be constituted *against* the partial and interested representations provided by this practical knowledge" (Bourdieu 1984a: 467, my translation).

17. Berger and Luckmann (1966: 48), typically, define social structure as "the sum total of [socially approved] typifications and of the recurrent patterns of interaction established by means of them." Blumer (1969) defends a kindred conception with his defi-

silence as well as for the emergent, objective configurations these strategies perpetuate or challenge. Neither can this kind of social marginalism explain why and according to what principles the work of social production of reality itself is produced. "If it is good to recall, against certain mechanistic visions of action, that social agents construct social reality, individually and also collectively, we must be careful not to forget, as the interactionists and the ethnomethodologists often do, that they have not constructed the categories they put to work in this work of construction" (Bourdieu 1989a: 47).

A total science of society must jettison *both* the mechanical structuralism which puts agents "on vacation" *and* the teleological individualism which recognizes people only in the truncated form of an "oversocialized 'cultural dope'" [18] or in the guise of more or less sophisticated reincarnations of *homo œconomicus*. Objectivism and subjectivism, mechanicalism and finalism, structural necessity and individual agency are false antinomies. Each term of these paired opposites reinforces the other; all collude in obfuscating the anthropological truth of human practice. [19] To transcend these dualities,

---

nition of society as "symbolic interaction," as does Garfinkel when he asserts that "organized social arrangements *consist of* various methods for accomplishing the accountability of a setting's organizational ways as a concerted undertaking" (1967: 33, my emphasis).

18. To combine two well-known expressions of Dennis Wrong (1961) and Harold Garfinkel (1967).

19. In anthropology, these oppositions crystallized in the 1960s and '70s in the polarized antagonism between symbolic anthropology (Geertz, Schneider, Victor Turner, Sahlins) and Lévi-Straussian structuralism (Leach, Needham, Mary Douglas) on the one side, and cultural ecology (Vayda, Rappoport, Marvin Harris) and political-economic and structural Marxist approaches (Eric Wolf, Maurice Bloch, Meillassoux, Godelier, Jonathan Friedman, June Nash) on the other. Sherry Ortner's (1984) recapitulation of the "acrimonious debates" of the 1960s among anthropologists brings out striking similarities with those that regularly pit proponents of objectivist and subjectivist brands of sociology (e.g., network theorists and symbolic interactionists, or human ecologists and advocates of postmodernist deconstruction in urban theory): "Whereas the cultural ecologists considered the symbolic anthropologists to be fuzzy-headed mentalists, involved in unscientific and unverifiable flights of subjective interpretation, the symbolic anthropologists considered cultural ecology to be involved with mindless and sterile scientism, counting calories and measuring rainfall, and willfully ignoring the one truth that anthropology had presumably established by that time: that culture mediates all human behavior. The Manichean struggle between 'materialism' and 'idealism,' 'hard' and 'soft' approaches, interpretive 'emics' and explanatory 'etics,' dominated the field" (see Bourdieu's [1987e] rejoinder to Ortner's article presenting a loosely defined "theory of practice" as the overcoming of this opposition).

Bourdieu turns what functions as the "world hypothesis" (Pepper 1942) of seemingly antagonistic paradigms into *moments* of a form of analysis designed to recapture the intrinsically double reality of the social world. The resulting *social praxeology*[20] weaves together a "structuralist" and a "constructivist" approach.[21] First, we push aside mundane representations to construct the objective structures (spaces of *positions*), the distribution of socially efficient resources that define the external constraints bearing on interactions and representations. Second, we reintroduce the immediate, lived experience of agents in order to explicate the categories of perception and appreciation *(dispositions)* that structure their action from inside. It should be stressed that, although the two moments of analysis are equally necessary, they are not equal: epistemological priority is granted to objectivist rupture over subjectivist understanding. Application of Durkheim's first principle of the "sociological method," the systematic rejection of preconceptions,[22] must come before analysis of the practical apprehension of the world from the subjective standpoint. For the viewpoints of agents will vary systematically with the point they occupy in objective social space (Bourdieu 1984a, 1989e).[23]

20. See the special issue of *Anthropologische Verkennungen* on Bourdieu's work as a praxeology (Coenen 1989, Mortier 1989, Verboven 1989, Vervaeck 1989).

21. Asked to label his work (in the context of a lecture at the University of California–San Diego in 1986), Bourdieu (1989e: 14) chooses the term "structuralist constructivism," which he immediately follows with the opposite designation of "constructivist structuralism" to stress the dialectical articulation of the two moments (objectivist and subjectivist) of his theory. Ansart (1990) identifies this aspect by the label of "genetic structuralism," as do Harker, Mahar, and Wilkes (1990: 3) with that of "generative structuralism."

22. Durkheim (1966: 32), it may be recalled, posited in *The Rules of the Sociological Method* that "the sociologist ought . . . , whether at the moment of the determination of his research objectives or in the course of his demonstrations, to repudiate resolutely the use of concepts originating outside of science for totally unscientific needs. He must emancipate himself from the fallacious ideas that dominate the mind of the layman; he must throw off, once and for all, the yoke of these empirical categories, which from long continued habit have become tyrannical."

23. Thus, if Bourdieu's vision of society can sometimes appear close to that of ethnomethodology or cognitive anthropology as practiced by Sturtevant or Goodenough (see the analysis of "Forms of Scholarly Classification" elaborated in *La noblesse d'Etat*), it is distinct from them in that it grounds the differential contents and *uses* of social taxonomies in the objectivity of material structures. However, this gap between Bourdieu and ethnomethodology has been narrowed by Aaron Cicourel (1990) who, in his recent work on communication processes, takes into account the underlying unequal distribution of cultural capital. For an interesting attempt to marry Garfinkel and Bour-

2   Classification Struggles and the Dialectic of Social and Mental Structures

A genuine science of human practice cannot be content with merely superimposing a phenomenology on a social topology. It must also elucidate the perceptual and evaluative schemata that agents invest in their everyday life. Where do these schemata (definitions of the situation, typifications, interpretive procedures) come from, and how do they relate to the external structures of society? This is where we encounter the second foundational hypothesis that anchors Bourdieu's (1989a: 7) sociology:

> There exists a correspondence between social structures and
> mental structures, between the objective divisions of the social
> world—particularly into dominant and dominated in the vari-
> ous fields—and the principles of vision and division that
> agents apply to it.

This, of course, is a reformulation and generalization of the seminal idea propounded in 1903 by Durkheim and Mauss (1963) in their classic study, "Some Primitive Forms of Classification." In that essay, the progenitor of the *Année sociologique* and his nephew argued that the cognitive systems operative in primitive societies are derivations of their social system: categories of understanding are collective representations, and the underlying mental schemata are patterned after the social structure of the group. Bourdieu extends the Durkheimian thesis of the "sociocentrism" of systems of thought in four directions. First, he argues that the correspondence between cognitive and social structures observed in traditional communities also obtains in advanced societies, in which their homology is for the most part produced by the functioning of school systems (Bourdieu 1967a).[24] Second, where

---

dieu, ethnomethodology and the theory of habitus, see Alain Coulon's (1991) study of the "practices of affiliation" of university students.

24. To be fair, Durkheim and Mauss did, in their analysis of Chinese thought (later pursued by Marcel Granet) and in the concluding section of their essay, suggest that the sociogenesis of ideas is operative in formations more advanced than the tribal societies of Australia and of the North American continent. But they did not apply their bold thesis to their own society, i.e., in particular, to their own thought. As Bourdieu (1982a: 10–11) points out, "the author of the 'Primitive Forms of Classification' never conceived the social history of the school system he proposed in 'The Evolution of Pedagogical Thought' as the genetic sociology of the categories of professorial understanding for which he nonetheless provided all the necessary tools."

Durkheim and Mauss's analysis lacked a sound causative mechanism for the social determination of classifications (Needham 1963: xxiv), Bourdieu proposes that social divisions and mental schemata are structurally homologous because they are *genetically linked:* the latter are nothing other than the embodiment of the former. Cumulative exposure to certain social conditions instills in individuals an ensemble of durable and transposable dispositions that internalize the necessities of the extant social environment, inscribing inside the organism the patterned inertia and constraints of external reality. If the structures of the objectivity of the second order (habitus) are the embodied version of the structures of the objectivity of the first order, then "the analysis of objective structures logically carries over into the analysis of subjective dispositions, thereby destroying the false antinomy ordinarily established between sociology and social psychology" (Bourdieu and de Saint Martin 1982: 47).[25] An adequate science of society must encompass both objective regularities and the process of internalization of objectivity whereby the transindividual, unconscious principles of (di)vision that agents engage in their practice are constituted.

Third, and most critically, Bourdieu submits that the correspondence between social and mental structures fulfills crucial political functions. Symbolic systems are not simply instruments of knowledge, they are also *instruments of domination* (ideologies in Marx's lexicon and theodicies in Weber's). As operators of cognitive integration they promote, by their very logic, the social integration of an arbitrary order: "The conservation of the social order is decisively reinforced by . . . the orchestration of categories of perception of the social world which, being adjusted to the divisions of the established order (and, therefore, to the interests of those who dominate it) and common to all minds structured in accordance with those structures, impose themselves with all appearances of objective necessity" (Bourdieu 1984a: 471, translation modified; see also 1971b). The socially consti-

---

Elsewhere, Bourdieu (1967a) writes, "The school system is one of the sites where, in differentiated societies, the systems of thought, which are the apparently more sophisticated equivalent of the 'primitive forms of classification,' are produced." This is the rationale behind Bourdieu's interest in education: his studies of the school system are chapters in a sociology of symbolic power defined as the power to impose and inculcate systems of classification that effect the naturalization of structures of domination (see especially Bourdieu 1989a, and Bourdieu and Passeron 1979: book 1).

25. For Connell (1983: 153), Bourdieu paves the way for a "realistic social psychology."

tuted classificatory schemes through which we actively construct society tend to represent the structures out of which they are issued as natural and necessary, rather than as the historically contingent fall-outs of a given balance of power between classes, "ethnic" groups, or genders.[26] But if we grant that symbolic systems are social products that contribute to making the world, that they do not simply mirror social relations but help *constitute* them, then one can, within limits, transform the world by transforming its representation (Bourdieu 1980g, 1981a).

It follows—this is the fourth way in which Bourdieu departs from the Durkheimian problematics—that systems of classification constitute a *stake in the struggles* that oppose individuals and groups in the routine interactions of daily life as well as in the solitary and collective contests that take place in the fields of politics and cultural production. In class-divided society, the social taxonomies (such as occupation or salary-scale) that organize the representation of groups are "at every moment produced by, and at stake in, the power relations between classes" (Bourdieu and Boltanski 1981: 149, translation modified).

Thus Bourdieu supplements the Durkheimian structural analysis with a *genetic and political* sociology of the formation, selection, and imposition of systems of classification. Social structures and cognitive structures are recursively and structurally linked, and the correspondence that obtains between them provides one of the most solid props of social domination. Classes and other antagonistic social collectives are continually engaged in a struggle to impose the definition of the world that is most congruent with their particular interests. The sociology of knowledge or of cultural forms is *eo ipso* a political sociology, that is, a sociology of symbolic power. Indeed, the whole of Bourdieu's work may be interpreted as a materialist anthropology of the

---

26. As Bourdieu (1987g: 234–35) puts it in his analysis of law: "The schemata of perception and appreciation which are at the root of our construction of the social world are produced by a collective historical labor but on the basis of the very structures of that world: as structured structures, historically constructed, our categories of thought *contribute* to producing the world, but only within the limits of their correspondence with pre-existing structures" (translation modified). Elsewhere: systems of classification "are not so much instruments of knowledge as instruments of power, subordinated to social functions and more or less openly geared to the satisfaction of the interests of a group" (Bourdieu 1984a: 477, translation modified).

specific contribution that various forms of symbolic violence make to the reproduction and transformation of structures of domination.

3 Methodological Relationalism

Against all forms of methodological monism that purport to assert the ontological priority of structure *or* agent, system *or* actor, the collective *or* the individual, Bourdieu affirms the *primacy of relations*. In his view, such dualistic alternatives reflect a commonsensical perception of social reality of which sociology must rid itself. This perception is embedded in the very language we use, which is "better suited to express things than relations, states than processes" (Bourdieu 1982a: 35). Norbert Elias (1978a: 113), another resolute advocate of the relational conception of the social, insists that ordinary language leads us to "draw involuntary conceptual distinctions between the actor and his activity, between structures and processes, or between objects and relations" that in effect prevent us from grasping the logic of social interweaving.[27] This linguistic proclivity to favor substance at the expense of relations is buttressed by the fact that sociologists are always competing with other specialists in the representation of the social world, and especially with politicians and media experts, who have a vested interest in such commonsense thinking. The opposition between the individual and society (and its translation into the antinomy of methodological individualism and structuralism) is one of those "endoxic propositions" that plague sociology because they are constantly reactivated by political and social oppositions (Bourdieu 1989f). Social science need not choose between these poles, for the stuff of social reality—of action no less than structure, and their intersection as history—lies in relations.

Bourdieu thus dismisses both methodological individualism and

---

27. The "process-reduction" characteristic of European languages (according to Benjamin Lee Whorf), and the reinforcement it receives from positivist philosophies of science, explain why "we always feel impelled to make quite senseless conceptual distinctions, like 'the individual *and* society,' which makes it seem that 'the individual' and 'society' were two separate things, like tables and chairs, or pots and pans" (Elias 1978a: 113; also 1987, part 1). The common root of Bourdieu's and Elias's stress on ordinary language as an obstacle to sociological thinking appears to be Cassirer, especially his analysis of "The Influence of Language Upon the Development of Scientific Thought" (Cassirer 1936).

holism, as well as their false transcendence in "methodological situationalism."[28] The relational perspective that forms the core of his sociological vision is not new. It is part and parcel of a broad, "polyphyletic and polymorphous" structuralist tradition that came to fruition in the postwar years in the work of Piaget, Jakobson, Lévi-Strauss, and Braudel, and that can be traced back to Durkheim and Marx (Merton 1975: 32).[29] Its most succinct and clearest expression was perhaps given by Karl Marx when he wrote in *Die Grundrisse* (1971: 77): "Society does not consist of individuals; it expresses the sum of connections and relationships in which individuals find themselves."[30] What is special about Bourdieu is the zeal and relentlessness with which he deploys such a conception, as evidenced by the fact that both of his key concepts of *habitus and field designate bundles of relations*. A field consists of a set of objective, historical relations between positions anchored in certain forms of power (or capital), while habitus consists of a set of historical relations "deposited" within individual bodies in the form of mental and corporeal schemata of perception, appreciation, and action.

In common with Philip Abrams, Michael Mann, and Charles Tilly, Bourdieu explodes the vacuous notion of "society" and replaces it with those of field and social space. For him, a differentiated society is not a seamless totality integrated by systemic functions, a common

28. Methodological individualism (a term coined by the economist Joseph Schumpeter) holds that all social phenomena are in principle explicable strictly in terms of the goals, beliefs and actions of individuals. Holism, in contrast, contends that social systems have emergent properties that cannot be derived from the properties of their component parts and that social explanation must start from the systemic level. Methodological situationalism takes the emergent properties of situated interaction as its core unit of analysis (Knorr-Cetina 1981: 7–15).

29. Bourdieu (1990a: 4; see also 1968b) credits structuralism for "having introduced into the social sciences the structural *method* or, more simply, the *relational* mode of thinking which, by breaking with the substantialist mode of thinking, leads us to characterize each element by the relations which unite it with all the others into a system from which it derives its meaning and function" (translation modified).

30. Bertell Ollman (1976: 14) has shown that "the relation is the irreducible minimum for all units in Marx's conception of reality. This is really the nub of our difficulty in understand Marxism, whose subject matter is not simply society but society conceived of 'relationally.'" The Japanese philosopher W. Hiromatsu has given a systematic and straightforwardly Cassirerian reading of Marx that highlights this (see the dialogue between Bourdieu, Hiromatsu and Imamura [1991]). For a sample of the structuralist tradition running from Marx to Lévi-Strauss, read DeGeorge and DeGeorge 1972.

culture, criss-crossing conflicts, or an overarching authority, but an ensemble of relatively autonomous spheres of "play" that cannot be collapsed under an overall societal logic, be it that of capitalism, modernity, or postmodernity. Much like Weber's *Lebensordnungen*, the economic, political, aesthetic, and intellectual "life-orders" into which social life partitions itself under modern capitalism (Gerth and Mills 1946: 331–59), each field prescribes its particular values and possesses its own regulative principles. These principles delimit a socially structured space in which agents struggle, depending on the position they occupy in that space, either to change or to preserve its boundaries and form. Two properties are central to this succinct definition. First, a field is a patterned system of objective forces (much in the manner of a magnetic field), a *relational configuration endowed with a specific gravity* which it imposes on all the objects and agents which enter in it. In the manner of a prism, it refracts external forces according to its internal structure:

> The effects engendered within fields are neither the purely additive sum of anarchical actions, nor the integrated outcome of a concerted plan. . . . It is the *structure* of the game, and not a simple effect of mechanical *aggregation*, which is at the basis of the transcendence, revealed by cases of inversion of intentions, of the objective and collective effect of cumulated actions.[31]

A field is simultaneously a *space of conflict and competition*, the analogy here being with a battlefield, in which participants vie to establish monopoly over the species of capital effective in it—cultural authority in the artistic field, scientific authority in the scientific field, sacerdotal authority in the religious field, and so forth—and the power to decree the hierarchy and "conversion rates" between all forms of authority in

31. Bourdieu (1987g: 248, translation modified). Thus what Samuelson calls "composition effects" and Boudon "counterintuitive effects" (two names for designating unintended consequences of action) are in fact *structural effects of fields* whose specific logic can and must be empirically uncovered in each particular case. For a demonstration of how the configuration of the field determines the ultimate effects of external forces and changes (morphological changes in particular), see Bourdieu 1987i, 1988a, 1987f, Bourdieu and de Saint Martin 1982, on the artistic field, the university field, the field of elite schools, and the religious field respectively. See Viala 1985, Fabiani 1989, and Charle 1990 for further historical illustrations.

the field of power.[32] In the course of these struggles, the very shape and divisions of the field become a central stake, because to alter the distribution and relative weight of forms of capital is tantamount to modifying the structure of the field. This gives any field a historical dynamism and malleability that avoids the inflexible determinism of classical structuralism. For instance, in his study of the local implementation of the housing policy of the French state in the 1970s, Bourdieu (1990b: 89) shows that even the "bureaucratic game," that is, the apparently inflexible organizational logic of public bureaucracies, allows for considerable uncertainty and strategic interplay. Any field, he insists, "presents itself as a structure of probabilities—of rewards, gains, profits, or sanctions—but always implies a measure of indeterminacy. . . . Even in the universe par excellence of rules and regulations, playing with the rule is part and parcel of the rule of the game."

So why is social life so regular and so predictable? If external structures do not mechanically constrain action, what then gives it its pattern? The concept of habitus provides part of the answer. Habitus is a *structuring mechanism* that operates from within agents, though it is neither strictly individual nor in itself fully determinative of conduct. Habitus is, in Bourdieu's words (1977a: 72, 95), "the strategy-generating principle enabling agents to cope with unforeseen and ever-changing situations . . . a system of lasting and transposable dispositions which, integrating past experiences, functions at every moment as a matrix of perceptions, appreciations and actions and makes possible the achievement of infinitely diversified tasks."[33] As the result of the internalization of external structures, habitus reacts to the solicitations of the field in a roughly coherent and systematic manner. As the collective individuated through embodiment or the biological individual "collectivized" by socialization, habitus is akin to the "intention in action" of Searle (1983: especially chapter 3)[34] or to the

32. Note that the field of power (see Bourdieu 1989a, Bourdieu and Wacquant 1991) is not situated on the same level as other fields (the literary, economic, scientific, state-bureaucratic, etc.) since it encompasses them in part. It should be thought of more as a kind of "meta-field" with a number of emergent and specific properties.

33. Habitus "expresses first the *result of an organizing action*, with a meaning close to that of words such as structure; it also designates a *way of being*, a *habitual state* (especially of the body) and, in particular, a *disposition, tendency, propensity,* or *inclination*" (Bourdieu 1977a: 214).

34. Mortier (1989) interprets Bourdieu's work as a redefinition of the structuralist problematic in an action-minded manner, leading to a formal praxeology that generalizes the theory of speech acts to comprise ritualistic conduct.

"deep structure" of Chomsky, except that, instead of being an anthropological invariant, this deep structure is a historically constituted, institutionally grounded, and thus socially variable, generative matrix (see Bourdieu 1987d). It is an operator of rationality, but of a practical rationality immanent in a historical system of social relations and therefore transcendent to the individual. The strategies it "manages" are systemic, yet ad hoc because they are "triggered" by the encounter with a particular field. Habitus is creative, inventive, but within the limits of its structures, which are the embodied sedimentation of the social structures which produced it.

Thus both concepts of habitus and field are relational in the additional sense that they function fully *only in relation to one another*. A field is not simply a dead structure, a set of "empty places," as in Althusserian Marxism, but a *space of play* which exists as such only to the extent that players enter into it who believe in and actively pursue the prizes it offers. An adequate theory of field, therefore, requires a theory of social agents:

> There is action, and history, and conservation or transformation of structures only because there are agents, but agents who are acting and efficacious only because they are not reduced to what is ordinarily put under the notion of individual and who, as socialized organisms, are endowed with an ensemble of dispositions which imply both the propensity and the ability to get into and to play the game. (Bourdieu 1989a: 59)

Conversely, the theory of habitus is incomplete without a notion of structure that makes room for the organized improvisation of agents. To understand just what this "social art" (Mauss) of improvisation consists of, we need to turn to Bourdieu's social ontology.

4   The Fuzzy Logic of Practical Sense

Bourdieu's philosophy of the social is monist in the sense that it refuses to establish sharp demarcations between the external and the internal, the conscious and the unconscious, the bodily and the discursive. It seeks to capture the intentionality without intention, the knowledge without cognitive intent, the prereflective, infraconscious mastery that agents acquire of their social world by way of durable immersion within it (this is why sports is of such theoretical interest to Bourdieu; see, for example, 1988f) and which defines properly human social practice. Drawing selectively on the phenomenologies of Husserl, Heidegger, and Merleau-Ponty, as well as on Wittgenstein's later philosophy, Bourdieu rejects the dualities—between body and mind, understanding and sensibility, subject and object, *En-soi* and *Pour-soi*—of Cartesian social ontology in order to "return to the social with which we are in contact by the mere fact of existing, and which we carry about inseparably with us before any objectification" (Merleau-Ponty 1962: 362). He builds in particular on Maurice Merleau-Ponty's idea of the intrinsic *corporeality of the preobjective contact between subject and world* in order to restore the body as the source of practical intentionality, as the fount of intersubjective meaning grounded in the preobjective level of experience. His is a structural sociology that incorporates a phenomenology of the "antepredicative unity of the world and our life" (Merleau-Ponty 1962: 61)[35] by treating the socialized body, not as an object, but as the repository of a generative, creative capacity to understand, as the bearer of a form of "kinetic knowledge" (Jackson 1983) endowed with a structuring potency.

The relation between the social agent and the world is not that between a subject (or a consciousness) and an object, but a relation of "ontological complicity"—or mutual "possession" as Bourdieu (1989a: 10) recently put it—between habitus, as the socially constituted principle of perception and appreciation, and the world which determines it. "Practical sense" operates at the preobjective, nonthetic level; it expresses this social sensitivity which guides us prior to our positing objects as such.[36] It constitutes the world as meaningful

35. "The body is in the social world but the social world is in the body" (Bourdieu 1982a: 38). Compare with Merleau-Ponty (1962: 401): "Inside and outside are wholly inseparable. The world is wholly inside and I am wholly outside myself." From this perspective, Bourdieu's project, however, is the exact opposite of that of interpretive sociology as defined by Ricoeur (1977: 158): "It is the task of interpretive sociology to ground . . . 'objectivity' in the preobjective layer of intersubjective experience *and* to show how the autonomy of the objects with which sociology deals proceeds from this preobjective sphere." For Bourdieu, sociology must subsume phenomenology not by pushing it aside, but by grounding intersubjectivity in historical objective structures via the genetic analysis of the constitution of habitus. By multiplying quotes from Merleau-Ponty to illustrate the logic of practical sense, I want to suggest that Bourdieu is his sociological heir, if one who innovates in ways that are sometimes incompatible with both the spirit and the letter of the phenomenologist's work. In particular, Bourdieu goes beyond the subjectivist apprehension of practical sense to investigate the social genesis of its objective structures and conditions of operation.

36. "As a person's fundamental, nonreflective familiarity with the world, habit is a precondition for the intentional determination of distinct objects of knowledge. . . .

by spontaneously anticipating its immanent tendencies in the manner of the ball player endowed with great "field vision" who, caught in the heat of the action, instantaneously intuits the moves of his opponents and teammates, acts and reacts in an "inspired" manner without the benefit of hindsight and calculative reason. Merleau-Ponty's (1963: 168–69) example of the soccer player is worth quoting extensively here because it expresses very clearly this "cohesion without concept" that guides our felicitous encounter with the world whenever our habitus matches the field in which we evolve.

> For the player in action the soccer field is not an "object," that is, the ideal term which can give rise to an indefinite multiplicity of perspectival views and remain equivalent under its apparent transformations. It is pervaded with lines of force (the "yard lines"; those which demarcate the "penalty area") and is articulated into sectors (for example, the "openings" between the adversaries) which call for a certain mode of action and which initiate and guide the action as if the player were unaware of it. The field itself is not given to him, but present as the immanent term of his practical intentions; the player becomes one with it and feels the direction of the "goal" for example, just as immediately as the vertical and the horizontal planes of his own body. It would not be sufficient to say that consciousness inhabits this milieu. At this moment consciousness is nothing other than the dialectic of milieu and action. Each maneuver undertaken by the player modifies the character of the field and establishes new lines of force in which the action in turn unfolds and is accomplished, again altering the phenomenal field.[37]

Neither programmed 'responses' nor routinized behaviors: habit is the embodied *sensitivity* to a sensitive world, and in this respect it provides for a field of behavioral possibilities in experience" (Ostrow 1990: 10).

37. One could also illustrate this immediate co-presence and mutual understanding of the body and the world with the famous example of the hammer given by Heidegger in *Being and Time*: competent use of a hammer presupposes both more and less than the conscious grasp of its instrumentality; it implies a mastery of its specific function *without* thematic knowledge of its structure. Empirical illustrations of such practical mastery are provided by Sudnow's (1978) ethnomethodological inquiry into the logic of jazz improvisation, Lord's (1960) analysis of the training of the *guslar* (Yugoslav bard) in the arts of poetic improvisation, Lave's (1989) anthropology of the uses of mathematics in

The "practical sense" *precognizes;* it reads in the present state the possible future states with which the field is pregnant. For in habitus the past, the present and the future intersect and interpenetrate one another. Habitus may be understood as virtual "sedimented situations" (Mallin 1979: 12) lodged inside the body that wait to be reactivated.[38] But the quote above is also of interest because it highlights two critical differences between Bourdieu's praxeology and Merleau-Ponty's theory of behavior. In the latter, there is no objective moment, and the soccer "field" remains a purely phenomenal form, grasped strictly from the standpoint of the acting agent.[39] This has the effect of blocking the investigation of the two-way relation between the subjectivist apprehension of the player and the underlying, objective configuration and rules of the game played. Again, as with Durkheimian objectivism, Merleau-Ponty's philosophy suffers from its inability to build a solid analytic link between internal and external structures, here between the sense of the game of the player and the actual constellation of the field. In addition, in soccer, the constraining regulations enforced by the referee are not the object of struggle, nor are the boundaries of the playground the subject of contention between teams (or between players and spectators who might want to enter the game). In short, Merleau-Ponty is silent on the twofold social genesis of the subjective and objective structures of the game.

It is important finally to emphasize that the lines of action engendered by habitus do not, indeed cannot, have the neat regularity of conduct deduced from a normative or juridical principle. This is because *"habitus is in cahoots with the fuzzy and the vague.* As a generative spontaneity which asserts itself in the improvised confrontation with endlessly renewed situations, it follows a *practical logic,* that of the fuzzy, of the more-or-less, which defines the ordinary relation to the world." Consequently, we should refrain from searching the productions of habitus for more logic than they actually contain: "the logic of practice is logical up to the point where to be logical would cease

---

everyday life, and by Wacquant's (1989a: 47–62) ethnography of the acquisition of boxing technique.

38. "Habits are our inherence in a field of time; through their functioning there is a concretion of past, present, and future" (Kestenbaum 1977: 91).

39. One must be careful here not to confuse Merleau-Ponty's notion of field, which merely denotes the soccer playground (*terrain* in French) and has no theoretical status, with Bourdieu's concept (*champ*).

being practical" (Bourdieu 1987a: 96).[40] The peculiar difficulty of sociology, then, is to produce a precise science of an imprecise, fuzzy, wooly reality. For this it is better that its concepts be polymorphic, supple, and adaptable, rather than defined, calibrated, and used rigidly.[41]

The concepts of habitus and field allow Bourdieu to forsake the false problems of personal spontaneity and social constraint, freedom and necessity, choice and obligation, and to sidestep the common alternatives of individual and structure, micro- (Blumer, Coleman) and macroanalysis (Blau, Skocpol)[42] that forces a polarized, dualistic social ontology: "One does not have to choose between structure and agents, between the field, which makes the meaning and value of the properties objectified in things or embodied in persons, and the agents who play with their properties in the space of play thus defined" (Bourdieu 1989a: 448), or between positions in a space of resources and the socialized urges, motives, and "intentions" of their occupants.

Just as he sidesteps the debate between microrationality and macrofunctionalism, Bourdieu rejects the alternative of submission and resistance that has traditionally framed the question of dominated cultures and which, in his eyes, prevents us from adequately understanding practices and situations that are often defined by their intrinsically double, skewed nature. If, to resist, I have no means other than to make mine and to claim aloud the very properties that mark me as dominated (according to the paradigm "black is beautiful"), in the manner of the sons of English proletarians proud to exclude themselves from school in the name of the ideal of masculinity borne by their class culture (Willis 1977), is that resistance? If, on the other hand, I work to efface everything that is likely to reveal my origins, or

40. See "The Devil of Analogy" (Bourdieu 1990b: 200–70) for a passionate argument against excessive logic and against the pursuit of anthropological coherence where it does not exist. As Don Levine (1985: 17) has argued, "the toleration of ambiguity can be productive if it is taken not as a warrant for sloppy thinking but as an invitation to deal responsibly with issues of great complexity."

41. To those who complain that his concepts are "blurred" (e.g., Joppke [1986: 61], who find that habitus is a "conceptual monster often applied in a blurred and metaphorical way"), Bourdieu could reply, with Wittgenstein (1980: 653), that "if a concept depends on a pattern of life, then there must be some indefiniteness in it."

42. The conceptual dyad of habitus and field also suggests a possible way out of the recurring aporias and built-in weaknesses of "role theory" (Wacquant 1990b).

to trap me in my social position (an accent, physical composure, family relations), should we then speak of submission? This, in Bourdieu's view, is an "unresolvable contradiction" inscribed in the very logic of symbolic domination. "Resistance can be alienating and submission can be liberating. Such is the paradox of the·dominated and there is no way out of it" (Bourdieu 1987a: 184).

But Bourdieu does not stop at pointing out the collaboration of the dominated to their own exclusion and subordination. He explains this collusion in a manner that avoids the naive psychologism or essentialism of La Boétie's "voluntary servitude." The solution to the riddle is given by an analysis of the historical genesis of the dispositions that "entrap" the dominated because, being homologous to the objective structures of the world of which they are issued, they render the bases of inequality literally invisible in their arbitrariness.

> If it is fitting to recall that the dominated always contribute to their own domination, it is necessary at once to be reminded that *the dispositions which incline them to this complicity are also the effect, embodied, of domination.* (Bourdieu 1989a: 12, my translation and emphasis)

Thus the submission of workers, women, minorities, and graduate students is most often not a deliberate or conscious concession to the brute force of managers, men, whites and professors; it resides, rather, in the unconscious fit between their habitus and the field they operate in. It is lodged deep inside the socialized body. In truth, it expresses the "somatization of social relations of domination" (Bourdieu 1990i).

It should be clear by now that those who understand Bourdieu's economy of practice as a generalized theory of economic determinism (e.g., Jenkins 1982, Honneth 1986, Caillé 1987a, Miller 1989, Gartman 1991) or, worse yet, as a variant of rational choice theory,[43] are victims of a twofold misreading of his sociology. First, they inject into the

---

43. The difference between Bourdieu and the latter is not whether agents make choices, as is sometimes argued by crude renderings of his perspective as a mechanical form of structuralism, as Van Parijs (1981), a proponent of "analytical Marxism," deplores. Bourdieu does not deny that agents face options, exert initiative, and make decisions. What he disputes is that they do so in the conscious, systematic, and intentional (in short, *intellectualist*) manner expostulated by rational-choice theorists. He insists to the contrary that deliberate decision making or rule following "is never but a makeshift aimed at covering up the misfirings of habitus" (Bourdieu 1972: 205).

concept of strategy the ideas of intentionality and conscious aiming, thereby transposing action *congruent* with, and potentially *actuated by,* certain "interests" into conduct rationally organized and deliberately directed toward clearly perceived goals.[44] Second, they restrict the historically variable notion of interest, understood as a socially constituted concern for, and desire to play, given social games, to an invariant propensity to pursue economic or material gain.[45] This double reduction, the intentionalist and the utilitarian, hides the paradoxical analytical movement that Bourdieu effects by means of the conceptual triad of habitus, capital, and field, which consist in *expanding the sphere of interest while reducing that of utility and consciousness.*

Bourdieu is at pains to emphasize that his economy of practice is neither intentionalist nor utilitarian. As argued above, he is staunchly opposed to the finalism of philosophies of consciousness that situate the mainspring of action in the voluntaristic choices of individuals. By strategy, he refers not to the purposive and preplanned pursuit of calculated goals (as does Coleman [1986]), but to the active deployment of objectively oriented "lines of action" that obey regularities and form coherent and socially intelligible patterns, even though they do not follow conscious rules or aim at the premeditated goals posited by a strategist.[46] With the concept of interest—a notion he has of late increasingly come to replace by that of *illusio* and, more recently still, by that of *libido*—Bourdieu seeks to do two things. First to break with

44. Thus, for Lash and Urry (1987: 293), "Bourdieu's central claim is that we consume not products but symbols with *the intention* of establishing distinctions" (my emphasis; see also Elster 1984a). Zuckerman (1988: 519) similarly reads Bourdieu's sociology of science as an analysis of "the *self-interest and calculations* of how best to survive the competition for resources and rewards" (my emphasis).

45. One example of this utilitarian reduction: according to Ory and Sirinelli's (1986: 229) interpretation of *Homo Academicus,* Bourdieu "concludes that career strategies and, more broadly, extra-ethical interests predominate over scientific and moral rationales, within a universe of conflicts flattened by multiple exchanges of favors and cascading networks of domination." Another illustration is Wippler's (1990) reduction of embodied cultural capital to "a special kind of human capital" à la Becker, which in effect destroys the logic of Bourdieu's theoretical architecture.

46. See Bourdieu's (1979d) analysis of strategies of honor for an empirical illustration. This conception of "strategy without a strategist" is not unlike Foucault's (see Dreyfus and Rabinow 1983: 187), except that the latter lacks the dispositional concept of habitus to link the objective structures bequeathed by history to the historical practices of agents and, therefore, a mechanism to account for the social patterning and objective meaning of strategies.

the "enchanted" vision of social action that clings to the artificial frontier between instrumental and expressive or normative behavior and refuses to acknowledge the various forms of hidden, nonmaterial profits that guide agents who appear "disinterested." Secondly, he wants to convey the idea that people are motivated, driven by, torn from a state of in-difference and moved by the stimuli sent by certain fields—and not others. For each field fills the empty bottle of interest with a different wine. A middle-class academic who has never been in a ghetto gym or attended fights in a small club can hardly, on first look, grasp the pugilistic interest *(libido pugilistica)* that leads subproletarian youngsters to value and willfully enter into the self-destructive occupation of boxing. Conversely, a high-school dropout from the inner city cannot apprehend the reason behind the intellectual's investment in the arcane debates of social theory, or his passion for the latest innovations in conceptual art, because he has not been socialized to give them value. People are "pre-occupied" by certain future outcomes inscribed in the present they encounter only to the extent that their habitus sensitizes and mobilizes them to perceive and pursue them. And these outcomes can be thoroughly "disinterested" in the common sense of the term, as can readily be seen in the fields of cultural production, this "economic world reversed" (Bourdieu 1983d, 1985d) where actions aimed at material profit are systematically devalued and negatively sanctioned. In other words,

> To break with economism in order to describe the universe of possible economies is to eschew the alternative of purely material and narrowly economic interest and of *disinterestedness*. It is to give ourselves the means of satisfying the principle of sufficient reason which demands that there be no action without a *raison d'être*, that is, without interest, or, if one prefers, without *investment in a game and in a stake, illusio, commitment*. (Bourdieu 1990a: 290, translation modified)

5   Against Theoreticism and Methodologism: Total Social Science

From this relational and anti-Cartesian conception of its subject matter, it follows that sociology must be a *total science*. It must construct "total social facts" (Mauss)[47] that preserve the fundamental unity of

47. "Total social facts" are facts that "set into motion in some cases the totality of society and its institutions . . . and in others a very large number of institutions" be-

human practice across the mutilating scissures of disciplines, empirical domains, and techniques of observation and analysis. This is the reason behind Bourdieu's opposition to premature scientific specialization and to the detailed division of labor it entails: habitus endows practice with a systematicity and an internal connectedness that cuts across these divides; social structures correspondingly perpetuate or transform themselves *undivided,* in all their dimensions simultaneously. This is best seen when studying the strategies of reproduction or conversion that groups develop to maintain or improve their position in an evolving class structure (Bourdieu and Boltanski 1977; Bourdieu 1974a, 1978b, and 1984a: 99–168). These strategies form a system *sui generis* that cannot be grasped as such unless one methodically connects realms of social life that are normally treated by separate sciences and with disparate methodologies. In the case of the ruling class examined in *La noblesse d'Etat* (The State Nobility, Bourdieu 1989a: 373–420), these involve fertility, education, prophylaxis, economic investment and patrimonial transmission, strategies of social investment (of which matrimonial strategies are a pivotal element) and, lastly, strategies of sociodicy which seek to legitimize their domination and the form of capital on which it rests. Although they are not the product of a deliberate strategic intention (even less, of a collective conspiracy), these strategies stand in objective relations of temporal succession, intergenerational interdependence, and functional solidarity such that only a totalization of knowledge can elucidate their internal coherence and external articulations. As soon as we recognize the underlying unity of social strategies and apprehend them as a dynamic totality, we can discern

> how artificial the ordinary oppositions between theory and research, between quantitative and qualitative methods, between statistical recording and ethnographic observation, between the grasping of structures and the construction of individuals can be. These alternatives have no function other than to provide a justification for the vacuous and resounding abstractions of theoreticism and for the falsely rigorous observations of

---

longing to the juridical, religious, economic, aesthetic, and morphological orders (Mauss 1950c: 274–75). This concept is useful in suggesting the need to shed narrow, rigidly compartmentalized observational approaches, but can itself become dangerous when it fosters a kind of loose "holism" used as a cover for lack of rigorous construction of the object.

positivism, or, as the divisions between economists, anthropologists, historians and sociologists, to legitimize the limits of *competency:* this is to say that they function in the manner of a *social censorship,* liable to forbid us to grasp a truth which resides precisely in the *relations* between realms of practice thus arbitrarily separated. (Bourdieu and de Saint Martin 1978: 7)

In light of this conception, it is not hard to see why Bourdieu decries the two opposed, yet complementary, forms of involution that currently plague social science: "methodologism" and "theoreticism." *Methodologism* may be defined as the inclination to separate reflection on methods from their actual use in scientific work and to cultivate method for its own sake. Bourdieu sees in "methodology," conceived as a distinct specialty severed from the workaday carrying-out of research, a form of *academicism* which, by falsely abstracting (*ab-trahere* means to separate) method from object, reduces the problem of the theoretical construction of the latter to the technical manipulation of empirical indicators and observations. Forgetting that "methodology is not the preceptor or the tutor of the scientist" but "always his pupil" (Schutz 1970: 315), such methodological fetishism is condemned to dress up preconstructed objects in the garb of science and risks inducing scientific myopia: "The sophistication of techniques of observation and proof can, if it is not accompanied by a redoubling of theoretical vigilance, lead us to see better and better fewer and fewer things" (Bourdieu et al. 1973: 88).[48] Indeed, it can turn into "art for art's sake" or, worse, into methodological imperialism, i.e., the forced definition of objects by existing techniques of analysis and data sets at hand (e.g., Rossi 1989). Methodology then carries over into an implicit theory of the social which makes researchers act in the manner of the late-night drunk evoked by Kaplan (1964) who, having lost the keys to his house, persists in searching for them under the nearest lamp post because this is where he has the most light. It is not the technical sophistication of methodological tools that Bourdieu criticizes but their mindless refinement to fill the vacuum created by the absence of theoretical vision.[49]

48. Bourdieu echoes a warning sounded by Mills (1959: 71–72) some thirty years ago: "Those in the grip of methodological inhibition often refuse to say anything about modern society unless it has been through the fine little mill of The Statistical Ritual."

49. Notwithstanding obvious differences in vocabulary and tone, there are numerous affinities between Bourdieu's position and the "in-house" critique of methodologism put forth by Stanley Lieberson (1984) in *Making It Count.*

The origins of Bourdieu's stance vis-à-vis methodology lie in his initial practical training as an anthropologist cum sociologist. Very early in his career, he developed a simultaneous and intimate familiarity with the methods of ethnography and statistical analysis. His first field experiences as a largely self-taught anthropologist and his collaboration with statisticians from INSEE in Algeria during 1958–62 (and later with mathematical statisticians from the school of "French data analysis") combined to give him an ingrained dislike for methodological monism or absolutism. Thus he openly asserts his "absolute rejection of the sectarian rejection of this or that method of research" (Bourdieu 1989a: 10).[50] It also convinced him that the practical organization and carrying out of data collection—or, to be accurate, data production—are so intimately bound up with the theoretical construction of the object that they cannot be reduced to "technical" tasks left to hired underlings, survey bureaucracies, or research assistants.[51] The conventional hierarchy of the tasks that make up the trade of the social scientist is but a *social* hierarchy ultimately rooted in a series of homologous and mutually reinforcing oppositions between high and low, mind and body, intellectual and physical labor,

50. Bourdieu (1989a: 10) continues: "The most elementary techniques of the sociology of science would suffice to establish that the denunciations that certain ethnomethodologists throw at sociologists, purely and simply identified with one manner, no doubt dominant in the American establishment, of conceiving social science, owe their mobilizing potency to the fact that they enable many sociologists to convert into an elective refusal certain deficiencies of their training. It would likewise reveal that the scorn of many methodologists for anything that strays in the slightest manner from the narrow canons they have erected as an absolute measure of rigor often serves to mask the routinized platitude of a practice devoid of imagination and almost always bereft of what no doubt constitutes the true precondition of true rigor: the reflexive critique of research techniques and procedures."

51. As is frequently the case in large-scale research projects in the United States, where graduate students can turn out to be the only ones to have any direct contact with the object of research of the professors they work for. By contrast, to this day, Bourdieu conducts much of the field observation, interviewing, and technical analysis that go into his writings himself. The account of the organization and implementation of the massive study (through surveys, in-depth interviews, ethnography, archival recollection) of elite schools that he and his collaborators conducted in the 1960s and 1980s (Bourdieu 1989a: 331–51) gives a very good idea of the practical translation of Bourdieu's principle of methodological vigilance. For a very interesting empirical study of the huge discrepancies, created by the social distance between (quantitative) methodologists and interviewers, between what the former think is done in a survey and what the latter actually do in the field in the main French survey institute, see Peneff 1988; see Merllié 1983 for another illustration. In France, Jean-Michel Chapoulie, Do-

the scientist who "creates" and the technician who "applies" routine procedures. This hierarchy is devoid of epistemological justification and must therefore be jettisoned.

Now, the methodological polytheism Bourdieu preaches and practices does not mean that "anything goes," as in the epistemological anarchism (or Dadaism) of a Feyerabend, but rather that, as Auguste Comte taught us long ago,[52] the array of methods used must fit the problem at hand and must constantly be reflected upon *in actu*, in the very movement whereby they are deployed to resolve particular questions. The upshot of Bourdieu's attack on "methodology" is clear: one cannot disassociate the construction of the object from the instruments of construction of the object and their critique.

Like method, theory properly conceived should not be severed from the research work that nourishes it and which it continually guides and structures. Just as he rehabilitates the practical dimension of practice as an object of knowledge, Bourdieu wishes to recover the practical side of theory as a knowledge-producing activity. His writings amply testify that he is not inimical to theoretical work. What he stands poised against is theoretical work done for its own sake, or the *institution* of theory as a separate, self-enclosed, and self-referential realm of discourse—what Kenneth Burke (1989: 282) labels "logology," that is, "words about words." Bourdieu has little time for such *conspicuous theorizing*, freed from connection to the practical constraints and realities of empirical work, and he shows little sympathy for the "splitting of Concepts and their endless rearrangement" (Mills

minique Merllié, Laurent Thévenot, and Alain Desrosières have critically analyzed the production of bureaucratic statistics from a standpoint influenced by Bourdieu.

52. "Method," writes Comte in the first volume of his *Cours de philosophie positive* (this quote opens Bourdieu's *Le métier de sociologue*) "is not liable to be studied apart from the research in which it is employed; or if it is, such a study is only a dead study (*étude morte*), incapable of inseminating the mind which devotes itself to it. Everything that can be said about it, when it is considered abstractly, is reduced to generalities so vague that they could have no influence on the intellectual regime." This is also one of the teachings of Georges Canguilhem's history of medical science, which exerted an important formative impact on Bourdieu's epistemology. In the United States, Abraham Kaplan (1964: 12) has advocated a kindred position by emphasizing the distinction between "reconstructed logic" and "logic-in-action": "The normative power of [reconstructed] logic does not necessarily improve logic-in-action," first because reconstructed logic focuses on what the scientist does *not* do at the expense of what he or she actually does; secondly, because it tends to idealize, as opposed to describe, scientific practice.

1959: 23) that defines much of contemporary theorizing, not to mention "metatheorizing."[53] His own relation to concepts is a pragmatic one: he treats them as "tool kits" (Wittgenstein) designed to help him solve problems. But this pragmatism does not open the door to rampant conceptual eclecticism (as in the "analytical theorizing" defended by Jonathan Turner [1987]), for it is anchored in, and disciplined by, the limited set of theoretical postulates and substantive concerns outlined in the foregoing.

Pierre Bourdieu will perhaps appear unduly harsh to many in his criticism of what he calls "theoreticist theory" (see below, part 2, section 5). In part, this is in reaction to a proximate intellectual environment that has traditionally rewarded philosophical and theoretical proficiency while nourishing strong resistance to empiricism (though the opposition between a "theoreticist Europe" and an "empiricist United States" nowadays owes more to a combination of scholarly stereotyping and cultural lag than to informed comparison). In the United States, where "instrumental positivism" has ruled virtually unchallenged since the 1940s (Bryant 1985) and where the interface between sociology and philosophy has been brittle at best, "theoreticians" may fulfill a more positive function by forcing the field to acknowledge its repressed pole. However, in recent years, the revival and autonomous development of theory (Giddens and Turner 1987; Alexander 1988: especially 89–93; Ritzer 1990b) has augmented the gap between pure thinkers and those who are often referred to in derision as "number crunchers."[54] As Sica (1989: 227) remarks: "The two cultures are well entrenched in sociology and neither seems likely to

53. Ritzer's (1990a) effort to "codify and solidify metatheory" (as the attainment of deeper understanding of theory, the creation of new theory or the development of overarching theoretical perspectives) characteristically proceeds in complete and deliberate seclusion from the real world and from the concerns of research. Bourdieu's conception of the relation of theory and research thus differs also from that of Giddens (1990a: 310–11; also 1989) who insists on the "relative autonomy" of theory from research and defends the value of conceptual and ontological work per se. Alexander (1987a, 1990) offers another energetic defense of the centrality of "generalized theoretical discourse."

54. Today, the sociological profession appears so organized in the United States that, to be recognized as a "theorist," it seems well-nigh mandatory to *not* conduct empirical research and to concentrate on writing exclusively recondite terminological treatises on concepts and other theories. Stinchcombe (1986: 44–45) has pointedly expressed the link between the level of abstraction of discourse, or its remoteness from the vulgarities of the real world, and the professional (or professorial) standing of theo-

give up any territory, despite the ritualized hope for theoretically informed research that is first sounded in graduate school and continues to the grave."[55]

In Bourdieu's view, the foibles of contemporary social theory do
not originate in what Jeffrey Alexander diagnoses as the "failure" to
achieve "presuppositional generality" and "multidimensionality" but
in a *social division of scientific labor* which splits, reifies, and compart-
mentalizes moments of the process of construction of the sociological
object into separate specialties, thereby rewarding the "audacity without rigor" of social philosophy and the "rigor without imagination" of
hyperempiricist positivism. While he would *in principle* likely support
their stated intent, Bourdieu believes that social theory has little to
expect from ventures in "theoretical logic" that are not grounded in a
concrete research practice. To call attention to the "dangers of conflation in scientific argument," to stress the "importance of multidimen-
sional thought at the most general presuppositional level" of action
and order, and to celebrate the "relative autonomy" of metaphysical,
methodological, and empirical commitments (Alexander 1980–82,
vol. 3: xvi) is all well and good. It remains a rhetorical exercise as long
as it is not part of a reflection on "actually existing" scientific practice
aimed at changing its *social organization*.[56]

---

rist: "it is the theories that are most divorced from blood, sweat and tears that have the
highest prestige."

55. Sica (1989: 230) adds: "Examine the journals most esteemed by members of the
guild with an eye toward which bodies of ideas, loosely called 'theory,' are connected,
even rhetorically, with sets of data and the requisite methods for reputable results. . . .
Most of these articles are *either openly theoryless* . . . or, *worse, cosmetically theoretical*"
(my emphasis). Randall Collins (1988: 494), another keen observer of the American
sociological scene, likewise reports that "there is considerable hostility between what is
seen as the methodological-quantitative side of the field and the theoretical-qualitative
side. Moreover, practitioners of one or another specialty tend to inhabit different intellectual networks, and hence to condemn each other's position *in absentia*, without
knowing much about it." Coleman (1990b: chap. 1) also notes the continuing and deep-
ening split between theory and research (though his diagnosis of its roots is quite
different).

56. "Max Weber reminds us that, in the art of warfare, the greatest progress originated, not in technical inventions, but in transformations of the social organization of
the warriors, as for instance with the case of the invention of the Macedonian phalanx.
One may, along the same line, ask whether a transformation of the social organization
of scientific production and circulation and, in particular, of the forms of communication and exchange through which logical and empirical control is carried out, would

Like his disciplined methodological pluralism, Bourdieu's rejection of the theory/research split finds its root in the intersection of his social trajectory, his primary scientific habitus and the peculiar conjuncture in which the latter was forged and initially tested, and which acted to exacerbate his sensitivity to the most elementary scientific operations. Reflecting upon his early field studies in Algeria at the end of the 1950s, Bourdieu (in Honneth, Kocyba, and Schwibs 1986: 39, translation modified) explains:

> I wanted to be useful in order to overcome my guilty conscience about being merely a participant observer in this appalling war. . . . This more or less unhappy integration into the intellectual field may well have been the reason for my activities in Algeria. I could not be content with reading left-wing newspapers or signing petitions; I had to do something as a scientist. . . . I could not be satisfied with just reading books and visiting libraries. In a historical situation in which at every moment, in every political statement, every discussion, every petition, the whole reality was at stake, it was absolutely necessary to be at the heart of events so as to form one's opinion, however dangerous it might have been—and dangerous it was. To see, to record, to photograph: I have never accepted the separation between the theoretical construction of the object of research and the set of practical procedures without which they can be no real knowledge.

Technological wizardry and conceptual logomachy that hide the lack of rigorous construction of the object and the adoption of commonsense conceptions do little to advance the *"empirical* science of concrete *reality"* of which Weber (1949: 72) spoke. Indeed, beyond their antagonism, methodological inhibition and the fetishism of concepts can conspire in the organized abdication of the effort to explain existing society and history.[57]

---

not be capable of contributing to the progress of scientific reason in sociology, and this more powerfully than the refinement of new technologies of measurement or the endless warnings and 'presuppositional' discussions of epistemologists and methodologists" (Bourdieu 1989f).

57. Similarly, for Mills (1959: 75), Grand Theory and abstracted empiricism "may be understood as insuring that we do not learn too much about man and society—the first by formal and cloudy obscurantism, the second by formal and empty ingenuity."

It is important to stress that Bourdieu does not call for more "interplay" between theory and research à la Merton. For the author of *Social Theory and Social Structure*, "there is two-way traffic between social theory and empirical research. Systematic empirical materials help advance social theory by imposing the task and by affording the opportunity for interpretation along lines often unpremeditated, and social theory, in turn, defines the scope and enlarges the predictive value of empirical findings by indicating the conditions under which they hold" (Merton 1968: 279). This formulation takes for granted, accepts as an incontestable given of sociological practice the scientific "apartheid" between the theorist and the survey researcher characteristic of American sociology in the postwar era (and personified, at the time when Merton wrote this essay, by the towering figures of Parsons and Lazarsfeld)[58] and reinforced by the current bureaucratic organization of academia and the rewarding of specialized competencies.[59] Instead of a continued separation between these two poles, mitigated only by intensified interaction, Bourdieu advocates the *fusion* of theoretical construction and practical research operations. He does not seek to connect theoretical and empirical work in a tighter

58. And evidenced by the division of Merton's (1968: chaps. 4 and 5) exposition into two mirror-image chapters, "The Bearing of Sociological Theory on Empirical Research," and "The Bearing of Empirical Research on Sociological Theory."

59. Alan Sica (1989: 228, 230, 231) remarks on the total absence of theoretical concerns among researchers: "Those who court the riches of routine research cannot afford to misallocate their attention by lingering over verbal complexity. They must manage their time and energy well, so if tedious theorizing cannot aid them adroitly in improving efficiency and productivity, however measured, it is either diluted to more manageable form or jettisoned altogether. . . . For the workaday sociologist some years out of graduate school and in determined pursuit of grants, the relationship between theory (or "ideas") and the other components of a successful grant application are not very troubling. . . . Everybody knows that the first question, *primus inter pares*, is how to get money for research. . . . After all, technique is saleable . . . mostly in the interest of grant-seeking, we eviscerate ourselves."

This is particularly visible in a sector of the sociological field such as poverty research which is simultaneously dominated scientifically (it is an intellectual backwater where theories and approaches long discredited in the more advanced regions of the field—for example, "culture of poverty," normative concepts of action, or moral concern for "social pathology"—still guide research and policy prescriptions, much as they survive in mass-produced undergraduate textbooks) and dominant in terms of academic power (it commands massive funding and is much in favor with scientific bureaucracies: witness the recent epidemic of programs of research on the "urban underclass" financed by various prominent foundations).

manner but to *cause them to interpenetrate each other* entirely. And this argument is not a plea *pro domo* tailored to elevate Bourdieu's own competency to the status of a universal yardstick of excellence but, rather, recognition of the immanent structure of "actually existing" social scientific practice which does, whether it wishes to acknowledge it or not, continually blend concept and percept, reflection and observation.[60]

Bourdieu maintains that every act of research is simultaneously empirical (it confronts the world of observable phenomena) and theoretical (it necessarily engages hypotheses about the underlying structure of relations that observations are designed to capture). Even the most minute empirical operation—the choice of a scale of measurement, a coding decision, the construction of an indicator, or the inclusion of an item in a questionnaire—involves theoretical choices, conscious or unconscious, while the most abstract conceptual puzzle cannot be fully clarified without systematic engagement with empirical reality. The most ethereal of theorists cannot afford not to "sully his hands with empirical trivia" (Bourdieu 1984a: 511). To be sure, theory will always retain a degree of epistemic primacy because, to speak like Bachelard in *The New Scientific Spirit* (1984: 4), the "epistemological vector" goes "from the rational to the real."[61] But to admit the priority of theory entails no contradiction here, since Bourdieu's understanding of theory itself is not logocentric but practical: for him, theory inheres not in discursive propositions but in the generative dispositions of the scientific habitus.[62]

60. "Any work of science, no matter what its point of departure, cannot become fully convincing until it crosses the boundary between the theoretical and the experimental" (Bachelard 1984: 3–4). On this point, see also Quine (1969).

61. "If the operations of practice are worth what the theory which founds them is worth, it is because theory owes its position in the hierarchy of operations to the fact that it actualizes the epistemological primacy of reason over experience" (Bourdieu, Chamboredon, and Passeron 1973: 88).

62. See below, part 2, sec. 5, and Brubaker (1989a). That Bourdieu's theory is the product of an active, working, scientific habitus makes it especially unsuitable for theoreticist readings or conceptual exegesis (yet another difference between his "method" and Giddens' structuration theory). For an example of how such theoreticist interpretation of Bourdieu's work can disfigure it, see Wallace (1988), who manages to read *into* it a theory of norms and of psychical contagion, and a concern for the dialectic of social and cultural structures construed as separable causal-explanatory variables in a hyperpositivist vein. Their nonlogocentric character also explains why Bourdieu has not exhibited the "obsessive preoccupation" with achieving unambiguous meaning in his

6   Epistemic Reflexivity

If there is a single feature that makes Bourdieu stand out in the landscape of contemporary social theory, it is his signature obsession with
reflexivity. From his early investigations of marriage practices in the
isolated village of the Pyrenees mountains where he was raised (Bourdieu 1962b, 1962c) to the hunt for *Homo academicus gallicus* (Bourdieu
1988a), the tribe he joined as a result of his upward social climb, Bourdieu has continually turned the instruments of his science upon himself—if in a manner not always immediately perceptible to some of his
readers. His analysis of intellectuals and of the objectifying gaze
of sociology, in particular, like his dissection of language as an instrument and arena of social power, imply very directly, and in turn rest
upon, a self-analysis of the sociologist as cultural producer and a reflection on the sociohistorical conditions of possibility of a science of
society (Wacquant 1990a).

Yet Bourdieu is neither the first nor the only social theorist to invoke the idea of reflexivity. Indeed, there are more than a few claims
to "reflexive sociology" floating about,[63] and, left without further
specification, the label is vague to the point of near vacuity. What
does the return (*re-flectere* means "to bend back") of science upon itself entail? What is its focus, how is it to be effected, and for what
purposes? I will argue that Bourdieu's brand of reflexivity, which may
be cursorily defined as the inclusion of a theory of intellectual practice
as an integral component and necessary condition of a critical theory
of society, differs from others in three crucial ways. First, its primary
target is not the individual analyst but the *social and intellectual unconscious* embedded in analytic tools and operations; second, it must be a
collective enterprise rather than the burden of the lone academic; and,
third, it seeks not to assault but to *buttress the epistemological security of
sociology*. Far from trying to undermine objectivity, Bourdieu's reflex-

---

concepts or the concern for specification, quantification, and elucidation characteristic
of Merton's theory of the middle range (Sztompka 1986: 98–101).

63. Among others, those of Garfinkel and ethnomethodology, of the "ethnography
as text" current in anthropology (Clifford, Marcus, Tyler, etc.), of strands in the "social
studies of science" led by David Bloor and Steve Woolgar, of advocates of
"postmodern" sociology such as Platt and Ashmore, and of Alvin Gouldner, Bennett
Berger, Anthony Giddens, and critical phenomenologist John O'Neill. The various
meanings and uses of reflexivity in science, the arts, and the humanities have been in-
ventoried by Malcom Ashmore (1989: chap. 2) in his "Encyclopedia of Reflexivity and

ivity aims at increasing the scope and solidity of social scientific knowledge, a goal which puts it at loggerheads with phenomenological, textual, and other "postmodern" forms of reflexivity (Platt 1989, Woolgar 1988).

Conceptions of reflexivity range from self-reference to self-awareness to the constitutive circularity of accounts or texts. Bloor (1976: 5), for instance, equates reflexivity with disciplinary self-reference when he writes: "in principle, [the] patterns of explanation [of the sociology of knowledge] would have to be applicable to sociology itself." In Bennett Berger's view (1981, 1991), reflexivity promotes self-awareness and serves to establish role distance (in the Goffmanesque sense) between the ethnographer-as-member-of-society and the ethnographer-as-analyst so as to undercut any noncognitive cathexis of the object. Taking cue from Riesman's *The Lonely Crowd*, Berger (1981: 222) defines reflexivity "as a psychological step or two beyond other-direction and role-taking because its distinctive preoccupation is with making those processes problematic; it attempts to cope with one's consciousness of the consequences of other-direction and role-taking in oneself [so as to] approach that dream of social science: the utterly detached observer." For ethnomethodologists (Garfinkel 1967, Cicourel 1974), reflexivity, along with "indexicality," is a key constituent property of social action, a "problematic phenomenon" woven into the fabric of the organized activities of everyday life. By that they mean that social action has to be accountable, as people universally and necessarily deploy "ethno-methods" to give sense to the practices of the daily round, and that accounts and reality are therefore mutually constitutive of one another.[64] Giddens (1984, 1987, 1990b), in turn, refers to reflexivity in all three senses and with three referents: agency, science, and society. Subjects are said to be reflexive insofar as they are "concept-bearing animals" who possess the capacity to "turn back upon" and monitor their own actions. Social science is reflexive in the sense that the knowledge it generates is "injected" back into the reality it describes.[65] Finally, society can be said to be reflexive as it

---

Knowledge" (though the self-consciously "innovative" and "outrageously inventive" [*sic*] form he gives to his inventory often muddies the notion more than it clarifies it).

64. On the distinction between endogenous and referential reflexivity in ethnomethodology, see the interesting piece by Pollner (1991); see also Collins 1988: 278–82.

65. "Social science tends to 'disappear' into the environment it is about . . . [and] has a very powerful impact upon the very constitution of that environment" (Giddens

evolves the capacity to control and program its own development (what Touraine puts under the notion of historicity).[66] What is missing from all these conceptions is the idea of reflexivity as a *requirement and form of sociological work*, that is, as an epistemological program in action for social science, and as a corollary a theory of intellectuals as the wielders of a dominated form of domination.

The distinctiveness of such a program may be highlighted by counterposing Bourdieu's conception of reflexivity with that of Alvin Gouldner (see also Friedrichs 1970 and O'Neill 1972 for kindred conceptions). For the author of *The Coming Crisis of Western Sociology* (Gouldner 1970: 483), Reflexive Sociology starts with the "very primitive assumption that theory is made by the praxis of men in all their wholeness and is shaped by the lives they lead." Calling for conscious self-referencing, it centers on the "sociologist's knowledge of himself and his position in the social world" (ibid., 489); in a manner akin to a prophetic practice (*vide* Gouldner's capitalization of the term), it aims at making a new cultural producer capable of generating a politically liberating sociology.[67] Like Berger, Gouldner makes the private person, the "I" of the sociologist, the pivot of reflexivity—both its object (or target) and its carrier.[68] Bourdieu acknowledges this concern; uncovering the social and personal pulsions that the analyst invests in his or her research is commendable and necessary. But he finds that it comes well short of identifying the key filters that alter sociological

---

1987: 197). This conception of the "double hermeneutic" is akin to a generalized version of Bourdieu's notion of the "theory-effect."

66. More recently, Giddens (1990b: 36–45, citation on p. 38) has made reflexivity, defined as "the fact that social practices are constantly examined and reformed in the light of incoming information about those very practices, thus constitutively altering their character," a defining property of modernity.

67. "The historical mission of a Reflexive Sociology . . . would be to *transform* the sociologist, to penetrate deeply into his daily life and work, enriching them with new sensitivities, and to raise the sociologist's self-awareness to a new historical level" (Gouldner 1970: 489).

68. "Reflexivity requires an 'I' and no apologies are needed" says Berger (1981: 220–21, also 236–39). The "roots of sociology pass through the sociologist as a total man," and "the question he must confront, therefore, is not merely how to *work* but how to *live*," echoes Gouldner (1970: 489). This quasi-messianic, existential transformation gives way to a kind of epistemic communalism when Gouldner (ibid.: 494) proclaims that we must "increasingly recognize the depth of our kinship with those whom we study . . . all men are basically akin to those we usually acknowledge as professional 'colleagues.'"

perception. For it ignores those limits of knowledge specifically associated with the analyst's membership and position in the intellectual field.[69]

To be more precise, Bourdieu suggests that three types of biases may blur the sociological gaze. The first is the one singled out by other advocates of reflexivity: the *social* origins and coordinates (class, gender, ethnicity, etc.) of the individual researcher. This is the most obvious bias and thus the more readily controlled one by means of mutual and self-criticism. The second bias is much less often discerned and pondered: it is that linked to the position that the analyst occupies, not in the broader social structure, but in the microcosm of the *academic* field, that is, in the objective space of possible intellectual positions offered to him or her at a given moment, and, beyond, in the field of power. The points of view of sociologists, like any other cultural producer, always owe something to their situation in a field where all define themselves in part in relational terms, by their difference and distance from certain others with whom they compete. Social scientists are furthermore situated near the dominated pole of the field of power and are therefore under the sway of the forces of attraction and repulsion that bear on all symbolic producers (Bourdieu 1971d, 1988a, 1989a).

But it is the third bias that is most original to Bourdieu's undertanding of reflexivity. The *intellectualist bias* which entices us to construe the world as a *spectacle,* as a set of significations to be interpreted rather than as concrete problems to be solved practically, is more profound and more distorting than those rooted in the social origins or location of the analyst in the academic field, because it can lead us to miss entirely the *differentia specifica* of the logic of practice (Bourdieu 1990a, 1990e). Whenever we fail to subject to systematic critique the "presuppositions inscribed in the fact of thinking the world, of retiring from the world and from action in the world in order to think that action" (Bourdieu 1990e: 382), we risk collapsing practical logic into

---

69. Gouldner (1970: 512) does warn "that it is not only forces external to intellectual life but also those *internal* to its own organization and embedded in its distinctive subculture, that are leading it to betray its own commitments." But instead of calling for an analysis of those "internal" factors (even loosely and narrowly defined in terms of "subculture"), he immediately goes on to flagellate "the acacemician and the university" for being "themselves active and willing agents in the dehumanizing of this larger world."

theoretical logic.[70] Given that these presuppositions are built into concepts, instruments of analysis (genealogy, questionnaires, statistical techniques, etc.), and practical operations of research (such as coding routines, "data cleaning" procedures, or rules of thumb in fieldwork), reflexivity calls less for intellectual introspection than for the permanent sociological analysis and control of sociological practice (Champagne et al. 1989).

For Bourdieu, then, reflexivity does not involve reflection *of* the subject *on* the subject in the manner of the Hegelian *Selbsbewusstsein*[71] or of the "egological perspective" (Sharrock and Anderson 1986: 35) defended by ethnomethology, phenomenological sociology, and Gouldner. It entails, rather, the systematic exploration of the "unthought categories of thought which delimit the thinkable and predetermine the thought" (Bourdieu 1982a: 10), as well as guide the practical carrying out of social inquiry. The "return" it calls for extends beyond the experiencing subject to encompass the organizational and cognitive structure of the discipline. What has to be constantly scrutinized and *neutralized, in the very act of construction of the object,* is the collective scientific unconscious embedded in theories, problems, and (especially national) categories of scholarly judgment (Bourdieu 1990j). It follows that the subject of reflexivity must ultimately be the social scientific field *in toto.* Thanks to the dialogic of public debate and mutual critique, the work of objectivation of the objectivating subject is carried out not by its author alone but by the occupants of all the antagonistic and complementary positions which constitute the scientific

70. "The incapacity of both philosophy and social science to comprehend practice . . . lies in the fact that, just as in Kant reason locates the principle of its judgments not in itself but in the nature of its objects, so the scholarly thinking of practice includes within practices the scholarly relation to practice" (Bourdieu 1983a: 5). In a recent address, Bourdieu (1990e: 382) goes as far as to propose that "there is a sort of incompatibility between our scholarly thinking and this strange thing that practice is. To apply to practice a mode of thinking which presupposes the bracketing of practical necessity and the use of instruments of thought constructed against practice . . . is to forbid ourselves from understanding practice as such." The epitome of this intellectualist fallacy is represented by Rational Action theory (e.g., Coleman 1986, Elster 1984a) which reifies its hyperrationalistic models of action and "injects" them into the minds of agents, thereby foreclosing an investigation of the actual *practical* rationality immanent in their conduct (Wacquant and Calhoun 1989: 47, 53–54).

71. Thus I disagree with Scott Lash (1990: 259), for whom "Bourdieu's reflexivity seems to be rather closer to this type."

field. If the latter is to produce and to reward reflexive scientific habituses, it must in effect institutionalize reflexivity in mechanisms of
training, dialogue, and critical evaluation. Correspondingly, it is the
social organization of social science, as an institution inscribed in
both objective and mental mechanisms, that becomes the target of
transformative practice.

Bourdieu clearly does not partake of the "mood of interpretivist
skepticism" (Woolgar 1988: 14) that fuels the "textual reflexiveness"
advocated by those anthropologists who have recently grown infatu-
ated with the hermeneutic process of cultural interpretation in the
field and with the (re)making of reality through ethnographic inscrip-
tion.[72] He is a merciless critic of what Geertz (1987: 90) has nicely
christened the "diary disease," for genuine reflexivity is not produced
by engaging in *post festum* "Reflections on Fieldwork" à la Rabinow
(1977); nor does it require the use of the first person to emphasize empathy, "difference" (or *différance*) or the elaboration of texts that situate the individual observer in the act of observation. "Rather it is
achieved by subjecting the *position* of the observer to the same critical
analysis as that of the constructed object at hand" (Barnard 1990: 75).[73]
It is not, as Rabinow (1977: 162) claims, Weberian "webs of significance" which separate the ethnographer from the native, but their
social condition, i.e., their differential distance to the necessity immanent to the universe under examination (Bourdieu 1990a: 14). It is
not the individual unconscious of the researcher but the epistemological unconscious of his discipline that must be unearthed: "What [has]
to be done [is] not magically to abolish this distance by a spurious
primitivist participation but to objectivize this objectivizing distance

72. Over the past decade, these "postmodern" anthropologists contend, the critique of colonialism and theorizing about the limits of representation (especially deconstruction) have undermined the authority of ethnographic accounts and revealed
ethnographies as rhetorical performances, "inescapably contingent, historical, and
contestable" representations whose persuasiveness and plausibility ultimately rests on
literary conventions (Clifford and Marcus 1986). Textual reflexivity refers to the notion
that "texts do not simply and transparently report an independent order of reality" but
are themselves "implicated in the work of reality-construction" (Atkinson 1990: 7). See
Spencer 1989 for a critical survey, and Marcus and Cushman 1982, Clifford and Marcus
1986, Geertz 1987, Tyler 1987, and Van Maanen 1988 for samples.

73. Barnard (1990: 58, 71) argues that Bourdieu "has shown how ethnography can be
reflexive without being narcissistic or uncritical" and offers "a way out of the cul-de-sac
that ethnographers and theorists of ethnography have created for themselves."

and the social conditions which make it possible, such as the externality of the observer, the techniques of objectivation he uses, etc." (Bourdieu 1990a: 14, translation modified).[74]

Bourdieu's quasi-monomaniacal insistence on the necessity of the reflexive return is thus not the expression of a sort of epistemological "sense of honor" but a principle that leads to constructing scientific objects differently. It helps produce objects in which the relation of the analyst to the object is not unwittingly projected, and that do not suffer the adulteration introduced by what he has, after John Austin, labeled the "scholastic fallacy" (Bourdieu 1990e). Bourdieu makes this plain in a discussion of the shift from "rule" to "strategy" which demarcates his views from those of Lévi-Straussian structuralism:[75]

> The change in the theory of practice provoked by theoretical
> reflection on the theoretical point of view, on the practical
> point of view and on their profound differences, is not purely

74. The gulf between epistemic and textual reflexivity is evident upon constrasting the main conclusions of Rabinow's *Reflections on Fieldwork in Morocco* and Rosaldo's *Culture and Truth* with Bourdieu's (1990a) preface to *The Logic of Practice*. Rabinow's return on his field experiences center on the Self in his intercourse with the Other and on the moral dimension implicit in the act of penetrating a foreign cultural universe. Fastening on the interaction of observation and participation, they evidence a nagging concern for "authenticity," leading to the conclusion that "all cultural facts are interpretations, and multivocal ones, and that is true for both the anthropologist and for his informant" (Rabinow 1977: 151). Similarly, for Rosaldo (1989: 169, 194, 206–7), "social analysts should explore their subjects from a number of positions," especially when individuals "belong to multiple, overlapping communities. . . . Social analysis thus becomes a relational form of understanding in which both parties actively engage in the 'interpretation of cultures.'" Bourdieu rejects this conflation of the interpretations of the ethnographer with those of the native, and has no interest in "authenticity." Rather than join Rosaldo (1989: 69) in trumpeting the banality that "no observer is either innocent nor omniscient," he wants to theorize the limits of anthropological knowledge.

Rabinow never considers the distortion implied in the disjuncture between his hermeneutic intent and the practical concerns of his informants. His revelation of fieldwork as "a process of intersubjective construction of liminal modes of communication" (Rabinow 1977: 155) indicates that, like Rosaldo, he has fallen into the scholastic trap of seeing the anthropologist and the native as jointly involved in interpretation (though passages of his narration evince a fleeting awareness that they "conceptualized [him] as a resource" in their own practical strategies, Rabinow [1977: 29] perceives his informants mainly as friends who are there to assist him in a hermeneutical task).

75. For an insightful comparison of Bourdieu's and Lévi-Strauss's anthropology and of their correlative conceptions of ethnographic practice, see Barnard 1990. For a comparison of Bourdieu with Geertz, see Lee 1988.

speculative: it is accompanied by a drastic change in the practical operations of research and by quite tangible scientific profits. For instance, one is led to pay attention to properties of ritual practice that structuralist logicism would incline to push aside or to treat as meaningless misfirings of the mythical algebra, and particularly to polysemic realities, underdetermined or indeterminate, not to speak of partial contradictions and of the fuzziness which pervade the whole system and account for its flexibility, its openness, in short everything that makes it "practical" and thus geared to respond at the least cost (in particular in terms of logical search) to the emergencies of ordinary existence and practice. (1990e: 384)

It is worth dwelling on this point, for it is this switch in perspective—i.e., the inclusion, at the heart of a theory of practice, of a theory of theoretical practice—that made possible Bourdieu's discovery of the logic of practice, just as he was led to ponder the specificity of theoretical logic by the empirical anomalies that the latter was stubbornly turning up in his field material (Bourdieu 1990a: 11–14). Here we come full circle and see how Bourdieu's understanding of reflexivity is of a piece with his conception of the interpenetration of theory and research. It is by laboring to puzzle out, empirically, down to the tiniest detail, all the correspondences and oppositions that make up the structure of Kabyle cosmogony that Bourdieu was forced to theorize the differences between abstract logic and practical logic.[76] Conversely, it is only because he continually reflected theoretically upon his own practice as an anthropologist that he could recognize and capture the discordance between them.

If reflexivity does make such a significant cognitive, as opposed to a rhetorical or existential, difference in the conduct of social inquiry, why is it not more widely practiced? Bourdieu suggests that the real sources of resistance to it are not so much epistemological as they are social.[77] Sociological reflexivity instantly raises hackles because it rep-

76. See the progressive working out of this empirical conundrum in Bourdieu (1972, 1973d, 1977a: 96–158, and 1990a: 200–275, especially the synoptic diagram on page 215).

77. Limitations of space forbid discussion of the three classical countercharges usually leveled against the possibility or desirability of reflexivity: narcissism, futility, and *regressio ad infinitum* leading to self-contradiction, solipsism, or radical cognitive relativism (Bloor 1976, Berger 1981: 222, Ashmore 1989, Woolgar 1988). The fact that no critic has raised them so far would seem to indicate that neither applies in any straightfor-

resents a frontal attack on the sacred sense of individuality that is so dear to all of us Westerners, and particularly on the charismatic self-conception of intellectuals who like to think of themselves as undetermined, "free-floating," and endowed with a form of symbolic grace.[78] For Bourdieu, reflexivity is precisely what enables us to escape such delusions by uncovering the social at the heart of the individual, the impersonal beneath the intimate, the universal buried deep within the most particular.[79] Thus, when he declines to enter the game of intimist confession, pointing instead to the generic features of his most formative social experiences (Bourdieu 1988a: xxvi; and below, part 2, section 7), he does nothing more than apply to himself the principle of his sociology (Bourdieu 1989a: 449) according to which

> persons, at their most personal, are essentially the *personi-fication* of exigencies actually or potentially inscribed in the structure of the field or, more precisely, in the position occupied within this field.

Bourdieu sees no need to make resounding private revelations to explain himself sociologically, for what happened to him is not singular: it is linked to a social trajectory. Again, everything inclines one to believe that, as his own theory would predict, Bourdieu's concern for reflexivity finds its roots in his social and academic trajectory and

---

ward manner to Bourdieu. Indeed, reviews of *Homo Academicus*, his main tract for, and exemplification of, epistemic reflexivity, have erred in exactly the opposite direction. They characteristically deal with the book's apparent object (the French university, the May '68 crisis), overlooking its deeper methodological and theoretical demonstration. Many also complain that the book contains a paucity of information on its author's personal experiences in academia, i.e., that Bourdieu is insufficiently narcissistic. The question of the futility or gratuitousness of reflexivity is addressed in Bourdieu and Wacquant 1989 and below, part 2, sec. 6.

78. "Intending to remain master and possessor of itself and of its own truth, wanting to know no determinism other than that of its own determinations (even if it concedes that they may be unconscious), the naive humanism deposited in every person experiences as 'sociologistic' or 'materialistic' reduction any attempt to establish that the meaning of the most personal and the most 'transparent' actions does not belong to the subject who accomplishes them but to the complete system of relations in and through which they accomplish themselves" (Bourdieu, Chamboredon, and Passeron 1973: 32).

79. As Durkheim (1965) wrote in *The Elementary Forms of Religious Life:* "It is not at all true that we are more personal as we are more individualized. . . . The essential element of the personality is the social part of us."

expresses the conditions of constitution of his early scientific habitus. It is first a product of the structural discrepancy between his primary (class) habitus and that required for smooth integration into the French academic field of the 1950s. Entering the world of intellectuals a stranger and a misfit gave Bourdieu a definite distance from the illusions of those professors to whom the "regal vision" of the social world goes without noticing because it is the vision of their class of origin.[80] The second major factor is the Algerian war of liberation: it was nearly impossible, under the horrendous circumstances created by the methodical efforts of the French military to suppress Algerian nationalism, not to be constantly interpellated about the peculiar privilege of the academic who withdraws from the world in order to observe it and who claims detachment from the subjects he studies. For even the normally innocuous activity of teaching could not but take, in this context, a highly charged political dimension that mandated an analytic return upon the analyst and his practice.[81] Third, this inclination to epistemic reflexivity may in part be a product of Bourdieu's reconversion from philosophy to social science, a reconversion that was not without costs (in terms of professional standing and self-image)[82] and thus was likely to encourage the questioning of one's practice and reflection on the differences between the posture of the social scientist and that of the philosopher.

But to account for Bourdieu's "taste" for reflexivity solely by reference to his habitus would be one-sided. Like his conception of theory

80. Bourdieu (1991a: 15) readily admits: "I have never been a happy member of the university and I have never experienced the amazement of the miracled oblate, even in the years of the novitiate." See Derrida's testimony on this in Casanova 1990.

81. In 1960 Bourdieu taught a course on "Algerian Culture" at the University of Algiers. This was viewed as a provocation by authorities and settler groups for whom the mere acknowledgment of the *existence* of something like an Algerian culture was tantamount to open support for the Nationalist Liberation Front. The impact of the Algerian war on the functioning of the French intellectual field is documented in Rioux and Sirinelli's (1991) collection.

82. In "An Aspiring Philosopher," Bourdieu (1991a: 17) evokes the nearly irresistible fascination exerted upon young would-be intellectuals by the towering model of the philosopher: "One became a 'philosopher' because one had been consecrated and one was consecrated by availing oneself to the prestigious identity of the 'philosopher.' The choice of philosophy was an expression of statutory assurance which reinforced statutory confidence (or arrogance)." Bourdieu's sensitivity to epistemological issues was also the result of his training in the history and philosophy of science with Canguilhem and Bachelard.

and research, this socially constituted disposition to problematize the sociological gaze found in the French intellectual field of the 1950s and 60s a propicious environment in which to actualize itself. A number of factors are relevant here: the existence of grand living models of the intellectual vocation—most prominently those incarnated by Lévi-Strauss and Sartre—and the sense of intellectual ambition and self-confidence imparted by passage through the Ecole normale supérieure when the prestige of the school was near its peak; the extraordinary concentration of scientific capital in Paris during a period of wholesale academic reconstruction (following the collapse of the war) and of unprecedented expansion of the social sciences; and Bourdieu's precocious insertion in an institution unique for its multidisciplinary orientation and its openness to foreign intellectual currents, as well as the protection afforded by being "sponsored" by perhaps the most prestigious trio of French social scientists of the postwar era, namely Lévi-Strauss, Braudel, and Aron (whose assistant Bourdieu was briefly upon returning precipitously from Algeria).[83]

In sum, Bourdieu's concern for reflexivity, like his social theory, is neither egocentric nor logocentric but quintessentially embedded in, and turned toward, scientific practice. It fastens not upon the private person of the sociologist in her idiosyncratic intimacy but on the concatenations of acts and operations she effectuates as part of her work and on the collective unconscious inscribed in them. Far from encouraging narcissism and solipsism, epistemic reflexivity invites intellectuals to recognize and to work to neutralize the specific determinisms to which their innermost thoughts are subjected and it informs a conception of the craft of research designed to strengthen its epistemological moorings.

83. Following a short teaching stint at the Sorbonne and at the University of Lille (to which he used to commute while residing in Paris), Bourdieu was nominated in 1964, at age 34, to the Ecole des hautes études en sciences sociales, at the behest of Braudel, Aron, and Lévi-Strauss (the back cover of his first English book, *The Algerians*, sported the endorsements of the latter two). Another important favorable factor is geographic stability: staying in the capital allowed Bourdieu to build a collective instrument of research as well as to accumulate and to concentrate intellectual connections over time, something that is made more difficult in the American academic field by the comparatively high spatial mobility of social scientists (which tends to increase with their rank in the scientific hierarchy). For a historical analysis of the Ecole des hautes études en sciences sociales from its creation through the early 1960s, see Mazon 1988 and Bourdieu's (1988j) brief preface.

7   Reason, Ethics, and Politics

Epistemic reflexivity has yet another payoff: it opens up the possibility of overcoming the opposition between the nihilistic relativism of postmodern "deconstruction" advocated by Derrida and the scientistic absolutism of "modernist" rationalism defended by Habermas. For it allows us to historicize reason without dissolving it, to found a *historicist rationalism* that reconciles deconstruction with universality, reason with relativity, by anchoring their operations in the objective—if historically given—structures of the scientific field. On the one side, like Habermas, Bourdieu believes in the possibility and desirability of scientific truth and, in that, he is passionately modernist.[84] But he holds, against the Frankfurt theorist, that the project of grounding reason in the transhistoric structures of consciousness or language partakes of a transcendentalist illusion of which historical sciences must rid themselves. On the other side, Bourdieu agrees with Derrida and Foucault that knowledge must be deconstructed, that categories are contingent social derivations and instruments of (symbolic) power possessing a constitutive efficacy—that the structures of discourse on the social world are often politically charged social preconstructions. Science is indeed, as Gramsci saw well,[85] an eminently political activity. Yet it is not for all that *merely* a politics and therefore incapable of yielding universally valid truths. To conflate the politics of science (knowledge) with that of society (power) is to make short shrift of the historically instituted autonomy of the scientific field and to throw the baby of sociology out with the bathwater of

84. Bourdieu does not "subscribe to Foucaultian power/knowledge assumptions" as Lash (1990: 255) maintains (see his critique of this notion in Bourdieu and Wacquant 1991). Although he is wary of its transcendentalization, he partakes wholeheartedly of the Enlightenment project of Reason: "Against this antiscientism which is the fashion of the day and which brings grist to the mill of the new ideologists, I defend science and even theory when it has the effect of providing a better understanding of the social world. One does not have to choose between obscurantism and scientism. 'Of two ills, Karl Kraus said, I refuse to choose the lesser'" (Bourdieu 1980b: 18). For a suggestive discussion of Bourdieu's work as a "sensible third path between universalism and particularism, rationalism and relativism, modernists and postmodernists," see Calhoun (1992).

85. "The problem of what 'science' itself is has to be posed. Is not science itself 'political activity' and political thought, in as much as it transforms men, and makes them different from what they were before?" (Gramsci 1971: 244).

positivism.[86] Here Bourdieu parts with poststructuralism: if deconstruction deconstructed itself, he contends, it would discover its historical conditions of possibility and therefore see that it itself presupposes standards of truth and rational dialogue rooted in the social structure of the intellectual universe.

In Bourdieu's view, then, reason is a historical product but a highly paradoxical one in that it can "escape" history (i.e., particularity) under certain conditions, conditions that must be continuously (re)produced by working very concretely to safeguard the *institutional bases for rational thought*. Far from challenging science, his analysis of the genesis and functioning of fields of cultural production aims at grounding scientific rationality in history, that is, in knowledge-producing relations objectified in the web of positions and "subjectified" in dispositions that together make up the scientific field as a historically unique social invention:

> We must, by taking historicist reduction to its logical conclusion, seek the origins of reason not in a human "faculty," that is, a *nature*, but in the very history of these peculiar social microcosms in which agents struggle, in the name of the universal, for the legitimate monopoly over the universal, and in the progressive institutionalization of a dialogical language which owes its seemingly intrinsic properties to the social conditions of its genesis and of its utilization. (Bourdieu 1990e: 389)

Bourdieu's notion of reflexivity runs counter, not to "modernist scientificity" as Lash (1990) claims, but to positivist conceptions of social science. Essential to the latter is a watertight separation between fact and value (Giddens 1977). For the author of *Distinction*, however,

86. While Bourdieu shares with Foucault a caesuralist and constructivist conception of rationality and a historicist understanding of knowledge (see his eulogy of Foucault entitled "The Pleasure of Knowing," in *Le Monde*, June 27, 1984), he rejects his *epochē* of the question of scientificity. Where Foucault, embracing a form of epistemological agnosticism, is content to suspend the question of meaning and truth by means of an "orthogonal double bracketing" (Dreyfus and Rabinow 1983) of the questions of causality and totality, Bourdieu recasts them by reference to the functioning of the scientific field. Here, as with the issues of "nonintentional" strategies or of power, the concept of field signals a profound divide between Bourdieu and Foucault.

empirical knowledge is not as discrepant from the discovery and pursuit of moral aims as followers of one or another brand of positivism would have us believe. In keeping with the Durkheimian project (Filloux 1970, Bellah 1973, Lacroix 1981), Bourdieu is intensely concerned with the moral and political significance of sociology. Though it is hardly reducible to it, his work conveys a moral message at two levels.

First, from the standpoint of the individual, it gives tools for distinguishing zones of necessity and of freedom, and thereby for identifying spaces open to moral action. Bourdieu (1989a: 47) argues that, as long as agents act on the basis of a subjectivity that is the unmediated internalization of objectivity, they cannot but remain the "apparent subjects of actions which have the structure as subject." *A contrario*, the more aware they become of the social within them by reflexively mastering their categories of thought and action, the less likely they are to be actuated by the externality which inhabits them. Socio-analysis may be seen as a collective counterpart to psycho-analysis: just as the logotherapy of the latter may free us from the individual unconscious that drives or constricts our practices, the former can help us unearth the *social* unconscious embedded into institutions as well as lodged deep inside of us. Whereas Bourdieu's work shares with all (post-)structuralisms a rejection of the Cartesian *cogito* (Schmidt 1985), it differs from them in that it attempts to make possible the historical emergence of something *like* a rational subject via a reflexive application of social-scientific knowledge.[87]

The moral dimension of reflexive sociology is also inherent in what we may call its *Spinozist function*. In Bourdieu's eyes, the business of the sociologist is to denaturalize and to defatalize the social world, that is, to destroy the myths that cloak the exercise of power and the

---

87. "Paradoxically, sociology frees us by freeing us from the illusion of freedom, or, more precisely, from misplaced belief in illusory freedoms. Freedom is not a given but a conquest, and a collective one. And I find regrettable that, in the name of a petty narcissistic libido, encouraged by an immature denegation of realities, people should deprive themselves of an instrument which enables one truly to constitute oneself—at least a little bit more—as a free subject, at the price of a work of reappropriation" (Bourdieu 1987a: 26). It is doubtful, therefore, that "Bourdieu would gladly participate in splashing the corrosive acid of deconstruction on the traditional subject," as Rabinow (1982: 175) asserts.

perpetuation of domination.[88] But debunking is not done for the purpose of castigating others and inducing guilt.[89] Quite the opposite: the mission of sociology is to "*necessitate* conducts, to tear them away from arbitrariness by reconstituting the universe of constraints which determine them, without justifying them" (Bourdieu 1989a: 143).

In rendering visible the links he perceives between a scientific sociology and the construction of "small-scale," day-to-day morals, Bourdieu joins with Alan Wolfe (1989a, 1989b) and Richard Maxwell Brown (1990) in bringing to the fore the inescapable ethical dimension of social science. However, he does not hold, as Wolfe does, that sociology can provide the operative moral philosophy of advanced societies. That would be tantamount to thrusting the sociologist back into the prophetic role of the Saint Simonian "theologian of the civil religion" of modernity.[90] For Bourdieu, sociology can tell us under what conditions moral agency is possible and how it can be institutionally enforced, not what its course ought to be.[91]

Bourdieu conceives of sociology as an *eminently political science* in that it is crucially concerned with, and enmeshed in, strategies and mechanisms of symbolic domination.[92] By the very nature of its object

88. In this, Bourdieu again concurs with Elias (1978a: 52), for whom "scientists are destroyers of myths." To those who would object that sociology should not be concerned with debunking accepted images of society, Bourdieu replies that "the discourse of science can seem disenchanting only to those who have an enchanted vision of the social world. It stands at equal distance from the utopianism which takes its wishes for reality and from the dampering evocation of fetishized laws" (untitled editorial introduction to the inaugural issue of *Actes de la recherche en sciences sociales*, 1975).

89. The sociologist is not "a kind of terrorist inquisitor, available for all operations of symbolic policing" (Bourdieu 1982a: 8).

90. Robert Bellah (1973: x) applies this expression to Durkheim. For Alan Wolfe (1989a: 22–23), "sociology ought to recover the moral tradition that was at the heart of the Scottish Enlightenment. . . . Social scientists are moral philosophers in disguise."

91. For instance, to guarantee that politicians or group leaders more generally act in pursuit of the collective interest, we must "institute social universes in which, as in the ideal Republic according to Machiavelli, agents have an interest in virtue and disinterestedness, in devotion to the public good, and to the commonweal." In politics as in science, "morality has some chance of being brought about if we work to create the institutional means of a politics of morals" (Bourdieu forthcoming b: 7).

92. Bourdieu (1977a: 165) holds that even epistemology is fundamentally political: "The theory of knowledge is a dimension of political theory because the specifically symbolic power to impose the principles of construction of reality—in particular social reality—is a major dimension of political power." Put otherwise: "The theory of knowl-

and the location of its practitioners in the dominated sector of the field of power, social science cannot be neutral, detached, apolitical. It will never reach the "uncontroversial" status of the natural sciences. Proof is the constant encounters it has with forms of resistance and surveillance (internal no less than external) that threaten to chip away at its autonomy and are largely unknown in the most advanced sectors of biology or physics. For Bourdieu (1975d: 101),

> it can hardly be otherwise because the stake of the internal struggle for scientific authority in the field of the social sciences, that is for the power to produce, to impose, and to inculcate the legitimate representation of the social world, is one of the stakes of the struggle between classes in the political field. It follows that positions in the internal struggle can never reach the degree of independence from positions in external struggles that can be observed in the field of the natural sciences. The idea of a neutral science is a fiction, and an interested fiction, which enables one to pass as scientific a neutralized and euphemized form of the dominant representation of the social world that is particularly efficacious symbolically because it is partially misrecognizable. By uncovering the social mechanisms which ensure the maintenance of the established order and whose properly symbolic efficacy rests on the misrecognition of their logic and effects, *social science necessarily takes sides in political struggles*. (Translation modified and emphasis added)

The specific dilemma of social science is that progress toward greater autonomy does not imply progress toward political neutrality. The more scientific sociology becomes, the more politically relevant it becomes, if only as a negative tool—a shield against forms of mystification and symbolic domination that routinely prevent us from becoming genuine political agents.[93]

---

edge and political theory are inseparable: every political theory contains, at least implicitly, a theory of perception of the social world organized according to oppositions very analogous to those that can be found in the theory of the natural world" (Bourdieu 1980b: 86, my translation).

93. "As a science which works to uncover the laws of production of science, [sociology] provides not means of domination but perhaps means to dominate domination" (Bourdieu 1980b: 49, my translation).

As the final section of the Chicago Workshop (part 2, section 7) makes evident, Bourdieu does not share the fatalistic vision of the world attributed to him by those who read in his work a politically sterile hyperfunctionalism. His is not a Nietzschean vision of "a universe of absolute functionality" (Rancière 1984: 34) where "every minute detail of social action [partakes] of a vast design for oppression" (Elster 1990: 89–90, 113). Bourdieu does not think, as did Mosca and Pareto, the "elite theorists" of the Italian school, that the social universe is inherently and forever divided into monolithic blocs of rulers and ruled, elite and nonelite. First of all because advanced societies are not a unified cosmos but differentiated, partially totalized entities made up of a set of intersecting but increasingly self-regulating fields, each with its dominant and its dominated. Besides, in each field, hierarchy is continually contested, and the very principles that undergird the structure of the field can be challenged and revoked. And the ubiquity of domination does not exclude the possibility of relative democratization. As the field of power becomes more differentiated, as the division of the work of domination becomes more complex (Bourdieu 1989a: 533–59), involving more agents, each with their specific interests, as the universal is invoked in more of the subfields that make up the space of play of the dominant class (in politics, in religion, in science, even in the economy, with the growing weight of legal reasoning in the day-to-day management and strategic steering of corporations), opportunities for pushing reason forward increase.

Second, Bourdieu does not hold that the social world obeys laws that are immutable. He wants no part of the "futility thesis," this figure of conservative (and sometimes radical) rhetoric that asserts that no collective action is worth undertaking since it will eventually prove incapable of redressing current inequity. Though Bourdieu pictures the social world as highly structured, he disagrees with the idea that it evolves "according to immanent laws, which human actions are laughably impotent to modify" (Hirschman 1991: 72). For him, social laws are temporally and spatially bound regularities that hold as long as the institutional conditions that underpin them are allowed to endure. They do not express what Durkheim (1956: 64) referred to as "ineluctable necessities" but rather historical connections that can often be politically undone, provided that one gains the requisite knowledge about their social roots.

Bourdieu's (1980b: 18) own political *Beruf* as a sociologist is apparently a modest one:

> My goal is to contribute to preventing people from being able to utter all kinds of nonsense about the social world. Schönberg said one day that he composed so that people could no longer write music. I write so that people, and first of all those who are entitled to speak, spokespersons, can no longer produce, apropos the social world, noise that has all the appearances of music.

No doubt Bourdieu's most significant political intervention consists indeed in his writings, particularly those on education, culture, and intellectuals.[94] Yet he has not for all that been inactive in the realm of official politics. While Bourdieu has persistently remained on the Left of the French political spectrum (in his survey of "French Intellectuals from Sartre to Soft Ideology," George Ross [1991: 248, n. 82] writes that "it is not uncommon to find Left-leaning sociologists in Paris these days lamenting that 'Bourdieu is all we have left'"),[95] his positions are little known outside of his homeland because his manner of intervening in the political arena is uncharacteristic of French intellectuals. It is parsimonious, restive and relatively low-key (for example, he rarely signs petitions, compared to other major—and minor—intellectual figures).[96] It is best typified by the somewhat uneasy combination of intense commitment with a rational distrust of organizational attachments (he belongs to no formal political grouping, party, or union) premised on the idea that, to be politically efficacious,

94. John Thompson (1991: 31) notes: "As a social scientist first and foremost, Bourdieu rarely engages in normative political theory, nor does he seek to formulate political programs or policies for particular social groups. But his relentless disclosure of power and privilege in its most varied and subtlest forms, and the respect accorded by his theoretical framework to the agents who make up the social world which he so acutely dissects, give his work an implicit critical potential."

95. Turner (1990) presents Bourdieu to a British audience as the "current doyen of hard-left social critique and a fierce opponent of the Continental 'philosophers' star system.'"

96. For a survey of the political involvements of French intellectuals since World War II and the central role of petitioning in them, see Ory and Sirinelli 1986: chaps. 8–10.

scientists must first constitute an autonomous and self-regulating ensemble.

In point of fact, the invariants of Bourdieu's political posture are premised on his sociological understanding of the historical genesis of intellectuals as bearers of a dominated form of capital (Bourdieu 1989d; see also Pinto 1984b, and Charle 1990). They are, first, a refusal of the compulsory exhibitions of "engagement"[97] which can paradoxically lead to a conformism of anticonformism that tends to undermine independence and, second, the will to put a properly scientific competency to work for political causes. Thus, in the 1950s, at the Ecole normale, Bourdieu joined in the resistance to the censorship that the Communist party was exerting on intellectual life with the zealous collaboration of many who have since become fervent anticommunists.[98] At the beginning of the decade of the 1960s, in Algeria, dissatisfied with moral denunciations and exhortations, he conducted surveys and fieldwork in the heart of the war zone, reporting in graphic detail some of the most brutal forms of colonial oppression, such as the "regrouping centers" analyzed in Le déracinement (The Uprooting, Bourdieu and Sayad 1964). His writings of this period comprise both scholarly works with a strong political tenor[99] and more exoteric interventions, such as the article "Revolution in the Revolution" (Bourdieu 1961) which forewarned of the unintended social effects and future pitfalls of the war of liberation.

In 1968 Bourdieu was again active before and during the uprising, speaking at various universities at the invitation of student groups, though The Inheritors (Bourdieu and Passeron 1979, originally published in 1964) contained a frontal attack of the theses of UNEF, the main student union, which portrayed its constituency as a unified "social class" by masking internal differences associated with class or-

97. See Bourdieu's evocation of Sayad's political positions in the war of Algeria (which he shared) in his preface to the latter's L'immigration, ou les paradoxes de l'altérité (Immigration or the Paradoxes of Otherness, Sayad 1991).

98. Bourdieu (1987a: 13) remembers that "Stalinist pressure was so exasperating that we had created, around 1951, with Bianco, Comte, Marin, Derrida, Pariente, and others, a Committee for the Defense of Liberties that Le Roy Ladurie denounced in the [Communist] cell of the school."

99. The cover of his first book, The Algerians (Bourdieu 1962), published in the United States by Beacon Press, displayed the flag of the yet-to-be-formed Republic of Algeria.

igins and gender.[100] Through the 1970s, swimming against the tide that swept a good many former communist intellectuals of the '50s and Maoists of the '70s toward a more or less openly conservative disenchantment, Bourdieu continued to assert progressive positions, far from the media spotlight and from the fads that ruled the journalistic scene (e.g., the so-called New Philosophers led by Glucksman, Bernard-Henri Lévy and Finkelkraut). He also opted not to participate in the quasi-ritualized demonstrations that mobilized a number of prominent intellectuals around a then-aging Sartre, choosing instead less ostentatious means of action. A resolute opponent of the conservative parties that ruled the country until 1981, Bourdieu became a constructive leftist critic of the Socialist administration on the heels of Mitterrand's election. After the return to power of the Left following the "cohabitation" intermezzo of 1986–88, he intervened more directly on a number of topics of his competency: education, television, publicity.[101] Over the years, Bourdieu has also been intermittently involved in antiracism struggles with the group SOS-Racisme, yet again without formally joining it. More recently, he has directed a large-scale study of social suffering, whose purpose is to short-circuit the institutions that normalize and censor the expression of social demands (see part 2, section 6). Emblematic of his stance of critical detachment and involvement (to recall Elias's [1987a] famed dyad) is the action in favor of Poland that Bourdieu organized with Michel Foucault to protest the meek reaction of France's Socialist government

100. See in particular the diagram contrasting the ideology and the sociology of the student milieu in Bourdieu and Passeron 1979: 52. Bourdieu also drafted the only known manifesto by professors to take sides with the May movement, while at the same time calling for measures designed to counteract the utopianism of student demands (see *Les idées de mai* 1978).

101. After drafting the "Report of the Collège de France on the Future of Education" (Bourdieu 1990g) that informed Mitterrand's 1988 presidential platform on education, and which he discussed with several trade union groups in various European countries, Bourdieu agreed to team up with biologist François Gros to head an advisory "Committee on the Reform of the Contents of Education" charged with spearheading the long-term school reform that was then the pet project of Rocard's Socialist administration. He also supported a highly politicized reform of spelling and he was instrumental in the creation of a publicly owned, European, cultural television channel (whose direction was entrusted to his colleague, medieval historian Georges Duby), and active in a pressure group pushing for the banning of publicity on public television.

to Jaruzelski's military coup in December of 1981, an action which constitutes one of his rare attempts to establish an organic linkage between intellectuals and the most innovative of French trade unions, the CFDT, with which he has continued to collaborate.[102]

But Bourdieu's most relentless, if perhaps least visible, political actions are those he has undertaken against what he perceives as the hidden vices of the intellectual world, in particular the growing influence of journalists and of scholars who use journalism as a means of acquiring in the intellectual field an authority they could not get otherwise (Bourdieu 1988a: especially 256–70, and 1980b). This is arguably the most significant difference between him and Sartre or Foucault: whereas the latter have used their intellectual capital primarily in the broader politics of society, Bourdieu has aimed his critical arsenal first and foremost at the forms of tyranny—in Pascal's sense—that threaten the intellectual field itself. In the manner of Karl Kraus (see below, p. 212, note 175), he has fought the imposture of those intellectuals who act as the Trojan horses of heteronomy in their own universe.

For Bourdieu, the genuine intellectual is defined by her or his independence from temporal powers, from the interference of economic and political authority. This autonomy asserts itself in the existence of institutionalized sites of regulated dialogue. *Liber: The European Review of Books* is one such site that Bourdieu helped create.[103] Conceived as a collective instrument of battle against intellectual provincialism and particularism, *Liber*'s goal is to promote a space where artists and scientists can debate according to their own norms, to "break the

102. See Bourdieu 1991c. See Eribon 1989: 316–24, for a detailed account of this resounding petition drive and ensuing series of demonstrations in favor of Solidarnosc, and Bourdieu's (1981e, also 1985e) piece in *Libération* appropriately titled "Reclaiming the Libertarian Tradition of the Left," in which he calls for the institutional recognition of the "anti-institutional current" of French political life born of May 1968 (i.e., ecology, feminism, the critique of authority, etc.). More recently, Bourdieu has publicly taken position on the Iraqi war ("Against War," an article co-signed with 80 other prominent French and Arab intellectuals, *Libération*, February 21, 1991) and on solidarity and immigration in *Die Tageszeitung* (interview on April 13, 1990). For a broader sample of his stances and thinking on the role of sociology in politics and current issues, see Bourdieu 1986d, 19871, 1988g, 1988h, 1989d; and Bourdieu, Casanova, and Simon 1975.

103. *Liber* has appeared as a supplement to major national newspapers in France, Italy, Great Britain, Spain, Portugal and Germany since 1989; its editorial board is composed of leading intellectuals from these countries, with Bourdieu as its editor-in-chief.

small circles of mutual admiration which are at the origin of so many national glories and, also paradoxically, of the international circulation of the false debates of essayism," as well as to free ideas from struggles over local professional status and dominion.[104] In Bourdieu's mind, *Liber* is meant to facilitate the formation of a European "collective intellectual" capable of acting as a continent-wide countervailing symbolic power. Similarly, *Actes de la recherche en sciences sociales*, the journal founded and edited by Bourdieu since 1975, follows a political cum scientific line that may be described as a form of scientific activism in favor of interdisciplinary research, alive to its sociopolitical implications and responsibility, yet thoroughly independent of any official political agenda. The journal operates in the manner of the intellectual as defined by Bourdieu: autonomous yet committed; engaged yet subject to no criteria of political "orthodoxy."[105]

The active promotion of such institutional sites of rational dialogue becomes all the more important in light of the unprecedented threats that symbolic producers face today (Bourdieu 1989d). These threats include the increasing encroachment of the state and penetration of economic interests into the world of art and science; the consolidation of the large bureaucracies that manage the television, press, and radio

104. P. Bourdieu, unpublished introductory editorial to *Liber*. Bourdieu explains the purpose of *Liber* thus to a British audience (cited by Turner 1990): "Intellectuals never create political movements but they can and should help. They can give authority, invest their cultural capital. Nowadays generally they don't. Good minds are frightened by the media and hide in their academies. Public forums are taken over by half-intellectuals—like the postmodernists—who invent emotive quarrels and false problems which waste everybody's time. The idea of *Liber* is to create a safe space in order to coax good minds out of hiding and into the world again. Intellectuals tend to overestimate their abilities as individuals and to underestimate the power they might have as a class. *Liber* is an attempt to bind intellectuals together as a militant force."

105. Issues of *Actes de la recherche en sciences sociales* have occasionally been direct intellectual-political interventions: e.g., the March 1986 issue on "Science and Current Issues" featured articles on the social foundations of the Solidarity movement in Poland, the Kanak uprising shaking the colonial society of New Caledonia, Sikhs in Indian history and politics, and Arab immigration in France. The November 1990 issue on "The Downfall of Leninism" tackled ongoing changes in Eastern Europe. The March and June 1988 issues ("Thinking the Political"), which sandwiched the French presidential and legislative elections of the Spring of 1988, included a debunking of the self-presentation of Chirac and Fabius (then current and immediate past prime ministers, and prominent members of the conservative Rally for the Republic and Socialist parties respectively) and of the (mis)uses of polls and television by politicians.

industries, forming an independent cultural establishment that imposes its own standards of production and consumption; and the tendency to strip intellectuals of their ability to evaluate themselves,
substituting instead journalistic criteria of topicality, readability, and
novelty. These pressures push cultural producers toward a forced
alternative between becoming "an expert, that is, an intellectual at
the service of the dominant" or remaining "an independent petty
producer in the old mode, symbolized by the professor lecturing in
his ivory tower" (in Bourdieu and Wacquant 1991: 31). To escape this
deadly choice, Bourdieu calls for the creation of a new form of intervention: the *collective intellectual*, allowing producers of knowledge to
influence politics as autonomous subjects by first asserting their independence as a group.

All the while, Bourdieu has shied away from stating his own values. Yet one may find in the prefaces and tributes he has written for
others admission of the kinds of stakes that motivate him. It is hard
not to discern, in his remarks on the tragic death of Maurice Halbwachs (his predecessor in the chair of Sociology at the Collège de
France) in a Nazi extermination camp, a manner of self-portrait by
proxy when he writes,

> I know too well that academic virtues are not much in favor
> these days and that it is all too easy to deride the mediocrely
> petty-bourgeois and vaguely social-democratic inspiration of
> any enterprise aimed at building, against all forms of particu-
> larism, a scientific humanism which refuses to split existence
> into two realms, the one devoted to the rigors of science, the
> other to the passions of politics, and which labors to put the
> weapons of reason at the service of the convictions of gener-
> osity. (Bourdieu 1987m: 166–67)

Anyone who has interacted, however briefly, with Bourdieu will
sense at once that, when he praises Halbwachs for faithfully main-
taining "an intellectual posture which leads to conceive the work of
the researcher as an activist task [*tâche militante*] (and conversely),"
when he talks of the latter's "generalized will to promote a politics of
scientific reason, and first of all within the specific order of its accomplishment, the world of the university," based on "a critical vision of
the institution," he is revealing some of his own deeply-cherished val-

ues.[106] This suggests, to conclude, that Bourdieu's sociology may also be read as a *politique* in the sense he gives to this term: an attempt to transform the principles of vision whereby we construct, and therefore may rationally and humanely shape, sociology, society and, ultimately, our selves.

106. This is made clear at the end of this eulogy, where Bourdieu (1987m: 170, 167) intimates that "we must resolutely assume the belief in the emancipatory virtues of scientific reason as professed by Maurice Halbwachs" before enjoining us to continue his "scientific enterprise."

II

The Purpose of Reflexive Sociology
(The Chicago Workshop)

Pierre Bourdieu and Loïc J. D. Wacquant

If I had to "summarize" Wittgenstein, I would say: He made changing the self the prerequisite of all changes.

Daniel Oster, *Dans l'intervalle*

1   Sociology As Socioanalysis

Loïc J. D. Wacquant: Let us begin with *Homo Academicus* (Bourdieu 1988a) since it is a work which in many ways stands at the epicenter of your sociological project (Wacquant 1990a: 678–79). In it, you offer both an empirical sociology of the academic institution and an analysis of the epistemological pitfalls and quandaries involved in analyzing one's own universe. One might have thought that it would be an easy book for you to write since it deals with French intellectuals, that is, a world in which you have been an actor, and a central one, for nearly three decades. Now, on the contrary, of all your studies, *Homo Academicus* appears to be the one that has cost you most in terms of time, of thinking, of writing, and in research effort—and also (I think this is revealing) in terms of anxiety: you mention in the foreword your apprehension about publishing such a book, and you devote the entire opening chapter to warding off, and to guarding yourself against, a wide variety of possible misreadings. Why so much difficulty?

Pierre Bourdieu: It is true that *Homo Academicus* is a book that I kept for a very long time in my files because I feared that it would slip away from me upon publication and that it would be read in a manner opposite to its deep intent, namely, as a pamphlet or as an instrument of self-flagellation.[1] There is always an extraordinary danger of losing

---

1. Reflecting on *Homo Academicus* shortly after its publication, Bourdieu (1987a: 116) writes with rare emotion: "Sociology can be an extremely powerful instrument of self-analysis which allows one better to understand what he or she is by giving one an understanding of one's own conditions of production and of the position one occupies in the social world. . . . It follows that this book demands a particular manner of reading. One is not to construe it as a pamphlet or to use it in a self-punitive fashion. . . . If

control of what you write. Everybody has repeated that since Plato's Seventh Letter, but this book did pose special problems when it came to publishing it. I was overwhelmed by the fear that the interests of my readers (which, given what I write, comprise a large majority of academics) would be so strong that all the work I had accomplished to prevent this kind of spontaneous reading would be swept away, and that people would bring down to the level of struggles within the academic field an analysis whose aim is to objectivize this competition and, thereby, to give the reader a certain mastery of it.

Homo Academicus is a book which is peculiar in that the ordinary work required by scientific objectivation is accompanied by a work—a labor in the psychoanalytic sense—upon the subject of objectivation. Working on such an object, one is reminded at every moment that the subject of the objectivation himself is being objectivized: the harshest and most brutally objectifying analyses are written with an acute awarenesss of the fact that they apply to he who is writing them. And, moreover, with the knowledge that many of those concerned by them will not think for one moment that the author of this or that apparently "cruel" sentence bears it along with them.[2] Consequently, they will denounce as gratuitous cruelty what is in fact a *labor of anamnesis*—a socioanalysis. (I have in mind here several passages which separated me from some of my best friends. I have had—I think that this is not of merely anecdotal significance—very dramatic clashes with colleagues who perceived very accurately the violence of the objectivation but who saw a contradiction in the fact that I could objectivize without thinking of myself, while of course I was doing it all the while.)

In the preface to the English-language edition, I give as the main factor to explain and understand the specificity of contemporary French philosophers (Foucault, Derrida, etc.) on the global intellectual scene the fact that most, if not all, of these heretical philosophers have been in that very odd position which consists of making an intel-

---

my book were read as a pamphlet, I would soon come to hate it and I would rather have it burned."

2. This was perceptively noticed by Bennett Berger (1989: 190): "The constant reflexivity of Bourdieu's style is a permanently reactivated reminder to the readers that he is subjected to the same relations between position, disposition, and predisposition as anybody else: it is also an invitation that he gives to his critics to uncover the distortions created by these relations."

lectual virtue out of a mundane necessity, of turning the collective fate of a generation into an elective choice. Normally bound to simple reproduction of the academic system by virtue of their academic success, which led them to the dominant positions within the system, they experienced the collapse of the school system from under their very feet and, following the May '68 movement and the ensuing transformation of the French university, they saw and lived the traditional dominant positions as untenable, unbearable. They were therefore led to a sort of anti-institutional disposition[3] which finds its roots, at least in part, in their relation to the university as an institution. Given my trajectory and position, I cannot deny that I partake of this anti-institutional mood. I am therefore well placed to know that any analysis that compels us to uncover the social determinants of a posture which tends to be experienced as a freely arrived-at, discretionary choice, or even as a more or less "heroic" rupture, must be to some degree unpleasant or irritating.

This native familiarity with the universe you study was thus an asset but also, on another level, an obstacle that you had to overturn. Is this why you base your work on such a large array of data (the mere listing of the sources takes up several appendixes) and yet display only a small portion of them?

It is indeed an ascetic book with regard to the use of data and with regard to writing. There is first of all an ascesis in the rhetoric of data presentation. There are a number of things that an analysis of my intellectual trajectory[4] would account for very well, such as a form of aristocratism that I owe to having followed one of the highest trajectories in the French educational sytem, to having been initially trained as a philosopher, etc. (This explains why my "invisible college" is found in part among philosophers, and why a certain form of positivistic exhibitionism is no doubt unconsciously forbidden to me as pedestrian.) Having said this, it is true that I have perhaps never handled more data than for that book. This is something that is not

3. The complexity, strength, and multivalence of this disposition is amply documented in the case of Foucault in Didier Eribon's (1991) masterful biography of the French philosopher.

4. See Bourdieu's firsthand recapitulation of his intellectual experiences in his interview with Honneth, Kocyba and Schwibs (1986) and in Bourdieu 1987a, 1987e. For his view of the French intellectual field since World War II, consult Bourdieu and Passeron 1967, Bourdieu 1987e and 1991a, and the preface to *Homo Academicus*.

always readily recognized in England and the United States,[5] no doubt in the name of a positivistic definition of data and of their usage which wrongly identifies science with an exhibitionism of data and procedures—where we would be better advised to display the conditions of construction and analysis of these data.

Second, there is an ascesis at the level of writing. I wrote a considerable number of pages which could have earned me a *succès de scandale* for being slightly polemical and caustic and which I ended up throwing out precisely because they would have encouraged a regression to the ordinary (i.e., polemical) vision of the field.[6] I should also add that the scientific rendering of an in-depth sociological analysis of this kind raises very thorny questions of writing. One would need to invent a whole new language to try to convey at once the sensible and the intelligible, the percept and the concept. (The journal that we edit at the Center for European Sociology, *Actes de la recherche en sciences sociales*, has been a laboratory for experimenting with such a new mode of sociological expression apt to transmit an *eye*: the principle of pertinence which constitutes a science.)[7] My

5. This comment on *Distinction* by Anthony Giddens (1986b: 302–3), whose reputation is paradoxically not staked on his empirical work, is indicative of this reaction: "Although it is rather distant from what most Anglo-Saxon sociologists would regard as a respectable research report, it is nonetheless informed by an extensive empirical investigation into the habits and attitudes of different social classes in France. Well over a thousand individuals, in fact, were interviewed in some detail." Murphy (1983: 40) is more abruptly dismissive in his assessment, going as far as to assert that Bourdieu's "effort to discredit empirical sociology [?] has led him into a profound ignorance of methods of systematic documentation and the unconvincing documentation of his own ideas," an ignorance he attributes to Bourdieu's alleged "vague anti-positivist humanism."

6. The paradigm (in the Platonic sense of exemplary instance) of such partial, interested and thus polemic views of the academic field is offered by Ferry and Renault's (1990) diatribe, *La pensée 68*, for France, and by Jacoby's lament, *The Last Intellectuals* (1987), for the United States. (See Wacquant 1990a for further discussion of this point.)

7. *Actes de la recherche en sciences sociales*, which publishes a wide range of writing formats, from polished articles to "rough" accounts of work-in-progress, accommodates different styles, sizes, and type fonts, and makes extensive use of pictures, facsimiles of primary documents, excerpts from field notes and interviews, along with statistical tables and graphs. The typographical, rhetorical, and stylistic innovations of the journal are premised on the idea that the substance and the form of a reflexive sociology are intimately linked, and that the manner in which a sociological object is elaborated is at least as important as the end result of the research process. As the name of the journal itself indicates, the "research acts" matter as much, if not more, than the

wish is to create a language that would enable producers of discourse on the social world to escape the deadly alternative between the dry objectivist detachment of scientific accounts and the more experientially sensitive involvement of literary forms. I had thought of doing in *Homo Academicus* what I attempted to do in *Distinction*, that is, create a "discursive *montage*"[8] that allows one to offer at once the scientific vision and the immediate intuition that this vision explains but also typically excludes. But this would have produced a "pinning" or labeling effect, given a violence to my analyses, such that I had to renounce the idea.

In fact, one of the central problems of a sociology of the intellectual milieu is that intellectuals are, as all social agents, "spontaneous sociologists" who are particularly skilled at objectivizing others. Being professionals of discourse and explication, however, intellectuals have a much greater than average capacity to transform their spontaneous sociology, that is, their self-interested vision of the social world, into the appearance of a scientific sociology.

---

finished product. "A social science which [takes] as its object social forms and social formalisms must reproduce in the presentation of its results the operation of desacralization which enabled it to produce them. We encounter here what is no doubt one of the specificities of social science: conquered over and against social mechanisms of dissimulation, its achievements can inform individual or collective practice only if their diffusion succeeds in escaping, if only partially, the laws that regulate all discourse on the social world. To communicate, in this case, is to offer, every time it is possible, the means to replicate, practically and not only verbally, the operations that made the conquest of the truth of practices possible. Having to provide instruments of perception and facts which can only be grasped through these instruments, social science must not only demonstrate *(démontrer)* but also designate and display *(montrer)*" (Pierre Bourdieu, untitled editorial introduction to the 1975 inaugural issue [no. 1, p. 2]). The lively format of the journal helps account for its circulation of over 8,000— the largest of any social science publication in the French language—which reaches well beyond the confines of academia.

8. This is fully visible only in the original edition of *Distinction* published by Editions de Minuit in 1979; for reasons of cost and stylistic conventions, the English-language translation replicates the textual layout of the original French volume only very partially. Barnard (1990: 81) has noted in his study "Bourdieu and Ethnography," that *Distinction* is "'dense with the machinery of "hard" sociology: graphs, charts, survey, interviews, and maps' (Warner). Yet the book also contains excerpts from magazines, photographs and the data obtained from participation in the milieu described. Furthermore, in this work like no other, all these elements are fused into a whole, so that there is no sense of priority being given to one mode of textual production or the other. If this is ethnography—and it certainly has elements which could not be thought of as otherwise . . .—it is certainly ethnography of an entirely novel kind."

In *Homo Academicus* you offer a sociology of your own intellectual universe. However, your aim is not simply to write a monograph on the French university and its faculty, but to make a much more fundamental point about the sociological method.

When I began that study in the mid-sixties—at a time when the crisis of the academic institution which was to climax with the student movement of '68 was rampant but not yet so acute that the contestation of academic "power" had become open—my intention was to conduct a sort of *sociological test about sociological practice itself.* I wanted to demonstrate that, contrary to the claims of those who pretend to undermine sociological knowledge or seek to disqualify sociology as a science on the grounds that sociologists necessarily adopt a socially determined point of view on the social world, sociology can escape to a degree from this historicist circle, by drawing on its knowledge of the social universe in which social science is produced to control the effects of the determinisms that operate in this universe and, at the same time, bear on sociologists themselves.

In that study, I pursue a double goal and construct a double object. First, the apparent object constituted by the French university as an institution, which requires an analysis of its structure and functioning, of the various species of power that are efficient in this universe, of the trajectories and agents who come to take up positions in it, of the "professorial" vision of the world, etc.; and, second, the deeper object: the reflexive return entailed in objectivizing one's own universe—that which is involved in objectivizing an institution socially recognized as founded to claim objectivity and universality for its own objectivations.

This device—using the university, that is, the setting of your professional life, as a pretext for studying the sociological gaze—is one that you had previously used when, in the early sixties, you conducted an investigation of marriage practices in your own village in southwestern France (Bourdieu 1962b, 1962c, 1977b) after completing a similar project among Algerian peasants (Bourdieu 1972, 1990a: 147–61).

Yes. *Homo Academicus* represents the culmination, at least in a biographical sense, of a very self-conscious "epistemological experiment" I started in the early sixties when I set out to apply to my most familiar universe the methods of investigation I had previously used to uncover the logic of kinship relations in a foreign universe, that of Algerian peasants and workers.

The idea behind this research was to overturn the natural relation of the observer to his universe of study, to make the mundane exotic and the exotic mundane, in order to render explicit what in both cases is taken for granted, and to offer a practical vindication of the possibility of a full sociological objectivation of the object *and* of the subject's relation to the object—what I call *participant objectivation.*[9] But I ended up putting myself in an impossible situation. Indeed, it turned out particularly difficult, if not impossible, to objectivize fully without objectivizing the interests that I could have in objectivizing others, without summoning myself to resist the temptation that is no doubt inherent in the posture of the sociologist, that of taking up the absolute point of view upon the object of study—here to assume a sort of intellectual power over the intellectual world. So in order to bring this study to a successful issue and to publish it, I had to discover the deep truth of this world, namely, that everybody in it struggles to do what the sociologist is tempted to do. I had to objectivize this temptation and, more precisely, to objectivize the form that it could take at a certain time in the sociologist Pierre Bourdieu.

Throughout your work, you have emphasized the need for a reflexive return on the sociologist and on his or her universe of production. You insist that it is not a form of intellectual narcissism but that it has real scientific consequences.

Indeed, I believe that *the sociology of sociology is a fundamental dimension of sociological epistemology.* Far from being a specialty among others, it is the necessary prerequisite of any rigorous sociological practice. In my view, one of the chief sources of error in the social sciences resides in an uncontrolled relation to the object which results in the projection of this relation onto the object. What distresses me when I read some works by sociologists is that people whose profession it is to objectivize the social world prove so rarely able to objectivize them-

---

9. "Objectivation has a chance to succeed only when it involves the objectivation of the point of view from which it proceeds. In short, only the ordinary alternatives of 'participant observation,' this necessarily mystified immersion, and the objectivism of the absolute gaze prevent us from grasping the possibility and the necessity of *participant objectivation.* . . . The most critical sociology is that which presupposes and implies the most radical self-criticism, and the objectivation of him or her who objectivizes is both a precondition for, and a product of, a full objectivation: the sociologist has a chance to succeed in his work of objectivation only if, observer observed, he submits to objectivation, not only everything he is, his own social conditions of production and thereby the 'limits of his mind,' but also his very work of objectivation, the hidden interests that are invested in it and the profits that it promises" (Bourdieu 1978a: 67–68).

selves, and fail so often to realize that what their apparently scientific discourse talks about is not the object but their relation to the object.

Now, to objectivize the objectivizing point of view of the sociologist is something that is done quite frequently, but in a strikingly superficial, if apparently radical, manner. When we say "the sociologist is inscribed in a historical context," we generally mean the "bourgeois sociologist" and leave it at that. But objectivation of any cultural producer demands more than pointing to—and bemoaning—his class background and location, his "race," or his gender. We must not forget to objectivize his position in the universe of cultural production, in this case the scientific or academic field. One of the contributions of *Homo Academicus* is to demonstrate that, when we carry out objectivations à la Lukács (and after him Lucien Goldmann [1975], to take one of the most sophisticated forms of this very commonplace sociologistic reductionism), that is, put in direct correspondence cultural objects and the social classes or groups for or by which they are presumed to be produced (as when it is said that such and such a form of English theater expresses "the dilemma of a rising middle class"), we commit what I call the *short-circuit fallacy* (Bourdieu 1988d). By seeking to establish a direct link between very distant terms, we omit the crucial mediation provided by the relatively autonomous space of the field of cultural production. This subspace is yet a social space with its own logic, within which agents struggle over stakes of a particular kind and pursue interests that can be quite disinterested from the standpoint of the stakes in currency in the larger social universe.

But to stop at this stage would still leave unexamined the most essential bias, whose principle lies neither in the social (class) location, nor in the specific position of the sociologist in the field of cultural production (and, by the same token, his or her situation in a space of possible theoretical, substantive, and methodological stances), but in the invisible determinations inherent in the intellectual posture itself, in the scholarly gaze that he or she casts upon the social world. As soon as we observe (*theorein*) the social world, we introduce in our perception of it a bias due to the fact that, to study it, to describe it, to talk about it, we must retire from it more or less completely. This *theoreticist* or *intellectualist bias* consists in forgetting to inscribe into the theory we build of the social world the fact that it is the product of a theoretical gaze, a "contemplative eye." A genuinely reflexive sociology must constantly guard itself against this epistemocentrism, or this "ethnocentrism of the scientist," which consists in ignoring everything that the analyst injects into his perception of the object by virtue of the fact that he is placed outside of the object, that he observes it from afar and from above.[10] Just as the anthropologist who constructs a genealogy entertains a relation to "kinship" that is worlds apart from the relation of the Kabyle head of clan who must solve the very practical and urgent problem of finding an appropriate spouse for his son, the sociologist who studies the American school system, for instance, has a "use" for schools that has little in common with those of a father seeking to find a good school for his daughter.

The upshot of this is not that theoretic knowledge is worth nothing but that we must know its limits and accompany all scientific accounts with an account of the limits and limitations of scientific accounts: theoretical knowledge owes a number of its most essential properties to the fact that the conditions under which it is produced are not that of practice.

In other words, an adequate science of society must construct theories which contain within themselves a theory of the gap between theory and practice.

Precisely. An adequate model of reality must take into account the distance between the practical experience of agents (who ignore the model) and the model which enables the mechanisms it describes to function with the unknowing "complicity" of agents. And the case of the university is a litmus test for this requirement, since everything here inclines us to commit the theoreticist fallacy. Like any social universe, the academic world is the site of a struggle over the truth of the academic world and of the social world in general. Very rapidly, we may say that the social world is the site of continual struggles to define what the social world is; but the academic world has this peculiarity today that its verdicts and pronouncements are among the most powerful socially. In academia, people fight constantly over the

10. The notion of "scholastic fallacy" is elaborated at length in *The Logic of Practice* (Bourdieu 1990a: book 1) and in "The Scholastic Point of View" (Bourdieu 1990e: 384): "Ignoring everything that is implicated in the 'scholastic point of view' leads us to commit the most serious epistemological mistake in the social sciences, namely, that which consists in putting 'a scholar inside the machine,' in picturing all social agents in the image of the scientist (of the scientist reasoning on human practice and not of the acting scientist, the scientist-in-action) or, more precisely, to place the models that the scientist must construct to account for practices into the consciousness of agents, to do as if the constructions that the scientist must produce to understand practices, to account for them, were the main determinants, the actual cause of practices."

question of who, in this universe, is socially mandated, authorized, to tell the truth of the social world (e.g., to define who and what is a delinquent or a "professional," where the boundaries of the working class lie, whether such and such a group, region, or nation exists and is entitled to rights, etc.). To intervene in it as a sociologist carries the temptation of claiming for oneself the role of the neutral arbiter, of the judge, to distribute rights and wrongs.

To put it differently, the intellectualist and theoreticist fallacy was the temptation par excellence for someone who, being a sociologist and thus party to the ongoing struggle over truth, set out to tell the truth of this world of which he is a part and of the opposed perspectives that are taken on it. This temptation to crush one's rivals by objectifying them, which was present at every moment during the objectivist phase of this research, is at the roots of serious *technical* mistakes. I emphasize "technical" here to stress the difference between scientific work and pure reflection. For everything that I have just said translates into very concrete research operations: variables added to or taken out of correspondence analyses, sources of data reinterpreted or rejected, new criteria inserted into the analysis, etc. Every single indicator of intellectual notoriety I use required an enormous amount of work to construct because, in a universe where identity is made largely through symbolic strategies, and rests in the final analysis on collective belief, the most minor piece of information had to be independently verified from different sources.

This return on the generic relation of the analyst to his object and on the particular location he or she occupies in the space of scientific production would be what distinguishes the kind of reflexivity you defend from that championed by Gouldner (1970), Garfinkel (1967; also Mehan and Wood 1975, Pollner 1991) or Bloor (1976).

Yes. Garfinkel is content with explicating dispositions that are very general, universal insofar as they are tied to the status of the agent as a knowing subject; his reflexivity is strictly phenomenological in this sense. In Gouldner, reflexivity remains more a programmatic slogan than a veritable program of *work*. [11] What must be objectivized is not (only) the individual who does the research in her biographical idiosyncracy but the position she occupies in academic space and the

---

11. Phillips (1988: 139) remarks that "Gouldner himself never followed up in any systematic way his call for a reflexive sociology, nor did he proceed to take his own advice."

biases implicated in the view she takes by virtue of being "off-sides" or "out of the game" *(hors jeu)*. What is lacking most in this American tradition, no doubt for very definite sociological reasons—among which the lesser role of philosophy in the training of researchers and the weaker presence of a critical political tradition can be singled out—is a truly reflexive and critical analysis of the academic institution and, more precisely, of the sociological institution, conceived not as an end in itself but as the condition of scientific progress.

I believe that the form of reflexivity I advocate is distinctive and paradoxical in that it is *fundamentally anti-narcissistic.* Psychoanalytic reflexivity is better tolerated and received because, if the mechanisms it makes us discover are universal, they are also tied to a unique history: the relation to the father is always a relation to a singular father in a singular history. What makes for the absence of charm, the painfulness even, of genuine sociological reflexivity is that it makes us discover things that are *generic,* things that are shared, banal, commonplace. Now, in the table of intellectual values, there is nothing worse than the common and the average. This explains much of the resistance that sociology, and in particular a non-narcissistic reflexive sociology, encounters among intellectuals.

This is to say that the sociology of sociology I argue for has little in common with a complacent and intimist return upon the private *person* of the sociologist[12] or with a search for the intellectual *Zeitgeist* that animates his or her work, as is the case with Gouldner's [1970] analysis of Parsons in *The Coming Crisis of Sociology.* I must also disassociate myself completely from the form of "reflexivity" represented by the kind of self-fascinated observation of the observer's writings and feelings which has recently become fashionable among some American anthropologists (e.g., Marcus and Fisher 1986, Geertz 1987, Rosaldo 1989, Sanjek 1990) who, having apparently exhausted the charms of fieldwork, have turned to talking about themselves rather than about their object of research. When it becomes an end in itself, such falsely radical denunciation of ethnographic writing as "poetics and politics" (Clifford and Marcus 1986) opens the door to a form of thinly veiled nihilistic relativism (of the kind that I fear also undergirds various versions of the "strong program" in the sociology of science) that stands as the polar opposite to a truly reflexive social science.

12. Bourdieu's (1988a: 21–35) distinction between "epistemic individual" and "empirical individual" is relevant here, as is "The Biographical Illusion" (Bourdieu 1987c).

There is thus an intellectualist bias inherent in the position of the social scientist who observes from the outside a universe in which she is not immediately involved. For you, it is this intellectualist relation to the world, which replaces the practical relation to practice that agents have with the scholastic relation between the observer and her object, that must be objectivized to fulfill the requirement of reflexivity.

This is one of the main things that separate me from Garfinkel and ethnomethodology. I grant that there is a primary experience of the social which, as Husserl and Schutz showed, rests on a relation of immediate belief in the facticity of the world that makes us take it for granted. This analysis is excellent as far as description is concerned but we must go beyond description and raise the issue of the conditions of possibility of this doxic experience. We must recognize that the coincidence between objective structures and embodied structures which creates the illusion of spontaneous understanding is a particular case of the relation to the world, namely the native relation. The great virtue of ethnological experience here is that it makes you immediately aware that such conditions are not universally fullfilled, as phenomenology would have us believe when it (unknowingly) universalizes a reflexion based on the particular case of the indigenous relation to one's own society.

I should add, in passing, that there is a positivism of ethnomethodologists who, in their struggle against statistical positivism, have accepted some of the presuppositions of their opponents, as when they counterpose data against data, video recording against statistical indices—this reminds us that, as Bachelard (1938: 20) wrote, "in a general manner, obstacles to scientific culture always present themselves in the form of couples." To be content with "recording" means to overlook the question of the construction or delimiting *(découpage)* of reality (think of photography). It entails accepting a preconstructed concrete which does not necessarily contain within itself the principles of its own interpretation. Interactions between a physician, an intern, and a nurse, for instance, are undergirded by hierarchical relations of power that are not always visible during the directly observable interaction.[13]

But this is not all. We need thoroughly to sociologize the phenomenological analysis of doxa as an uncontested acceptance of the daily lifeworld, not simply to establish that it is not universally valid for all

13. Bourdieu refers to research by Aaron Cicourel (1985) on discursive interactions and the social logic of medical diagnosis in a hospital.

perceiving and acting subjects, but also to discover that, when it realizes itself in certain social positions, among the dominated in particular, it represents the most radical form of acceptance of the world, the most absolute form of conservatism. This relation of prereflexive acceptance of the world grounded in a fundamental belief in the immediacy of the structures of the *Lebenswelt* represents the ultimate form of conformism. There is no way of adhering to the established order that is more undivided, more complete than this infrapolitical relation of doxic evidence; there is no fuller way of finding natural conditions of existence that would be revolting to somebody socialized under other conditions and who does not grasp them through categories of perception fashioned by this world.[14]

This alone explains a good number of misunderstandings between intellectuals and workers, where the latter take for granted and find acceptable, even "natural," conditions of oppression and exploitation that are sickening to those "on the outside"—which in no way excludes practical forms of resistance and the possibility of a revolt against them (Bourdieu et al. 1963; Bourdieu 1980d and 1981c). But the best illustration of the political import of doxa is arguably the symbolic violence exercised upon women.[15] I think in particular of the sort of socially constituted agoraphobia that leads women to exclude themselves from a whole range of public activities and ceremonies from which they are structurally excluded (in accordance with the dichotomies public/male versus private/female), especially in the realm of formal politics. Or which explains that they can confront these situations, at the cost of an extreme tension, only in proportion to the effort necessary for them to overcome the recognition of their exclusion inscribed deep in their own bodies (see Bourdieu 1990i). Thus, what comes with a narrowly phenomenological or ethnomethodological analysis is the neglect of the historical underpinnings of this relation of immediate fit between subjective and objective structures and the elision of its political significance, that is, depoliticization.

14. The two-way relation (of conditioning on the one hand, of structuring on the other) between a position in a social space and the categories of perception that come with it, and which tend to mirror its structure, is captured by Bourdieu with the notion of "point of view as a view taken from a point" (see Bourdieu 1988e, 1989d and 1988d, on "Flaubert's Point of View"; and 1989a: part 1, pp. 19–81 in particular). It is discussed in some detail below, sec. 4.

15. On the symbolic violence of gender, see Bourdieu 1990i and below, sec. 5.

2 The Unique and the Invariant

Homo Academicus deals exclusively with a particular case at a particular time: French academics in the 1960s. How does one generalize the analyses that you propose in it? For example, can the underlying structure of the French academic universe be found in another country at another time, say the United States in the 1990s?

One of the goals of the book is to show that *the opposition between the universal and the unique, between nomothetic analysis and idiographic description, is a false antinomy.* The relational and analogical mode of reasoning fostered by the concept of field enables us to grasp particularity within generality and generality within particularity, by making it possible to see the French case as a "particular case of the possible," as Bachelard (1949) says. Better, the unique historical properties of the French academic field—its high degree of centralization and institutional unification, its well-delimited barriers to entry—make it a highly propitious terrain for uncovering some of the universal laws that tendentially regulate the functioning of all fields.

One can and must read *Homo Ac idemicus* as a program of research on *any* academic field. In fact, by m ans of a mere mental experimentation, the American (Japanese, Brazilian, etc.) reader can do the work of transposition and discover, through homological reasoning, a good number of things about his or her own professional universe. Of course, this is no substitute for a thorough scientific study of the American scientific field. I toyed with the idea of doing such a study a few years back; I had begun gathering data and documents during a previous sojourn in the United States. At the time I even thought of putting together a team with some American colleagues to try to cumulate all advantages, those of the theoretical mastery of a comparative model and those of primary familiarity with the universe to be analyzed. I believe that, in the American case, such a project would in some ways be easier, given that there exist series of yearly statistics that are much more elaborate and readily available, on professors, on the various student bodies, and on universities, particularly university hierarchies and rankings of departments. (In the French case I had to build, often from scratch, a whole battery of indicators that had not existed.) I even think that a very worthwhile first pass could be done on the basis of a secondary analysis of data already compiled.

My hypothesis is that we would find the same main oppositions, in particular that between *academic capital* linked to power over the instruments of reproduction and *intellectual capital* linked to scientific renown, but that this opposition would be expressed in different forms. Would it be more or less pronounced? Is the capacity of an academic power devoid of scientific grounding to perpetuate itself greater in France or in the United States? Only a full study could tell us the answer. Such research could also give an empirical answer to the question (raised periodically, both by the American sociology of the French university system and by the French uses of the American model as an instrument of critique of the French system) of whether this American system that presents itself as more competitive and "meritocratic" is more favorable to scientific autonomy from social forces than the French system.

Does this not also raise the problem of the relation of academics to the powers that be?

Here, too, we would need to have very precise measurements of the relation of American scholars to the various institutions that are part of what I call the "field of power."[16] In France, you have indicators

---

16. On the notion of field of power, by which Pierre Bourdieu seeks to get away from the substantialist cast of the concept of "ruling class," see Bourdieu 1989a, esp. pp. 373–427; Bourdieu and Wacquant 1991; and below, part 3, sec. 2. A liminary definition is the following: "The field of power is a *field of forces* defined by the structure of the existing balance of forces between forms of power, or between different species of capital. It is also simultaneously a *field of struggles for power among the holders of different forms of power*. It is a space of play and competition in which the social agents and institutions which all possess the determinate quantity of specific capital (economic and cultural capital in particular) sufficient to occupy the dominant positions within their respective fields [the economic field, the field of higher civil service or the state, the university field, and the intellectual field] confront one another in strategies aimed at preserving or transforming this balance of forces. . . . This struggle for the imposition of the dominant principle of domination leads, at every moment, to a balance in the sharing of power, that is, to what I call a *division of the work of domination*. It is also a struggle over the legitimate principle of legitimation and for the legitimate mode of reproduction of the foundations of domination. This can take the form of real, physical struggles, (as in "palace revolutions" or wars of religion for instance) or of symbolic confrontations (as in the discussions over the relative ranking of *oratores*, priests, and *bellatores*, knights, in Medieval Europe). . . . The field of power is organized as a chiasmatic structure: the distribution according to the dominant principle of hierarchization (economic capital) is inversely symmetrical to the distribution according to the dominated principle of hierarchization (cultural capital)" (unpublished lecture, "The Field of Power," University of Wisconsin at Madison, April 1989).

such as membership in official administrative commissions, governmental committees, advisory boards, unions, etc. In the United States, I think that one would have to focus on scientific "blue-ribbon" panels, expert reports, and especially on the large philanthropic foundations and institutes of policy research that play a crucial, albeit largely hidden, role in defining the broader directions of research. On this count, my hypothesis would be that the structural ties between the university field and the field of power are stronger in the United States. Of course, one would need to take into consideration another difference: the specificity of the very structure of the American political field, characterized, very cursorily, by federalism, the multiplication of and conflicts between different levels of decision making, the absence of leftist parties and of a strong tradition of oppositional trade unionism, the weak and weakening role of "public intellectuals" (Gans 1989), and so on.

Those who dismiss my analyses on account of their "Frenchness" (every time I visit the United States, there is somebody to tell me that "in the mass culture of America, taste does not differentiate between class positions")[17] fail to see that what is truly important in them is not so much the substantive results themselves as the process through which they are obtained. "Theories" are research programs that call not for "theoretical debate" but for a practical utilization that either refutes or generalizes them or, better, specifies and differentiates their claim to generality. Husserl taught that you must immerse yourself in the particular to find in it the invariant. And Koyré (1966), who had attended Husserl's lectures, showed that Galileo did not have to repeat the experiment of the inclined plane to understand the phenomenon of the fall of bodies. A particular case that is well constructed ceases to be particular.

17. The denial—or denegation—of class distinctions in matters of culture in America has a long and distinguished pedigree, tracing its roots back to Tocqueville and accelerating with the sacralization of upper-class cultural forms at the turn of the century (Levine 1988, DiMaggio 1991b). Thus Daniel Bell (cited in Gans 1975: 6) could safely write in 1970: "Art [as representative of high-class culture] has become increasingly autonomous, making the artist a powerful taste-maker in his own right; the 'social location' of the individual (his social class or other position) no longer determines his life-style and his values. . . . For the majority of the society . . . this general proposition may still hold true. But it is increasingly evident that, for a significant proportion of the population, the relation of social position to cultural style—particularly if one thinks in gross dimensions such as working class, middle class and upper class—no longer holds." DiMaggio and Useem (1978) have effectively put this view to rest.

Another criticism, already raised against *Distinction* by some of your British and American commentators, is that the data are dated.[18]

One of the purposes of the analysis is to uncover *transhistorical invariants*, or sets of relations between structures that persist within a clearly circumscribed but relatively long historical period. In this case, whether the data are five or fifteen years old matters little. Proof is that the main opposition that emerges, within the space of scholarly disciplines, between the college of arts and sciences on the one hand and the schools of law and medicine on the other, is nothing other than the old opposition, already described by Kant in *The Conflict of the Faculties,* between the faculties that depend directly upon temporal powers and owe their authority to a sort of social delegation and the faculties that are self-founded and whose authority is premised upon scientificity (the faculty of sciences being typical of this category).[19]

Yet another proof, perhaps the most solid, of the propositions I put forth in the realm of education, and of the analysis of cultural consumption, is given by the fact that the surveys conducted at great expense every four years by the French Ministry of Culture regularly confirm the findings obtained twenty-five years ago (to the great outrage of that same Ministry) by our surveys of museum attendance, of the practice of photography, or of the fine arts, etc. And hardly a week goes by without the publication of a book or an article showing that the mechanisms of class reproduction that I described in the sixties, against the dominant representation of the time (in particular the enduring myth of America as the paradise of social mobility), are at work in countries as different as the United States, Sweden, and

18. E.g., Hoffman 1986. Jenkins (1986: 105) gives a version of that criticism so extreme as to verge on the comical when he writes: "The time lag between data collection and publication . . . renders much of the book incomprehensible to all but dedicated cultural archeologists."

19. In his latest book, *La noblesse d'Etat,* Bourdieu (1989a; also Bourdieu and de Saint Martin 1987) carries out another experimental verification of the durability of fields by showing that the structure of the field of the French *Grandes écoles,* conceived as a set of objective positional differences and distances among elite graduate schools, and between them and the social positions of power which lead to them and to which they in turn lead, has remained remarkably constant, nearly identical in fact, over the twenty-year period from 1968 to the present, the spectacular proliferation of business schools and continued decline of the university notwithstanding. Likewise for the position and structure of the subfield of the French episcopate in the field of power over the period 1930–1980 (Bourdieu and de Saint Martin 1982).

Japan (Bourdieu 1989c).[20] All of this seems to suggest that if France is an exception, as has often been said in reaction to my work, perhaps it is so only insofar as it has been studied in an exceptional, that is, nonconformist manner.

Precisely. Numerous commentators of various persuasions (e.g., Bidet 1979, DiMaggio 1979, Collins 1981a, Jenkins 1982, Sulkunen 1982, Connell 1983, Aronowitz and Giroux 1985, Wacquant 1987, Gartman 1991) have criticized your models for being overly static and "closed," leaving little room for resistance, change, and the irruption of history.[21] _Homo Academicus_ gives at least a partial answer to this concern by putting forth an analysis of a political and social rupture, the May '68 protest, which seeks to dissolve the opposition between reproduction and transformation and between structural history and event history.[22]

I willingly concede that my writings may contain arguments and expressions that render plausible the systematic misreadings that they have suffered. (I must also say in all candor that in many cases I find these criticisms strikingly superficial, and cannot help thinking that those who make them have paid more attention to the titles of my books than to the actual analyses they develop.) In addition to the title of my second book on the educational system, _Reproduction_, whose brutal conciseness helped to establish a simplified vision of my vision of history, I think that some formulas born of the will to break with the ideology of the "liberating school" can appear to be inspired by what I call the "functionalism of the worst case."[23] In fact,

20. E.g., Collins 1979, Oakes 1985, Cookson and Persell 1985a and 1985b, Brint and Karabel 1989, Karabel 1986, Weis 1988, and Fine 1991 on the United States; Broady and Palme 1990 on Sweden; Miyajima et al. 1987 on Japan; Rupp and de Lange 1989 on the Netherlands; and for a wider historical and comparative analysis, Detleff, Ringer and Simon 1987.

21. Two representative criticisms: Karabel et Halsey (1977: 33) contend that Bourdieu's "is not, properly speaking, a conflict theory of education at all, for its scheme leaves no room for working-class resistance to the cultural hegemony of the bourgeoisie"; Giroux (1983: 92) asserts that, for the French sociologist, "working-class domination . . . appears as part of an Orwellian nightmare that is as irreversible as it is unjust."

22. This is acknowledged by Randall Collins (1989: 463), who had previously taken Bourdieu to task for his lack of concern for historical change: "With this analysis, Bourdieu makes a move to shore up a gap in his earlier work . . . [and] has set himself on the path to a more dynamic analysis."

23. Or what Jon Elster (1990: 113) calls an "inverted sociodicy" based on "the assumption that all is for the worst in the worst possible world."

I have repeatedly denounced both this pessimistic functionalism and the dehistoricizing that follows from a strictly structuralist standpoint (e.g., Bourdieu 1968b, 1980b, and 1987a: 56ff.). Similarly, I do not see how relations of domination, whether material or symbolic, could possibly operate without implying, activating resistance. *The dominated, in any social universe, can always exert a certain force,* inasmuch as belonging to a field means by definition that one is capable of producing effects in it (if only to elicit reactions of exclusion on the part of those who occupy its dominant positions).[24]

24. It has become customary, indeed, almost ritual, particularly in educational sociology, to counterpose Bourdieu's "structural reproduction" model (e.g., McLeod 1987, Wexler 1987, Connell 1983: 151) to approaches that highlight—and often celebrate—resistance, struggle and the "creative praxis" of the dominated, a position often said to be exemplified by writers associated with the Birmingham Centre for Contemporary Cultural Studies—Richard Hoggart, Stuart Hall, Dick Hebdige, Paul Corrigan, Paul Willis, John Clarke, etc.—or by some strands of Frankfurt-style Marxism. Foley (1989: 138) notes that Willis "is often celebrated here in America for putting subjectivity, voluntarism, that is, people, the heroic working class, back into class analysis. . . . [He] rescues class analysis from the structural determinism of 'reproduction theorists' such as Bowles and Gintis (1976) and Bourdieu and Passeron (1977)."

This opposition misrepresents both Bourdieu's position (as I argued earlier; see also Thapan 1988, and Harker, Mahar, and Wilkes 1990) and his relation to the Birmingham school. First, Bourdieu's heavy emphasis on the "conservative function" of schooling stems from his desire to "twist the stick in the other direction," to use a sentence of Mao Zedong that he is fond of quoting by provocation. It must be understood, that is, against the backdrop of the theoretical climate of the 1960s, a climate suffused with the ideas of achievement, meritocracy, and the "end of ideology" (Bourdieu 1989c). It is deliberately that Bourdieu chooses to emphasize those functions and processes that are least visible and whose efficacy is in large part an effect of their being hidden from view—it might even be argued that this inclination is a self-conscious scientific principle informing all of this work.

Second, active resistance by students can, and often does, objectively collude with the reproduction of class and gender hierarchies, as Willis (1977) demonstrates beautifully in his monograph on the "counter-school culture" of working-class "lads" in a British industrial city (as Berger [1989: 180] puts it, Willis "describes ethnographically the interpenetration of 'habitus' and 'action' that Bourdieu outlines so persuasively in theoretical terms"; also Zolberg 1990: 158). In the end, it is an empirical matter, not a conceptual one, whether resistance manages to overturn existing patterns of domination or not. Bourdieu himself has often expressed surprise, even astonishment, at the degree to which structures of class inequality remain impervious to the individual agency of students—see for example, his analysis of how the cultural and political preferences of students among French elite schools help perpetuate their relative position (Bourdieu 1989a: 225–64). The rigid determinisms he highlights are for him observable facts that he has to report, no matter how much he may dislike them (see below, sec. 6).

The logic of adjustment of dispositions to position allows us to understand how the dominated can exhibit more *submission* (and less resistance and subversion) than those who see them through the eyes, i.e., the habitus, of the dominant or the dominated dominant, that is, less than intellectuals would envision. Having said this, there is no denying that there exist dispositions to resist; and one of the tasks of sociology is precisely to examine under what conditions these dispositions are socially constituted, effectively triggered, and rendered politically efficient.[25] But, when they go in the direction of a sort

---

Finally, Bourdieu and the Birmingham group have entertained early and cooperative relations that suggest a complementarity rather than an opposition between their works (Eldridge 1990: 170). For example, *The Uses of Literacy*, the classic study of working-class culture by Richard Hoggart (1967), the first director of the Centre, was published in translation (with a long introduction by Jean-Claude Passeron) in Bourdieu's series by Editions de Minuit as early as 1970. In 1977, at Bourdieu's request, Paul Willis published an article in *Actes de la recherche en sciences sociales* summarizing the main findings of his book *Learning to Labour*. Stuart Hall (1977: 28–29) was then also acquainted with, and quite favorably inclined towards, Bourdieu's work (in part thanks to the mediation of Raymond Williams, who had presented his own work to Bourdieu's seminar at the Ecole normale and also published work in *Actes de la recherche* in 1977). Richard Nice, Bourdieu's main translator, worked at the Birmingham CCS in the mid-1970s where he circulated early translations of Bourdieu's key articles (e.g., *Two Bourdieu Texts*, CCCS Stenciled paper no. 46, 1977). In his editorial introduction to the July 1980 issue of *Media, Culture and Society* devoted to Bourdieu's work (vol. 2, no. 3: 208), Garnham points to the "remarkable congruity" of "Bourdieu's enterprise" with the position advocated in the same issue by Corrigan and Willis, seing in it a movement "towards the fulfilment of that promise of a properly materialist theory of culture and of a cultural practice and a politics based on it."

25. In his analysis of the transformation of marital practices of his home region of Béarn, Bourdieu (1989b: 20–25) shows that it is the relative autonomy and closure of the microcosm of the local peasantry (weak penetration of market relations, geographic isolation reinforced by poor transportation routes, cultural isolation in the absence of modern forms of communication) that permitted and rendered efficacious a form of cultural resistance capable of posing peasant values, not simply as alternate, but as *antagonistic* to the dominant urban culture (see also the analysis of the uses of photography by peasants in Bourdieu et al. 1965). Suaud (1978) offers a detailed historical analysis of the impact of the "opening" (or modernization) of local social spaces upon religious practice and sacerdotal vocations in rural Vendée; Pinçon (1987) depicts the crumbling of working-class traditions with the economic restructuring of a mono-industrial city in Northeastern France. Rogers (1991), by contrast, gives an account of the dialectic of economic transformation and cultural resilience in a French rural community of Aveyron in the postwar era. Bourdieu's work on the Algerian urban (sub)proletariat and peasantry deals in detail with the sociohistorical conditions of cultural resilience and resistance in the context of colonialism (Bourdieu and Sayad 1964, Bour-

of spontaneist populism, theories of resistance (e.g., Giroux 1983, Scott 1990) often forget that the dominated seldom escape the antinomy of domination. For example, to oppose the school system, in the manner of the British working-class "lads" analyzed by Willis (1977), through horseplay, truancy, and delinquency, is to exclude oneself from the school, and, increasingly, to lock oneself into one's condition of dominated. On the contrary, to accept assimilation by adopting school culture amounts to being coopted by the institution. The dominated are very often condemned to such dilemmas, to choices between two solutions which, each from a certain standpoint, are equally bad ones (the same applies, in a sense, to women or to stigmatized minorities).[26]

In the realm of culture, historically and broadly speaking, this translates into an alternative between, on the one hand, the celebration or canonization of "popular culture," whose hyperbolic limit is the *Proletkult* that entraps the working class into its historical being and, on the other, what I call "populi-culture," that is, policies of cultural upgrading aimed at providing the dominated with access to dominant cultural goods or, at least, to a degraded version of this culture (to transform workers into petty bourgeois subscribing to the Bolshoi). This problem is a very vexing and complex one and it is easy to see why debates on this issue so often reveal more about those who

---

dieu 1979c). See also his analysis of magic as a form of resistance to the monopolization of the means of production and manipulation of religious goods (Bourdieu 1971b).

26. Philippe Bourgois (1989: 629, 627) offers a striking illustration of this antinomy of domination in his study of the "culture of terror" embraced by crack dealers in East Harlem to operate successfully in the flourishing illegal drugs economy. He shows how "the violence, crime, and substance abuse plaguing the inner city can be understood as the manifestations of a 'culture of resistance' to mainstream, white racist, and economically exclusive society. This 'culture of resistance,' however, results in greater oppression and self-destruction. . . . Tragically, it is that very process of struggle against—yet within—the system that exacerbates the trauma" of the contemporary American ghetto. Another analysis of the counterintuitive effects of class resistance is found in Pialoux's (1979) study of the labor market strategies of working-class youth from the stigmatized housing projects of the Parisian "Red Belt." Pialoux demonstrates that resistance to superexploitation and rejection of the cultural and personal indignity involved in traditional factory work leads these youth to accept, even actively seek, degraded forms of temporary work *(travail intérimaire)* that correspond closely to the needs of a growing segment of industrial employers and ends up entrenching their social and economic marginality.

engage in them—about their relation to the school, to culture, and to the "people"—than about their apparent object.[27]

We could say of certain populist exaltations of "popular culture" that they are the "pastorals" of our epoch. As the pastoral according to Empson (1935), they offer a sham inversion of dominant values and produce the fiction of a unity of the social world, thereby confirming the dominated in their subordination and the dominant in their superordination. As an inverted celebration of the principles that undergird social hierarchies, the pastoral confers upon the dominated a nobility based on their adjustment to their condition and on their submission to the established order (think of the cult of *argot* or slang and, more generally, of "popular language," of the *passéiste* extolling of the peasants of old or, in another genre, of the glorifying description of the criminal underground or, today, of the veneration of rap music in certain circles).

Your rejection of the notion of "popular culture"[28] has been denounced by some as elitist or even politically conservative. Where do you stand on this question?

To accuse me, as has sometimes been done, of consecrating the difference between so-called popular culture and "high" culture, in sum, of *ratifying* the superiority of bourgeois culture (or the opposite, depending on whether one purports to be "revolutionary" or conservative) is to ignore the Weberian distinction between a judgment of value and a reference to values (Weber 1949). It amounts to mistaking a reference to values that agents actually effect in objectivity for a

27. In a lecture on "The Uses of 'The People,'" Bourdieu (1987a: 180) argues that discourses on the "popular" cannot be elucidated without recognizing that this notion is first and foremost a stake of struggle in the intellectual field: "The different representations of 'the people' thus appear as so many transformed expressions (according to the censorship and norms of stylization specific to each field) of a fundamental relation to the people which depends on the position occupied in the field of specialists [of cultural production]—and, beyond, in social space—as well as on the trajectory which led to this position." For a critique of the notion of "popular language" (and slang) along these lines, that is, as an intellectual construct, born of scholastic distance, which destroys the very reality it claims to capture, see "Did You Say 'Popular'?" (in Bourdieu 1991e).

28. "The question is not to know whether there is or is not *for me* a 'popular culture.' The question is to know whether there is in reality something which resembles what people put under the label of 'popular culture.' And to this question my answer is no" (Bourdieu 1980b: 15).

value judgment passed by the scientist who studies them. We touch here on one of the great difficulties of sociological discourse. Most discourses on the social world aim at saying, not what the realities under consideration (the state, religion, the school, etc.) *are*, but what they are worth, whether they are good or bad. Any scientific discourse of simple enunciation is strongly liable to be perceived either as ratification or as denunciation. Thus I have been criticized just as often for celebrating dominant culture and its values (at the cost of a radical misunderstanding of the notion of legitimacy) as for glorifying popular lifestyles (based, for instance, on my analysis of dining among the working class).[29] To act as if one had only to reject in discourse the dichotomy of high culture and popular culture that exists in reality to make it vanish is to believe in magic. It is a naive form of utopianism or moralism (Dewey, however laudable his stances in matters of art and education, did not escape this kind of moralism fostered by both his epoch and his national philosophical and political traditions). Irrespective of what *I* think of this dichotomy, it exists in reality in the form of hierarchies inscribed in the objectivity of social mechanisms (such as the sanctions of the academic market) as well as in the subjectivity of schemata of classifications, systems of preferences, and tastes, which everybody knows (in practice) to be themselves hierarchized.[30]

Verbally to deny evaluative dichotomies is to pass a morality off for a politics. The dominated in the artistic and the intellectual fields have always practiced that form of radical chic which consists in rehabilitating socially inferior cultures or the minor genres of legitimate culture (think, for instance, of Cocteau's spirited defense of jazz at the turn of the century). To denounce hierarchy does not get us anywhere. What must be changed are the conditions that make this hierarchy exist, both in reality and in minds. We must—I have never stopped repeating it—work to *universalize in reality the conditions of ac-*

29. Grignon and Passeron (1989) analyze this twofold temptation of "populism" (the inverted celebration of the autonomy and integrity of popular cultural forms) and "miserabilism" (the reduction of popular culture to a passive side effect of the cultural rule of the dominant class).

30. Lawrence W. Levine's (1988) historical study of the "sacralization" of the fine arts reveals, in the case of the United States, the process whereby the distinction between highbrow and lowbrow culture was progressively instituted in the form of organizations and categories of aesthetic judgment and appreciation. See also DiMaggio 1991b.

cess to what the present offers us that is most universal, instead of talking about it.[31]

You are aware that there are first-degree readings of *Distinction* **or** *The Love of Art* **(Bourdieu 1984a; Bourdieu, Darbel, and Schnapper 1966) that portray sociology as a war machine against culture and the sociologist as the high priest of a Boeotian hatred of art or philosophy.**

If I could express myself in such pretentious terms, I would say that this is to mistake the iconologist for the iconoclast. In all sincerity, I cannot deny that a certain iconoclasm of the disenchanted believer could have facilitated the break with primary belief necessary to produce an objectifying analysis of cultural practices (and of philosophical and artistic practices in particular). But spectacular transgressions and aggressive provocations—out of which some artists make artistic "statements"—can still be expressions of a disappointed faith turned against itself. What is sure is that mastery of iconolatrous and iconoclastic pulsions is the primary condition for progress toward knowledge of artistic practice and experience. Much as negative theology, artistic nihilism is still another manner of sacrificing to the cult of the God of Art. (This could be shown very clearly by revealing how, no matter how liberating and enlightening they may seem, the fulgurations and fulminations of Nietzsche against culture and education remain trapped within the limits attached to their social conditions of production, that is, to the position of Nietzsche in social space and, more specifically, within academic space.)

I believe that a definite break with the more naive forms of artistic belief is the necessary condition for the very possibility of constituting art and culture as an object. This explains why the sociology of art

31. Elsewhere, Bourdieu (1990e: 385–86) asks: "What do we do, for instance, when we talk of a 'popular aesthetics' or when we want at all costs to credit the 'people' *(le peuple)*, who do not care to have one, with a 'popular culture'? Forgetting to effect the *epoché* of the social conditions of the *epoché* of practical interests that we effect when we pass a pure aesthetic appreciation, we purely and simply *universalize* the particular case in which we are placed or, to speak a bit more roughly, we, in an unconscious and *thoroughly theoretical* manner, grant the economic and social privilege which is the precondition of the pure and universal aesthetic point of view to all men and women. . . . Most of the human works that we are accustomed to treating as universal—law, science, the fine arts, ethics, religion, etc.—cannot be disassociated from the scholastic point of view and from the social and economic conditions which make the latter possible."

will always shock the believers or those pharisees of culture who, as we recently saw both in the United States and in France, rise to the defense of High Culture (or the Great Books, etc.) and who are equally distant from the liberated unself-consciousness of the aristocratic lover as they are from the provocative freedom of the avant-garde artist. Needless to say, if I sometimes happen to feel close to the latter—perhaps by virtue of a homology of position—I do not take up stances in the artistic field properly speaking. (I turned down, a few years ago, a chance to collaborate with conceptual painter Alain de Kérily, who has since made a name for himself in New York, who wanted to exhibit a statistical table excerpted from my book *The Love of Art* along with a recording of a dialogue between the artist and the sociologist.) Thus, even though, as a "lover" of art, I have preferences among painters engaged in the field (which means that I am not indifferent to or, worse still, systematically hostile to art, as some would like to think), I do not intervene in the field but, rather, I take it as an object. I describe the space of positions which constitute it as a field of production of this modern fetish that the work of art is, that is, as a universe objectively oriented toward the *production of belief* in the work of art (Bourdieu 1980a). (Thus the analogy, which has often struck analysts, between the artistic field and the religious field. Nothing is more like a pilgrimage to a holy shrine than one of those trips to Salzburg that tour operators will organize in the thousands for the Year of Mozart.)[32] It is only then that, as I did for the literary field in Flaubert's time or for the artistic field in Manet's (Bourdieu 1983d, 1987j, 1988d, 1987i), I can raise the question of the relation between the space of positions occupied by different producers and the space of works (with their themes, form, style, etc.) which correspond to them.

In short, I observe that position-takings (preferences, taste) closely correspond to positions occupied in the field of production on the side of producers and in social space on the side of consumers. This is to say that all forms of artistic faith, whether blind belief or pharisaic piety, or even the belief freed from the observances of cultural ritualism (to which a scouring sociology can give access), have social conditions of possibility. This strikes a devastating blow to the mystical

---

32. "The sociology of culture is the sociology of the religion of our time" (Bourdieu 1980b: 197). See especially "High Fashion and High Culture" and "But Who Created the Creators?" in Bourdieu 1980a: 196–206, 207–21; and 1988b.

representation of the artistic "encounter" and to the primary cult of art and the artist, with its holy places, its perfunctory rites, and its routinized devotions. And it is particularly devastating for all those "poor whites" of culture who desperately cling to the last vestiges of difference, that is, humanist culture, Latin, spelling, the classics, the West, and so on. But what can I do about it? All I can wish for is that iconoclastic critique, which can use the weapons of sociological analysis, will be able to promote an artistic experience shorn of ritualism and exhibitionism.

So your work is not a "blanket condemnation of the aesthetic as a mere class signal and as conspicuous consumption" (Jameson 1990: 132; also Bürger 1990, Garnham 1986), and it does not sentence us to a leveling relativism.

Of course not. The artistic field is the site of an objectively oriented and cumulative process engendering works which, from purification to purification, from refinement to refinement, reach levels of accomplishment that decisively set them apart from forms of artistic expression that are not the product of such a history. (I have an unpublished postface to *Distinction* where I tackle the problem of cultural relativism. I took it out of the book because I thought: I have effected a critical questioning of aesthetic belief, of the fetishism of art shared; and now, at the very end, I give them an escape? The God of Art is dead and I am going to resuscitate him?)

Durkheim (1965) raises this question in *The Elementary Forms of Religious Life* when he asks: is there not something universal about culture? Yes, ascesis. Everywhere culture is constructed against nature, that is, through effort, exercise, suffering; all human societies put culture above nature. Thus if we can say that avant-garde paintings are superior to the lithographs of suburban shopping malls, it is because the latter are a product without history (or the product of a negative history, that of the divulgence of the high art of the preceding epoch), whereas the former are accessible only on condition of mastering the relatively cumulative history of previous artistic production, that is, the endless series of refusals and transcendences necessary to reach the present—as, for instance, with poetry as antipoetry or antipoetics.

It is in this sense that we can say that "high" art is more universal. But, as I noted, the conditions of appropriation of this universal art are not universally allocated. I showed in *The Love of Art* that access to "high" art is not a question of virtue or individual gift but of (class) learning and cultural inheritance.[33] The universality of the aesthetes is the product of privilege, for they have a monopoly over the universal. We may concede that Kant's aesthetics is true, but only as a phenomenology of the aesthetic experience of those who are the product of *scholē*, leisure, distance from economic necessity, and practical urgency. To know this leads to a cultural politics that is just as opposed to the "absolutism" of the knights of Culture constituted as the preserve of a happy few (Bloom) as it is to the relativism of those who, forgetting to include in their theory and practice differences inscribed in reality, merely ratify and accept the fact of the cultural dispossession of the majority: an ethical or political program aimed at universalizing the conditions of access to what the present offers us as most universal (see Bourdieu 1990e).

But what could the social bases of such a cultural policy be, and can we reasonably expect those who have a monopoly over the universal to work to undermine their own privilege?

This is indeed one of the major contradictions of any cultural policy. We could go on and on enumerating the strategies of bad faith through which the privileged of culture tend to perpetuate their monopoly, very often under the appearance of sacrificing it—whether it be verbal deplorations of cultural dispossession (nowadays imputed to the alleged bankruptcy of the school system) or the rehabilitations, as spectacular as they are inefficacious, aimed at universalizing cultural exigencies without universalizing the conditions that make them attainable.

Reflexive vigilance must be exercised with special force whenever we deal with culture, art, or science, to say nothing of philosophy and sociology: so many objects of direct interest to thinkers and scientists, in which they are deeply invested. It is especially necessary, in these cases, to break with spontaneous representations in currency in the intellectual world. It behooves the sociology of culture, of art, of sci-

33. "The sociologist establishes, theoretically and experimentally, that . . . in its learned form, aesthetic pleasure presupposes learning and, in this particular case, learning by familiarization and exercise, so that this pleasure, an artificial product of art and artifice, which is experienced or is meant to be experienced as if it were natural, is in reality a cultivated pleasure" (Bourdieu and Darbel 1966: 162).

ence, of philosophy, in sum, of all cultural works that claim universality, to accomplish the rupture, no matter how painful it may be for the one who effects it as well as for others, with the scholarly doxa and with all the "professional" ideologies of the professionals of thought. This is the reason I gave these objects the privileged place, the kind of absolute priority they occupy in my work.

Homo Academicus is not only an exercise in methodical reflexivity. In it, you also tackle the problem of historical crisis, the question of whether social science can account, if only partially, for what may at first glance appear to be a contingent conjuncture, a singular event or series of events, and you confront the more general question of the relations between social structure and historical change.

In *Homo Academicus* I try to account, as completely as possible, for the crisis of May '68 and, at the same time, to put forth some of the elements of an invariant model of crises or revolutions. In the course of the analysis of this specific event, I discovered a number of properties that seem to me to be quite general. First I show that the crisis internal to the university was the product of the meeting of two partial crises provoked by separate, autonomous evolutions. On the one hand we have a crisis among the faculty triggered by the effects of the rapid and massive swelling of its ranks and by the resulting tensions between its dominant and subordinate categories: full professors, and assistant professors and teaching assistants. On the other hand, we find a crisis of the student body due to a whole range of factors, including the overproduction of graduates, the devaluation of credentials, changes in gender relations, etc. These partial, local crises converged, providing a base for conjunctural alliances. The crisis then spread along lines that were very determinate, toward instances of symbolic production in particular (radio and television stations, the church, and so on), that is, in all those universes in which there was an incipient conflict between the established holders of the legitimacy of discourse and the new contenders.

Thus I have never overlooked the contradictions and the conflicts of which the academic field is the site and which are at the very root of the ongoing changes through which it perpetuates itself—and remains more unchanged than may appear at first sight. The very notion of field implies that we transcend the conventional opposition between structure and history, conservation and transformation, for the relations of power which form the structure provide the underpinnings of both resistance to domination and resistance to subversion, as we can clearly see in May 1968. Circularity is only apparent here, and one need only enter into the detail of a particular historical conjuncture to see how struggles that only an analysis of positions in the structure can elucidate account for the transformation of this structure.

More generally, could you clarify the place of history in your thinking?

Obviously, this is an immensely complex question and I can only answer it in the most general terms.[34] Suffice it to say that *the separation of sociology and history is a disastrous division,* and one totally devoid of epistemological justification: all sociology should be historical and all history sociological. In point of fact, one of the functions of the theory of fields that I propose is to make the opposition between reproduction and transformation, statics and dynamics, or structure and history, vanish. As I tried to demonstrate empirically in my research on the French literary field in Flaubert's time and on the artistic field around Manet's time (Bourdieu 1983d, 1987i, 1987j, 1988d), we cannot grasp the dynamics of a field if not by a synchronic analysis of its structure and, simultaneously, we cannot grasp this structure without a historical, that is, genetic analysis of its constitution and of the tensions that exist between positions in it, as well as between this field and other fields, and especially the field of power.

The artificiality of the distinction between history and sociology is most evident at the highest level of the discipline: I think that great historians are also great sociologists (and often vice versa). But, for various reasons, they feel less bound than sociologists to forge concepts, to construct models, or to produce more or less pretentious theoretical or metatheoretical discourses, and they can bury under elegant narratives the compromises that often go hand in hand with discretion. On the other hand, in the present state of the social sciences, I think that, too often, the kind of "macrohistory" that many sociologists practice when they tackle processes of rationalization, bureaucratization, modernization, and so on, continues to function as one of the last refuges of a thinly veiled social philosophy. There are of course many exceptions, and fortunately their number has

34. See Bourdieu and Chartier 1989, Bourdieu, Chartier and Darnton 1985, and Bourdieu 1980d for elements of a more extended reply.

grown in recent years. I have in mind here works, such as that of Charles Tilly (1990) on the formation of European states, that managed to escape the trap of the more or less openly functionalist evolutionism implied by a unidimensional framework, and have paved the way for a genuinely genetic sociology by a theoretically guided use of the comparative method. What we need, in effect, is a form of structural history that is rarely practiced, which finds in each successive state of the structure under examination both the product of previous struggles to maintain or to transform this structure, and the principle, via the contradictions, the tensions, and the relations of force which constitute it, of subsequent transformations.

The intrusion of pure historical events, such as May '68 or any other great historical break, becomes understandable only when we reconstruct the plurality of "independent causal series" of which Cournot (1912) spoke to characterize chance *(le hasard)*, that is, the different and relatively autonomous historical concatenations that are put together in each universe, and whose collision determines the singularity of historical happenings. But here I will refer you to the analysis of May 1968 that I develop in the last chapter of *Homo Academicus* and which contains the embryo of a theory of symbolic revolution that I am presently developing.

There are numerous affinities between your work, particularly your historical studies on the French artistic field in late-nineteenth-century France, and that of several major cultural and social historians. I think here immediately of people such as Norbert Elias, E. P. Thompson, Eric Hobsbawm, William H. Sewell, Moshe Lewin, Alain Corbin, or even Charles Tilly—and I could name many others.[35] These historians share a focus on enduring processes of constitution of mental, cultural, and sociopolitical structures: categories of conduct, appreciation, and feeling, cultural expressions, forms of collective action, and social groupings. These concerns are also central to your own research, if on a different scale. Why have you not made these intellectual kinships more visible? The absence of an open rapprochement with history is all the

35. See, for example, Elias 1978b, 1983; E. P. Thompson 1963; Sewell 1980, 1987; Lewin 1985; Corbin 1986, 1990; and Tilly 1986. One could also add Nathalie Zemon Davis 1975; Lynn Hunt 1984; and Fritz Ringer (1990, 1991), who recently proposed a recasting of intellectual history in terms of Bourdieu's concept of field (see the rejoinders to his programmatic essay by Jay [1990] and Lemert [1990]). The convergence between Bourdieu's theory of practice and historical sociology broadly conceived is noted by Philip Abrams (1982).

more puzzling when one considers that much of the research published in *Actes de la recherche en sciences sociales* is historical in the strongest sense of the term, and also that many, if not most, of your close colleagues and friends are themselves historians (e.g., Roger Chartier, Robert Darnton, Louis Marin, Joan Scott, and Carl Schorske).[36]

Perhaps the bombast with which some sociologists have seemingly "discovered" history in recent years has discouraged me from highlighting the convergences and affinities that exist, and have existed for a long time.[37] It is true that I have a deep-seated suspicion of the great tendential laws that have flourished in Marxism and its macroscopic rivals (structural-functionalism, developmentalism, historism, etc.). Among the professional reflexes I try to inculcate is defiance toward superficial and careless comparisons between two states of a given social system (as, for instance, with the question of the "democratization" of higher education), because such comparisons so easily lead to normative judgments and teleological reasoning. Besides the teleological fallacy, there is also the tendency to pass description off as explanation. In short, there is a whole range of things that make me feel ill at ease.

Now, the problematic of Elias, for instance, is certainly one with which I have a great deal of intellectual sympathy, because it is indeed based on the historical psychosociology of an actual grand historical process, the constitution of a state which progressively monopolizes first physical violence and second—this is what I want to add with my current work on the genesis of the state—symbolic violence.[38] This is not the place to discuss everything that separates me from Elias beyond our agreement on a small number of fundamental principles, most often derived from Durkheim or Weber, which are, in my eyes, constitutive of sociological thinking. But I must at least mention

36. The intellectual affinities are evident upon reading Chartier 1988a, Darnton 1984, Marin 1988, Schorske 1981, and Scott 1988, all of whom have published articles in *Actes de la recherche en sciences sociales* (as have E. P. Thompson, Eric J. Hobsbawm, Norbert Elias, and Moshe Lewin before them). See also the partial parallels with the "New Cultural History" (Hunt 1989); the exchange between Bourdieu, Chartier, and Darnton (1985) touches on several of the more significant differences between Bourdieu and the latter.

37. For instance, in 1975, Bourdieu (1980b: 251–63) gave a concluding address entitled "Strikes and Political Action" to a conference on European social history organized by the Maison des Sciences de l'Homme, in which Hobsbawm, Thompson, and Tilly participated.

38. See Bourdieu 1989a, Bourdieu and Wacquant 1991 and below, sec. 5.

what my work on the emergence of the state has led me to discover: that, just like Weber before him, Elias always fails to ask who benefits and who suffers from the monopoly of the state over legitimate violence, and to raise the question (addressed in *La noblesse d'Etat* [Bourdieu 1989a]) of the domination wielded *through* the state.

Elias is also more sensitive than I am to continuity. Historical analysis of long-term trends is always liable to hide critical breaks. Take the example of the program of historical research on sports that Elias outlines in his well-known "Essay on Sport and Violence."[39] By sketching a continuous genealogy running from the games of Antiquity to the Olympic Games of today, this piece carries the danger of masking the fundamental ruptures introduced, among other things, by the rise of educational systems, English colleges and boarding schools, etc., and by the subsequent constitution of a relatively autonomous "space of sports."[40] There is nothing in common between ritual games such as the medieval *soule* and American football. We find the same problem when we study artists or intellectuals: we use the same word, "artist," the same lexicon of aesthetic expression, creation, creator, etc., to speak of Piero della Francesca or of Pissaro and Munch. But in fact there are extraordinary discontinuities and a con-

39. This long article was first published in French in *Actes de la recherche en sciences sociales* (no. 6, November 1976) and subsequently reprinted in a shorter version in Elias and Dunning (1986: 150–74).

40. "The Space of Sports" is the topic of two recent issues of *Actes de la recherche en sciences sociales* (79 and 80, September and November 1989), which include articles on tennis, golf, and squash; the significance and uses of soccer in Brazil, in a small mining town of France, and inside the automobile firm Peugeot; the historical separation of the two games of rugby in Great Britain; the social evolution of sky-diving; the struggle over sports among the nobility at the turn of the century; boxing in black Chicago; and the symbolism of the 1936 Olympic games in Berlin. Bourdieu is virtually alone among major sociologists—Elias being the other one—to have written seriously on sports (see Bourdieu 1978c, 1988f, and in *Distinction*) and he has exerted a strong influence on physical educationalists, as MacAloon's (1988) "A Prefatory Note to Pierre Bourdieu's 'Program for a Sociology of Sport'" indicates (for instance, the study of the social roots, organization, and meaning of rugby in Southern France by Pociello [1981], a physical education specialist, owes much to Bourdieu's theoretical direction). This interest in sport—a minor sociological topic by any measure of the hierarchy of scientific objects— is related to the centrality that Bourdieu accords the body in his theory and to the fact that it offers what Merton (1987) calls a "strategic research site" for uncovering the logic of "practical sense" (as well as an "opportunistic research" site [Riemer 1977]: Bourdieu was a noted rugby player in his youth).

tinuous genesis of discontinuity. When we retrospectively project the concept of artist before the 1880s, we commit absolutely fantastic anachronisms: we overlook the genesis, not of the character of the artist or the writer, but of the *space* in which this character can exist as such.

And the same is true of politics. We take the risk of formidable historical fallacies when we fail, as do some historians who, today, take a fancy to "political philosophy," to pose the question of the social genesis of the political field (Bourdieu 1981a) and of the very notions that political philosophy eternalizes by treating them as transhistorical essences. What I just said about the words "art" and "artist" would apply to notions such as "democracy" and "public opinion" (see Bourdieu 1979e, Bourdieu and Champagne 1989, Champagne 1990). Paradoxically, historians often condemn themselves to anachronism because of their ahistorical, or dehistoricized, usage of the concepts they employ to think the societies of the past. They forget that these *concepts* and the reality they capture are themselves the product of a historical construction: the very history to which they apply these concepts has in fact invented, created them, oftentimes at the cost of an immense—and largely forgotten—historical work.[41]

3   The Logic of Fields

The notion of field is, together with those of habitus and capital, the central organizing concept of your work, which includes studies of the fields of artists and intellectuals, class lifestyles, *Grandes écoles*, science, religion, the field of power, of law, of housing construction, and so on.[42] You use the notion of field in a highly

41. This fruitful tension between history and sociology encouraged by Bourdieu is particularly well illustrated by the historical research of his colleagues and collaborators Christophe Charle (1987, 1990, 1991), Dario Gamboni (1989), Alain Viala (1985) and Victor Karady, who has undertaken an ambitious long-term project in the historical sociology of Hungary and other Eastern European countries (see Karady 1985, Don and Karady 1989, Karady and Mitter 1990). On the question of historical discontinuity and the temporal rootedness of conceptual categories or *épistémés*, there are many parallels between Bourdieu and Foucault, some of which can be traced directly back to their common training in the history of science and medicine under Canguilhem (Bourdieu 1988e: 779). The major differences are rooted in Bourdieu's historicizing of reason via the notion of field.

42. On the intellectual and artistic field, see Bourdieu 1971a, 1975b, 1975c, 1983a, 1983d, 1988a; on the space of classes and class lifestyles, Bourdieu 1978b, 1984a, 1987b; on

technical and precise sense that is perhaps partly hidden behind its commonsense meaning. Could you explicate where the notion comes from (for Americans, it is likely to evoke the "field theory" of Kurt Lewin) and what its meaning and theoretical purposes are?

I do not like professorial definitions much, so let me begin with a brief aside on their usage. I could refer here to *Le métier de sociologue* (Bourdieu, Chamboredon, and Passeron 1973), which is a didactic, almost scholastic, book,[43] but a book which nevertheless contains a number of theoretical and methododological principles that would make people understand that many of the gaps or shortcomings for which I am sometimes reproached are in fact conscious refusals and deliberate choices. For instance, the use of *open concepts*[44] is a way of rejecting

---

cultural goods, Bourdieu 1980h, 1985d, and Bourdieu and Delsaut 1975; on the religious field, Bourdieu 1971b, 1987h, Bourdieu and de Saint Martin 1982; on the scientific field Bourdieu 1981d, 1987e, 1990e; on the juridical field and the field of power, Bourdieu 1981a, 1986c, 1987g, 1989a, and Bourdieu and de Saint Martin 1978, 1982, 1987; the field of private housing construction is explored in Bourdieu et al. 1987 and in the articles that make up the March 1990 issue of *Actes de la recherche en sciences sociales*.

Others studies of fields conducted at the Center for European Sociology include, *inter alia*, the fields of comic books (Boltanski 1975) and of children's book publishing (Chamboredon and Fabiani 1977), the field of the French university and intellectuals at the turn of the century (Charle 1983 and 1990, Karady 1983, Fabiani 1989), the field of power under the Third Republic (Charle 1987), and the fields of religion (Grignon 1977), the arts and sciences in the classical age (Heinich 1987), seventeenth-century literature (Viala 1985), the management of the "elderly" (Lenoir 1978), peasant trade-unionism (Maresca 1983), social work (Verdès-Leroux 1976, 1978), political representation (Champagne 1988, 1990), and feminist studies in France (Lagrave 1990).

43. This book (whose translation was for years blocked for obscure copyright reasons and has just been published by Walter de Gruyter) is essential to an understanding of Bourdieu's sociological epistemology. It consists of a dense exposition of the foundational principles of "applied rationalism" in the social sciences, and of a selection of texts (by historians and philosophers of science, Marx, Durkheim, Weber, Mauss, and other sociologists) that illustrate key arguments. Each comprises three parts which theorize the three stages that Bourdieu, following French epistemologist Gaston Bachelard, considers central to the production of sociological knowledge and that he encapsulates in the following formula: "Facts are conquered [through rupture with common sense], constructed, confirmed (*les faits sont conquis, construits, constatés)"* (Bourdieu, Chamboredon, and Passeron 1973: 24). A worthwhile critical introduction to Bachelard's philosophy can be found in Tiles 1984; see MacAllester 1991 for a selection of texts.

44. For examples of criticisms of Bourdieu for the lack of closure or rigor of his concepts, see DiMaggio 1979: 1467, Swartz 1981: 346–48, Lamont and Larreau 1988: 155–58.

positivism—but this is a ready-made phrase. It is, to be more precise, a permanent reminder that concepts have no definition other than systemic ones, and are designed to be *put to work empirically in systematic fashion.* Such notions as habitus, field, and capital can be defined, but only within the theoretical system they constitute, not in isolation.[45]

This also answers another question that is often put to me in the United States: why do I not propose any "laws of the middle range"? I think that this would first of all be a way of satisfying a positivistic expectation, of the kind represented in earlier times by a book by Berelson and Steiner (1964) which was a compilation of small, partial laws established by the social sciences. This kind of positivistic gratification is something that science must deny itself. Science admits only systems of laws (Duhem showed this long ago for physics, and Quine has since developed this fundamental idea).[46] And what is true of concepts is true of relations, which acquire their meaning only within a system of relations. Similarly, if I make extensive use of correspondence analysis, in preference to multivariate regression for instance, it is because correspondance analysis is a relational technique of data analysis whose philosophy corresponds exactly to what, in my view, the reality of the social world is. It is a technique which "thinks" in terms of relation, as I try to do precisely with the notion of field.[47]

To think in terms of field is to *think relationally.*[48] The relational

45. The distinction between relational or "systemic concepts" (rooted in a theoretical problematics of the object) and "operational concepts," defined in terms of the pragmatic requirements and constraints of empirical measurement, is elaborated in Bourdieu, Chamboredon, and Passeron 1973: 53–54.

46. The now famous "Duhem-Quine hypothesis" states that science is a complex network that faces the test of empirical experience as a whole: evidence impinges not on any particular proposition or concept but on the entire net they form.

47. The technique of correspondence analysis is a variant of factor analysis developed by the school of "French Data Analysis" (J. P. Benzécri, Rouanet, Tabard, Lebart, Cibois), which has elaborated tools for a relational use of statistics that are increasingly being employed by social scientists in France, the Netherlands, and Japan in particular. Two useful and accessible presentations in English are Greenacre 1984 and Lebart et al. 1984; correspondence analysis has recently been included on standard computer packages by SAS and BMDP.

48. Bourdieu (1982a: 41–42, my translation) explains: "To think in terms of field demands a conversion of the whole ordinary vision of the social world which fastens only on visible things: the individual, this *ens realissimum* to which we are attached by a sort of primordial ideological interest; the group, which is only in appearance defined solely by the temporary or durable relations, formal or informal, between its members; and

(rather than more narrowly "structuralist") mode of thinking is, as Cassirer (1923) demonstrated in *Substanzbegriff und Funktionsbegriff*, the hallmark of modern science, and one could show that it lies behind scientific enterprises apparently as different as those of the Russian formalist Tynianov,[49] of the social psychologist Kurt Lewin, of Norbert Elias, and of the pioneers of structuralism in anthropology, linguistics and history, from Sapir and Jakobson to Dumézil and Lévi-Strauss. (If you check, you will find that both Lewin and Elias draw explicitly on Cassirer, as I do, to move beyond the Aristotelian substantialism that spontaneously impregnates social thinking.) I could twist Hegel's famous formula and say that *the real is the relational:* what exist in the social world are relations—not interactions between agents or intersubjective ties between individuals, but objective relations which exist "independently of individual consciousness and will," as Marx said.

In analytic terms, a field may be defined as a network, or a configuration, of objective relations between positions. These positions are objectively defined, in their existence and in the determinations they impose upon their occupants, agents or institutions, by their present and potential situation *(situs)* in the structure of the distribution of species of power (or capital) whose possession commands access to the specific profits that are at stake in the field, as well as by their objective relation to other positions (domination, subordination, homology, etc.).

In highly differentiated societies, the social cosmos is made up of a number of such relatively autonomous social microcosms, i.e., spaces of objective relations that are the site of a logic and a necessity that are *specific and irreducible* to those that regulate other fields. For instance, the artistic field, or the religious field, or the economic field all follow specific logics: while the artistic field has constituted itself by rejecting

---

even relations understood as *interactions,* that is, as intersubjective, actually activated connections. In fact, just as the Newtonian theory of gravitation could only be constructed against Cartesian realism which wanted to recognize no mode of action other than collision, direct contact, the notion of field presupposes a break with the realist representation which leads us to reduce the effect of the *environment* to the effect of direct action as actualized during an interaction."

49. Jurii Tynianov (1894–1943) was, with Roman Jakobson and Vladimir Propp, a leading member of the Russian Formalist school which advocated a structuralist approach to the study of literature and language.

or reversing the law of material profit (Bourdieu 1983d), the economic field has emerged, historically, through the creation of a universe within which, as we commonly say, "business is business," where the enchanted relations of friendship and love are in principle excluded.

You often use the analogy of a "game" to give a first intuitive grasp of what you understand by field.

We can indeed, with caution, compare a field to a game *(jeu)* although, unlike the latter, a field is not the product of a deliberate act of creation, and it follows rules or, better, regularities,[50] that are not explicit and codified. Thus we have *stakes (enjeux)* which are for the most part the product of the competition between players. We have an *investment in the game, illusio* (from *ludus,* the game): players are taken in by the game, they oppose one another, sometimes with ferocity, only to the extent that they concur in their belief *(doxa)* in the game and its stakes; they grant these a recognition that escapes questioning. Players agree, by the mere fact of playing, and not by way of a "contract," that the game is worth playing, that it is "worth the candle," and this *collusion* is the very basis of their competition. We also have *trump cards,* that is, master cards whose force varies depending on the game: just as the relative value of cards changes with each game, the hierarchy of the different species of capital (economic, social, cultural, symbolic) varies across the various fields. In other words, there are cards that are valid, efficacious in all fields—these are the fundamental species of capital—but their relative value as trump cards is determined by each field and even by the successive states of the same field.

This is so because, at bottom, the value of a species of capital (e.g., knowledge of Greek or of integral calculus) hinges on the existence of a game, of a field in which this competency can be employed: a species of capital is what is efficacious in a given field, both as a weapon and as a stake of struggle, that which allows its possessors to wield a power, an influence, and thus to *exist*, in the field under consideration, instead of being considered a negligible quantity. In empirical work, it is one and the same thing to determine what the field is, where its limits lie, etc., and to determine what species of capital are

50. On the difference between rules and regularities and the equivocations of structuralism between those two terms, see Bourdieu 1986a, and 1990a: 30–41.

active in it, within what limits, and so on. (We see here how the notions of capital and field are tightly interconnected.)

At each moment, it is the state of the relations of force between players that defines the structure of the field. We can picture each player as having in front of her a pile of tokens of different colors, each color corresponding to a given species of capital she holds, so that her *relative force in the game*, her *position* in the space of play, and also her *strategic orientation toward the game*, what we call in French her "game," the moves that she makes, more or less risky or cautious, subversive or conservative, depend both on the total number of tokens and on the composition of the piles of tokens she retains, that is, on the volume and structure of her capital. Two individuals endowed with an equivalent overall capital can differ, in their position as well as in their stances ("position-takings"), in that one holds a lot of economic capital and little cultural capital while the other has little economic capital and large cultural assets. To be more precise, the strategies of a "player" and everything that defines his "game" are a function not only of the volume and structure of his capital *at the moment under consideration* and of the game chances (Huygens spoke of *lusiones*, again from *ludus*, to designate objective probabilities) they guarantee him, but also of the *evolution over time* of the volume and structure of this capital, that is, of his social trajectory and of the dispositions (habitus) constituted in the prolonged relation to a definite distribution of objective chances.

But this is not all: players can play to increase or to conserve their capital, their number of tokens, in conformity with the tacit rules of the game and the prerequisites of the reproduction of the game and its stakes; but they can also get in it to transform, partially or completely, the immanent rules of the game. They can, for instance, work to change the relative value of tokens of different colors, the exchange rate between various species of capital, through strategies aimed at discrediting the form of capital upon which the force of their opponents rests (e.g., economic capital) and to valorize the species of capital they preferentially possess (e.g., juridical capital).[51] A good number of struggles within the field of power are of this type, notably

---

51. For an illustration of the growing conflict between juridical and economic capital involved in the rise of new legal professions (notably "bankruptcy experts") at the intersection of the two fields, see Dezalay 1989.

those aimed at seizing power over the state, that is, over the economic and political resources that enable the state to wield a power over all games and over the rules that regulate them.

This analogy displays the links between the core concepts of your theory, but it does not tell us how one determines the existence of a field and its boundaries.

The question of the limits of the field is a very difficult one, if only because it is *always at stake in the field itself* and therefore admits of no *a priori* answer. Participants in a field, say, economic firms, high fashion designers, or novelists, constantly work to differentiate themselves from their closest rivals in order to reduce competition and to establish a monopoly over a particular subsector of the field. (I should immediately correct this sentence for its teleological bias, the very bias attributed to me by those who construe my analysis of cultural practices as based on a search for distinction. There is a production *of* difference which is in no way the product of a *search for* difference. There are many agents—I think for instance of Gustave Flaubert—for whom to exist in a given field consists *eo ipso* in differing, in being different, in asserting one's difference, oftentimes because they are endowed with properties such that they should not be there, they should have been eliminated at the entrance to the field.) Their efforts to impose this or that criterion of competency, of membership, may be more or less successful in various conjunctures. Thus the boundaries of the field can only be determined by an empirical investigation. Only rarely do they take the form of juridical frontiers (e.g., *numerus clausus*), even though they are always marked by more or less institutionalized "barriers to entry."

We may think of a field as a space within which an effect of field is exercised, so that what happens to any object that traverses this space cannot be explained solely by the intrinsic properties of the object in question. The limits of the field are situated at the point where the effects of the field cease. Therefore, you must try by various means to measure in each case the point at which these statistically detectable effects decline. In the work of empirical research the construction of a field is not effected by an act of imposition. For instance, I seriously doubt that the ensemble of cultural associations (choirs, theater groups, reading clubs, etc.) of a given American state or of a French region form a field. By contrast, the work of Jerry Karabel (1984) suggests that major American universities are linked by objective relations such that the structure of these (material and symbolic) relations has effects within each of them. Similarly for newspapers: Michael Schudson (1978) shows that you cannot understand the emergence of the modern idea of "objectivity" in journalism if you do not see that it arose in newspapers concerned with standards of respectability, as that which distinguishes "news" from the mere "stories" of tabloids. It is only by studying each of these universes that you can assess how concretely they are constituted, where they stop, who gets in and who does not, and whether at all they form a field.

What are the motor causes of the functioning and transformation of a field?

The principle of the dynamics of a field lies in the form of its structure and, in particular, in the distance, the gaps, the asymmetries between the various specific forces that confront one another. The forces that are active in the field—and thus selected by the analyst as pertinent because they produce the most relevant differences—are those which define the specific capital. *A capital does not exist and function except in relation to a field.* It confers a power over the field, over the materialized or embodied instruments of production or reproduction whose distribution constitutes the very structure of the field, and over the regularities and the rules which define the ordinary functioning of the field, and thereby over the profits engendered in it.

As a space of potential and active forces, the field is also a *field of struggles* aimed at preserving or transforming the configuration of these forces. Furthermore, the field as a structure of objective relations between positions of force undergirds and guides the strategies whereby the occupants of these positions seek, individually or collectively, to safeguard or improve their position and to impose the principle of hierarchization most favorable to their own products. The strategies of agents depend on their position in the field, that is, in the distribution of the specific capital, and on the perception that they have of the field depending on the point of view they take *on* the field as a view taken from a point *in* the field.[52]

52. Bourdieu takes pains to emphasize the discontinuity between a social field and a magnetic field, and therefore between sociology and a reductionistic "social physics": "Sociology is not a chapter of mechanics and social fields are fields of forces but also fields of struggles to transform or preserve these fields of forces. And the relation, practical or reflective, that agents entertain with the game is part and parcel of the game and may be at the basis of its transformation" (Bourdieu 1982a: 46, my translation).

What difference is there between a field and an apparatus or a system as theorized by Luhmann for instance?

An essential difference: struggles, and thus historicity! I am very much against the notion of apparatus, which for me is the Trojan horse of "pessimistic functionalism": an apparatus is an infernal machine, programmed to accomplish certain purposes no matter what, when, or where.[53] (This fantasy of the conspiracy, the idea that an evil will is responsible for everything that happens in the social world, haunts critical social thought.) The school system, the state, the church, political parties, or unions are not apparatuses but fields. In a field, agents and institutions constantly struggle, according to the regularities and the rules constitutive of this space of play (and, in given conjunctures, over those rules themselves), with various degrees of strength and therefore diverse probabilities of success, to appropriate the specific products at stake in the game. Those who dominate in a given field are in a position to make it function to their advantage but they must always contend with the resistance, the claims, the contention, "political" or otherwise, of the dominated.

Now, under certain historical conditions, which must be examined empirically, a field may start to function as an apparatus.[54] When the dominant manage to crush and annul the resistance and the reactions of the dominated, when all movements go exclusively from the top down, the effects of domination are such that the struggle and the dialectic that are constitutive of the field cease. There is history only as long as people revolt, resist, act. Total institutions—asylums, prisons, concentration camps—or dictatorial states are attempts to institute an end to history. Thus apparatuses represent a limiting case, what we may consider to be a pathological state of fields. But it is a limit that is never actually reached, even under the most repressive "totalitarian" regimes.[55]

53. "As a game structured in a loose and weakly formalized fashion, a field is not an *apparatus* obeying the quasi-mechanical logic of a *discipline* capable of converting all action into mere *execution*" (Bourdieu 1990b: 88). See Bourdieu 1987g: 210–12 for a brief critique of the Althusserian concept of "legal apparatus."

54. For historical examples of the opposite evolution, from apparatus to field, see Fabiani (1989: chap. 3) on French philosophy at the end of the nineteenth century, and Bourdieu (1987i) on the birth of impressionist painting.

55. The notion of apparatus also makes it possible to elude the question of the production of social agents who can operate in them and make them operate, a question

As for systems theory, it is true that it has a number of surface similarities with field theory. One could easily retranslate the concepts of "self-referentiality" or "self-organization" by what I put under the notion of autonomy; in both cases, indeed, the process of differentiation and autonomization plays a pivotal role. But the differences between the two theories are nonetheless radical. For one thing, the notion of field excludes functionalism and organicism: the products of a given field may be systematic without being products of a system, and especially of a system characterized by common functions, internal cohesion, and self-regulation—so many postulates of systems theory that must be rejected. If it is true that, in the literary or artistic field, for instance, one may treat the stances constitutive of a space of possibles as a system, they form a system of differences, of distinctive and antagonistic properties which do not develop out of their own internal motion (as the principle of self-referentiality implies) but via conflicts internal to the field of production. The field is the locus of relations of force—and not only of meaning—and of struggles aimed at transforming it, and therefore of endless change. The coherence that may be observed in a given state of the field, its apparent orientation toward a common function (in the case of the French *Grandes écoles*, to reproduce the structure of the field of power; see Bourdieu

---

that cannot be dodged by a field analysis insofar as "a field can function only if it finds individuals socially predisposed to behave as responsible agents, to risk their money, their time, sometimes their honor or their life, to pursue the games and to obtain the profits it proposes" (Bourdieu 1982a: 46; see also Bourdieu's [1987i] analysis of the historical genesis of the artistic field as the "institutionalization of anomie" in aesthetic matters).

The fictitious character of the notion of apparatus is further emphasized by Bourdieu (1988i) in his critique of the notion of "totalitarianism" as developed by French political theorists such as Lefort and Castoriadis, following Hannah Arendt. For Bourdieu, the very concept of "totalitarianism" is what Kenneth Burke would call a "terministic screen" which has masked the reality, however repressed, of ongoing social contention in Soviet-type societies, just as, in the case of the court society under the absolute monarchy of Louix XIV, "the appearance of an apparatus, in fact, conceals a field of struggles in which the holder of 'absolute power' himself must participate" (Bourdieu 1981c: 307). At the same time, Bourdieu (1981a) has highlighted opposite tendencies in the functioning of the political field, where a range of factors related to the lack of cultural capital among the dominated classes tend to foster the concentration of political capital and therefore a drift of leftist parties toward an apparatus-like functioning. For an analysis of the French Communist Party that critically assesses tendencies and countertendencies toward "totalization" and of the social fabrication of members fit to carry them out, see Verdès-Leroux 1981 and Pudal 1988, 1989.

1989a) are born of conflict and competition, not of some kind of immanent self-development of the structure.[56]

A second major difference is that a field does not have parts, components. Every subfield has its own logic, rules and regularities, and each stage in the division of a field (say the field of literary production) entails a genuine qualitative leap (as, for instance, when you move down from the level of the literary field to that of the subfield of novel or theater).[57] Every field constitutes a potentially open space of play whose boundaries are *dynamic borders* which are the stake of struggles within the field itself. A field is a game devoid of inventor and much more fluid and complex than any game that one might ever design. But to see fully everything that separates the concepts of field and system one must put them to work and compare them via the empirical objects they produce.[58]

Briefly, how does one carry out the study of a field and what are the necessary steps in this type of analysis?

An analysis in terms of field involves three necessary and internally connected moments (Bourdieu 1971d). First, one must analyze the position of the field vis-à-vis the field of power. In the case of artists and writers (Bourdieu 1983d), we find that the literary field is contained within the field of power where it occupies a dominated position. (In common and much less adequate parlance: artists and writers, or intellectuals more generally, are a "dominated fraction of the dominant

56. The necessity expressed in the structure and functioning of a field is "the product of a historical process of progressive collective creation which obeys neither a plan nor an obscure immanent Reason without being for that abandoned to chance" (Bourdieu 1989a: 326). Luhmann's conception of law as a system is briefly discussed in Bourdieu 1987g: 212; for a methodical comparison of Bourdieu and Luhmann, see Cornelia Bohn's (1991) *Habitus und Kontext*.

57. The concept of field can be used at different levels of aggregation: the university (Bourdieu 1988a), the totality of disciplines or the faculty of the human sciences; in the housing economy (Bourdieu 1990c), the market made up of all home-builders or the individual construction firm "considered as a relatively autonomous unit."

58. Contrast, for instance, the way in which Bourdieu (1990b, 1990c, 1990d; Bourdieu and Christin 1990) conceptualizes the internal dynamics of the industrial sector of single-family home production in France as an economic field and its interface with other fields (notably the bureaucratic field, i.e., the state) with Luhmann's (1982) and Parsons and Smelser's (1956) abstract theorization of the boundaries between the economy and other formal subsystems.

class.") Second, one must map out the objective structure of the relations between the positions occupied by the agents or institutions
who compete for the legitimate form of specific authority of which
this field in the site. And, third, one must analyze the habitus of
agents, the different systems of dispositions they have acquired by in-
ternalizing a determinate type of social and economic condition, and
which find in a definite trajectory within the field under consideration
a more or less favorable opportunity to become actualized.

The field of positions is methodologically inseparable from the
field of stances or position-takings *(prises de position)*, i.e., the structured system of practices and expressions of agents. Both spaces, that
of objective positions and that of stances, must be analyzed together,
treated as "two translations of the same sentence" as Spinoza put it. It
remains, nevertheless, that, in a situation of equilibrium, *the space of
positions tends to command the space of position-takings.* Artistic revolutions, for instance, are the result of transformations of the relations of
power constitutive of the space of artistic positions that are themselves made possible by the meeting of the subversive intentions of a
fraction of producers with the expectations of a fraction of the audience, thus by a transformation of the relations between the intellectual field and the field of power (Bourdieu 1987i). And what is true of
the artistic field applies to other fields: one can observe the same "fit"
between positions within the academic field on the eve of May 1968
and the political stances taken by the various protagonists of these
events, as I show in *Homo Academicus,* or between the objective position of banks in the economic field and the advertising and personnel
management strategies they deploy, etc.

**In other words, the field is a critical mediation between the practices of those who
partake of it and the surrounding social and economic conditions.**

First, the external determinations that bear on agents situated in a
given field (intellectuals, artists, politicians, or construction com-
panies) never apply to them directly, but affect them only through the
specific mediation of the specific forms and forces of the field, after
having undergone a *re-structuring* that is all the more important the
more autonomous the field, that is, the more it is capable of imposing
its specific logic, the cumulative product of its particular history. Second, we can observe a whole range of structural and functional *homologies* between the field of philosophy, the political field, the literary

field, etc., and the structure of social space (or class structure): each has its dominant and its dominated, its struggles for usurpation and exclusion, its mechanisms of reproduction, and so on. But every one of these characteristics takes a specific, irreducible form in each field (a homology may be defined as a resemblance within a difference). Thus, being contained within the field of power, the struggles that go on in the philosophical field, for instance, are always overdetermined, and tend to function in a double logic. They have political effects and fulfill political functions by virtue of the homology of position that obtains between such and such a philosophical contender and such and such a political or social group in the totality of the social field.[59]

A third general property of fields is that they are *systems of relations that are independent of the populations which these relations define.* When I talk of the intellectual field, I know very well that in this field I will find "particles" (let me pretend for a moment that we are dealing with a physical field) that are under the sway of forces of attraction, of repulsion, and so on, as in a magnetic field. Having said this, as soon as I speak of a field, my attention fastens on the primacy of this system

59. "The specifically ideological function of the field of cultural production is performed quasi-automatically on the basis of the homology of structure between the field of cultural production, organized around the opposition between orthodoxy and heterodoxy, and the field of struggles between the classes, for the maintenance or subversion of the symbolic order. . . . The homology between the two fields causes the struggles for the specific objectives at stake in the autonomous field to produce *euphemized* forms of the ideological struggles between the classes" (Bourdieu 1979b: 82, translation modified).

At the core of Bourdieu's theory of symbolic domination is the notion that ideological legitimation (or "naturalization") of class inequality operates via a correspondence which is effected only between systems. It does not require that cultural producers intentionally endeavor to mask or to serve the interests of the dominant—indeed, the function of "sociodicy" of culture is more effectively fulfilled when the opposite is true. It is only by genuinely pursuing their specific interest as specialists in symbolic production that intellectuals *also* legitimate a class position: "Ideologies owe their structure and their most specific functions to the social conditions of their production and circulation, i.e., to the functions they fulfill *first for the specialists* competing for the monopoly of the competence in question (religious, artistic, etc.), and *secondarily and incidentally* for the non-specialists" (Bourdieu 1979b: 81–82, my emphasis).

For analyses of how the homology with the structure of class relations obtains and with what effects, see Bourdieu and Delsaut 1975 on high fashion, Bourdieu 1980a on tastes in theater and art, Bourdieu 1988b on philosophy and Bourdieu 1989a on elite professional schools.

of objective relations over the particles themselves. And we could say, following the formula of a famous German physicist, that the individual, like the electron, is an *Ausgeburt des Felds:* he or she is in a sense an emanation of the field. This or that particular intellectual, this or that artist, exists *as such* only because there is an intellectual or an artistic field. (This is very important to help solve the perennial question that historians of art have raised time and again, namely, at what point do we move from the craftsman to the artist? This is a question which, posed in this fashion, is almost meaningless, since this transition is made progressively, along with the constitution of an artistic field within which something like an artist can come to exist.)[60]

The notion of field reminds us that the true object of social science is not the individual, even though one cannot construct a field if not through individuals, since the information necessary for statistical analysis is generally attached to individuals or institutions. It is the field which is primary and must be the focus of the research operations. This does not imply that individuals are mere "illusions," that they do not exist: they exist as *agents*—and not as biological individuals, actors, or subjects—who are socially constituted as active and acting in the field under consideration by the fact that they possess the necessary properties to be effective, to produce effects, in this field. And it is knowledge of the field itself in which they evolve that allows us best to grasp the roots of their singularity, their *point of view* or position (in a field) from which their particular vision of the world (and of the field itself) is constructed.

This is because, at every moment, there is something like an "admission fee" that each field imposes and which defines eligibility for participation, thereby selecting certain agents over others.

People are at once founded and legitimized to enter the field by their possessing a definite configuration of properties. One of the goals of research is to identify these active properties, these efficient charac-

---

60. Bourdieu's analysis of the historical formation of the artistic field in late nineteenth-century France and of the correlative "invention" of the modern artist is the centerpiece of a forthcoming book entitled *The Economics of Cultural Goods.* For preliminary sketches, see Bourdieu 1971a, 1971c, 1971d, 1983d, 1988d. A concise statement of his sociology of aesthetics and art is Bourdieu 1987d; several of these articles are contained in Bourdieu forthcoming c.

teristics, that is, these forms of *specific capital.* There is thus a sort of hermeneutic circle: in order to construct the field, one must identify the forms of specific capital that operate within it, and to construct the forms of specific capital one must know the specific logic of the field. There is an endless to and fro movement in the research process that is quite lengthy and arduous.[61]

To say that the structure of the field—note that I am progressively building a *working* definition of the concept—is defined by the structure of the distribution of the specific forms of capital that are active in it means that when my knowledge of forms of capital is sound I can differentiate everything that there is to differentiate. For example, and this is one of the principles that guided my work on intellectuals, one cannot be satisfied with an explanatory model incapable of differentiating people—or, better, positions—who ordinary intuition in the specific universe tells us are quite different. In such a case, one should search for what variables have been omitted which permit us to differentiate. (Parenthesis: ordinary intuition is quite respectable; only, one must be sure to introduce intuitions into the analysis in a conscious and reasoned manner and to control their validity empirically,[62] whereas many sociologists use them unconsciously, as when they build the kind of dualistic typologies that I criticize at the beginning of *Homo Academicus,* such as "universal" vs. "parochial" intellectuals.) Here intuition raises questions: "Where does the difference come from?"

One last and critical point: *social agents are not "particles"* that are mechanically pushed and pulled about by external forces. They are, rather, bearers of capitals and, depending on their trajectory and on the position they occupy in the field by virtue of their endowment (volume and structure) in capital, they have a propensity to orient

61. For a detailed illustration of this "hermeneutic circle," through which the population of relevant individuals or institutions and the efficient assets or forms of capital are mutually specified, see Bourdieu's study of the reform of governmental housing policy in France in the mid-1970s (Bourdieu and Christin 1990, esp. 70–81).

62. "Far from being, as certain 'initiatory' representatives of the 'epistemological break' would have us believe, a sort of simultaneously inaugural and terminal act, the renunciation of first-hand intuition is the end product of a long dialectical process in which intuition, formulated in an empirical operation, analyses and verifies or falsifies itself, engendering new hypotheses, gradually more firmly based, which will be transcended in their turn, thanks to the problems, failures and expectations which they bring to light" (Bourdieu 1988a: 7).

themselves actively either toward the preservation of the distribution of capital or toward the subversion of this distribution. Things are of course much more complicated, but I think that this is a general proposition that applies to social space as a whole, although it does not imply that all small capital holders are necessarily revolutionaries and all big capital holders are automatically conservatives.

Let us grant that the social universe, at least in advanced societies, is made up of a number of differentiated fields that have both invariant properties (this justifies the project of a general theory of fields) and varying properties rooted in their specific logic and history (which requires a genetic and comparative analysis of each of them). How do these diverse fields relate to one another? What is the nature of their articulation and their differential weight?

The question of the interrelation of different fields is an extremely complex one. It is a question that I would normally not answer because it is too difficult, and I risk saying things that are relatively simple and might thereby reawaken modes of analysis phrased in terms of "instance" and "articulation," that allowed some Marxists to give rhetorical solutions to problems that only empirical analysis can tackle. I believe indeed that there are *no transhistoric laws of the relations between fields*, that we must investigate each historical case separately. Obviously, in advanced capitalist societies, it would be difficult to maintain that the economic field does not exercise especially powerful determinations. But should we for that reason admit the postulate of its (universal) "determination in the last instance"? An example from my research on the artistic field will, I believe, suggest how complicated this question is.

When we study this question historically, we observe that a process began with the Quattrocento which led the artistic field to acquire its true autonomy in the nineteenth century. From then on, artists are no longer subjected to the demands and commands of sponsors and patrons, they are freed from the state and from academies, etc. Most of them begin to produce for their own restricted market in which a sort of deferred economy operates (Bourdieu 1983d, 1987i). Everything would lead us to believe that we are dealing with an irreversible and irresistible movement toward autonomy, and that art and artists have once and for all achieved their freedom from external forces. Now, what do we observe today? A return of patronage, of direct dependency, of the state, of the most brutal forms of censorship, and suddenly the idea of a linear and indefinite process of autonomization is reopened. Look at what happened to a painter such as Hans Haacke who uses artistic tools to question interferences with the autonomy of artistic creation.[63] He exhibited at the Guggenheim Museum a painting displaying the origins of the financial resources of the Guggenheim family. Now, the Director of the Museum had no alternative other than to resign or be dismissed by his funders, or to ridicule himself in the eyes of artists by refusing to exhibit the painting. This artist gave a function back to art and immediately he ran into trouble. Thus we discover that the autonomy acquired by artists, originally dependent for both the content and the form of their work, implied a submission to necessity: artists had made a virtue out of necessity by arrogating to themselves the absolute mastery of the form, but at the cost of a no less absolute renunciation of function. As soon as they want to fulfill a function other than that assigned to them by the artistic field, i.e., the function which consists in exercising no social function ("art for art's sake"), they rediscover the limits of their autonomy.

This is only one example, but it has the merit of reminding us that relations between fields—the artistic and the economic field in this case—are not defined once and for all, even in the most general tendencies of their evolution. The notion of field does not provide ready-made answers to all possible queries, in the manner of the grand concepts of "theoreticist theory" which claims to explain everything and in the right order. Rather, its major virtue, at least in my eyes, is that it promotes a mode of construction that has to be rethought anew every time. It forces us to *raise* questions: about the limits of the universe under investigation, how it is "articulated," to what and to what degree, etc. It offers a coherent system of recurrent questions that saves us from the theoretical vacuum of positivist empiricism and from the empirical void of theoreticist discourse.

In a recent issue of *Actes de la recherche en sciences sociales* (March 1990) devoted to the "Economy of Housing," that is, the set of social spaces that have to be taken into account to understand the production and circulation of this peculiar economic good that the single-family home is, you have been led to analyze the genesis of

---

63. The sociological significance of Haacke's work is underlined by Howard Becker and John Walton (1986).

state policies which, in this case, enter directly in the determination of the functioning of an economic market. In so doing, you have begun to outline a theory of the state as a sort of meta-field.[64]

Indeed, it seems to me that, when you take a close look at what goes on inside what we call the "state," you immediately annul most of the *scholastic* problems that scholars, armchair Marxists and other speculative sociologists, keep raising about the state, that quasi-metaphysical notion that must be exploded in order to "go to the things themselves," as Edmund Husserl said in a different context. I think for instance of the consecrated theoretical alternative between "correspondence" (or dependance) and "autonomy." This alternative presupposes that the state is a well-defined, clearly bounded and unitary reality which stands in a relation of externality with outside forces that are themselves clearly identified and defined (for instance, in the case of Germany, on which so much ink has been spilled because of the famous *Sonderweg,* the traditional landed aristocracy of the Junkers, or the wealthy industrial bourgeoisie, or, in the case of England, the urban entrepreneurial bourgeoisie and the country gentry). In fact, what we encounter, concretely, is an ensemble of administrative or bureaucratic fields (they often take the empirical form of commissions, bureaus and boards) within which agents and categories of agents, governmental and nongovernmental, struggle over this peculiar form of authority consisting of the power to *rule* via legislation, regulations, administrative measures (subsidies, authorizations, restrictions, etc.), in short, everything that we normally put under the rubric of state policy as a particular sphere of practices related, in this case, to the production and consumption of housing.

The state, then, if you insist on keeping this designation, would be

64. The analysis of the structuring role of the state in the economics of housing is found in Bourdieu 1990b, and Bourdieu and Christin 1990. Bourdieu was first led to address the question of the state frontally in *La noblesse d'Etat,* when he came to the conclusion that the "contemporary technocracy" are the "structural (and sometimes genealogical) inheritors" of the *noblesse de robe* which "created itself [as a corporate body] by creating the state," and formulated the hypothesis that "the state nobility . . . and educational credentials are born of complementary and correlative inventions" (Bourdieu 1989a: 544, 540). Bourdieu's course at the Collège de France in 1988–91 has been devoted to this topic, in the form of an investigation of the genesis and effects of the modern state understood as the organizational expression of the concentration of symbolic power, or "public trove of material and symbolic resources guaranteeing private appropriations" (Bourdieu 1989a: 540).

the ensemble of fields that are the site of struggles in which what is at stake is—to build on Max Weber's famed formulation—the *monopoly of legitimate symbolic violence,*[65] i.e., the power to constitute and to impose as *universal* and *universally applicable* within a given "nation," that is, within the boundaries of a given territory, a common set of coercive norms. As I showed in the case of state housing policy in France between 1970 and 1980, these fields are the locus of a constant confrontation between forces belonging both to the private sector (banks and bankers, construction and architectural firms, etc.) and to the public sector (ministries, administrative divisions within these ministries, and the *grands corps d'Etat* who staff them),[66] that is, sub-universes themselves organized as fields that are both united by and divided over internal cleavages and external oppositions. The notion of "state" makes sense only as a convenient stenographic label—but, for that matter, a very dangerous one—for these spaces of *objective relations* between *positions* of power (assuming different forms) that can take the form of more or less stable networks (of alliance, cooperation, clientelism, mutual service, etc.) and which manifest themselves in phenomenally diverse interactions ranging from open conflict to more or less hidden collusion.

As soon as you examine in detail how "private" agents or organizations (say, banks interested in the passing of certain regulations likely to boost the diffusion of given kinds of housing loans), which are themselves in competition with one another, work to orient "state" policy in each of their domains of economic or cultural activity (the same processes can be observed in the case of an educational reform), how they form coalitions and ties with other bureaucratic agents

65. For developments, see Bourdieu 1989a: part 5, and Bourdieu and Wacquant 1991: 100: "The state is in the final analysis the great fount of symbolic power which accomplishes acts of consecration, such as the granting of a degree, an identity card or a certificate—so many acts through which the authorized holders of an authority assert that a person is what she is, publicly establish what she is and what she has to be. It is the state, as the reserve bank of consecration, that vouchsafes these official acts and the agents who effect them and, in a sense, carries them out via the agency of its legitimate representatives. This is why I distorted and generalized Max Weber's famous words to say that *the state is the holder of a monopololy, not only over legitimate physical violence, but over legitimate symbolic violence* as well."

66. The *grands corps* are corporate bodies made up of graduates of the country's top *Grandes écoles* which traditionally reserve for themselves certain upper-level administrative positions within the French state. (On *Grandes écoles*, see p. 231, n. 22.)

whose preference for a given type of measure they share, how they confront yet other organizational entities with their own interests and resources (e.g., the properly bureaucratic capital of management of regulations), you cannot but jettison all speculations about correspondence and autonomy. To be truthful, I feel closer, on this count, to the analyses of Edward Laumann (Laumann and Knoke 1988), though I differ from him in other respects, than to those of Nicos Poulantzas (1973) or Theda Skocpol (1979), to cite two names emblematic of traditional positions on correspondence and autonomy. By this, I mean to point out also that, in such matters as elsewhere, the "armchair Marxists," those materialists without materials, whom I ceaselessly opposed at the time of their apogee in the 1960s, have done much to help the perpetuation of scholastic issues.

More generally, this illustrates what makes for much of the difficulty of my position in the sociological field. On the one hand, I can appear very close to the "Grand Theoreticians" (especially the structuralists) insofar as I insist on structural configurations that cannot be reduced to the interactions and practices through which they express themselves. At the same time, I feel a kinship and a solidarity with researchers who "put their noses to the ground" (particularly symbolic interactionists, and all those who, through participant observation or statistical analysis, work to uncover and to debunk the empirical realities that Grand Theoreticians ignore because they look down upon social reality from such heights), even though I cannot agree with the philosophy of the social world which often undergirds their interest in the minutiae of daily practices and which, in this case, is in fact imposed upon them by this "close-up view" and by the theoretical myopia or the blindness to objective structures, to relations of force that are not immediately perceivable, that this view encourages.

What, then, would separate your analysis of the state as a set of partially overlapping bureaucratic fields from Laumann and Knoke's (1988) notion of the "organizational state" or from network theory more broadly?
I could recall here the distinction I established, against Max Weber in particular, between structure and interaction or between a structural relation which operates in a permanent and invisible fashion, and an effective relation, a relation actualized in and by a particular exchange (see Bourdieu 1971b, 1971e, 1987h). In fact, the structure of a field,

understood as a space of objective relations between positions defined by their rank in the distribution of competing powers or species
of capital, is different from the more or less lasting networks through
which it manifests itself. It is this structure that determines the possibility or the impossibility (or, to be more precise, the greater or lesser
probability) of observing the establishment of linkages that express
and sustain the existence of networks. The task of science is to uncover the structure of the distribution of species of capital which
tends to determine the structure of individual or collective stances
taken, through the interests and dispositions it conditions. In network analysis, the study of these underlying structures has been sac-
rificed to the analysis of the particular linkages (between agents or
institutions) and flows (of information, resources, services, etc.)
through which they become visible—no doubt because uncovering
the structure requires that one put to work a relational mode of thinking that is more difficult to translate into quantitative and formalized
data, save by way of correspondence analysis.

I could pursue this argument by drawing on the research I have
been conducting over the past few years on the historical genesis of
the state. I could argue, to simplify greatly, that there has occurred,
since the construction of the dynastic state and, later, of the bureaucratic state, a long-term process of concentration of different species
of power, or capital, leading, in a first stage, to private monopolization—by the king—of a public authority at once external and superior
to all private authorities (lords, bourgeoisie, etc.). The concentration
of these different species of capital—economic (thanks to taxation),
military, cultural, juridical and, more generally, symbolic—goes hand
in hand with the rise and consolidation of the various corresponding
fields. The result of this process is the emergence of a specific capital,
properly statist capital, born of their cumulation, which allows the state
to wield a power over the different fields and over the various forms
of capital that circulate in them. This kind of *meta-capital* capable of
exercising a power over other species of power, and particularly over
their rate of exchange (and thereby over the balance of power between
their respective holders), defines the specific power of the state. It follows that the construction of the state goes hand in hand with the
constitution of the field of power understood as the space of play in
which holders of various forms of capital struggle *in particular* for
power over the state, that is, over the statist capital that grants power

over the different species of capital and over their reproduction (via the school system in particular).

4   Interest, Habitus, Rationality

Your use of the notion of interest has often called forth the charge of "economism."[67] What theoretical role does interest play in your method of analysis?

The notion of interest imposed itself upon me as an instrument of rupture with a philosophical anthropology, a naive conception of human conduct that was dominant when I started working in the social sciences. I have often quoted a remark of Weber about law which says that social agents obey a rule only insofar as their interest in following it outweighs their interest in overlooking it. This sound materialist principle reminds us that, before claiming to describe the rules according to which people act, we should ask what makes those rules operative in the first place.

Thus, building upon Weber, who utilized an economic model to uncover the specific interests of the great protagonists of the religious game, priests, prophets, and sorcerers (Bourdieu 1971b, 1987h), I introduced the notion of interest into my analysis of cultural producers in reaction to the dominant vision of the intellectual universe, to question the ideology of the *freischwebende Intelligenz*. I much prefer to use the term *illusio*, since I always speak of specific interest, of interests that are both presupposed and produced by the functioning of historically delimited fields. Paradoxically, the term interest has brought forth the knee-jerk accusation of economism.[68] In fact, the

67. E.g., Paradeise 1981, Caillé 1981 and 1987a, Richer 1983, Adair 1984, Kot and Lautier 1984, Rancière 1984: 24, Joppke 1986, Sahlins 1989: 25. Thus Fiske (1991: 238) lumps Gary Becker and Bourdieu together as defenders of "the selfish rationality assumption" that constitutes one of his four models of social relations. The opposite interpretation is vigorously defended by Harker, Mahar, and Wilkes (1990: 4–6), Thompson (1991) and Ostrow (1990: 117), among others, who commend Bourdieu for his rejection of economism.

68. Bourdieu's opposition to economism is clear from his first ethnographic pieces on the sense of honor among the Kabyles (Bourdieu 1965 and 1979d). It is argued at great length in *Esquisse d'une théorie de la pratique* and in *The Logic of Practice*: "Economism is a form of ethnocentrism. Treating precapitalist economies, in Marx's phrase, 'as the Fathers of the Church treated the religions that preceded Christianity,' it applies to them categories, methods (economic accounting, for instance), or concepts (such as the notions of interest, investment, or capital, etc.) that are the historical product of

notion as I use it is the means of a deliberate and provisional reductionism that allows me to import the materialist mode of questioning into the cultural sphere from which it was expelled, historically, when the modern view of art was invented and the field of cultural production won its autonomy (Bourdieu 1987d), and in which it is therefore particularly offensive.

To understand the notion of interest, it is necessary to see that it is opposed not only to that of disinterestedness or gratuitousness but also to that of *indifference*. To be indifferent is to be unmoved by the game: like Buridan's donkey, this game makes no difference to me. Indifference is an axiological state, an ethical state of nonpreference as well as a state of knowledge in which I am not capable of differentiating the stakes proposed. Such was the goal of the Stoics: to reach a state of ataraxy (*ataraxia* means the fact of not being troubled). *Illusio* is the very opposite of ataraxy: it is to be invested, taken in and by the game. To be interested is to accord a given social game that what happens in it matters, that its stakes are important (another word with the same root as interest) and worth pursuing.[69]

This is to say that the concept of interest, as I construe it, is totally disjoint from the transhistorical and universal interest of utilitarian theory. It would be easy to show that Adam Smith's self-interest is nothing more than an unconscious universalization of the form of interest engendered and required by a capitalist economy. Far from being an anthropological invariant, interest is a *historical arbitrary*,[70] a historical construction that can be known only through historical analysis, *ex post*, through empirical observation, and not deduced a

capitalism, and which therefore induce a radical transformation of their object, similar to the historical transformation from which they arose" (Bourdieu 1990a: 113, translation modified, and passim; see also Bourdieu 1986b: 252–53).

69. "What, for a 'well-socialized' Kabyle, is a matter of life and death, a crucial stake, might leave *indifferent* an agent lacking the principles of differentiation which enable him to make the difference and to be taken in by the games of honor" (Bourdieu 1987e: 7).

70. This is one of the conclusions of Mauss's inquiry into the logic of gift giving: "If some equivalent motivation actuates Trobiander or American chiefs and Adaman clan members, or actuated generous Hindus and the Germanic or Celtic nobles of yesteryear to make gifts or expenses, it is not the cold rationale of the trader, the banker or the capitalist. In these civilizations, one is *interested, but in a manner other than during our times*" (Mauss 1950a: 270–71, my emphasis). Bourdieu is seconded by Hirschman (1987) in this revisionist interpretation of the notion of interest.

priori from some fictitious—and so evidently ethnocentric—conception of "Man."

This implies that there are as many "interests" as there are fields, that each field simultaneously presupposes and generates a specific form of interest incommensurable with those that have currency elsewhere.

Precisely. Each field calls forth and gives life to a specific form of interest, a specific *illusio*, as tacit recognition of the value of the stakes of the game and as practical mastery of its rules. Furthermore, this specific interest implied by one's participation in the game differentiates itself according to the position occupied in the game (dominant vs. dominated or orthodox vs. heretic) and with the trajectory that leads each participant to this position. Anthropology and comparative history show that the properly social magic of institutions can constitute just about anything as an interest, and as a realistic interest, i.e., as an investment (in the double meaning that the word has in economics and in psychoanalysis) that is objectively paid back by a specific "economy."

Beyond interest and investment, you have borrowed from economic language several other concepts, such as market, profit and capital (e.g., Bourdieu 1985d, 1986b), which evoke the economic mode of reasoning. Moreover, both your earliest and your latest research have been squarely in the realm of economic sociology. Your very first work on Algerian peasants and workers sought, among other things, to explain the differential emergence of a rational, calculative disposition towards the economy—the habitus of homo œconomicus—among various fractions of the Algerian proletariat, and the social and economic consequences of the failure of the urban subproletariat to master such dispositions objectively required by the capitalist economy thrust upon them by French colonialism. In your recent book-length study of the economics of single-family home production and consumption in France analyzed as a field, you investigate the social genesis of the system of preferences and strategies of buyers, on the one hand, and the organization and dynamics of the space of suppliers (housing construction firms) and products on the other. And you find that the state—or what you call the bureaucratic field—plays a crucial role in both, and especially in structuring their encounter: the market is a sociopolitical construction that results from the refraction, at various territorial levels of the "bureaucratic field," of the claims and desiderata of a range of social and economic agents

unequally equipped to obtain consideration of their interests.[71] What sets your theoretical approach apart from an "economic approach to human behavior" à la Gary Becker (1976)?

The only thing I share with economic orthodoxy (by this I mean the multistranded and diverse stream that dominates today's economic science, which, we must not forget, is itself a highly differentiated field) are a number of words. Take the notion of investment. By investment I mean the propensity to act that is born of the relation between a field and a system of dispositions adjusted to the game it proposes, a sense of the game and of its stakes that implies at once an *inclination* and an *ability* to play the game, both of which are socially and historically constituted rather than universally given. The general theory of the economy of fields that emerges progressively from generalization to generalization (I am presently working on a book in which I attempt to isolate, at a more formal level, the general properties of fields) enables us to describe and to identify the *specific form* taken by the most general mechanisms and concepts such as capital, investment, interest, within each field, and thus to avoid all kinds of reductionisms, beginning with economism, which recognizes nothing but material interest and the deliberate search for the maximization of monetary profit.

A general science of the economy of practices that does not artificially limit itself to those practices that are socially recognized as economic must endeavor to grasp capital, that "energy of social physics" (Bourdieu 1990a: 122), in all of its different forms, and to uncover the laws that regulate their conversion from one into another.[72] I have

71. There exist obvious and large zones of overlap and convergence between Bourdieu's older and newer work in that area and the concerns of the "New Economic Sociology" (e.g., Swedberg, Himmelstrand, and Brulin 1987; Zelizer 1988; Zukin and DiMaggio 1990; Granovetter 1985 and 1990), although neither seems to have connected with the other yet (but see DiMaggio 1990, and Powell and DiMaggio 1991).

Bourdieu's economic sociology of Algeria is found in Bourdieu 1962a, 1964, 1973a, 1979c; Bourdieu et al. 1963; and Bourdieu and Sayad 1964. For the study of the housing economy in France, see Bourdieu 1990b, 1990c, 1990d; Bourdieu and de Saint Martin 1990; Bourdieu and Christin 1990.

72. Bourdieu (1986b: 241) defines capital thus: "Capital is accumulated labor (in its materialized form or its 'incorporated,' embodied, form) which, when appropriated on a private, i.e., exclusive, basis by agents or groups of agents, enables them to appropriate social energy in the form of reified or living labor." For an interesting critical discussion of Bourdieu's conceptualization of capital, see Grossetti 1986.

shown that *capital presents itself under three fundamental species* (each with its own subtypes), namely, economic capital, cultural capital, and social capital (Bourdieu 1986b). To these we must add symbolic capital, which is the form that one or another of these species takes when it is grasped through categories of perception that *recognize* its specific logic or, if you prefer, misrecognize the arbitrariness of its possession and accumulation.[73] I shall not dwell on the notion of economic capital. I have analyzed the peculiarity of cultural capital, which we should in fact call *informational capital* to give the notion its full generality, and which itself exists in three forms, embodied, objectified, or institutionalized.[74] Social capital is the sum of the resources, actual or virtual, that accrue to an individual or a group by virtue of possessing a durable network of more or less institutionalized relationships of mutual acquaintance and recognition. Acknowledging that capital can take a variety of forms is indispensable to explain the structure and dynamics of differentiated societies. For example, to account for the shape of social space in old social democratic nations such as Sweden or in Soviet-type societies, one must take into consideration this peculiar form of social capital constituted by political capital which has the capacity to yield considerable profits and privileges, in a manner similar to economic capital in other social fields, by operating a "patrimonialization" of collective resources (through unions and the Labor party in the one case, the Communist party in the other).

Orthodox economics overlooks the fact that practices may have principles other than mechanical causes or the conscious intention to maximize one's utility and yet obey an immanent economic logic. *Practices form an economy,* that is, follow an immanent reason that cannot be restricted to economic reason, for the economy of practices may be defined by reference to a wide range of functions and ends. To reduce the universe of forms of conduct to mechanical reaction or

73. The notion of symbolic capital is one of the more complex ones developed by Pierre Bourdieu, and his whole work may be read as a hunt for its varied forms and effects. See Bourdieu 1972: 227–43; 1977a: 171–83; 1990a: 112–21; 1989a: part 5; and 1991e for successive elaborations.

74. The acquisition, transmission, conversion, and social effects of these three forms of cultural capital is extensively illustrated in the varied articles that make up the October 1989 issue of *Sociologie et Sociétés* devoted to "Culture as Capital." See in particular de Saint Martin's (1989b) analysis of the dynamics of gender and cultural capital in the determination of "intellectual vocations."

purposive action is to make it it impossible to shed light on all those practices that are *reasonable* without being the product of a reasoned purpose and, even less, of conscious computation.

Thus my theory owes nothing, despite appearances, to the transfer of the economic approach. And I hope one day to be able to demonstrate fully that, far from being the founding model, economic theory (and rational action theory which is its sociological derivative) is probably best seen as a particular instance, historically dated and situated, of the theory of fields.

You have clarified the concepts of field and of capital. There is a third central category which constitutes a theoretical bridge between them by providing the mechanism that "propels" definite agents, endowed with certain valences of capital, to take up this or that strategy, subversion or conservation—or, one might add, indifference, exit from the game. If I understand you correctly, the notion of habitus is the conceptual linchpin by which you rearticulate the apparently economic notions of capital, market, interest, etc., into a model of action radically discontinuous with that of economics.[75]

I have explained the meaning and function of the concept of habitus so often that I hesitate to return to it once more, lest I only repeat myself and simplify without necessarily clarifying things. . . All I want to say here is that the main purpose of this notion is to break with the intellectualist (and intellectualocentric) philosophy of action represented in particular by the theory of homo œconomicus as rational agent, which rational choice theory has recently brought back in fashion at the very time when a good number of economists have repudiated it (often without saying so or realizing it fully). It is to account for the actual logic of practice—an expression in itself oxymoronic since the hallmark of practice is to be "logical," to have a logic without having logic as its principle—that I have put forth a theory of practice as the product of a *practical sense*, of a socially constituted "sense of

---

75. On the development and successive reworkings of the concept of habitus in Bourdieu's work, see Bourdieu 1967a, 1967b, 1971c, 1972, 1977a, 1980d, 1984a, 1990a: chap. 3, 1986c, and 1985c, which provides a condensed recapitulation of its history and functions. Again, to grasp adequately the aims and meaning of the concept, one must focus on its uses, that is, see how Bourdieu invokes it in the course of concrete empirical analyses and with what *analytical effects*. There seems to be a drift, over time, from a more mentalist to a more corporeal emphasis, perhaps partly due to the heavier influence of the linguistic model of structuralism in Bourdieu's earlier work.

the game" (Bourdieu 1977a, 1990a). I wanted initially to account for practice in its humblest forms—rituals, matrimonial choices, the mundane economic conduct of everyday life, etc.—by escaping both the objectivism of action understood as a mechanical reaction "without an agent" and the subjectivism which portrays action as the deliberate pursuit of a conscious intention, the free project of a conscience positing its own ends and maximizing its utility through rational computation.

A second major function of the notion of habitus, of which I must also say that it designates first and foremost a posture (or, if you wish, a scientific habitus), that is, a definite manner of constructing and understanding practice in its specific "logic" (including temporal), is to break with another opposition that is no less deadly and no doubt considerably more difficult to overcome: against positivistic materialism, the theory of practice as practice posits that objects of knowledge are *constructed*, and not passively recorded; against intellectualist idealism it reminds us that the principle of this construction is found in the socially constituted system of structured and structuring dispositions acquired in practice and constantly aimed at practical functions. Following the program suggested by Marx in the *Theses on Feuerbach*, it aims at making possible a materialist theory of knowledge that does not abandon to idealism the notion that all knowledge, be it mundane or scholarly, presupposes a work of construction.[76] But it emphasizes that this work has nothing in common with intellectual work, that it consists of an activity of practical construction, even of practical reflection, that ordinary notions of thought, consciousness, knowledge prevent us from adequately thinking. I believe that all those who used this old concept or similar ones before me, from Hegel's *ethos*, to Husserl's *Habitualität*, to Mauss's *hexis*, were inspired (without always knowing it explicitly) by a theoretical intention akin to mine, which is to escape from under the philosophy of the subject without doing away with the agent (Bourdieu 1985c), as well as from under the phi-

76. Marx's third thesis *Ad Feuerbach*, with which Bourdieu (1977a: vi) opens the *Outline of a Theory of Practice*, reads as follows: "The principal defect of all materialism up to now—including that of Feuerbach—is that the external object, reality, the sensible world, is grasped in the form of an *object or an intuition;* but not as *concrete human activity,* as *practice,* in a subjective way. This is why the active aspect was developed by idealism, in opposition to materialism—but only in an abstract way, since idealism naturally does not know real concrete activity as such."

losophy of the structure but without forgetting to take into account the effects it wields upon and through the agent. But the paradox is that most commentators completely overlook the significant difference between my usage of this notion and the totality of previous usages (Héran 1987)—I said habitus so as *not* to say habit—that is, the generative (if not creative) capacity inscribed in the system of dispositions as an *art*, in the strongest sense of practical mastery, and in particular as an *ars inveniendi*. In short, they keep to a mechanistic vision of a notion constructed *against mechanism*.

Some authors, such as Victor Kestenbaum (1977) and James Ostrow (1990), have drawn parallels between your theory of habitus and the philosophical tradition of American pragmatism, and John Dewey in particular. Do you recognize yourself in this portrayal?

I came across these studies very recently and they stimulated me to take a closer look at Dewey's philosophy, of which I had only very partial and superficial knowledge. Indeed, the affinities and convergences are quite striking, and I believe I understand what their basis is: my effort to react against the deep-seated intellectualism characteristic of all European philosophies (with the rare exceptions of Wittgenstein, Heidegger, and Merleau-Ponty) determined me, unwittingly, to move very close to philosophical currents that the European tradition of "depth" and obscurity is inclined to treat as foils, negative reference points.

At bottom and in short—I cannot consider here all the relevant commonalities and differences—I would say that the theory of practical sense presents many similarities with theories, such as Dewey's, that grant a central role to the notion of habit, understood as an active and creative relation to the world, and reject all the conceptual dualisms upon which nearly all post-Cartesian philosophies are based: subject and object, internal and external, material and spiritual, individual and social, and so on.[77]

---

77. Dewey (1958: 104) writes in *Art as Experience:* "Through habits formed in intercourse with the world, we also in-habit the world. It becomes a home, and the home is part of our every experience." His definition of "mind" as the "active and eager background which lies in wait and engages whatever comes its way" has obvious kinship with Bourdieu's habitus.

Such a conception of social action puts you in frontal opposition to this wide, if heterogeneous, current that has gained strength across the social sciences in recent years under the label of rational action theory or rational choice theory (Elster 1986, Coleman 1990b; see Wacquant and Calhoun 1989 for a critical survey).

A typical instance of the scholastic fallacy—of the ordinary error of professionals of logic, namely, that which consists in "taking the things of logic for the logic of things," as Marx said of Hegel—rational action theory (RAT) puts the mind of the scientist who conceptualizes practice in the place of the socially constituted practical sense of the agent. The actor, as it construes him or her, is nothing other than the imaginary projection of the knowing subject *(sujet connaissant)* into the acting subject *(sujet agissant)*, a sort of monster with the head of the thinker thinking his practice in reflexive and logical fashion mounted on the body of a man of action engaged in action. RAT recognizes nothing but the "rational responses" to potential or actual opportunities of an agent who is both indeterminate and interchangeable. Its "imaginary anthropology" seeks to found action, whether "economic" or not, on the intentional choice of an actor who is himself or herself economically and socially unconditioned. This narrow, economistic conception of the "rationality" of practices ignores the individual and collective *history* of agents through which the structures of preference that inhabit them are constituted in a complex temporal dialectic with the objective structures that produced them and which they tend to reproduce.

Isn't one of the purposes of the notion of habitus, which some critics (e.g., Jenkins 1982) have made into the conceptual hub of a philosophy of history allegedly aimed

---

There has recently been a resurgence of interest in the notion of habit and in its neglect or denigration in social theory (see, for example, Perinbanayagam 1985, Camic 1986, Baldwin 1988, and Connerton 1989: esp. 22–30, 84–95, and the discussion of "inscribing" and "incorporating" practices in chap. 3), in part in reaction to the overly "rationalist models of cognition and decision-making" that have come to dominate American social science (Collins 1981b: 985). Dewey and Mead are the authors most frequently "rediscovered" for their early formulation of a sociology of action based on habit; the critical relevance of Merleau-Ponty's work on the corporeality of the preobjective, nonthetic contact between world and subject is brought out by Ostrow (1990) and Schmidt (1985, esp. chaps. 3 and 4). It will be interesting to see whether this view gains strength in America and connects with Bourdieu.

at negating history, precisely to remind us of the historicity of the economic agent, of the historical genesis of her aspirations and preferences?

Human action is not an instantaneous reaction to immediate stimuli, and the slightest "reaction" of an individual to another is pregnant with the whole history of these persons and of their relationship. To explain this, I could mention the chapter of *Mimesis* entitled "The Brown Stocking," in which Erich Auerbach (1953) evokes a passage of Virginia Woolf's *To the Lighthouse*, and the representations or, better, the repercussions that a minor external event triggers in Mrs. Ramsay's consciousness. This event, trying on a stocking, is but a point of departure which, though it is not wholly fortuitous, takes value only through the indirect reactions it sets off. One sees well, in this case, that knowledge of stimuli does not enable us to understand much of the resonances and echoes they elicit unless one has some idea of the habitus that selects and amplifies them with the whole history with which it is itself pregnant.

This means that one can genuinely understand practices (including economic practices) only on condition of elucidating the economic and social conditions of production and actualization of the habitus that provides their dynamic principle.

By converting the immanent law of the economy into a universal and universally realized norm of adequate practice, RAT forgets—and hides—the fact that the "rational," or, better, reasonable, habitus which is the precondition of an adequate economic practice is the product of a particular economic condition, defined by the possession of the minimum economic and cultural capital necessary actually to perceive and seize the "potential opportunities" formally offered to all. All the capacities and dispositions it liberally grants to its abstract "actor"—the art of estimating and taking chances, the ability to anticipate through a kind of practical induction, the capacity to bet on the possible against the probable for a measured risk, the propensity to invest, access to economic information, etc.—can only be acquired under definite social and economic conditions. They are in fact always a function of one's power in, and over, the specific economy.[78]

78. Bourdieu (1979c: 68 and passim) shows in *Algeria 1960* that Algerian sub-proletarians could not reach the "threshold of modernity" which constituted the boundary between them and the stable working class, and beneath which the formation of the "rational habitus" demanded by a rationalized (capitalist) economy was im-

Because it must postulate *ex nihilo* the existence of a universal, pre-constituted interest, RAT is thoroughly oblivious to the social genesis of historically varying forms of interests.

Moreover, the theory of habitus explains why the finalism of rational choice theory, although anthropologically false, may appear empirically sound. Individualistic finalism, which conceives action as determined by conscious aiming at explicitly posed goals, is indeed a well-founded illusion: the sense of the game which implies an anticipated adjustment of habitus to the necessities and probabilities inscribed in the field does present itself under the appearance of a successful "aiming at" a future. Likewise, the structural affinity of habituses belonging to the same class is capable of generating practices that are convergent and objectively orchestrated outside of any collective "intention" or consciousness, let alone "conspiracy." In this fashion it explains many phenomena of quasi teleology which can be observed in the social world, such as those forms of collective action or reaction that pose such insuperable dilemmas to RAT.[79]

The efforts of the proponents of one or another version of rational action theory remind me of Tycho Brahé trying to salvage the Ptolemaic paradigm after Copernicus. It is amusing to see them go back and forth, sometimes from one page to the next, between a mechanism that explains action by the direct efficacy of causes (such as market constraints) and a finalism which, in its pure form, wants to see nothing but the choices of a pure mind commanding a perfect will or which, in its more temperate forms, makes room for choices under

---

possible, so long as their "entire occupational existence was placed under the rule of the arbitrary" imposed by permanent insecurity and extreme deprivation (further exacerbated, in this case, by the cultural shock created by the disappearance of the assurances and supports formerly guaranteed by peasant society). In the absence of a minimum distance from economic necessity, agents cannot develop the temporal dispositions necessary for conceiving the possibility of a future pregnant with options and inviting meaningful decisions (a jobless man from the city of Constantine sums this up well: "When you are not sure of today, how can you be sure of tomorrow?").

79. The most famous of these dilemmas is that of the "free rider" (Olson 1965). Bourdieu dissolves this problem by showing that "the objective homogenizing of group or class habitus which results from the homogeneity of conditions of existence is what enables practices to be objectively harmonized outside of any strategic computation and outside of any conscious reference to a norm, and to be mutually adjusted *in the absence of any direct interaction* and, a fortiori, of any explicit co-ordination" (Bourdieu 1990a: 58, translation modified).

constraints—as with "bounded rationality," "irrational rationality," "weakness of the will," etc., the variations are endless. The unfortunate hero of this untenable paradigm is arguably Jon Elster (1984b) who, the same causes producing the same effects, repeats Sartre's analyses of bad faith and oath in *Ulysses and the Sirens*.[80]

Doesn't the notion of habitus also have the function of sidestepping the alternative between the individual and society, and thus between methodological individualism and holism?

To speak of habitus is to assert that the individual, and even the personal, the subjective, is social, collective. Habitus is a socialized subjectivity. This is where I part for instance with Herbert Simon and his notion of "bounded rationality" (Simon 1955; March 1978). Rationality is bounded not only because the available information is curtailed, and because the human mind is generically limited and does not have the means of fully figuring out all situations, especially in the urgency of action, but also because the human mind is *socially* bounded, socially structured. The individual is always, whether he likes it or not, trapped—save to the extent that he becomes aware of it—"within the limits of his brain," as Marx said, that is, within the limits of the system of categories he owes to his upbringing and training. (I notice that I have never cited Marx as often as I do nowadays, that is, at a time when he has been made the scapegoat of all the ills of the social world—no doubt an expression of the same rebellious dispositions that inclined me to cite Weber at the time when the Marxist orthodoxy was trying to ostracize his work. . .)

The proper object of social science, then, is neither the individual, this *ens realissimum* naively crowned as the paramount, rock-bottom reality by all "methodological individualists," nor groups as concrete sets of individuals sharing a similar location in social space, but the *relation between two realizations of historical action*, in bodies and in things. It is the double and obscure relation between habitus, i.e., the durable and transposable systems of schemata of perception, appre-

80. See Bourdieu (1990a: 42–51) for a thorough critique of Sartrean phenomenology and Elster's rational choice theory along these lines. Elsewhere, Bourdieu (1990e: 384) writes: "The rational calculator that the advocates of Rational Action Theory portray as the principle of human practices is no less absurd . . . than the *angelus rector*, the far-seeing pilot to which some pre-Newtonian thinkers attributed the regulated movement of the planets."

ciation, and action that result from the institution of the social in the body (or in biological individuals), and fields, i.e., systems of objective relations which are the product of the institution of the social in things or in mechanisms that have the quasi reality of physical objects; and, of course, of everything that is born of this relation, that is, social practices and representations, or fields as they present themselves in the form of realities perceived and appreciated.

What is the nature of this "double and obscure relation" (you speak somewhere of an "ontological correspondence") between habitus and field, and how does it work itself out more precisely?

The relation between habitus and field operates in two ways. On one side, it is a relation of *conditioning:* the field structures the habitus, which is the product of the embodiment of the immanent necessity of a field (or of a set of intersecting fields, the extent of their intersection or discrepancy being at the root of a divided or even torn habitus). On the other side, it is a relation of knowledge or *cognitive construction.* Habitus contributes to constituting the field as a meaningful world, a world endowed with sense and value, in which it is worth investing one's energy. Two things follow. First, the relation of knowledge depends on the relation of conditioning that precedes it and fashions the structures of habitus. Second, social science is necessarily a "knowledge of a knowledge" and must make room for a sociologically grounded phenomenology of the primary experience of the field or, to be more precise, of the invariants and variations of the relation between different types of fields and different types of habitus.

Human existence, or habitus as the social made body, is this thing of the world for which there are things. As Pascal more or less put it, *le monde me comprend mais je le comprends* (in short, "the world encompasses me but I understand it"). Social reality exists, so to speak, twice, in things and in minds, in fields and in habitus, outside and inside of agents. And when habitus encounters a social world of which it is the product, it is like a "fish in water": it does not feel the weight of the water, and it takes the world about itself for granted.[81] I could, to make sure that I am well understood, explicate Pascal's for-

81. "Habitus never practically masters its field of action more than when it is fully inhabited by the field of forces because its structures are the product of this field" (Bourdieu 1989a: 327).

mula: the world encompasses me *(me comprend)* but I comprehend it *(je le comprends)* precisely *because* it comprises me. It is because this world has produced me, because it has produced the categories of thought that I apply to it, that it appears to me as self-evident. In the relation between habitus and field, history enters into a relation with itself: a genuine ontological complicity, as Heidegger and Merleau-Ponty suggested, obtains between the agent (who is neither a subject or a consciousness, nor the mere executant of a role, the support of a structure or actualization of a function) and the social world (which is never a mere "thing," even if it must be constructed as such in the objectivist phase of research).[82] This relation of practical knowledge is not that between a subject and an object constituted as such and per-ceived as a problem. Habitus being the social embodied, it is "at home" in the field it inhabits, it perceives it immediately as endowed with meaning and interest. The practical knowledge it procures may be described by analogy with Aristotle's *phronesis* or, better, with the *orthē doxa* of which Plato talks in *Meno:* just as the "right opinion" "falls right," in a sense, without knowing how or why, likewise the coincidence between dispositions and position, between the "sense of the game" and the game, explains that the agent does what he or she "has to do" without posing it explicitly as a goal, below the level of calculation and even consciousness, beneath discourse and representation.

But it seems to me that this analysis should lead you to forsake the idiom of strategy entirely, yet the latter is central to your work (Bourdieu 1986a).

Indeed, far from being posited as such in an explicit, conscious project, the strategies suggested by habitus as a "feel for the game"

---

82. "The relationship to the social world is not the mechanical causality between a 'milieu' and a consciousness, but rather a sort of ontological complicity. When the same history inhabits both habitus and habitat, both dispositions and position, the king and his court, the employer and his firm, the bishop and his see, history in a sense commu-nicates with itself, is reflected in its own image. History as 'subject' discovers itself in history as 'object'; it recognizes itself in 'antepredicative,' 'passive syntheses,' struc-tures that are structured prior to any structuring operation or any linguistic expression. The doxic relation to the native world, a quasi-ontological commitment flowing from practical experience, is a relationship of belonging and possessing in which a body, ap-propriated by history, absolutely and immediately appropriates things inhabited by the same history" (Bourdieu 1981c: 306, translation modified).

aim, on the mode of "protension" so well characterized by Husserl (1982) in *Ideen*, towards the "objective potentialities" immediately given in the immediate present. And one may wonder, as you do, whether we should then talk of "strategy" at all. It is true that the word is strongly associated with the intellectualist and subjectivist tradition which, from Descartes to Sartre, has dominated modern Western philosophy, and which is now again on the upswing with RAT, a theory so well suited to satisfy the spiritualist *point d'honneur* of intellectuals. This is not a reason, however, not to use it with a totally different theoretical intention, to designate the objectively oriented lines of action which social agents continually construct in and through practice.[83]

Paradoxically, then, the very cases in which the immediate agreement between habitus and field obtains are the ones most likely to lead one to contest the reality of habitus and to doubt its scientific utility.

To give this paradox its full weight, one could even say that the theory of habitus may allow you to cumulate explanation by *vis dormitiva* (why does someone make petty-bourgeois choices? Because he has a petty bourgeois habitus!) and *ad hoc* explanation. I do not deny that some users of the concept may have succumbed to one or the other of these dangers, or to both, but I would be ready to dare my critics to find one such instance in my writings—and not only because I have been keenly aware of this danger all along. In reality, every time it is confronted with objective conditions identical with or similar to those of which it is the product, habitus is perfectly "adapted" to the field without any conscious search for purposive adaptation, and one could say that the effect of habitus is then redundant with the effect of field. In such a case, the notion can seem less indispensible, but it still has the virtue of pushing aside interpretations in terms of "rational choice" that the "reasonable" character of the situation seems to warrant.

Habitus is what you have to posit to account for the fact that, without being rational, social agents are *reasonable*—and this is what

83. "The problem of the conscious or unconscious character of strategies, thus of the good faith or cynicism of agents which is of such great interest to petty-bourgeois moralism" becomes "nonsensical" (Bourdieu 1990d: 37, note 3) once it is recognized that it is the encounter of habitus with the peculiar conjuncture of the field that drives them.

makes sociology possible. People are not fools; they are are much less bizarre or deluded than we would spontaneously believe precisely because they have internalized, through a protracted and multisided process of conditioning, the objective chances they face. They know how to "read" the future that fits them, which is made for them and for which they are made (by opposition to everything that the expression "this is not for the likes of us" designates), through practical anticipations that grasp, at the very surface of the present, what unquestionably imposes itself as that which "has" to be done or said (and which will retrospectively appear as the "only" thing to do or say).

But there are also cases of discrepancy between habitus and field in which conduct remains unintelligible unless you bring into the picture habitus and its specific inertia, its hysteresis. The situation I observed in Algeria, in which peasants endowed with a precapitalist habitus were suddenly uprooted and forcibly thrown into a capitalist cosmos (Bourdieu 1979a) is one illustration. Another example is given by historical conjunctures of a revolutionary nature in which changes in objective structures are so swift that agents whose mental structures have been molded by these prior structures become obsolete and act inopportunely (à contre-temps) and at cross purposes; they think in a void, so to speak, in the manner of those older people of whom we may justly say that they are "out of sync." In short, the ongoing dialectic of subjective hopes and objective chances, which is at work throughout the social world, can yield a variety of outcomes ranging for perfect mutual fit (when people come to desire that to which they are objectively destined) to radical disjunction (as with the Don Quixote effect dear to Marx).[84]

84. The internalization of objective chances in the form of subjective hopes and mental schemata plays a key role in Bourdieu's analysis of social strategies, whether it be in schools, in labor and marriage markets, in science, or in politics (see Bourdieu 1974a, 1979b, 1977b, for major statements). Since it has often been misconstrued as implying that agents' expectations necessarily and mechanically replicate their objective opportunities (e.g., Swartz 1977: 554; McLeod 1987), it is useful to quote Bourdieu's strong rejection of this view at some length: "The tendency to persevere in their being that groups owe, among other reasons, to the fact that the agents who compose them are endowed with durable dispositions capable of surviving the economic and social conditions of their own production, can be at the basis of *maladjustment as well as adjustment, of revolt as well as resignation*. It suffices to evoke other possible forms of the relation between dispositions and conditions to see in the anticipated adjustment of habitus to objective conditions a 'particular case of the possible' and *to avoid uncon-*

Another reason why we cannot do without the notion of habitus is that it alone allows us to take into account, and to account for, the constancy of dispositions, tastes, preferences, which gives so much trouble to neomarginalist economics (many economists of consumer behavior have observed that the structure and level of expenses are not affected by short term variations in income and that consumption outlays display a high degree of inertia owing to the fact that they strongly depend on prior consumption patterns). However, the virtue, at once heuristic and explanatory, of the concept is never seen better than in the case of practices that are often studied separately either by the same science, such as marital behavior and fertility, or by different sciences, as with the linguistic hypercorrection, low fertility, and strong propensity to save of the upwardly mobile fractions of the petty bourgeoisie (see Bourdieu 1984a: chap. 6).

In brief, the theory of habitus not only has the merit (forgive me but I feel called upon to defend it) of better accounting for the actual logic of actual practices (especially economic practices) than rational choice theory, which destroys them, pure and simple. It also offers a matrix of hypotheses which have received numerous empirical verifications, and not in my work alone.

Does the theory of habitus rule out strategic choice and conscious deliberation as one possible modality of action?

Not at all. The immediate fit between habitus and field is only one modality of action, if the most prevalent one ("We are empirical," said Leibniz, by which he meant practical, "in three quarters of our actions"). The lines of action suggested by habitus may very well be accompanied by a strategic calculation of costs and benefits, which tends to carry out at a conscious level the operations that habitus carries out in its own way. Times of crises, in which the routine adjustment of subjective and objective structures is brutally disrupted, constitute a class of circumstances when indeed "rational choice" may take over, at least among those agents who are in a position to be rational.

---

sciously universalizing the model of the quasi-circular relation of near-perfect reproduction which is completely valid only in the case where the conditions of production of habitus are identical or homologous to its conditions of functioning" (Bourdieu 1990a: 62–63, translation modified and emphasis added). Similar statements can be gleaned from earlier writings, for example, Bourdieu 1974a, on the "Causality of the Probable."

Does the introduction of the mediating concept of habitus really free us from the "iron cage" of structuralism? To many of your readers, the notion seems to remain overly deterministic: if habitus, as the "strategy-generating principle enabling agents to cope with unforeseen and ever-changing situations," results from the incorporation of the durable objective structures of the world, if the improvisation it regulates is itself "regulated" by those structures (Bourdieu 1977a), where does the element of innovation and agency come from? [85]

Before I answer this question, I would like to invite you to ask yourself why this notion, in a sense very banal (everyone will readily grant that social beings are at least partly the product of social conditionings), has triggered such reactions of hostility, if not rage, among some intellectuals, and even among sociologists. What is it about it that is so *shocking*? The answer is, I think, that it collides head on with the illusion of (intellectual) mastery of oneself that is so deeply ingrained in intellectuals. To the three "narcissistic wounds" evoked by Freud, those visited upon humanity by Copernicus, Darwin, and Freud himself, one should add that which sociology inflicts upon us, especially when it applies to "creators." Sartre, of whom I have often said that he has given intellectuals their "professional ideology" or, better, to speak like Weber, the "theodicy of their own privilege," elaborated the most accomplished version of the founding myth of the uncreated creator with his notion of "original project" (Bourdieu

85. Again, the notion of habitus is one which interpreters and critics of Bourdieu hardly agree upon. For Gartman (1991), Giroux (1982), and Jenkins (1982), among others, habitus reinforces determinism under the appearance of relaxing it. Giroux (1983: 90) contends that "its definition and use constitute a conceptual straight-jacket that provides no room for modification or escape. Thus the notion of habitus smothers the possibility for social change and collapses into a mode of management ideology." On the contrary, according to Harker (1984), Miller and Branson (1987: 217–18), Thapan (1988), Schiltz (1982: 729), Harker et al. (1990: 10–12) and Sulkunen (1982), it is a mediating, and not a structural, concept which introduces a degree of free play, creativity, and unpredictability in social action. Fox (1985: 199) expresses this interpretation thus: "habitus portrays social life and cultural meaning as a constantly developing practice, akin to the conception of culture as always in the making." Sahlins (1985: 29, 51, 53), Powell and DiMaggio (1991), and Calhoun (1982: 232–33) find both dimensions to be present in the concept. According to Ansart (1990: 40), it is the notion of habitus that allows Bourdieu to break out of the structuralist paradigm by developing an active conception of social conduct, a view shared by Lemert (1990: 299): "habitus is the most powerful idea from which Bourdieu generates a theory of structures unique for its sensitivity to the riddle upon which theories of structure most often falter: How does agency survive the constraining power of structuring?"

1971a), which is to the notion of habitus as the myth of genesis is to the theory of evolution. (The "original project" is, as you recall, this sort of free and conscious act of self-creation whereby a creator assigns to himself his life's designs, and that Sartre [1981–91] situated toward the end of childhood in his study of Flaubert.) The notion of habitus provokes exasperation, even desperation, I believe, because it threatens the very idea that "creators" (especially aspiring ones) have of themselves, of their identity, of their "singularity." Indeed, only the (experienced) seriousness of this stake can explain the fact that so many fine minds reacted not to what I wrote but to what they thought they had read.

Habitus is not the fate that some people read into it. Being the product of history, it is an *open system of dispositions* that is constantly subjected to experiences, and therefore constantly affected by them in a way that either reinforces or modifies its structures.[86] It is durable but not eternal! Having said this, I must immediately add that there is a probability, inscribed in the social destiny associated with definite social conditions, that experiences will confirm habitus, because most people are statistically bound to encounter circumstances that tend to agree with those that originally fashioned their habitus.

In truth, the problem of the genesis of the socialized biological individual, of the social conditions of formation and acquisition of the generative preference structures that constitute habitus as the social embodied, is an extremely complex question. I think that, for logical reasons, there is a *relative irreversibility* to this process: all the external stimuli and conditioning experiences are, at every moment, perceived through categories already constructed by prior experiences. From that follows an inevitable priority of originary experiences and consequently a *relative* closure of the system of dispositions that constitute habitus.[87] (Aging, for instance, may be conceived as the increasing

86. Aside from the effects of certain social trajectories, habitus can also be transformed via socio-analysis, i.e., via an awakening of consciousness and a form of "self-work" that enables the individual to get a handle on his or her dispositions, as Bourdieu suggests below. The possibility and efficacy of this kind of self-analysis is itself determined in part by the original structures of the habitus in question, in part by the objective conditions under which the awakening of self-consciousness takes place (see, for instance, the "anti-institutional" disposition of French philosophers touched upon above in sec. 1).

87. "The very logic of its genesis explains that habitus is a chronologically ordered series of structures in which a structure of a given rank-order specifies the structures of

closure of these structures: the mental and bodily schemata of a person who ages become more and more rigid, less and less responsive to external solicitations.) Moreover, everything leads me to believe that certain basic structures, such as the opposition male/female, are organized extremely early on. Recent research in developmental psychology by Eleanor Maccoby (1988) reveals that girls and boys learn in nursery school, before age three, how to behave differently with a boy or a girl, and what to expect of each: blows from the one and kisses from the other. If we hold, as I do, that the principle of gender opposition plays a very fundamental role, for instance in politics (all the major political oppositions are overlaid with sexual connotations), if we hold that the bodily schemata of perception of the division of sexual labor and of the sexual division of labor are constitutive of the perception of the social world (Bourdieu 1977d),[88] then we must admit that, to some extent, primary social experiences have a disproportionate weight.

---

lower rank-order (i.e., genetically anterior) and structures the structures of higher ranking through the structuring action it exercises upon the structured experiences generative of these structures. Thus, for instance, the habitus acquired in the family is at the basis of the structuring of school experiences . . . ; the habitus transformed by the action of the school, itself diversified, is in turn at the basis of all subsequent experiences . . . and so on, from restructuring to restructuring" (Bourdieu 1972: 188, my translation).

88. From the first, gender oppositions have been at the very heart of Pierre Bourdieu's thinking (he once half-facetiously confessed that "it was women who 'taught' [him] sociology"). He wrote extensively on this topic at the start of his career. His first major articles, based upon research in his home region of Béarn and in Algeria, concern "The Relation Between the Sexes in Peasant Society" (Bourdieu 1962c), "Bachelorhood and the Condition of Peasants" (Bourdieu 1962b), and the ethos of masculinity that underpins "The Sentiment of Honor in Kabyle Society" (Bourdieu 1965). His famous "The Berber House, or the World Reversed" (written in 1968 and reprinted in Bourdieu 1979c) revolves around the male/female oppositions that structure Kabyle cosmogony and domestic ritual practices. Discussion of sexual differences and categorizations abound in *Outline of a Theory of Practice* and *Distinction*. Yet, since the early 1960s, Bourdieu had never launched a frontal attack on the issue. This is remedied in the recent article entitled "Male Domination," in which Bourdieu (1990i) argues that gender domination constitutes the paradigm of all domination and is perhaps its most persistent form. It is at once the most arbitrary and the most misrecognized dimension of domination because it operates essentially via the deep, yet immediate, agreement of embodied schemata of vision of the world with the existing structures of that world, an agreement whose original roots go back thousands of years and can be found in the exclusion of women from the games of symbolic capital. See the discussion in sec. 5, below.

But I would also like to dispel another difficulty. Habitus reveals itself—remember that it consists of a system of dispositions, that is, of virtualities, potentialities, eventualities—only in reference to a definite situation. It is only *in the relation to* certain structures that habitus produces given discourses or practices. (Here you can see the absurdity of reducing my analyses of cultural heredity to a direct and mechanical relation between the occupation of the father and that of the son.) We must think of it as a sort of spring that needs a trigger and, depending upon the stimuli and structure of the field, the very same habitus will generate different, even opposite, outcomes. I could take here an example from my work on bishops (Bourdieu and de Saint Martin 1982). Bishops live to be very old, and when I interviewed them in synchrony I found myself talking with men ranging anywhere from 35 to 80 years of age, that is, to people who had become bishops in 1936, 1945, and 1980, and who had therefore been constituted in very different states of the religious field. The sons of nobles who, in the 1930s, would have been bishops in Meaux, and would have asked the worshipers of their parish to kiss their ring in a quasi-feudal aristocratic tradition, are today "red bishops" in Saint Denis,[89] that is, radical clergymen active in the defense of the downtrodden. The same aristocratic habitus of highness, distance, and separation from the "middle," the "petty," the average, i.e., from the middle classes and the petty bourgeois, and thereby from the banal, the trivial, the commonplace, can produce diametrically opposed conducts due to the transformation of the situation in which they operate.

You thus reject the deterministic schema sometimes attributed to you with the formula "structures produce habitus, which determine practices, which reproduce structures" (Bidet 1979: 203; also Jenkins 1982, Gorder 1980, Giroux 1982: 7), that is, the idea that position in the structure directly determines social strategy. In truth, the determinations attached to a given position always operate through the multilayered filter of dispositions acquired and active over the social and biographical trajectory of the agent, as well as through the structural history of this position in social space.

Circular and mechanical models of this kind are precisely what the notion of habitus is designed to help us destroy (Bourdieu 1980d, 1988c, 1990a). At the same time, I can understand such misinterpreta-

---

89. Meaux is a traditionalist provincial town in a small religious district whose bishop is generally of noble descent. Saint Denis is an archetypal working-class suburb north of Paris and a historic stronghold of the Communist party.

tions: insofar as dispositions themselves are socially determined, one could say that I am in a sense hyperdeterminist. It is true that analyses that take into account both effects of position and effects of disposition can be perceived as formidably deterministic. The notion of habitus accounts for the fact that social agents are neither particles of matter determined by external causes, nor little monads guided solely by internal reasons, executing a sort of perfectly rational internal program of action. Social agents are the *product of history*, of the history of the whole social field and of the accumulated experience of a path within the specific subfield. Thus, for example, in order to understand what professor A or B will do in a given conjuncture (say, May '68) or in any ordinary academic situation, we must know what position she occupies in academic space but also how she got there and from what original point in social space, for the way in which one accedes to a position is inscribed in habitus. To put it differently, social agents will *actively* determine, on the basis of these socially and historically constituted categories of perception and appreciation, the situation that determines them. One can even say that *social agents are determined only to the extent that they determine themselves.* But the categories of perception and appreciation which provide the principle of this (self-) determination are themselves largely determined by the social and economic conditions of their constitution.

This being said, one can utilize such analyses precisely to step back and gain distance from dispositions. The Stoics used to say that what depends upon us is not the first move but only the second one. It is difficult to control the first inclination of habitus, but reflexive analysis, which teaches that we are the ones who endow the situation with part of the potency it has over us, allows us to alter our perception of the situation and thereby our reaction to it. It enables us to monitor, up to a certain point, some of the determinisms that operate through the relation of immediate complicity between position and dispositions.

At bottom, determinisms operate to their full only by the help of unconsciousness, with the complicity of the unconscious.[90] For deter-

90. "The 'unconscious' . . . is indeed never but the forgetting of history that history itself produces by turning the objective structures it itself engenders into those quasi natures that habituses are" (Bourdieu 1990a: 56, translation modified). Put differently: "As long as the principles which orient practices are left in a state of unconscious, the interactions of ordinary existence are, according to Marx's expression, 'relations be-

minism to exert itself unchecked, dispositions must be abandonned to their free play. This means that agents become something like "subjects" only to the extent that they consciously master the relation they entertain with their dispositions. They can deliberately let them "act" or they can on the contrary inhibit them by virtue of consciousness. Or, following a strategy that seventeenth-century philosophers advised, they can pit one disposition against another: Leibniz argued that one cannot fight passion with reason, as Descartes claimed, but only with "slanted wills" *(volontés obliques)*, i.e., with the help of other passions. But this work of management of one's dispositions, of habitus as the unchosen principle of all "choices," is possible only with the support of explicit clarification. Failing an analysis of such subtle determinations that work themselves out through dispositions, one becomes accessory to the unconsciousness of the action of dispositions, which is itself the accomplice of determinism.

Substituting the constructed relation between habitus and field for the apparent relation between the "actor" and the "structure" is also a means of bringing time to the core of social analysis.[91] And it reveals, *in contrario*, the shortcomings of the detemporalized conception of action that informs both structural and rational-choice views of action.

---

tween men mediated by things': the structure of the distribution of economic and cultural capital and the principles of perception and appreciation which are its transfigured form interpose themselves between the one who judges and the one who is judged, in the form of the unconscious of the 'subject' of the judgment" (Bourdieu 1989a: 13, my translation).

91. Bourdieu's interest in time is a long-standing one, going back to his days as a student of philosophy in the 1950s when he undertook a systematic reading of Husserl and Heidegger. Much of his early anthropological research in Algeria deals with the contrasted social structuring and uses of time in the capitalist and the traditional sectors of the Algerian economy. Several of his earlier publications, for instance, "The Obsession of Unemployment Among Algerian Workers" (Bourdieu 1962d), "The Algerian Subproletariate" (Bourdieu 1973a, originally published in 1962), and "The Attitude of the Algerian Peasant Toward Time" (Bourdieu 1964) explore the dialectic of "Economic Structures and Temporal Structures" (to recall the subtitle of the first and longest essay in *Algeria 1960*, Bourdieu 1979c). It is in good part by restoring the temporality of practice that Bourdieu breaks with the structuralist paradigm. Time is also at the center of Bourdieu's analysis in that it is built into his conceptualization of social space. The model of the structure of social space put forth in *Distinction* is a three-dimensional one: in addition to the volume and structure of capital possessed by social agents, it takes into account the evolution over time of these two properties.

The relation between habitus and field as *two modes of existence of history* allows us to found a theory of time that breaks simultaneously with two opposed philosophies of time: on the one hand the metaphysical vision which treats time as a reality in itself, independent of the agent (as in the metaphor of the river) and, on the other hand, a philosophy of consciousness. Far from being a condition *a priori* and transcendent to historicity, time is what practical activity produces in the very act whereby it produces itself. Because practice is the product of a habitus that is itself the product of the em-bodiment of the immanent regularities and tendencies of the world, it contains within itself an anticipation of these tendencies and regularities, that is, a nonthetic reference to a future inscribed in the immediacy of the present. Time is engendered in the actualization of the act, or the thought, which is by definition presentification and de-presentification, that is, the "passing" of time according to common sense.[92]

We have seen how practice need not—except by way of exception—explicitly constitute the future as such, as in a project or a plan posited through a conscious and deliberate act of will. Practical activity, insofar as it is *makes sense*, as it is *sensée*, reasonable, that is, engendered by a habitus adjusted to the immanent tendencies of the field, is an act of temporalization through which the agent transcends the immediate present via practical mobilization of the past and practical anticipation of the future inscribed in the present in a state of objective potentiality. Because it implies a practical reference to the future implied in the past of which it is the product, habitus temporalizes itself in the very act through which it is realized. This analysis obviously demands considerable elaboration and differentiation. All I want to suggest here is that we can see how the theory of practice condensed in the notions of field and habitus allows us to do away with the metaphysical representation of time and history as realities in themselves, external and anterior to practice, without for all that embracing the philosophy of consciousness which underpins the vision of temporality found in Husserl or in rational action theory.[93]

92. As Merleau-Ponty (1962: 239–40) writes: "In every focusing moment my body unites present, past and future, it secretes time. . . . My body takes possession of time; it brings into existence a past and a future for a present, it is not a thing, but creates time instead of submitting to it."

93. "To reintroduce uncertainty is to reintroduce time, with its rhythm, its orientation, and its irreversibility, substituting the dialectic of *strategies* for the mechanics of

Your reflection on time has led you to embrace a radical historicism, founded upon the identification of (social) being with history (or time).

Habitus, as a structuring and structured structure, engages in practices and in thoughts practical schemata of perception issued out of the embodiment—through socialization, ontogenesis—of social structures, themselves issued out of the historical work of succeeding generations—phylogenesis. Asserting this *double historicity of mental structures* is what distinguishes the praxeology I propose from the efforts to construct a universal pragmatics in the manner of Apel and Habermas. (It differs from the latter also in that it rejects the reductionist and coarse distinction between instrumental and communicative action, a distinction which is completely inoperative in the case of precapitalist societies and never fully accomplished even in the most differentiated societies. To realize that, it suffices to analyze institutions typical of the capitalist world such as business gifts or public relations.) Praxeology is a universal anthropology which takes into account the historicity, and thus the relativity, of cognitive structures, while recording the fact that agents *universally* put to work such historical structures.

This double historicity of habitus is what allows you to provide an anthropological foundation for the actual logic of social reproduction.

Far from being the automatic product of a mechanical process, the reproduction of social order accomplishes itself only through the strategies and practices via which agents temporalize themselves and make the time of the world (which does not prevent them from often experiencing it as a transcendent reality upon which they have no control, as with waiting, impatience, uncertainty, etc.). For instance, we know that social collectives such as bureaucracies have built-in propensities to perpetuate their being, something akin to a memory or a loyalty that is nothing other than the "sum" of routines and conducts of agents who, relying on their know-how (*métier*), their habitus, engender (within the limits of the constraints inscribed in the relations of force constitutive of the field of which they partake and of the struggles which oppose them) lines of action adapted to the situation such as their habitus inclines them to perceive it, thus tailor made

the *model*, but without falling over into the imaginary anthropology of the theories of the 'rational actor'" (Bourdieu 1990a: 99, translation modified; see also Bourdieu 1986a).

(without being designed as such) to reproduce the structure of which their habitus is the product.

The tendency toward self-reproduction of the structure is realized only when it enrolls the collaboration of agents who have internalized its specific necessity in the form of habitus and who are *active producers* even when they consciously or unconsciously contribute to reproduction. Having internalized the immanent law of the structure in the form of habitus, they realize its necessity in the very spontaneous movement of their existence. But what is necessary to reproduce the structure is still a historical action, accomplished by true *agents*. In sum, the theory of habitus aims at excluding the "subjects" (which are always possible as a kind of limiting ideal case) dear to the tradition of philosophies of consciousness without annihilating agents to the benefit of a hypostatized structure, even though these agents are the product of this structure and continually make and remake this structure, which they may even radically tranform under definite structural conditions.

But I am not very satisfied with this answer because I am keenly aware that, despite the qualifications I have attached to it, verbally and mentally (nobody hears the latter, but a good reader, one careful to apply the "principle of charity," should append them on his or her own), I am still inclined or drawn to simplifications which, I fear, are the inescapable counterpart of "theoretical talk." In truth, the most adequate reply to all the questions you have put to me on this matter, particularly on the logic of social reproduction, is for me contained in the five hundred pages of *La noblesse d'Etat* (1989a), that is to say, in the whole set of empirical and theoretical analyses which alone can articulate in its full complexity the system of relations between mental structures and social structures, habitus and fields, and unravel their immanent dynamics.

5   Language, Gender, and Symbolic Violence

In *Language and Symbolic Power* (Bourdieu 1982b, 1991e),[94] you develop a sweeping critique of structural linguistics, or what one might call the "pure" study of language.

94. Much as *Esquisse d'une théorie de la pratique* and *Outline of a Theory of Practice* differ substantially in content and organization, *Language and Symbolic Power* (Bourdieu 1991e) and *Ce que parler veut dire* (literally "What Speaking Means," Bourdieu 1982b) are almost different books, even though the former is, formally, the translation of the

You put forth an alternative model which, to simplify greatly, makes language an instrument or a medium of power relations, rather than a mere means of communication, that must be studied within the interactional *and* structural contexts of its production and circulation. Could you summarize the gist of this critique?

What characterizes "pure" linguistics is the primacy it accords to the synchronic, structural, or internal perspective over the historical, social, economic, or external determinations of language. I have sought, especially in *The Logic of Practice* and *Ce que parler veut dire* (Bourdieu 1990a: 30–41, and 1982b: 13–98, respectively), to draw attention to the relation to the object and to the theory of practice implicit in this perspective. The Saussurian point of view is that of the "impartial spectator" who seeks understanding as an end in itself and thus leads to impute this "hermeneutic intention" to social agents, to construe it as the principle of their practices. It takes up the posture of the grammarian, whose purpose is to study and codify language, as opposed to that of the orator who seeks to act in and upon the world through the performative power of the word. Those who treat it as an *object* of analysis rather than use it to think and to speak with are led to constitute language as a *logos*, in opposition to a *praxis*, as a "dead letter" without practical purpose or no purpose other than that of being interpreted, in the manner of the work of art.

This typically scholastic opposition is a product of the scholarly apperception and situation—another instance of the scholastic fallacy we encountered earlier. This scholarly bracketing neutralizes the functions implied in the ordinary usage of language. Language, according to Saussure, or in the hermeneutic tradition, is treated as an instrument of intellection and an object of analysis, a dead language (written and foreign as Bakhtin points out), a self-contained system completely severed from its real uses and denuded from its practical and *political* functions (as in Fodor's and Katz's pure semantics). The illusion of autonomy of the "purely" linguistic order which is asserted by the privilege granted to the internal logic of language, at the expense of the social conditions and correlates of its social usage, opens the way to all subsequent theories which proceed as if the theoretical

latter. The English-language book, as constructed by John B. Thompson, includes several additional pivotal essays that make explicit the intimate connection between Bourdieu's sociological linguistics and his theory of the political field and of the politics of group formation. All quotes in this section are my translation from the French book.

mastery of the code sufficed to confer practical mastery of socially appropriate usages.

By that, do you mean to assert, against the claims of structural linguistics, that the meaning of linguistic utterances cannot be derived, or deduced, from the analysis of their formal structure?

Yes, and, to put it more strongly, that grammaticality is not the necessary and sufficient condition of the production of meaning, as Chomsky (1967) might lead us to believe by overlooking the fact that language is made not for linguistic analysis but to be spoken and to be spoken *à propos*. (The Sophists used to say that what is important in learning a language is to learn the appropriate moment, *kairos*, for saying the appropriate thing.) All the presuppositions, and all the subsequent difficulties, of all structuralisms—and this is true both in anthropology and in sociology—derive from the *intellectualist philosophy of human action that underpins it;* they are contained in nutshell in this initial operation that reduces the speech act to mere execution. It is this primeval distinction between language *(langue)* and its realization in speech *(parole)*, that is, in practice and in history, which is at the root of the inability of structuralism to think the relation between two entities other than as the model and its execution, essence and existence, and which amounts to putting the scientist, keeper of the model, in the position of a Leibnizian God to whom the objective meaning of practices is given.

In challenging this posture, I am also trying to overcome the shortcomings of both the economic and the purely linguistic analysis of language, to destroy the ordinary opposition between materialism and culturalism. What is it that they both forget? Essentially, to sum up a long and difficult demonstration in one sentence, that *linguistic relations are always relations of symbolic power* through which relations of force between the speakers and their respective groups are actualized in a transfigured form. Consequently, it is impossible to elucidate any act of communication within the compass of linguistic analysis alone.[95] Even the simplest linguistic exchange brings into play a complex and ramifying web of historical power relations between the speaker, endowed with a specific social authority, and an audience, which recog-

95. See Bourdieu and Boltanski 1975, Bourdieu 1975a, 1977c, 1983b, and Bourdieu 1980b: 95–112, 121–142 for further developments.

nizes this authority to varying degrees, as well as between the groups to which they respectively belong. What I sought to demonstrate is that a very important part of what goes on in verbal communication, even the content of the message itself, remains unintelligible as long as one does not take into account the totality of the structure of power relations that is present, yet invisible, in the exchange.

Could you give us an illustration of this?

Let me take the example of communication between settlers and natives in a colonial or postcolonial context. The first question that arises is, what language will they use? Will the dominant embrace the language of the dominated as a token of his concern for equality? If he does, there is a good chance that this will be done through what I call a strategy of condescension (Bourdieu 1984a: 472–73): by temporarily but ostentatiously abdicating his dominant position in order to "reach down" to his interlocutor, the dominant profits from this relation of domination, which continues to exist, by denying it. Symbolic denegation (in the Freudian sense of *Verneinung*), i.e., the fictitious bracketing of the relation of power, exploits this relation of power in order to produce the recognition of the relation of power that abdication elicits. Let us turn now to the situation, which in fact is by far the most frequent one, where it is the dominated who is obliged to adopt the language of the dominant—and here the relation between standard, white English and the black American vernacular provides a good illustration. In this case, the dominated speaks a *broken language*, as William Labov (1973) has shown, and his linguistic capital is more or less completely devalued, be it in school, at work, or in social encounters with the dominant. What conversation analysis leaves out too easily, in this case, is that every linguistic interaction between whites and blacks is constrained by the encompassing structural relation between their respective appropriations of English, and by the power imbalance which sustains it and gives the arbitrary imposition of middle-class, "white" English its air of naturalness.

To push this analysis further, one would need to introduce all kinds of positional coordinates, such as gender, level of education, class origins, residence, etc. All these variables intervene at every moment in the determination of the objective structure of "communicative action," and the form taken by linguistic interaction will hinge substantially upon this structure, which is unconscious and works almost wholly "behind the backs" of locutors. In short, if a French person talks with an Algerian, or a black American to a WASP, it is not two persons who speak to each other but, through them, the colonial history in its entirety, or the whole history of the economic, political, and cultural subjugation of blacks (or women, workers, minorities, etc.) in the United States. This shows, incidentally, that the "fixation on readily visible orderliness" (Sharrock and Anderson 1986: 113) of ethnomethodologists and the concern to keep the analysis as close to "concrete reality" as possible which inspires conversational analysis (e.g., Sacks and Schegloff 1979), and fuels the "micro-sociological" intention, can prompt us entirely to miss a "reality" that escapes immediate intuition because it resides in structures that are transcendent to the interaction they inform.[96]

96. "Contrary to all forms of the occasionalist illusion which inclines one to relate practices directly to properties inscribed in the situation, it has to be pointed out that 'interpersonal' relations are only apparently person-to-person relations and that the truth of the interaction never lies entirely in the interaction" (Bourdieu 1990a: 291). The clearest theoretical presentation of the distinction between structural and interactional levels and modes of analysis is found in Bourdieu's critical exegesis of Weber's sociology of religion (1971b, 1971e: esp. the diagram on pages 5–6, 1987h). Bourdieu reformulates in terms of structure the relations between religious agents described by Weber in terms of interaction, thereby dissolving a number of the difficulties that Weber could not resolve. This distinction between the structural and the interactional level of analysis is further illustrated in his study of the discursive strategies that sellers and buyers of individual homes deploy in the information and bargaining phase of their encounter. This leads him to show that "by searching for them in discourse alone, 'discourse analysis' prevents itself from finding the laws of construction of discourse which lie in the laws of construction of the social space of production of discourse" (Bourdieu and Christin 1990: 79). The same distinction is stressed in his analysis of post-election television debates below, part 3, sec. 5.

This "occasionalist fallacy" is illustrated in Marjorie Harness Goodwin's remarkable ethnography of communication among black children in the natural setting of their Philadelphia neighborhood. It is all well and good to treat "children as *actors actively engaged* in the creation of their social worlds" via the medium of linguistic games (Goodwin 1990: 284) as long as one realizes that the structure of those worlds is already predefined by broader racial, gender, and class relations. Only within the narrow framework of the immediate face-to-face situation can one argue that "speech events can themselves *provide for* social organization, shaping alignments and the social identities of participants." Furthermore, they do so according to rules and oppositions that are not contained within the situation (in this case, the opposition between blacks and whites, who are absent from the "natural setting," or between the school and the street). Only by overlooking the macro-sociopolitical construction of the "frame" (in Goffman's sense) of linguistic interaction can one assert "the primacy of conversational

You argue that every linguistic utterance is an act of power, if a covert one. But are there not domains of practice in which linguistic exchanges (such as "small talk," conversation between intimates, or other mundane "forms of talk" as analyzed by Goffman [1981]) are either orthogonal or irrelevant to structures of inequality, and where verbal behavior is not embedded in relations of domination?

Every linguistic exchange contains the *potentiality* of an act of power, and all the more so when it involves agents who occupy asymmetric positions in the distribution of the relevant capital. This potentiality can be "bracketed," as often happens in the family and within relations of *philia* in Aristotle's sense of the term, where violence is suspended in a kind of pact of symbolic nonaggression. However, even in these cases, the refusal to wield domination can be part of a strategy of condescension or a way of taking violence to a higher degree of denegation and dissimulation, a means of reinforcing the effect of misrecognition and thereby of symbolic violence.

You also denounce the "illusion of linguistic communism" (Bourdieu and Boltanski 1975) according to which the social competence to speak is given equally to all.

Any speech act or any discourse is a conjuncture, the product of the encounter between, on the one side, a *linguistic habitus*, that is, a set of socially constituted dispositions that imply a propensity to speak in certain ways and to utter determinate things (an expressive interest), as well as a competence to speak defined inseparably as the linguistic ability to engender an infinite array of discourses that are grammatically conforming, and as the social ability to adequately utilize this competence in a given situation; and, on the other side, a *linguistic market*, i.e., a system of relations of force which impose themselves as a system of specific sanctions and specific censorship, and thereby help fashion linguistic production by determining the "price" of linguistic products. This, because the practical anticipation of the price that my discourse will fetch contributes to determining the form and contents of my discourse,[97] which will be more or less "tense,"

---

materials in anthropological understandings of how people structure their lives" (Goodwin 1990: 287).

97. Lest this sentence be understood as falling back into a simple rationalistic, economic model of language, it must be stressed that "[t]his anticipation, which owes nothing to conscious computation, is the deed of the linguistic habitus which, being the product of a primordial and prolonged relation to the laws of a definite market, tends to function as a sense of the acceptability and of the probable value of its own linguistic

more or less censored, sometimes to the point of annulment—as in the silence of intimidation. The more official or "tense" the linguistic market, that is, the more it practically conforms to the norms of the dominant language (think of all the ceremonies of official politics: inaugurations, speeches, public debates), the greater the censorship, and the more the market is dominated by the dominant, the holders of the legitimate linguistic competence.

Linguistic competence is not a simple technical ability, but a statutory ability. This means that not all linguistic utterances are equally acceptable, and not all locutors equal.[98] Saussure (1974), borrowing a metaphor used before him by Auguste Comte, says that language is a "treasure," and he describes the relation of individuals to language as a sort of mystical participation in the common treasure universally and uniformly accessible to all the "subjects who belong to the same community." The illusion of "linguistic communism," which haunts all of linguistics (Chomsky's theory of competence has at least the great merit of making explicit the idea of a "universal treasure" which remained tacit in the Saussurian tradition), is the illusion that everyone participates in language as they enjoy the sun, the air, or water—in a word, that language is not a rare good. In fact, access to legitimate language is quite unequal, and the theoretically universal competence liberally granted to all by linguists is in reality monopolized by some. Certain categories of locutors are deprived of the capacity to speak in certain situations—and often acknowledge this deprivation in the manner of the farmer who explained that he never thought of running for mayor of his small township by saying: "But I don't know how to speak!"

Inequalities of linguistic competence constantly reveal themselves in the market of daily interactions, that is, in the chatter between two

---

products and of those of others on the different markets. It is this sense of acceptability, and not one or another form of rational computation aimed at maximizing symbolic profits, which determines corrections and all forms of self-censorship, those concessions that we grant to a social universe by the fact of accepting to become acceptable in it, by inclining us to take into account in the phase of production the probable value of our discourse" (Bourdieu 1982b: 75–76, my translation).

98. "Because competence is not reducible to the specifically linguistic capacity to generate a certain type of discourse but involves all the properties constituting the speaker's *social personality* . . . the same linguistic productions may obtain radically different profits depending on the transmitter" (Bourdieu 1977c: 654).

persons, in a public meeting, a seminar, a job interview, and on the radio or television. Competence effectively functions differentially, and there are monopolies on the market of linguistic goods, just as on the market of economic goods. This is perhaps most visible in politics, where spokespersons, being granted a monopoly over the legitimate political expression of the will of a collective, speak not only in favor of those whom they represent but also very often in their place.[99]

This ability that spokespersons have to shape reality by projecting a definite representation of reality (classificatory schemes, concepts, definitions, etc.), raises the question of the power of words: where does the social efficacy of words reside? Here, you argue once more against the pure "communicational" model represented by Austin, and especially by Habermas, according to which the linguistic substance of a discourse accounts for its effects.

We must be grateful to philosophers of language, and particularly to Austin (1962), for having asked how it is that we can "do things with words," that utterances can produce effects. How is it that if I tell somebody "Open the window!" under certain conditions, this person opens it? (And if I am an old British lord reading his weekend newspaper, lounging in an easy chair, it might even be enough for me to say "John, don't you think that it's getting a bit chilly?" and John will close the window.) When we stop to think about it, this ability to make things happen with words, the power of words to give orders and to bring order is quite magical.

To try to understand linguistically the power of linguistic expressions, to try to ground in language the principle and mechanisms of the efficacy of language, is to forget that *authority comes to language from the outside*, as Benveniste (1969: 30–37) reminds us in his analysis of the *skeptron* handed, according to Homer, to the orator about to deliver a speech. The efficacy of speech does not lie in "illocutionary expressions" or in discourse itself, as Austin suggests, for it is nothing other than the *delegated power* of the institution. (To be fair, Austin himself accorded a central place to institutions in the analysis of lan-

99. This is what Bourdieu (1985b; also 1981a) calls the "oracle effect": the "legitimate trickery," whose possibility is inscribed in the very logic of delegation, whereby the spokesperson passes his words, and thereby his world, off as those of the people he or she represents, and imposes his own definition of their situation, condition, and interests. Maresca (1983) offers an exemplary study of this effect among the French peasantry. See Wacquant 1987 for an extended analysis.

guage, but his commentators, especially Récanati [1982], have generally twisted his theory of the performative toward an inquiry into its intrinsic properties.)[100] Symbolic power, the power to constitute the given by stating it, to act upon the world by acting upon the representation of the world, does not reside in "symbolic systems" in the form of an "illocutionary force." It is defined in and by a definite relation that creates belief in the legitimacy of the words and of the person who utters them, and it operates only inasmuch as those who undergo it recognizes those who wield it. (This is clearly visible in the sudden decline in the potency of religious language that accompanies the crumbling of the world of social relations that constitutes it.) Which means that to account for this action at a distance, this real transformation effected without physical contact, we must, as with magic according to Marcel Mauss (1950a), reconstruct the totality of the social space in which the dispositions and beliefs that make the efficacy of the magic of language possible are engendered.[101]

Your analysis of language, then, is not an accidental "incursion" into the domain of linguistics but, rather, the extension, into a new empirical realm, language and speech or discursive practices more generally (including those of linguists), of the method of analysis you have applied to other cultural products.[102]

Yes. I have spent my entire life fighting arbitrary boundaries that are pure products of academic reproduction and have no epistemological

100. In his speech-act theory, Austin (1962) analyzes a class of utterances (e.g., "I name this ship the Queen Elizabeth"), which he labels "performatives," that cannot be said to be true or false but only "felicitous" or "infelicitous," depending on whether they respect certain "conventional procedures." Thus the British philosopher clearly suggests that symbolic efficacy depends on institutional conditions but, rather than analyze the *social* character of those conditions (of agent, time, place, authority, etc.), he retreats into a linguistic distinction between locutionary, perlocutionary, and illocutionary acts (see Thompson 1984: 47–48 for a discussion of this point). Fornel (1983) offers a more detailed theoretical examination of Austin's notion of "felicity" from the standpoint of a linguistic pragmatics inspired by Bourdieu's political economy of language.

101. Mauss's (1950a) "Outline of a General Theory of Magic" originally published in 1902–3 in the *Année sociologique* is also the direct inspiration behind Bourdieu and Delsaut's (1975) study of the social magic of the *griffe* (designer's signature) in the field of high fashion.

102. John Thompson (1991) argues this point very cogently. This is also discussed in Snook's (1990) essay on the influence of Nietzsche and Wittgenstein on Bourdieu's conception of language.

foundation whatsoever, between sociology and anthropology, sociology and history, sociology and linguistics, the sociology of art and the sociology of education, the sociology of sport and the sociology of politics, etc. Here again is a situation where the transgression of disciplinary boundaries is a prerequisite for scientific advance.

I think that one cannot fully understand language without placing linguistic practices within the full universe of compossible practices: eating and drinking habits, cultural consumptions, taste in matters of arts, sports, dress, furniture, politics, etc. For it is the whole class habitus, that is, the synchronic and diachronic position occupied in the social structure, that expresses itself through the linguistic habitus which is but one of its dimensions. *Language is a technique of the body*,[103] and linguistic (and especially phonological) competency is a dimension of bodily *hexis* in which the whole relation to the social world expresses itself. Everything suggests, for instance, that the bodily schema characteristic of a social class determines the system of phonological traits that characterize a class pronunciation, via what Pierre Guiraud (1965) calls the "articulatory style." This articulatory style is part and parcel of a lifestyle that has become embodied, *fait corps*, and stands in linked relation with the usages of the body and of time that properly define this lifestyle. (It is no happenstance if bourgeois distinction invests its relation to language with the same distancing intention it engages in its relation to the body.)

An adequate sociology, at once structural and genetic, of language presupposes that we theoretically found and empirically restore the unity of human practices, of which linguistic practices are but one figure, so as to take as its object the relation that unites structured systems of sociologically pertinent linguistic differences to similarly structured systems of social differences.[104]

Let me try to sum up what you are arguing. The meaning and social efficacy of a message is determined only within a given field (e.g., journalism or philosophy), itself nested in a network of hierarchical relations with other fields. Without an understanding of the entire structure of objective relationships that define positions

103. The notion of "technique of the body" is borrowed from Mauss's (1950b) seminal essay bearing the same title.

104. Laks (1983) gives a detailed empirical illustration of the systematic correspondence between social practices and linguistic practices among a group of teenagers from a Parisian suburb via a fine-grained construction of their individual class habitus.

in this field, of the specific forms of censorship each imposes, and without knowledge of the trajectories and linguistic dispositions of those who occupy these positions, it is impossible to fully explicate processes of communication—why something is said or not said, by whom, what is meant, what is understood, and, most importantly, with what social effects.

This is what I tried to demonstrate in my study *The Political Ontology of Martin Heidegger* (Bourdieu 1975c and 1988b).[105] Indeed, it is the logic of my research on language and on the notion of field that led me to concern myself with Heidegger. The work of Heidegger (with which I became intimately familiar very early on, at a time of my youth when I was preparing a book on the phenomenology of affective life and temporal experience) appeared to me a particularly propitious terrain to verify my hypotheses on the effect of censorship exerted by fields of cultural production. Heidegger is a master—I am inclined to say *the* master—of double talk or, if you wish, of polyphonic discourse. He manages to speak simultaneously in two keys, that of scholarly philosophical language and that of ordinary language. This is particularly visible in the case of the apparently "pure" concept of *Fürsorge* which plays a central role in the Heideggerian theory of time and which, in the expression *soziale Fürsorge*, social assistance, refers to the political context and to the condemnation of the welfare state, of paid vacations, of health insurance, etc. But Heidegger interested me also as the exemplary incarnation of the "pure philosopher" and I wanted to show, in what is apparently the most unfavorable case for the sociology of cultural works as I conceive it, that the method of analysis I propose can not only account for the sociopolitical conditions of production of the work but also lead to a better understanding of the work itself, that is, in this case, the central thrust of Heideggerian philosophy, namely, the ontologization of historicism.

The value of Heidegger as the paradigmatic "pure," ahistorical thinker who explicitly forbids and refuses to relate the thought to the thinker, to his biography, and, even less, to the social and economic conditions of his time (and who has always been read in a profoundly dehistoricized manner), is to force us to rethink the links between

---

105. This study, which Bourdieu wrote in Germany during a sojourn at the Max Plank Institut für Sozialforschung, was originally published in German by Syndicat Verlag of Frankfurt in 1976 and in French as an article in *Actes de la recherche en sciences sociales* in 1975. It was subsequently revised and published as a book in French in 1988.

philosophy and politics. This is what I meant by the title I gave to my study: the ontology is political and politics become ontology. But, in this case perhaps more than in any other, the intelligible relation that exists between the "philosophical führer" and German politics and society, far from being a direct one, is established only via the structure of the philosophical microcosm. An adequate analysis of Heidegger's discourse must thus be founded on a twofold refusal: it rejects both the claim of the philosophical text to absolute autonomy and its correlative rejection of external reference; and it rejects the direct reduction of the text to the most general contexts of its production and circulation.[106]

This twofold refusal is also the guiding principle behind your sociology of literature, of painting, of religion or of law (see, respectively, Bourdieu 1988d, 1983d; 1987i; 1971b, forthcoming a; 1987g). In each of these cases, you propose to relate cultural works to the field of their specialized production, and you reject both internal readings and reduction to external factors.

Indeed. By taking into account the field of specific production and its autonomy which is the product of the field's proper history, itself irreducible to "general" history, you avoid two complementary mistakes that function as mutual foils and mutual alibis: that which consists in treating works as self-sufficient realities, and that which reduces them directly to the most general social and economic conditions.[107] Thus, for instance, those who clash over the question of Heidegger's Nazism always grant his philosophical discourse either too much or too little autonomy: it is an undisputed fact that Heidegger was a member of the Nazi party but neither the early nor the mature Heidegger was a Nazi ideologist in the way that the rector Krieck was. The external,

---

106. "We can acknowledge [the] independence [of philosophical discourse] but only on condition that we clearly see that it is but another name for its dependence upon the specific laws of the functioning of the philosophical field. We can acknowledge dependence but only as long as we take into account the systematic transformations that its effects undergo due to the fact that this dependence operates only via the specific mechanisms of the philosophical field" (Bourdieu 1988b: 10).

107. To claim, as Bürger (1990: 23) does, that "Bourdieu takes a radical position: the external perspective" in his analysis of art and other cultural practices involves a fundamental misunderstanding of Bourdieu's theory, since it amounts to effacing the notion of field of symbolic production, as is clear from his earliest pieces (e.g., the 1966 article on "Creative Project," Bourdieu 1971a: 185).

iconoclastic interpretation and the internal, celebratory interpretation have in common their ignorance of the effect of philosophical stylization *(mise en forme):* they overlook the possibility that Heidegger's philosophy might have been only the *philosophical sublimation,* imposed by the specific censorship of the field of philosophical production, of the same political and ethical principles that determined his adherence to nazism. To see this, it is necessary to forsake the opposition between political reading and philosophical reading and to submit to a *double reading,* inseparably philosophical and political, writings that are fundamentally defined by their ambiguity, that is, by their constant simultaneous reference to two social spaces to which two mental spaces correspond.

Thus, to grasp Heidegger's thought, you have to understand not only all the "accepted ideas" of his time (as they were expressed in newspaper editorials, academic discourses, prefaces to philosophical books, and conversations between professors, etc.) but also the specific logic of the philosophical field in which the great specialists, i.e., the neo-Kantians, phenomenologists, neo-Thomists, etc., entered in contention. To effect the "conservative revolution" that he operated in philosophy, Heidegger had to draw on an extraordinary capacity for technical invention, that is, an exceptional philosophical capital (see the virtuosity he exhibits in his treatment of *Kant and the Problem of Metaphysics*) and an equally exceptional ability to give his positions a philosophically acceptable form, which itself presupposed a practical mastery of the totality of the positions of the field, a formidable sense of the philosophical game. In contrast with mere political pamphleteers such as Spengler, Junger, or Niekisch, Heidegger truly *integrates* philosophical stances hitherto perceived as incompatible into a new philosophical position. This mastery of the space of possibles can be seen most clearly in the second Heidegger, who constantly defines himself relationally, countering by anticipation and denegation the representations of his past and present stances that one could produce on the basis of other positions in the philosophical field.

You derive Heidegger's political thought not so much from the study of its context but from the reading of the text itself and the elucidation of the multiple semantic frames in which it functions.

It is the reading of the work itself in a double key, of its double meanings and double entendre, that revealed some of the most unforeseen political implications of Heideggerian philosophy: the rejection of the welfare state hidden at the heart of the theory of temporality, the anti-semitism sublimated as a condemnation of "wandering," the refusal to denounce his former support of the Nazis inscribed in the tortuous allusions of his dialogue with Junger, etc. All of this could be readily found in the texts themselves, as I showed in 1975, but it stood beyond the grasp of the guardians of the orthodoxy of philosophical reading who, in the manner of downclassed aristocrats, responded to the threat that the progress of sciences which elude them posed for their difference by clinging to the sacred boundary between ontology and anthropology. Purely logical and purely political analysis are equally incapable of accounting for a double discourse whose truth resides in the relation between the declared system and the repressed system.

Contrary to what is often thought, the adequate understanding of a philosophy does not require this dehistoricization through eternalization effected by the atemporal reading of canonical texts construed as *philosophia perennis* or, worse, by their endless revamping to fit the issues and debates of the day, sometimes at the cost of properly incredible contortions and distortions. (When I hear that "Heidegger helps us think the Holocaust," I have to believe that I am dreaming—or could it be that I am not "postmodern" enough!) It arises, rather, from a genuine historicization which allows us to discover the underlying principle of the work by reconstructing the problematics, the space of possibles in relation to which it was constructed, and the *specific effect of field* that gave it the specific form it took.[108]

The publication in French of *The Political Ontology of Martin Heidegger* in book form, over a decade after its initial publication in German, was also an opportunity for raising in a very pointed manner the question of the political blindness of philosophy, or at least of the political uses of philosophy by some of its practicioners.

108. Bourdieu (1988a: 118) summarizes this point as follows: "Heidegger's thought . . . is a structural equivalent, in the 'philosophical' order, of the 'conservative revolution' of which Nazism was another figure, produced according to other laws of formation, and therefore truly unacceptable for those who could not and cannot recognize it in any form other than the sublimated form that the philosophical alchemy gives it." Likewise, it is only by fully historicizing Flaubert, that is, by reconstructing his literary practice as the product of the encounter between the field and his habitus as mediated by his trajectory, that "we can understand how he tore himself away from the strict historicity of less heroic fates" (Bourdieu 1988d: 557).

I used the controversy that erupted around the work of Heidegger,[109] and in which certain philosophers (Lacoue-Labarthe and Lyotard notably) displayed more clearly than ever before their profound political irresponsibility, to highlight the politically ambiguous implications of a certain way of conceiving philosophy that has spread in France since the 1960s: a vision of philosophy, especially through the exaltation of the works of Nietzsche or Heidegger, that leads to an *aestheticism* of transgression, to a form of "radical chic," as some of my American friends put it, that is extremely ambiguous intellectually and politically.

From this angle, my work—I think in particular of *The Love of Art* (Bourdieu, Darbel, and Schnapper 1966)[110] or *Distinction*—stands as the very antithesis of the philosophical role which, since Sartre, has always entailed an aesthetic dimension: the critique, not of culture, but of the *social uses of culture as a capital and an instrument of symbolic domination*, is incompatible with the aestheticist entertainment often concealed behind a scientific front, as in Barthes or *Tel Quel* (not to mention Baudrillard), dear to those French philosophers who have taken the aestheticization of philosophy to a degree hitherto unequalled. Derrida is, on this point, no doubt the most skilled and the most ambiguous insofar as he manages to give the appearance of a radical break to analyses which always stop short of the point where they would fall into "vulgarity," as I showed in the postscriptum to *Distinction* (1984a: 485–500): situating himself both inside and outside

109. The publication of Farias' (1987, Eng. trans. 1989) study documenting Heidegger's support of, and involvement in, Nazi politics triggered a heated and politically charged intellectual controversy into which all the "heavyweights" of the French intellectual field were drawn. It was the occasion of a vigorous exchange between Derrida and Bourdieu in the pages of the left-leaning daily *Libération* and of many acrimonious debates, both public and private. The "affair" has since become international (and partly entangled with the "Paul de Man affair") and continues to rage as of this writing. Books are pouring off the presses almost weekly that claim to prove or refute accusations levied against Heidegger, and argue over their upshot for his philosophy. For a sample of this debate in France and Germany, see the articles by Gadamer, Habermas, Derrida, Blanchot, Lacoue-Labarthe, and Levinas in Davidson 1989, Margolis and Brunell 1990, and the Winter 1989 issue of the *New German Critique*. As Rudof Augstein, the editor of *Der Spiegel* who obtained the famous "posthumous" interview of Heidegger emphasized (cited by Robert Maggiori in his review of the book in *Libération*, 10 March 1988, p. vi), Bourdieu's study of the links between Heidegger and Nazism predates by a full decade this "affair."

110. On the social determinants and uses of art, see also Bourdieu et al. 1965, and Bourdieu 1968a, 1971c, 1974c, 1985d, 1987d.

the game, on the field and on the sidelines, he plays with fire by brushing against a genuine critique of the philosophical institution without completing it.

Thus the "Heidegger affair" was for me an opportunity to show that philosophical aestheticism is rooted in a social aristocratism which is itself at the base of a contempt for the social sciences that is highly unlikely to facilitate a realistic vision of the social world and which, without necessarily determining political "mistakes" as monstrous as Heidegger's *grosse Dummheit*, have very serious implications for intellectual life and, indirectly, for political life. It is not by chance that the French philosophers of the sixties, whose philosophical project was formed in a fundamentally ambivalent relation with the "human sciences," and who never fully repudiated the privileges of caste associated with the status of philosopher, have given a new life, throughout the world but especially in the United States, to the old philosophical critique of the social sciences, and fueled, under the cover of "deconstruction" and the critique of "texts," a thinly veiled form of irrationalism sometimes labeled, without our knowing too much why, "postmodern" or "postmodernist."

Your analysis of Heidegger, and of the social production and functioning of philosophical discourse more generally,[111] thus presupposes, and calls forth, an analysis of the objective position of sociology in relation to philosophy.

Since the second half of the nineteenth century, European philosophy has constantly defined itself in opposition to the social sciences, against psychology and against sociology in particular, and through

111. Aside from Heidegger's ontology, Bourdieu has analyzed the discourse and institution of philosophy as the ideal-typical case of an intellectual practice that claims to be "free floating" and mystifies both itself and others by refusing to face up to its historical determinacy (Bourdieu 1983a and 1985e). Among other topics, the French sociologist has critically examined the rhetoric of Althusserian Marxism, Sartre's invention of the figure of the "total intellectual," the "scholarly myths" of Montesquieu, and the meaning of the vocation of philosophy in the French university of the 1950s (see Bourdieu 1975b, 1980e, 1980f, and 1991a respectively). Substantial analyses of the field of philosophy by his students and collaborators include Boschetti (1988) on Sartre, Fabiani (1989) on the philosophers of the Third Republic, and Pinto (1987) on contemporary philosophy.

It would appear that, for Bourdieu (1983c), short of dissolving itself into social science, philosophy can fully realize itself only by exercising the kind of reflexivity he advocates, that is, socially locating its problematics, categories, and practices, *and*

them, against any form of thought that is explicitly and immediately directed at the "vulgar" realities of the social world. The refusal to derogate by studying objects deemed inferior or by applying "impure" methods, be it statistical survey or even the simple historiographic analysis of documents, castigated at all times by philosophers as "reductionist," "positivist," etc., goes hand in hand with the refusal to plunge into the fleeting contingency of historical things that prompts those philosophers most concerned with their statutory dignity always to return (sometimes by the most unexpected routes, as Habermas testifies today), to the most "universal" and "eternal" thought.[112]

A good number of the specific characteristics of French philosophy since the 1960s can be explained by the fact that, as I demonstrate in *Homo Academicus*, the university and intellectual field came, for the first time, to be dominated by specialists in the human sciences (led by Lévi-Strauss, Dumézil, Braudel, etc.). The central focus of all discussions at the time shifted to linguistics, which was constituted into the paradigm of all human sciences, and even of such philosophical enterprises as Foucault's. This is the origin of what I have called the "-logy effect" to designate the efforts of philosophers to borrow the methods, and to mimic the scientificity, of the social sciences without giving up the privileged status of the "free thinker": thus the literary semio*logy* of Barthes, the archeo*logy* of Foucault, the grammato*logy* of Derrida, or the attempt of the Althusserians to pass the "scientific" reading of Marx off as a self-sufficient and self-contained science, and yardstick of all science (Bourdieu 1975b; see Kauppi 1991 and forthcoming for a fuller analysis of the "-logy effect" in the French intellectual field of the 1960s and '70s).

This sounds like a call for the end of philosophy. Is there a specific mission, a meaningful epistemological space left for philosophy, besieged as it is from all quarters by the various social sciences? Is sociology bound to dethrone the queen

---

acknowledging the social laws that regulate its own internal functioning, if only because this will help it transcend the limitations inscribed in its historical grounding.

112. According to Bourdieu (1983c), philosophy suffers from the incapacity to resolve the antinomy of historicity and truth other than by means of exegetical readings which actualize past works in such a way that they more or less completely negate historicity. The solutions to this antinomy proposed by Hegel (the dialectic which preserves and transcends), Kant (the retrospective construction of past philosophies), and Heidegger (the revelation of originary revelation) converge in their refusal of history.

discipline and to make it obsolete? Is the time ripe for the idea of a "sociological philosophy" (Collins 1988–89; see Addelson 1990 for a similar argument from the philosophical side) or is the latter an oxymoron?

To recall the conditions under which philosophical thinking is accomplished, be it the scholastic situation of *scholē*, the closure onto itself of the academic world, with its protected market and its secure clienteles, or, more broadly, its distance from all manner of necessities and urgencies, has nothing of a polemical denunciation aimed at relativizing all knowledge and thought. Far from leading to its destruction, a genuine sociological analysis of philosophy that replaces it in the field of cultural production and in historical social space is the only means of understanding philosophies and their succession and thus of *freeing philosophers from the unthought inscribed in their heritage.* [113] It would enable them to discover everything that their most common instrument of thought, concepts, problems, taxonomies, owe to the social conditions of their (re)production and to the determinations inscribed in the social philosophy inherent in the function and functioning of the philosophical institution. And thereby to reappropriate the social unthought of this thought.

If the historical social sciences pose a threat for philosophy, it has less to do with their seizing domains hitherto monopolized by philosophy than with the fact that they tend to impose a definition of intellectual activity whose explicit or implicit (historicist and yet rationalist) philosophy is at loggerheads with that objectively inscribed into the post and the posture of the professional philosopher (Bourdieu 1983a and 1983c). Thus I can understand why philosophers, supposed or real, are so strongly inclined, especially in France, to cling in the manner of fallen aristocrats to the external signs of their endangered grandeur.

But would you say that your work belongs to philosophy?

This is a question that does not worry me too much, and I know too well what would be the answer of those philosophers most concerned

---

113. "It is on condition of taking the risk of putting in question and in jeopardy the philosophical game itself, to which their existence as philosophers is linked, that philosophers could avail themselves of the freedom from everything that authorizes and founds them to think and to present themselves as philosophers" (Bourdieu 1983c: 52; see also Bourdieu 1990e).

to defend their turf. If I wanted to give a somewhat idealized vision of my intellectual journey, I could say that it is an enterprise that has allowed me to realize, in my own eyes, the idea that I had of philosophy—which is another way of saying that those who are ordinarily called philosophers do not all and always conform to this idea. It would be a somewhat fictitious vision because there is an enormous component of chance in any biography; I have not truly chosen most of the things that I have done. At the same time, there would be a kernel of truth in this answer because I believe that, given the development of the social sciences, it becomes more and more untenable to deprive yourself of the achievements and techniques of these sciences—although this does not seem to bother most philosophers. I think that I was very lucky to escape the illusion of the "white page and the pen." It suffices for me to read a certain recent treatise in political philosophy to imagine what I could have said if my sole intellectual equipment had been my philosophical training. Which I nonetheless think is absolutely crucial. Hardly a day goes by when I do not read or reread philosophical works, and especially British and German authors I must admit. I am constantly at work with philosophers and putting them to work. But the difference, for me, is that philosophical skills—this may be a bit desacralizing—are on exactly the same level as mathematical techniques: I do not see an ontological difference between a concept of Kant or Plato and a factorial analysis.

Since we are talking "theory," let me bring up a puzzle. You are frequently billed, and certainly read, as a "social theorist" (and, as you well know, this is a very definite type in the gallery of possible sociological personas in the United States). Yet I keep being struck by how seldom, in your work, you make purely "theoretical" statements or arguments. Instead, you refer time and again to particular research problems and dilemmas encountered while gathering, coding, or analyzing data, or thinking through a substantive issue. In your research seminar at the Ecole des hautes études en sciences sociales in Paris (see below, part 3), you warn your audience upfront repeatedly that they shall not get from this course "neat presentations on habitus and field." You are also extremely reluctant to discuss the concepts that you have coined and use in your work in isolation from their empirical supports. Could you explicate the place that theory occupies in your work?

I need not remind you that the perception of a work depends on the intellectual tradition and even on the political context in which its readers are situated (Bourdieu 1990j). The structure of the field of reception stands between the author (or the text) and its readers, via the mental structures it imposes on all who belong to it, and in particular through the structuring oppositions that organize current debates (e.g., today, reproduction versus resistance in Great Britain, and micro-macro in the United States). The upshot of this is a whole series of distortions, often quite surprising and sometimes a bit painful. In my case, the most striking result of this filtering process is the discrepancy between the reception of my work in France and in foreign countries. For a number of reasons—notably because those who could have been attuned to them, such as philosophers, did not want to see them, and more so because they were obfuscated by what was perceived as a political, critical, and even polemical dimension in my work—the anthropological foundations and theoretical implications of my work (the theory of practice and the philosophy of action that founds it) have gone largely unnoticed in France. Instead, typically scholastic discussions, linked to an outdated state of the intellectual debate, on freedom and determinism, on relativism, and other *tristes topiques* of the interwar period, perpetuated in part by the submission of many intellectuals to Marxism and by the inertia of academic problematics handed down in philosophy classes. The important point, I believe, is that what was in my eyes an attempt to construct a general anthropology premised on a historical analysis of the specific properties of contemporary societies was interpreted as a set of political *theses*—on the school system or on culture in particular.

No doubt this obfuscation of my intentions owes something to the fact that I have never resigned myself to producing a general discourse on the social world, and, even less, a universal metadiscourse on knowledge of this world. I hold indeed that discourse on scientific practice is quite disastrous when it takes the place of scientific practice. For a true theory is one which accomplishes and abolishes itself in the scientific work it has helped produce. I do not have much liking for theory that shows itself, that shows off, against theory made to be shown and seen, or, as we say in French, *tape à l'oeil*, gaudy, flashy theory. I am aware that it is not a taste that is too common these days.

Too often, we have an idea of epistemological reflexion that leads us to construe theory or epistemology as a sort of empty and vague discourse on an absentee scientific practice. For me, theoretical reflection manifests itself only by dissimulating itself under, or within, the scientific practice it informs. And I could invoke here the character of the Sophist Hippias. In Plato's *The Lesser Hippias*, Hippias appears as a sort of dunce, incapable of elevating himself above the particular case. Asked about the essence of the Beautiful, he obstinately answers by listing specific instances: a beautiful boiling pot, a beautiful girl, etc. In fact, as Dupréel (1978) showed, he obeys the explicit intention to refuse generalization and the reification of abstraction that it favors. I do not share Hippias's philosophy (although I fear the reification of abstractions that is so frequent in the social sciences more than anything else) but I think that one cannot think well except in and through theoretically constructed empirical cases.

Yet you cannot deny that there is a theory *in* your work or, to be more precise, a set of "thinking tools," to use a notion from Wittgenstein, of wide—if not universal—applicability.

No, but these tools are only visible through the results they yield, and they are not built as such. The ground for these tools—the notion of cultural capital,[114] for instance, that I proposed in the early sixties to account for the fact that, after controlling for economic position and social origin, students from more cultured families not only have higher rates of academic success but exhibit different modes and patterns of cultural consumption and expression in a wide gamut of domains—lies in research, in the practical problems and puzzles encountered and generated in the effort to construct a phenomenally diverse set of objects in such a way that they can be treated, thought of, comparatively.

The thread which leads from one of my works to the next is the *logic of research*, which is in my eyes *inseparably empirical and theoretical*. In my practice, I found the theoretical ideas that I consider most important conducting an interview or coding a survey questionnaire. For instance, the critique of social taxonomies that led me to rethink the problem of social classes from top to bottom (Bourdieu and Boltanski 1981, Bourdieu 1984a, 1985a, 1987b) was born of reflections on the concrete difficulties encountered in classifying the occupations of respondents. This is what enabled me to escape the vague and wordy generalization on classes that reenact the eternal and fictitious confrontation of Marx and Weber.

114. See Bourdieu 1979a on the "three forms" (embodied, objectified and institutionalized) of cultural capital, and Bourdieu 1986b on the relations between cultural, social, economic, and symbolic capital.

What is the difference between "theoreticist theory" and theory as you conceive it?

For me, theory is not a sort of prophetic or programmatic discourse which originates by dissection or by amalgamation of other theories for the sole purpose of confronting other such pure "theoreticist theories" (of which the best example remains, a decade after his death, Parsons' AGIL scheme that some today are trying to resurrect).[115] Rather, scientific theory as I construe it emerges as a program of perception and of action—a scientific habitus, if you wish—which is disclosed only in the empirical work that actualizes it. It is a *temporary construct which takes shape for and by empirical work.*[116] Consequently, it has more to gain by confronting new objects than by engaging in theoretical polemics that do little more than fuel a perpetual, self-sustaining, and too often vacuous metadiscourse around concepts treated as intellectual totems.

To treat theory as a *modus operandi* which practically guides and structures scientific practice obviously implies that we give up the somewhat fetishistic accommodativeness that "theoreticians" usually establish with it. It is for this reason that I never felt the urge to retrace the genealogy of the concepts I have coined or reactivated, like those of habitus, field, or symbolic capital. Not having been born of theoretical parthenogenesis, these concepts do not gain much by being re-situated vis-à-vis previous usages. Their construction and use emerged in the practicalities of the research enterprise, and it is in this context that they must be evaluated. The function of the concepts I employ is first and foremost to designate, in a kind of shorthand, within the research procedure, a theoretical stance, a principle of methodological choice, negative as well as positive. Systematization necessarily comes *ex post*, as fruitful analogies emerge little by little, as the useful properties of the concept are successfully tried and tested.[117]

115. For Bourdieu (Bourdieu, Chamboredon, and Passeron 1973: 44–47), the traditional representation of theory as the cumulative compilation, classification, or elaboration of concepts (he likens the labors of Talcott Parsons and Georges Gurvitch to that of medieval canonists) is a component of the "scholarly common sense" with which sociology must break decisively on pain of reintroducing into its practice a continuist and positivist philosophy of science that stands in contradiction with what Bachelard characterizes as the "new scientific spirit."

116. Cf. Bourdieu and Hahn 1970; Bourdieu, Chamboredon, and Passeron 1973, part 1; and below for elaborations.

117. For instance, it is only after utilizing the notion of "social capital" for a number of years and in a wide variety of empirical settings, from the matrimonial relations of

I could paraphrase Kant and say that *research without theory is blind, and theory without research is empty*. Unfortunately, the socially dominant model of sociology today is still predicated on a clear-cut distinction, and a practical divorce, between research (I think here in particular of this "science without a scientist" epitomized by public opinion research and of that scientific absurdity called "methodology") and the "theory without object" of pure theoreticians, presently exemplified by the trendy discussion raging around the so-called "micro-macro link" (e.g., Alexander et al. 1987). This opposition between the pure theory of the *lector* devoted to the hermeneutic cult of the scriptures of the founding fathers (if not of his own writings), on the one hand, and survey research and methodology on the other is an entirely *social* opposition. It is inscribed in the institutional and mental structures of the profession, rooted in the academic distribution of resources, positions, and competencies, as when whole schools (e.g., conversational analysis or status attainment research) are based almost entirely on one particular method.

Perhaps a better way to make you explicate your conception of "theoretical work," then, would be to ask you how concretely, in your scientific practice, you embed theoretical construction into the research process by reflecting upon a particular object on which you have worked over a period of time. I am thinking here of a paper you recently published, in a rather obscure journal, *Etudes rurales,* on bachelorhood among the peasants of Béarn, your home region, under the title "Reproduction Forbidden: The Symbolic Bases of Economic Domination" (Bourdieu 1989b). What I found most interesting in this article is that, in it, you return to the very same topic you had studied three decades before in a book-long piece entitled "Celibacy and the Condition of Peasants" (Bourdieu 1962b), published in the same journal, to adumbrate a general theory of the *contribution* of symbolic violence to economic domination on the basis of a particular case.

The point of departure of this research is a very personal experience that I recounted in the article, but in a veiled form, because at the time I felt compelled to "disappear." I contrived to used impersonal sen-

---

peasants to the symbolic strategies of research foundations, or from designers of high fashion to alumni associations of elite schools (see, respectively, Bourdieu 1977b, 1980a, 1980b, 1981b; Bourdieu and Delsaut 1975), that Bourdieu wrote a paper outlining some of its generic characteristics (Bourdieu 1980c). For an empirical illustration dealing with the French nobility, see de Saint Martin 1980 and 1985.

tences so as never to write "I" and I described in as neutral a manner as possible the initial scene: a small-village ball on a Saturday evening, on Christmas Eve, in a rural tavern where a friend of mine had taken me some thirty years ago. There, I witnessed a very stunning scene: young men and women from the neighboring city were dancing in the middle of the room while another group of older youths, about my age at the time, all still bachelors, were standing idly on the sides. Instead of dancing, they were intently scrutinizing the ball and, unconsciously, moving forward so that they were progressively shrinking the space used by the dancers. I saw this initial scene as a sort of challenge: at the time I had in the back of my mind the idea of taking as an object of analysis a universe of which I had a familiar knowledge. Having worked in Kabylia, a foreign universe, I thought it would be interesting to do a kind of *Tristes tropiques* (Lévi-Strauss 1970) but in reverse (this book was one of the great intellectual models that we all had in mind at the time): to observe the effects that objectivation of my native world would produce in me. Thus I had a small theoretical purpose and the ballroom scene raised questions. I embarked on an attempt to go beyond the ordinary explanations that still are current both among natives and among journalists. Every year, at the time of the "singles' fairs" that then took place in a number of villages, it was said that "girls don't want to stay in the countryside any more" and that is it. So I listened to people who experienced as profoundly scandalous the fact that older boys, that is, those who are normally legitimated to reproduce themselves, could no longer marry. I then gathered statistics and constructed bachelorhood ratios according to a number of variables. The details are in the long article written in 1960 (Bourdieu 1962b).

Then in the mid-1970s, I was asked by an English publisher to revise this article into a book. I thought the analysis was no longer up to date, so I reworked it entirely. Out of this overhaul came another article entitled "Marriage Strategies in the System of Strategies of Reproduction" [118] in which I tried to uncover what seemed to me to be

---

118. The exact title of this paper ended up being "Marriage Strategies as Strategies of Social Reproduction" (Bourdieu 1977b), which loses the original idea that strategies form a system *sui generis*, because the editors of the history journal *Annales: Economies, sociétés, civilisations* did not like the stylistic ring of it (Bourdieu 1987a: 85). The various strategies of reproduction and their interrelations are explored in depth in *La noblesse d'Etat* (Bourdieu 1989a: 386–427).

the implicit philosophy of what I had done. I had tried to substitute for the model of kinship theories that was dominant at the time, i.e., structuralist theory, a way of looking at matrimonial exchanges that has since become rather trivial, especially among historians of the family, which consisted of conceiving marriages as complex strategies of reproduction[119] (Medick and Warren 1984, Crow 1989, Morgan 1989, Hareven 1990, Woolf 1991) in which any number of parameters are involved, from the size of the estate and the birth rank to the residence, the age or wealth differentials between potential spouses, etc. It was a first revision from which we can extract the following teaching, particularly for those who like to speak of "rupture": *scientific rupture is not effected at once*, it is not a sort of originary act as in initiatory philosophies (and Althusserian Marxism). It can take thirty years. Whence the fact that we sometimes have to return to the same object ten times, even at the risk of having critics complain that we are repeating the same thing over and over.

Thus I did a first revision which, I believe, raised a number of propositions contained in the initial analysis to a much higher degree of explicitness, and suggested a shift to a more dynamic, "strategic" form of analysis. Which should also make us think about the notion of "intuition." When it is said of a sociologist that he or she has a lot of "intuition," it is rarely meant as a compliment. Yet I can say that I spent nearly twenty years trying to understand why I chose that village ball. . . I even believe—this is something that I would never have dared say even ten years ago—that the feeling of sympathy (in the strongest sense of the term) that I felt then and the sense of pathos that exuded from the scene I witnessed were surely at the root of my interest in this object.

Yet the 1989 article both extends your earlier analyses and breaks with them . . .

In this article, as indicated in the subtitle, I tried to rethink this case as a particular case of a general theory—I always hesitate to use such words—of symbolic violence. To understand what happens to bachelors—to the elder sons of landowning families (these are small peasants, the majority of whom own a dozen acres at the most), who

---

119. Bourdieu (1986a) discusses this paradigmatic shift "From Rules to Strategy" and its implications for social theory and the practical operations of research (what type of data to gather, how to code them, etc.).

were privileged in a previous state of the system and are now the victims of their own privilege and fated to bachelorhood, "forbidden to reproduce," because they cannot lose caste, derogate, and adapt to the new matrimonial rules—to understand this phenomenon, I must construct things that were implicit, hidden in the scene of the ball. Or, to be more precise, things that this scene both unveiled and veiled, revealed and obscured at the same time: the ball is a concrete incarnation of a matrimonial market, just as a concrete market (say the flower market in Amsterdam) is a concrete incarnation of the market of neoclassical economics, though one that has little in common with it.

What I had seen was the matrimonial market in a practical state, the locus of the new, emerging form of exchange, the concrete realization of the "open market" which had only a few years before replaced the protected market of the past, controlled by the family—here I could cite Polanyi. The bachelors who stood like so many wallflowers around the dance floor were the victims of the replacement of a closed market by an open market where everyone must manage on his own and can count only on his own assets, on his own symbolic capital: his ability to dress, to dance, to present himself, to talk to girls and so on. This transition from a protected matrimonial regime to a matrimonial regime of "free exchange" had made victims, and these victims were not randomly distributed. At this stage, I returned to my statistics to show how it affected men differently depending on their residence, degree of "citification," education, etc. And I can now quote the passage of the article that sums up the meaning of what I had witnessed (Bourdieu 1989b: 29–30):

> Statistics establish that, when they manage to marry, the sons of peasants marry daughters of peasants whereas the daughters of peasants are more often wedded to nonpeasants. By their very antagonism, these split matrimonial strategies express the fact that [members of] the group do not want for their daughters what they want for their sons or, worse, that at bottom they do not want their sons for their daughters, even if they want some of their daughters for their sons. By having recourse to diametrically opposed strategies, depending on whether they have to receive or to give women, peasant families betray the fact that, under the effect of symbolic violence,

the violence of which one is both the subject and the object, all are divided against themselves. Whereas endogamy testified to the unicity of criteria of evaluation and thereby to the agreement of the group with itself, the duality of matrimonial strategies brings to light the duality of criteria that the group uses to assess the value of an individual, and thus its own value as a class of individuals.

This is a more or less coherent formulation of what I tried to demonstrate.[120] We see how far we have traveled from the originary intuitive perception of the ballroom scene.

This case study of bachelorhood is interesting because it connects with an extremely important economic phenomenon: France has eliminated a large chunk of its peasantry in the space of three decades without any state violence (except to repress demonstrations), whereas the Soviet Union employed the most brutal means to rid itself of its peasants. (This is schematic, but if you read the article you will see that I have said all that in a more nuanced and respectable fashion.) In other words, under definite conditions and at a definite cost, symbolic violence can do what political and police violence can do, but more efficiently. (It is one of the great weaknesses of the Marxist tradi-

---

120. Bourdieu (1989b: 30–33, my translation) continues: "Everything happens as if the symbolically dominated group conspired against itself. By acting as if its right hand ignored what its left hand does, it helps bring about the conditions for the celibacy of inheritors and of the rural exodus, which it happens to deplore as a social curse. By giving away its girls, which it used to marry upward, to city-dwellers, it reveals that, consciously or unconsciously, it takes over as its own the urban representation of the actual and expected value of peasants. Always present, yet repressed, the urban image of the peasant imposes itself even in the consciousness of the peasant. The crumbling of the *certitudo sui* which peasants had managed to preserve over and against all forms of symbolic assault, including those of the integrative pull of schooling, exacerbates the effects of the questioning which triggers it. . . . The interior defeat, felt at the level of each individual, which is at the root of these isolated treasons, carried out under the cover of the anonymous solitude of the market, leads to this unintended collective result, the fleeing of women and the celibacy of men. It is this same mechanism that undergirds the conversion of the peasant's attitude toward the school system. . . . These mechanisms have not only the effect of cutting the peasant off from their means of biological and social reproduction; they also tend to foster the emergence, in the consciousness of peasants, of a catastrophic image of their collective future. And the technocratic prophecy which proclaims the disappearance of peasants cannot but reinforce this representation."

tion to have failed to make room for these "soft" forms of violence which operate even in the economic realm.)

To finish, let me read one footnote that I wrote, on the last line of the last page, for those who would not see the so-called theoretical stakes of this text (but who would look for "Grand Theory" in a text on bachelorhood published in *Rural Studies*?):

> Though I hardly like the typically scholastic exercise which consists in reviewing all other rival theories in order to distinguish one's own—if only because it can lead some to believe that this analysis could have no principle other than the search for distinction—I would like to stress everything that separates Foucault's theory of domination as discipline or "drilling," or, in another order, the metaphor of the open and capillary network from a concept such as that of field.

In brief, though I take pains not to say it—except in a footnote that I deleted three times before finally putting it back in the text—important theoretical issues can be at stake in the humblest empirical work.

In that paper, you invoke the notion of symbolic violence. This notion plays a pivotal theoretical role in your analysis of domination in general. You contend that it is indispensible to account for phenomena apparently as different as the class domination exercised in advanced societies, relations of domination between nations (as in imperialism or colonialism), and, even more so, gender domination. Could you say more precisely what you designate by this notion and how it operates? [121]

Symbolic violence, to put it as tersely and simply as possible, is the *violence which is exercised upon a social agent with his or her complicity.* Now, this idiom is dangerous because it may open the door to scholastic discussions on whether power comes "from below," or why the agent "desires" the condition imposed upon him, etc. To say it more rigorously: social agents are knowing agents who, even when they are subjected to determinisms, contribute to producing the efficacy of

121. Bourdieu's writings on religion, law, politics, and intellectuals offer different angles on the same basic phenomenon. He treats law, for instance, as "the form par excellence of the symbolic power of naming and classifying that creates the things named, and particularly groups; it confers upon the realities emerging out of its operations of classification all the permanence, that of things, that a historical institution is capable of granting to historical institutions" (Bourdieu 1987g: 233–34, translation modified).

that which determines them insofar as they structure what determines them. And it is almost always in the "fit" between determinants and the categories of perception that constitute them as such that the effect of domination arises. (This shows, incidentally, that if you try to think domination in terms of the academic alternative of freedom and determinism, choice and constraint, you get nowhere.)[122] I call *misrecognition* the fact of recognizing a violence which is wielded precisely inasmuch as one does not perceive it as such.

What I put under the term of "recognition," then, is the set of fundamental, prereflexive assumptions that social agents engage by the mere fact of taking the world for granted, of accepting the world as it is, and of finding it natural because *their mind is constructed according to cognitive structures that are issued out of the very structures of the world.* What I understand by misrecognition certainly does not fall under the category of influence; I never talk of influence. It is not a logic of "communicative interaction" where some make propaganda aimed at others that is operative here. It is much more powerful and insidious than that: being born in a social world, we accept a whole range of postulates, axioms, which go without saying and require no inculcating.[123] This is why the analysis of the doxic acceptance of the world, due to the immediate agreement of objective structures and cognitive structures, is the true foundation of a realistic theory of domination and politics. Of all forms of "hidden persuasion," the most implacable is the one exerted, quite simply, by the *order of things.*

One may wonder in this respect if some of the most frequent misunderstandings of which your work has been the object in Britain and the United States (much more so

122. "Any symbolic domination presupposes on the part of those who are subjected to it a form of complicity which is neither a passive submission to an external constraint nor a free adherence to values. . . . The specificity of symbolic violence resides precisely in the fact that it requires of the person who undergoes it an attitude which defies the ordinary alternative between freedom and constraint" (Bourdieu 1982b: 36).

123. This is one of the main differences between Bourdieu's theory of symbolic violence and Gramsci's (1971) theory of hegemony: the former requires none of the active "manufacturing," of the work of "conviction" entailed by the latter. Bourdieu (1989e: 21) makes this clear in the following passage: "Legitimation of the social order is not . . . the product of a deliberate and purposive action of propaganda or symbolic imposition; it results, rather, from the fact that agents apply to the objective structures of the social world structures of perception and appreciation which are issued out of these very structures and which tend to picture the world as evident."

than in Germany or other Continental countries for instance) do not originate in the tendency of the academic mind unconsciously to universalize its particular structures, that is, its national university tradition, both in terms of standards of theory (as with those who compare you to Parsons) and methods, but also in terms of style.

Some review articles are wonderful object lessons in this kind of ethnocentrism at once triumphant and completely trapped in the iron cage of its conceit. I think in particular of a recent essay on *Homo Academicus* (Jenkins 1989) whose author invites me to return to college—and to an English college of course—so as to learn how to write ("Could somebody pass Professor Bourdieu a copy of Gower's *Plain Words*?"). Would Mr. Richard Jenkins write this about Giddens or Parsons, not to mention Garfinkel? By reproaching my alleged attachment to what he mistakenly takes to be a French tradition ("he is playing the game with a long and successful tradition in French academic life"), Mr. Jenkins betrays his undiscussed adherence to a writing tradition that cannot itself be separated from the *doxa*—since such is the word—which, better than any oath, unites an academic body. Thus, for instance, when he goes so far as to excoriate me for an expression such as "the doxic modality of utterances," he reveals not only his ignorance ("doxic modality" is an expression of Husserl that has not been naturalized by ethnomethodologists) but also and more significantly his ignorance of his own ignorance and of the historical and social conditions that make it possible.

If, adopting the mode of thinking suggested in *Homo Academicus*, Mr. Jenkins had turned a reflexive gaze on his critique, he would have discovered the deeply anti-intellectual dispositions which hide themselves behind his eulogy of simplicity, and he would not have offered in such *plain* view the naively ethnocentric prejudices that are at the base of his denunciation of my stylistic particularism (which is at any rate more Germanic than French). Before launching into one of those false polemical objectivations against which I warn and relentlessly try to protect myself in *Homo Academicus* ("What is *really* being communicated is the great man's distinction"), he might have asked if the cult of "plain words," of plain style, plain English, or of understatement (which may lead the virtuosi of this rhetoric of antirhetoric, such as Austin, to mimic in the title of their books or articles the naive simplicity of children's ditties), is not associated with another academic tradition, *his own*, thus instituted as the absolute yardstick of any possible stylistic performance. And if he had understood the true intention of *Homo Academicus,* he would have found in his disconcertment, nay his disgust at my writing, an opportunity to question the arbitrariness of stylistic traditions imposed and inculcated by the various national school systems; that is, an opportunity to ask himself whether the exigencies that British universities impose in matters of language do not constitute a *censorship,* all the more formidable in that it can remain almost tacit, through which operate certain ignored limitations and mutilations that school systems inflict upon us all.[124]

We realize here the function of the concept of *cultural arbitrary* (a concept that has often been questioned by my critics), namely, to serve as an instrument of rupture with the intellectualocentric doxa.[125] Intellectuals are often among those in the least favorable position to discover or to become aware of symbolic violence, especially that wielded by the school system, given that they have been subjected to it more intensively than the average person and that they continue to contribute to its exercise.

Recently, you have further elaborated this concept of symbolic violence in an essay on gender (Bourdieu 1990i) in which you draw upon an unusual combination of sources—your ethnographic materials on traditional Algerian society, the literary vision of Virginia Woolf, and the so-called great texts of philosophy (from Kant to Sartre) treated as "anthropological documents"—to tease out the theoretical and historical specificity of male domination.

To try to unravel the logic of gender domination, which seems to me to be the paradigmatic form of symbolic violence, I chose to ground my analysis in my ethnographic research among the Kabyle of Algeria and this for two reasons. First, I wanted to avoid the empty

124. For Pierre Bourdieu, one of the obstacles to "free trade" in ideas across countries is the fact that foreign works are interpreted through domestic schemata of understanding of which the importer may be completely unaware. It is thus imperative that academics free themselves from conceptual and judgmental biases embedded in *national* academic traditions, for the "internationalization (or 'denationalization') or categories of thought is a condition of intellectual universalism" (Bourdieu 1990j: 10).

125. This concept is discussed extensively in *Reproduction in Education, Culture, and Society* (Bourdieu and Passeron 1977). Another instrument of rupture with scholarly doxa is the social history of intellectual tools and especially the sociology of the genesis and social uses of "The Categories of Professorial Judgment" (Bourdieu 1988a: 194–225, and Bourdieu 1989a: part 1).

speculation of theoretical discourse and its clichés and slogans on gender and power which have so far done more to muddle the issue than to clarify it. Second, I use this device to circumvent the critical difficulty posed by the analysis of gender: we are dealing in this case with an institution that has been inscribed for millennia in the objectivity of social structures and in the subjectivity of men-mental structures, so that the analyst has every chance of using as *instruments* of knowledge categories of perception and of thought which he or she should treat as *objects* of knowledge. This mountain society of North Africa is particularly interesting because it is a genuine cultural repository that has kept alive, through its ritual practices, its poetry, and its oral traditions, a system of representations or, better, a system of principles of vision and di-vision common to the entire Mediterranean civilization, and which survives to this day in our mental structures and, for a part, in our social structures. Thus, I treat the Kabyle case as a sort of "aggrandized picture" on which we can more easily decipher the fundamental structures of the male vision of the world: the "phallonarcissistic" cosmology of which they give a collective and public (re)presentation haunts our own unconscious.

This reading shows, first of all, that male order is so deeply grounded as to need no justification: it imposes itself as self-evident, universal (man, *vir*, is this particular being which experiences himself as universal, who holds a monopoly over the human, *homo*). It tends to be taken for granted by virtue of the quasi-perfect and immediate agreement which obtains between, on the one hand, social structures such as those expressed in the social organization of space and time and in the sexual division of labor and, on the other, cognitive structures inscribed in bodies and in minds. In effect, the dominated, that is, women, apply to every object of the (natural and social) world and in particular to the relation of domination in which they are ensnared, as well as to the persons through which this relation realizes itself, unthought schemata of thought which are the product of the embodiment of this relation of power in the form of paired couples (high/low, large/small, inside/outside, straight/crooked, etc.), and which therefore lead them to construct this relation from the standpoint of the dominant, i.e., as natural.

The case of gender domination shows better than any other that *symbolic violence accomplishes itself through an act of cognition and of mis-*

recognition that lies beyond—or beneath—the controls of consciousness and will, in the obscurities of the schemata of habitus that are at once gendered and gendering.[126] And it demonstrates that we cannot understand symbolic violence and practice without forsaking entirely the scholastic opposition between coercion and consent, external imposition and internal impulse. (After two hundred years of pervasive Platonism, it is hard for us to think that the body can "think itself" through a logic alien to that of theoretical reflection.) In this sense, we can say that gender domination consists in what we call in French a *contrainte par corps*, an imprisonment effected via the body. The work of socialization tends to effect a progressive somatization of relations of gender domination through a twofold operation: first by means of the social construction of the vision of biological sex which itself serves as the foundation of all mythical visions of the world; and, second, through the inculcation of a bodily hexis that constitutes a veritable *embodied politics*. In other words, male sociodicy owes its specific efficacy to the fact that it legitimates a relation of domination by inscribing it in a biological which is itself a biologized social construction.

This double work of inculcation, at once sexually differentiated and sexually differentiating, imposes upon men and women different sets of dispositions with regard to the social games that are held to be crucial to society, such as the games of honor and war (fit for the display of masculinity, virility) or, in advanced societies, all the most valued games such as politics, business, science, etc. The masculinization of male bodies and feminization of female bodies effects a somatization of the cultural arbitrary which is the durable construction of the un-

126. The immediate agreement of a gendered habitus with a social world suffused with sexual asymmetries explains how women can come to collude with and even actively defend or justify forms of aggression which victimize them, such as rape. Lynn Chancer (1987) provides a vivid demonstration of this process in her case study of the negative reactions of Portuguese women to the highly publicized group rape of another Portuguese woman in Bedford, Massachusetts, in March of 1983. The following comments by two women who marched in defense of the six rapists on trial reveal the deeply taken-for-granted nature of assumptions about masculinity and femininity as they are socially defined within this community: "I am Portuguese and proud of it. I'm also a woman, but you don't see me getting raped. If you throw a dog a bone, he's gonna take it—if you walk around naked, men are just going to go for you." "They did nothing to her. Her rights are to be at home with her two kids and to be a good mother. A Portuguese woman should be with her kids and that's it" (Chancer 1987: 251).

conscious.[127] Having shown this, I shift from one extreme of cultural space to the other to explore this originary relation of exclusion from the standpoint of the dominated as expressed in Virginia Woolf's (1987) novel *To the Lighthouse*. We find in this novel an extraordinarily perceptive analysis of a paradoxical dimension of symbolic domination, and one almost always overlooked by feminist critique, namely the domination of the dominant by his domination: a feminine gaze upon the desperate and somewhat pathetic effort that any man must make, in his triumphant unconsciousness, to try to live up to the dominant idea of man. Furthermore, Virginia Woolf allows us to understand how, by ignoring the *illusio* that leads one to engage in the central games of society, women escape the *libido dominandi* that comes with this involvement, and are therefore socially inclined to gain a relatively lucid view of the male games in which they ordinarily partake only by proxy.

There remains to be explained the riddle of the inferior status that is almost universally assigned to women. Here you propose a solution congruent with, yet different from, some feminist responses (e.g., O'Brien 1981).

To account for the fact that women are, throughout most known societies, consigned to inferior social positions, it is necessary to take into account the asymmetry of status ascribed to each gender in the economics of symbolic exchanges. Whereas men are the *subjects* of matrimonial strategies through which they work to maintain or to increase their symbolic capital, women are always treated as *objects* of these exchanges in which they circulate as symbols fit for striking alliances. Being thus invested with a symbolic function, women are forced continually to work to preserve their symbolic value by conforming to the male ideal of feminine virtue defined as chastity and candor, and by endowing themselves with all the bodily and cosmetic attributes liable to increase their physical value and attractiveness. This object status granted to women is best seen in the place that the Kabyle mythico-ritual system gives to their contribution to reproduction. This system paradoxically negates the properly female labor of gestation (as it negates the corresponding labors of the soil in the

127. Henley (1977) shows how women are taught to occupy space, to walk, to adopt bodily postures appropriate to their role in the division of labor between the sexes, that is, how social organization profoundly shapes our soma in a gender-specific way.

agrarian cycle) to the benefit of the male intervention in the sexual act. Likewise in our societies, the privileged role that women play in properly symbolic production, within the household as well as outside of it, is always devalued if not dismissed (e.g., de Saint Martin 1990b on women writers).

Male domination is thus founded upon the logic of the economics of symbolic exchanges, that is, upon the fundamental asymmetry between men and women instituted in the social construction of kinship and marriage: that between subject and object, agent and instrument. And it is the relative autonomy of the economy of symbolic capital that explains how male domination can perpetuate itself despite transformations of the mode of production. It follows that the liberation of women can come only from a collective action aimed at a symbolic struggle capable of challenging practically the immediate agreement of embodied and objective structures, that is, from a symbolic revolution that questions the very foundations of the production and reproduction of symbolic capital and, in particular, the dialectic of pretention and distinction which is at the root of the production and consumption of cultural goods as signs of distinction.[128]

6 For a *Realpolitik* of Reason

In a paper published in 1967 in *Social Research* (Bourdieu and Passeron 1967: 212), you expressed the hope that, "just as American sociology was able, for a time, by its empirical rigor, to act as the scientific bad conscience of French sociology," French sociology might, "by its theoretical stringency, become the philosophical bad conscience of American sociology." Twenty years later, where does this wish stand?

Bachelard teaches us that epistemology is always conjunctural: its propositions and thrust are determined by the principal threat of the moment. Today *the main danger we face is the growing split between theory*

---

128. "Indeed, everything inclines us to think that women's liberation has as its prerequisite a genuine collective mastery of the social mechanisms of domination which prevent us from conceiving culture, that is, the ascesis and sublimation in and through which humanity institutes itself, other than as a social relation of *distinction* asserted against a nature which is never anything other than the naturalized fate of dominated groups—women, the poor, the colonized, stigmatized minorities, etc. For it is clear that, even though they are not completely and always identified with a nature serving as a foil for all the games of culture, women enter into the dialectic of pretension and distinction more as objects than as subjects" (Bourdieu 1990i: 20).

and research that can be observed everywhere, and which fuels the concurrent growth of methodological perversion and theoretical speculation. So I think that it is the very distinction between theory and research implied by this statement that must be challenged, and challenged practically, not rhetorically. If French sociology is ever to become the scientific bad conscience of American sociology (or vice versa), then it must first succeed in overcoming this separation by putting forth a new form of scientific practice founded at once upon greater theoretical exigency and increased empirical rigor.

In what sense can we speak of scientific progress then? Has sociology moved forward in the past several decades or are we still battling the same evils of "Grand Theory" and "Abstracted Empiricism" identified by C. Wright Mills (1959) in the late 1950s?

At one level, the sociological landscape has not changed much over the past quarter century. On the one side, the brunt of empirical research continues to address questions that are more frequently the product of "scholarly common sense" than of serious scientific thinking. And such research often justifies itself by "methodology" too often conceived as a specialty in itself consisting of a collection of recipes and technical precepts that one must respect, not to know the object, but to be seen as knowing how to know the object. On the other side, you have the return of a form of Grand Theory severed from any research practice. *Positivist research and theoreticist theory go hand in hand, complement and compliment one another.* Yet, at another level, the social sciences have witnessed momentous changes. Since the breakdown of the Lazarsfeld-Parsons-Merton orthodoxy in the sixties, a number of movements and developments have emerged and opened up a new space for debate (Bourdieu 1988e). I think here, among other currents, of the "microsociological revolution" (Collins 1985) led by symbolic interactionism and ethnomethodology or of a number of works inspired by feminism. The resurgence of a strong historical current in "macro-sociology" and now in cultural sociology, as well as some of the new work in organizational and economic sociology, etc., have definitely had positive effects.

But, instead of progress, I would rather speak of *obstacles to progress* and of the means of overturning these obstacles. There is undoubtedly progress, and sociology is a considerably more advanced science than observers, even its practitioners, are willing to grant. Consciously or not, we often assess the state of a discipline in terms of an implicit evolutionary model: Auguste Comte's famous table of the hierarchy of sciences still haunts our minds as a sort of ideal hit-parade, and the "hard" sciences are still seen as the yardstick by which "soft" sciences have to evaluate themselves.[129] One factor that makes scientific progress difficult in the social sciences is the fact that there have been in the past attempts to mimic the structure of the so-called hard sciences: namely the spongy and false paradigm that crystallized around Parsons after World War II and which dominated American sociology and most of world sociology until the mid-sixties.

Scientific orthodoxies are the product of a simulation of scientific order which conforms not to the actual agonistic logic of science but to the representation of science projected by a certain positivist epistemology.[130] (One of the merits of Kuhn [1970] was to explode this sort of positivist orthodoxy on the basis of which a scientific orthodoxy could be mimicked under the banner of cumulation, codification, etc.) Thus we had the simulation of a simulacrum of science which, in effect, acted as a factor of regression. For, indeed, a genuine scientific field is a space where researchers agree on the grounds of disagreement and on the instruments with which to resolve these disagreements and on nothing else.

129. It may be recalled that, in his *Positive Philosophy*, Comte drew up a hierarchy of the sciences based on the Law of the Three Stages which ranked them by degree of increasing complexity: in ascending order, astronomy, physics, chemistry, biology and, crowning them all, sociology.

The value assessed to the "hard" sciences is very visible in the objectively asymmetric relations that obtain between sociology and economics, where the amused and contemptuous skepticism of the economists towards sociology is reinforced by the often fascinated and envious admiration of sociologists for economics. In a book of interviews with leading economists and sociologists working at the frontier between the two disciplines, Swedberg (1990: 322) shows that "the pecking order seems to be the following: physics, mathematics, and biology all have higher status than economics; and economics has higher status than sociology, psychology, and history. The more one uses sophisticated mathematics, the higher status one has." Proof that the scientistic project of imitating the natural sciences is still alive in social theory is administered by Wallace's (1988) postulation of a "disciplinary matrix" which opens the recent *Handbook of Sociology* edited by Neil Smelser (see Coser 1990 for a dissenting view on the viability of such a project).

130. On the agonistic nature of science, see Bourdieu 1975d. See also Bryant's (1985) dissection of the "instrumental positivism" that has informed, and continues to suffuse, American sociology since World War II.

For you, what should the sociological field look like? Could you outline your vision of the scientific field?

The American academic orthodoxy of the 1950s organized itself by means of a tacit bargain: one brings "Grand Theory," the other "multivariate statistics," and the last "middle-range theories," and you have the Capitoline triad of a new Academic Temple. Then you say that U.S. sociology is the best in the world and that all the others are imperfect versions of it, and pretty soon you get a Terry Clark (1973) to write a pseudohistory of Durkheimian and French sociology showing that the latter is but a provisional stage on the way to the development of genuine scientific sociology which begins (and naturally ends) in America.[131] It was against all this that I had to battle when I entered sociology.

Another way of mimicking science consists of occupying a position of academic power so as to control other positions, programs of training, teaching requirements, etc., in short the mechanisms of reproduction of the faculty (Bourdieu 1988a), and to impose an orthodoxy. Such situations of monopoly have nothing to do with a scientific field. A scientific field is a universe in which researchers are autonomous and where, to confront one another, they have to drop all nonscientific weapons—beginning with the weapons of academic authority. In a genuine scientific field, you can freely enter free discussions and violently oppose any contradictor with the arms of science because your position does not depend on him or because you can get another position elsewhere. Intellectual history shows that a science that is controversial, alive with genuine (i.e., scientific) conflicts, is more advanced than one where a soft consensus reigns, predicated on elastic concepts, vague programs, editorial truces and edited volumes.[132]

A field is all the more scientific the more it is capable of channeling, of converting unavowable motives into scientifically proper behavior. In a loosely structured field characterized by a low level of autonomy, illegitimate motives produce illegitimate strategies and, furthermore, strategies that are scientifically worthless. In an autonomous field

131. See Chamboredon 1975 for a meticulous critique of Clark's *Prophets and Patrons*, uncovering the implicit evolutionary Americocentrism of its image of the French university.

132. Bachelard writes in *The Philosophy of No:* "Two people, if they truly wish to agree, must first have contradicted one another. Truth is the daughter of debate and not that of sympathy."

such as the mathematical field today, by contrast, a top mathematician who wants to triumph over his opponents is compelled by the force of the field to produce mathematics to do so, on pain of excluding himself from the field. Being aware of this, we must work to constitute a Scientific City in which the most unavowable intentions have to sublimate themselves into scientific expression. This vision is not utopian at all, and I could propose a number of very concrete measures designed to make it come true. For instance, where we have one national referee or evaluator, we can institute an international panel of three foreign judges (of course, we must then control for the effects of international networks of mutual knowledge and alliances). When a research center or a journal enjoys a situation of monopoly, we can work to create a rival one. We can raise the level of scientific censorship by a series of actions designed to upgrade the level of training, the minimum amount of specific competency required to enter the field, etc.

In short, we must create conditions such that the worst, the meanest, and the most mediocre participant is compelled to behave in accordance with the norms of scientificity in currency at the time. The most advanced scientific fields are the site of such an alchemy whereby scientific *libido dominandi* is forcibly transmuted into *libido sciendi*. This is the rationale behind my resistance to a soft consensus which, in my eyes, is the worst possible situation. If nothing else, let us at least have conflicts!

Besides the split of research and theory, you have pointed out a number of dualisms or antinomies that stand in the way of the development of an adequate science of society.[133] What explains their resilience?

These dualisms are indeed enduring, and I sometimes wonder whether they can be neutralized. One of the major tasks of a genuine epistemology, that is, an epistemology built on knowledge of the social conditions under which scientific schemata actually function, is to confront the problems raised by the existence of these dualisms.

133. Among the "false antinomies of social science," Bourdieu (1988e) lists the split between theory and research or methodology, the oppositions between disciplines, and the division of writers into theoretical denominations (Marxist, Weberian, Durkheimian, etc.), the alternatives of structure and action (or history), micro and macro, qualitative and quantitative methods, and the fundamental antinomy of objectivism and subjectivism.

There are antinomies (take, for instance, the opposition between the individual and society, or between individualism and holism, or total-itarianism: I really don't know what to put at the other pole) which are devoid of any meaning and have been destroyed a thousand times in the course of scientific history. But they can easily be brought back to life and—this is very important—those who revive them gain great profits from doing so. In other words, these antinomies are enor-mously costly to demolish because they are inscribed in social reality. Thus the social sciences have a Sisyphean task ahead of them: they must always break, start their work of demonstration and argumenta-tion anew, knowing that all of this work may be destroyed in a flash at any moment by being forced back into these false antinomies. Alain once said that "conversation always proceeds at the level of the dumb-est." In the social sciences, even the dumbest can always invoke com-mon sense and find support in it.

There are people who, since the birth of the social sciences—in France since Durkheim—have announced time and again the "return of the subject," the *resurrection* of the individual, savagely crucified by the social sciences. And every time they are hailed and applauded. One of the reasons why the sociology of literature or of art is so back-ward is that these are realms in which investments in personal iden-tity are formidable. And therefore when the sociologist arrives on the scene and carries out banal scientific operations, when she reminds us that the stuff of the social is made of relations, not individuals, she encounters enormous obstacles. She is at every moment liable to be brought back down to the level of common sense. As soon as science pushes its rock uphill a little, there is someone to say, "Did you hear that? So-and-so denies that individuals exist! How shocking!" (or, "Mozart is so much better than Frank Sinatra!"). And he gains a lot. And he is thought to be a thinker . . .

In reality, the debate between the "philosophy of the subject" (as "philosophers of the subject" such as Paul Ricoeur and others used to put it in the 1960s) is but one of the forms assumed by the struggle between the social sciences and philosophy. Philosophy has always found it hard to put up with the existence of the social sciences, per-ceived as a threat to its hegemony, and to accept the fundamental principles of scientific knowledge of the social world—in particular the "right to objectivation" arrogated by every sociologist or historian worthy of the name. The philosophies and philosophers that may be loosely characterized as spiritualist, idealist, "personalist," etc., are naturally on the frontline of this battle (this was obvious in Durkheim's time but it remains true, though in a more veiled manner, in the time of John Paul II and of "human rights"). Thus the "return of the subject" celebrated with clamor by today's cultural magazines hardly comes as a surprise to those who are cognizant of the logic of the periodic alternation between these "worldviews." As we had explained in an article published at the time (Bourdieu and Passeron 1967), the triumph in the '60s of the "philosophy without subject" (encapsulated by the "death of Man" and other formulas deftly coined to shock the readers of *Esprit*) was nothing other than the "resurrection" (but more chic) of the "philosophy without subject," incarnated by Durkheimian sociology, against which the generation of the immediate postwar era—the Aron of *Une introduction à la philosophie de l'histoire* no less than the Sartre of *Being and Nothingness*—established themselves, and that existentialism had held up to public obloquy. (I am thinking here of the book by Monnerot [1945] entitled *Les faits sociaux ne sont pas des choses* [Social Facts Are Not Things], now forgotten even by those, including some "sociologists," who parrot it today while believing they are breaking new ground.) And the reaction of the new entrants of the 1970s and '80s against those who dominated the field then (and in particular against Foucault)—whom one antisociological *essayiste* lumped together, in a daunting if paradoxical stroke of sociologism, under the label "la pensée 68"[134]—had, thanks to the highly propitious environment offered by a political conjuncture of restoration, to trigger a return to the defense of the individual and the person, of Culture and the West, of Human Rights and Humanism.

These apparent conflicts, which attract journalists and *essayistes* and those participants of the scientific field in search of a surplus of notoriety, hide true oppositions that are themselves only rarely directly related to "worldly" conflicts. The space in which social scientists situate themselves is not that of "current issues," whether political or in-

134. Bourdieu alludes to the book by Ferry and Renault (1989) entitled *La pensée 68* ("The Thought of 1968: An Essay on Contemporary Anti-Humanism"), which offers a blanket critique of the "intellectual generation of the '60s" as a "hyperbolic" reincarnation of the nihilistic strands of German philosophy partaking of a project of "demonization of Europe and of Western values," with Foucault as the representative of "French Nietzscheism," Derrida the exponent of "French Heidegerianism," Lacan the advocate of "French Freudianism," and Bourdieu holding the banner of "French Marxism."

tellectual, as we say to designate what is debated in the book review section of the major cultural magazines and newspapers. It is the thoroughly international and relatively atemporal space of Marx and Weber, Durkheim and Mauss, Husserl and Wittgenstein, Bachelard and Cassirer, but also Goffman, Elias, or Cicourel—of all those who have contributed to produce the problematic which researchers confront today and which has little to do with the problems posed to or by those whose eyes are glued to current issues.

Isn't the same true of most dualisms?

Why are these dualisms so persistent? In good part because they are predisposed to serve as rallying points for forces that are organized around antagonistic divisions in a field. They are, in a sense, the *logical expression of social spaces constituted around dualist divisions*. If this is correct, it follows that, to kill a dualism, it is not enough to refute it— that is a naive and dangerous intellectualist illusion. Pure epistemology is very often plainly impotent if it is not accompanied by a sociological critique of the conditions of validity of epistemology. You cannot, with epistemological arguments alone, destroy a *Streit* in which people have vital—and real—interests. (Indeed, I think that if you wanted to retard social science, all you would have to do is to throw around some silly *Streiten*, in the way one throws a bone to a pack of dogs.)

But this is not all. I think indeed that the curse of these dualisms, of these apparently scientific antinomies rooted in social antagonisms, is that they find another social support in pedagogy. I have written somewhere that professors are perhaps the main obstacle to the progress of scientific knowledge, at least in the social sciences. I know from experience (I have taught for some thirty years) that professors have a pressing need for simple oppositions for purposes of teaching. These dualisms come in handy: first part consensus (or micro), second part conflict (macro), and third part me . . . A number of false controversies, long dead and buried (for example, internal versus external analysis in literary studies, qualitative versus quantitative techniques in "methodology") exist only because professors need them to organize their course syllabi and exam questions.

The sociology of sociology cannot destroy these forces by itself (true ideas do not have intrinsic force) but it can at least weaken them. By developing reflexivity, it can teach people always to be aware that when they say or think something, they can be moved by causes as well as by reasons. And if you build the utopia of a Scientific City in which the sociology of sociology would be uniformly and universally diffused, that is, in which this "martial art of the mind" would be available to all, you can see that scientific life would be completely different. This, on condition that it does not become this quite perverse professorial game which consists in reducing sociology to the vision of Thersites.[135] (As you can see, one cannot put forth a piece of practical advice without at once counter-advising against the probable use of this advice.)

How can we translate this knowledge of the special difficulties of social science into concrete forms of action or organization aimed at reinforcing scientific autonomy and reflexivity?

The existence of a common body of instruments of reflexivity, collectively mastered and collectively utilized, would be a formidable instrument for autonomy (the lack of minimal epistemological culture explains why researchers often construct theories of their practice that are less interesting than their practice of theory). But we would also have to consider the issue of funding. The difference between sociology and other intellectual endeavors—especially philosophy—is that it costs a lot (and yields little profit). And it is all too easy to become ensnared in the logic of one proposal calling forth the next proposal, a logic of which it is hard to tell whether it serves the needs of research, the needs of the researcher, or those of his funders. We would need to elaborate a rational politics of the management of relations with the suppliers of research funds, be they governments, foundations or private patrons. (For instance, based on epistemological reflection as well as political intuition, we might posit the principle that grants or contracts shall be accepted only for research that has already been conducted and on problems for which the answer is already roughly worked out. This is a means of safeguarding your autonomy, of ensuring that no command is brutally or surreptitiously imposed upon you.)

135. In Shakespeare's *Troilus and Cressida*, Thersites is a foot soldier whose envy and ressentiment leads him to disparage his superiors and to embrace a naively finalist view of history. See Bourdieu's (1988a: 3) discussion of this notion in *Homo Academicus*.

I would add to these another principle: you need to build into the conception of your research program the actual conditions of its realization. A superb questionnaire, a splendid body of hypotheses, a magnificent protocol of observation that do not include the practical conditions of their realization are void and worthless. Now, this form of scientific realism is neither taught nor spontaneously inscribed in the habitus of most people who enter the social sciences. I come across hundreds of truly remarkable research proposals that meet sudden death because they have not integrated the social conditions of possibility of their program conceived *in abstracto*. In sum, you must learn to *avoid being the toy of social forces in your practice of sociology*.

You defend reflexivity as an instrument for increasing scientific autonomy. But there is another source of autonomy or heteronomy: that built into certain positions in the academic field. Without going as far as evoking Lysenko or the Camelot affair, it is obvious that not all positions in the space of the social sciences enjoy the same degree of independence from external powers. Reflexivity may be within the reach of a tenured professor at the University of Chicago (and of a professor at the Collège de France) but is it available to the same degree to an assistant professor at a community college or to a government researcher?

Naturally, by itself, reflexivity is hardly enough to guarantee autonomy. I see what you are driving at with the example of the Chicago professor: you mean that there are positions of guaranteed statutory independence that allow you to say "the hell with you" to worldly authorities while others do not give you that luxury. Aristotle put this in more palatable terms: "Virtue requires a certain ease." The virtue of freedom does not come without the social conditions of freedom and, for many people, to say "to hell with you" to funders or to the state is structurally forbidden (which, incidentally, does not mean that those who do say it to government or business have no merit, because there are many scientists who have all the requisite social conditions in the world and who never do it). Thus autonomy does not come without the social conditions of autonomy; and these conditions cannot be obtained on an individual basis.

In the final analysis, a necessary condition of autonomy is the existence of an autonomous scientific capital. Why? Because scientific capital consists of instruments of defense, construction, argument, etc., but also because *recognized scientific authority protects you from the temptation of heteronomy.* There is a social law applicable to all the fields of cultural production I have studied, to art, literature, religion, science, etc.: that heteronomy is introduced by those agents who are dominated according to the specific criteria of the field.[136] The paradigm of this is Hussonnet in Flaubert's *A Sentimental Education.* Hussonnet is a failed writer who ends up heading the Commission for Cultural Affairs, and who uses his position in government to wield a terrifying authority over his former friends. He is the most heteronomous of the lot, the one who has succeeded least according to the specific criteria of the literary field, and thus is the most sensitive to the seduction of mermaids—the state, prominent society personalities, political parties.

The difficulty that social science experiences in breaking decisively with common sense, in establishing its specific *nomos,* owes much to the fact that there are always people who, being scientifically dominated, are spontaneously on the side of the preconstructed, who have vital interests in de-constructing the constructed, in misunderstanding the understood, and thus in trying to bring everybody back to the starting line. They can be found outside of the field but also inside the field; and those on the outside would be much less influential if not for those who assist them on the inside.[137] One of the key reasons why sociology has so much difficulty in acquiring its autonomy is that those who peddle common sense always have their chance in the field according to a principle familiar to economists: bad money chases away good.

136. "Who in the social world, asks Bourdieu (1982a: 25–26), has interest in the existence of an autonomous science of the social world? At any rate, it is not those who are most deprived scientifically: structurally inclined to seek in the alliance with external powers, whatever they may be, a reinforcement or a revenge against the constraints and the controls born of internal competition, they can always find in political denunciation a facile substitute for scientific critique. It is not the holders of temporal or spiritual power either, who cannot view a truly autonomous social science as anything but a competitor."

137. "*Sociology partakes at once of two radically discrepant logics:* the logic of the political field, in which the force of ideas is mainly a function of the power of the groups which take them to be true; and the logic of the scientific field which, in its most advanced states, knows and recognizes only the 'intrinsic force of the true idea' of which Spinoza spoke." It follows that "endoxic propositions," statements "that are not probable" in the terms of science but "plausible—in the etymological sense of the word—that is, liable to receive the assent and *applause* of the majority," can have currency in sociology and even survive logical critique and empirical refutation (Bourdieu 1989f).

For you, the specific obstacles that sociology finds in its path, its peculiar "difficulty in becoming a science like the others" (Bourdieu 1982a: 34) is due to its extreme vulnerability to social forces, not to the fact that it deals with meaningful action, "texts" that require interpretation and empathy rather than explanation, as the interpretive current claims (e.g., Geertz 1974, Rabinow and Sullivan 1979).

Indeed, I hold that, all the scholastic discussions about the distinctiveness of the human sciences notwithstanding, the human sciences are subject to the same rules that apply to all sciences. You have to produce coherent explanatory systems of variables, propositions assembled into parsimonious models that account for a large number of empirically observable facts and which can be opposed only by other, more powerful models which have to obey the same conditions of logical coherence, systematicity, and empirical falsifiability.[138] I am struck, when I speak with my friends who are chemists, physicians, or neurobiologists, by the similarities between their practice and that of the sociologist. The typical day of a sociologist, with its experimental groping, statistical analysis, reading of scholarly papers, and discussion with colleagues, looks very much like that of an ordinary scientist to me.

Many of the difficulties that sociology encounters are due precisely to the fact that we always want it to be a science different from the others. We both expect too much and too little of sociology. And there are always too many "sociologists" to respond to the most grandiose requests. If I were to make a list of all the topics on which journalists ask to interview me, you would be alarmed: it runs the gamut from the threat of nuclear war and the length of skirts to the evolution of Eastern Europe, hooliganism, racism, and AIDS. People confer upon sociologists the role of a prophet able to give coherent and systematic answers to all matters of social existence. This function is disproportionate and untenable; it is insane to bestow it on anybody.[139] But at

138. Bourdieu wishes to "deny sociology the epistemological status of an exception." However, his rejection of the Dilthean dualism which separates the interpretative understanding of culture from the causal explanation of nature does not lead him to equate sociology with a natural science of society: "For the question as to whether or not sociology is a science, and a science like the others, we must substitute the question of the type of organization and of functioning of the Scientific City most favorable to the emergence and development of research subjected to strictly scientific controls. One cannot answer this new question in all-or-nothing terms" (Bourdieu, Chamboredon, and Passeron 1973: 103, my translation).

139. Bourdieu is quite scornful of those social scientists who, donning the mantle of

the same time, people refuse the sociologist what she has every right to claim, which is the ability to give precise and verifiable answers to questions that she is able to construct scientifically.

The peculiarity of sociology owes a lot to the social image that lay people (and often scholars as well) have of it. Durkheim liked to say that one of the major obstacles to the constitution of a science of society resides in the fact that everybody, in such matters, believes that they have the *science infuse*, innate knowledge of the social world. For instance, journalists, who would never even dare think of discussing a discovery in biology or physics, or interfere in a philosophical debate betwen a physicist and a mathematician, rarely hesitate to expound "social problems," and to judge a scientific analysis of the functioning of the university or the intellectual world without having the slightest idea of the specific *stakes* of this analysis—for instance, the question of the relation between social structures and cognitive structures—which, as in every science, are the product of the autonomous history of scientific research and debate. (I think of the journalist who, upon publication of my book *La noblesse d'Etat*, asked me in all candor to speak for three minutes "in favor" of the *Grandes écoles* in a face-to-face debate with the president of the Ecole nationale d'administration who would speak "against" them . . . How could I possibly agree to do that?) It is a social fact of the greatest importance that *sociology is amenable to immediate, direct judgment by outsiders:* any technocrat or politician can take a public stand in the newspapers or on television about a problem of which he knows nothing without the slightest risk of being ridiculed or disqualified.

The difficulty that social science encounters in "taking off" is explained thus: it constantly faces a very strong demand for answers to questions that touch everybody and sometimes bear on matters of "life and death" (as does prophecy according to Weber); and it does not always enjoy all the conditions of autonomy and the instruments

---

the "officially accredited prophet" (Weber), offer "false systematizations of the answers that spontaneous sociology gives to the existential questions that ordinary experience encounters in extended order" (Bourdieu, Chamboredon, and Passeron 1973: 42, my translation). He reveals how they overstep the bounds of their specific competency and often serve their interests as intellectuals under the guise of serving public or "universal" causes (which oftentimes turn out to be no more than the current concerns of agents of the state). For an epistemological critique of the "temptation of prophetism in sociology," see ibid., 41–43.

necessary to resist the pressures of external demands, this situation itself being the product of the past domination of these demands upon the discipline.[140] This is so, in particular, because it is not in a position to discourage, discredit, or exclude those who seek immediate profits by agreeing to respond at the lowest possible cost to all demands, that is, without doing the necessary—and difficult—work required to transform the "social problems" of the general public into sociological problems liable to scientific solutions.

You are truly relentless in your advocacy of the autonomy of the intellectual field.

Yes, I am a resolute, stubborn, absolutist advocate of scientific autonomy (this may seem puzzling to some but I believe that my sociology is not suspected of collusion with the established order). I think that *sociology ought to define its social demand and functions on its own*. Now, some sociologists feel an obligation to justify their existence as sociologists, and to fulfill that obligation they feel obliged to serve. To serve whom or what? Sociology must first assert its autonomy; it must be ever so touchy and supercilious on the question of its independence.[141] It is only in this manner that it will acquire rigorous instruments and thus gain political relevance and potency. Whatever political potency it may have will be due to its properly scientific authority, that is, to its autonomy.[142]

---

140. In *Questions de sociologie*, Bourdieu (1980b: 8) lists several other handicaps faced by social science in its entanglement with public debate: "In the struggle against the discourse of mouthpieces, politicians, essayists, and journalists, everything works to the disadvantage of scientific discourse: the difficulties and slowness of its elaboration which causes it, more often than not, to 'arrive after the battle'; its unavoidable complexity liable to discourage simplistic and prejudiced minds or, simply, those who do not have the cultural capital necessary for deciphering it; its abstract impersonality which hinders identification and all forms of gratifying projections; and especially its distance from received ideas and primary convictions" (my translation).

141. "Social science can constitute itself only by refusing the social demand for instruments of legitimation or manipulation. Though he or she may deplore it, the sociologist has no mandate, no mission other than that which he or she assigns herself by virtue of the logic of her research" (Bourdieu 1982a: 27–28, my translation).

142. For Bourdieu, there is no opposition between autonomy and engagement. In point of fact, the "unstable combination" of these two dimensions, the scientific and the political, is for him what defines the specificity of the modern intellectual as a "bidimensional, paradoxical being" historically wedded to the "corporatism of the universal" (Bourdieu 1989d).

Strengthening the autonomy of the scientific field can result only from collective reflection and action designed to bolster the *institutional conditions of rational communication* in the social sciences. Weber (1978: 1148–50) reminds us that the greatest progress in the art of warfare came not from technological inventions but from innovations in the social organization of warriors, such as the Macedonian phalanx. Likewise, it is by working to build and to strengthen all the institutional mechanisms capable of thwarting the tendencies of different national traditions toward isolationism or even imperialism—toward all forms of scientific intolerance—in order to promote more open forms of communication and a confrontation of ideas, that social scientists will contribute most efficaciously to the progress of their sciences.[143]

If there exist, *pace* Habermas, no transhistorical universals of communication, there certainly exist forms of social organization of communication that are liable to foster the production of the universal. We cannot rely on moral exhortation to abolish "systematically distorted" communication from sociology. Only a realistic politics of scientific reason can contribute to the transformation of structures of communication, by helping to change both the modes of functioning of those universes where science is produced and the dispositions of the agents who compete in these universes, and thus the institution that contributes most to fashioning them, the university.

Implicit in the vision of the scientific field you propose is a philosophy of the history of science that argues for the transcendence of yet another major antinomy, one that has been with us at least since Kant and Hegel and which lay at the heart of the German *Methodenstreit*, and of which the debate between Habermas and the advocates of "postmodernism" is in many ways an avatar: that between historicism and rationalism.

I believe indeed that science is thoroughly historical without for that matter being relative or reducible to history. There are historical con-

---

143. Three recent actions of Bourdieu's are designed to promote what he calls "a genuine scientific internationalism": first, the creation of *Liber: The European Review of Books*; second, the working conference on "The International Circulation of Ideas" held at the Collège de France in February of 1991 to organize a Europe-wide research program on transnational intellectual exchanges; third, his participation as co-chair, with James Coleman, of the Russell Sage conference on Social Theory in a Changing Society, held in Chicago in May of 1989 (see Bourdieu 1989f, 1990j, and Bourdieu and Coleman 1991).

ditions for the genesis and progress of reason in history.[144] When I say that a situation of open conflict (even if it is not fully scientific) is to be preferred over a situation of false academic consensus, of "working consensus," as Goffman would put it, it is in the name of a philosophy of history according to which there can be a politics of Reason. I do not think that reason lies in the structure of the mind or of language. It resides, rather, in certain types of historical conditions, in certain social structures of dialogue and nonviolent communication. There is in history what we may, after Elias, call a *process of scientific civilization*, whose historical conditions are given with the constitution of relatively autonomous fields within which all moves are not allowed, in which there are immanent regularities, implicit principles and explicit rules of inclusion and exclusion, and admission rights which are being continually raised. Scientific reason realizes itself when it becomes inscribed not in the ethical norms of a practical reason or in the technical rules of a scientific methodology, but in the apparently anarchical social mechanisms of competition between strategies armed with instruments of action and of thought capable of regulating their own uses, and in the durable dispositions that the functioning of this field produces and presupposes.[145]

One does not find scientific salvation alone. Just as one is not an artist alone, but by participating in the artistic field, likewise we can say that it is the scientific field which makes scientific reason possible through its very functioning. Habermas notwithstanding, reason itself has a history: it is not Godgiven, already inscribed in our thinking or language. Habitus (scientific or otherwise) is a transcendental but a *historical transcendental* bound up with the structure and history of a field.

144. For Bourdieu, the scientific field is both a field like all others and a unique space of struggles in that it is capable of yielding products (true knowledge) that transcend their historical conditions of production. This "peculiarity of the history of scientific reason" is argued in Bourdieu 1991f, and can be highlighted by contrast with the functioning of the "juridical field" (Bourdieu 1987g).

145. Against all forms of transcendentalism, Bourdieu proposes a radical historicization of the Kantian-Hegelian problematic to solve the antinomy of reason and history: "We must admit that reason realizes itself in history only to the extent that it is inscribed in the objective mechanisms of a regulated competition capable of obliging interested pretensions to monopoly to convert themselves into forced contributions to the universal" (Bourdieu 1991f).

In other words, if there is a freedom of the intellectual, it is not the individual freedom of a Cartesian *cogito* but a freedom collectively conquered through the historically dated and situated construction of a space of regulated discussion and critique. [146]

This is something very seldom recognized by intellectuals, who are typically inclined to think in a singular key and who expect salvation from individual liberation, in the logic of wisdom and initiatory conquest. Intellectuals too often forget that there is a politics of intellectual freedom. On the basis of everything I have said, one can clearly see that an emancipatory science is possible only if the social and political conditions that make it possible are present. This requires, for instance, an end to the effects of domination which distorts scientific competition by preventing people who want to enter into the game from doing so—by turning down meritorious applications for fellowships or by cutting off research funds (this is the more brutal form of censorship but we must not forget that it is exercised on a daily basis). There are softer formulas, such as censorship through academic propriety *(bienséance):* by obliging somebody who has a lot to contribute to expend a considerable portion of his or her time providing the full proof, according to the positivistic canons of the time, of each and every one of her propositions, you can prevent her from producing a great many new propositions whose full validation could be left to others. As I showed in *Homo Academicus,* it is mainly through the control of time that academic power is exercised. [147]

The universal subject is a historical achievement that is never completed once and for all. It is through historical struggles in historical spaces of forces that we progress toward a little more universality (Bourdieu and Schwibs 1985). It is on condition that we engage in the struggle for reason and that we engage reason in history—that we practice a "*Realpolitik* of Reason" (Bourdieu 1987k)—for instance through interventions to reform the university system or through actions aimed at defending the possibility of publishing books with small audiences, by demonstrating against the exclusion of assistant professors on political grounds, or by fighting the use of pseudo-

146. With his notion of a "collective intellectual," Bourdieu (1989d) seeks a synthesis and transcendence of the two main political models of intellectual activity in the postwar era, the "total intellectual" (as incarnated by Sartre) and the "specific intellectual" epitomized by Foucault.

147. See "Time and Power" in Bourdieu 1988a: 90–105.

scientific arguments in issues of racism, etc., that we can push reason forward.[148]

But isn't one root of the many foibles and ills of sociology to be found in the fact that it often misplaces its capacity to take as object all human practices, including practices that claim universality such as science, philosophy, law, art, etc.—in short, in the fact that it does not always measure up to its own claims to be "meta"?

It all depends on what you mean by "meta." To be meta is to be above, and, very often in scientific struggles, people try to be meta in the sense of being above others. I am reminded of a very elegant experiment conducted by the ethologist W. N. Kellogg to illustrate this. Kellogg puts up a banana beyond the reach of a group of monkeys kept in a room; the monkeys immediately notice it and they all jump up and try to reach it. Finally, Sultan, who is the smartest of the pack, pushes his little she-monkey friend under the banana, quickly jumps on top of her, grabs the fruit and eats it. What happens next is that the monkeys all stand around under the banana with one foot up in the air, waiting for the opportunity to climb up on each other's back. Think about it for a minute and you will realize that this paradigm fits many scientific discussions. Very often these debates are completely sterile because people seek not to understand but to get up on top of each other. One of the unconscious motivations of the vocation of the sociologist is that it is a manner of being meta. For me, sociology ought to be meta but *always vis-à-vis itself*. It must use its own instruments to find out what it is and what it is doing, to try to know better where it stands, and must refuse a polemical use of the "meta" which serves only to objectivize others.

One might well object here that this reflexive return runs the serious risk of becoming an end in itself. Is this reflection on the intellectual world a self-contained project or is it the means to a more rigorous science of the social capable of producing stronger political effects because it is more rigorous?

Such an analysis has two kinds of effects, the one scientific and the other political, scientific effects in turn generating political effects. Just as I said earlier regarding individual agents that unconsciousness is complicit with determinism, likewise I would argue that the collec-

148. See the discussion of Bourdieu's politics, and especially of his academic politics, above in part 1, sec. 7.

tive unconsciousness of intellectuals is the specific form taken by the complicity of intellectuals with the dominant sociopolitical forces. I believe that the blindness of intellectuals to the social forces that rule the intellectual field, and therefore their practices, is what explains how, collectively, often under quite radical airs, the intelligentsia contributes to the perpetuation of dominant forces. I am aware that such a blunt statement is shocking because it goes against the image of themselves that intellectuals have fabricated: they like to think of themselves as liberators, as progressive (or at worst as neutral, disengaged, especially in the United States). And it is true that they have often taken sides with the dominated—for structural reasons, by virtue of their position as dominated among the dominant.[149] But they have been so much less often than they could have been and especially much less than they like to believe.

Is this the reason why you reject the label of "critical sociology"? You have always studiously kept aloof from anything that marches under the self-proclaimed banner of "radical" sociology or "critical" theory.

You are right. I can even say that one of my first reflexes as a young sociologist was to constitute myself against a certain image of the Frankfurt school.[150] I think that ignorance of the collective mecha-

149. For Bourdieu, intellectuals (or symbolic producers more generally: artists, writers, scientists, professors, journalists, etc.) constitute the "dominated fraction of the dominant class," or, in a more recent—and in his eyes more adequate—formulation, they occupy the dominated pole of the field of power (Bourdieu 1984a: 260–67, 283–95, 315–17; Bourdieu 1989a: 373–85 and 482–86; Bourdieu 1989d). They are "dominant as possessors of the power and privileges conferred upon possession of cultural capital and even, for some of them at least, possession of a volume of cultural capital sufficient to wield a power over cultural capital." But they are "dominated in relation to the holders of political and economic power." Their contradictory position as dominated among the dominant, or, by homology with the political field, as the left wing of the right, explains the ambiguity of their stances, for "alliances based on homology of position (dominated dominant = dominated) are always more uncertain, more fragile than solidarities based on identity of position and, thereby, of condition and habitus" (Bourdieu 1987a: 172–74). Bishops are a paradigmatic realization of the specific contradictions of the dominated dominant in the field of power: they wield a temporal power in the universe of the spiritual, yet possess neither temporal authority nor spiritual authority (Bourdieu and de Saint Martin 1982).

150. "I have always entertained a somewhat ambivalent relation with the Frankfurt school: though the affinities between us are obvious, I felt a certain irritation at the aristocratism of that totalizing critique which retained all the features of grand theory, no

nisms of political and ethical subordination and overestimation of the freedom of intellectuals have too often led the most sincerely progressive intellectuals (such as Sartre) to remain complicit with the forces they thought they were fighting, and this in spite of all the efforts invested in trying to escape the shackles of intellectual determinism. Because this overestimation encouraged them to engage in forms of struggle that are unrealistic, naive, "adolescent" if you wish.

Part of the difficulty here is that, among the risks that one must take to defend positions such as mine, there is that of disappointing adolescents (in the sociological sense of the term, that is, in particular younger scholars and graduate students). All intellectuals dream of being the "corrupters of youth" . . . Granted, it is disappointing to tell adolescents that their subversive intentions are often immature, i.e., oneiric, utopian, unrealistic. There is a whole range of such strategies of subversion that are in effect strategies of displacement. One of the goals of my work on intellectuals is to show that the principle of all these malversations, of all this double talk and *doubles jeux*, resides in bad faith in one's relation to one's insertion in the intellectual field.

Intellectuals are particularly inventive when it comes to masking their specific interests. For instance, after '68, there was a kind of *topos* in the French intellectual milieu which consisted in asking: "But from where are you speaking? From what place am I speaking?" This false, narcissistic confession, vaguely inspired by psychoanalysis, served as a screen in the Freudian sense of the word and blocked a genuine elucidation, that is, the discovery of the *social* location of the locutor: in this case, the position in the university hierarchy. It is not by chance that I first elaborated the notion of field in the case of the intellectual and artistic world.[151] I deliberately constructed this notion to destroy intellectual narcissism and that particularly vicious legerdemain *(escamotage)* of objectivation which consists of making objectivations either singular, and here psychoanalysis comes in handy, or so broad that the individual under consideration becomes the token of a category so large that his or her responsibility vanishes entirely. To

---

doubt out of a concern not to dirty its hands in the kitchens of empirical research" (Bourdieu 1987a: 30). Gartman (1991) offers a critical comparison of Bourdieu's theory of culture with the Frankfurt school's.

151. The first developments of the concept are found in Bourdieu 1971a, 1971b, 1971d.

proclaim "I am a bourgeois intellectual, I am a slimy rat!" as Sartre liked to do, is devoid of implications. But to say "I am an assistant professor at Grenoble and I am speaking to a Parisian professor" is to force oneself to ask whether it is not the relation between these two positions that is speaking through my mouth.

If I understand you correctly, then, science is still the best tool we have for the critique of domination. You fall squarely in line with the modernist project of the *Aufklärung* (and in sharp disagreement with the postmodernists) in that you argue that sociology, when it is scientific, constitutes an inherently politically progressive force.[152] But isn't there a paradox in the fact that, on the one hand, you enlarge the possibility of a space of freedom, of a liberating awakening of self-consciousness that brings within rational reach historical possibilities hitherto excluded by symbolic domination and by the misrecognition implied in the doxic understanding of the social world, while, on the other hand, you simultaneously effect a radical disenchanting that makes this social world in which we must continue to struggle almost unlivable? There is a strong tension, perhaps a contradiction, between this will to provide instruments for increasing consciousness and freedom and the demobilization that an overly acute awareness of the pervasiveness of social determinisms threatens to produce.

As exemplified in *Homo Academicus*, I use the instruments provided by reflexivity to try to control the biases introduced by unreflexivity and to make headway in the knowledge of the mechanisms that can alter reflection. *Reflexivity is a tool to produce more science, not less.* It is not designed to discourage scientific ambition but to help make it more realistic. By helping the progress of science and thus the growth of knowledge about the social world, *reflexivity makes possible a more responsible politics*, both inside and outside of academia. Bachelard wrote that "there is no science but of that which is hidden." This effect of unveiling carries an unintended critique that will be all the stronger the more powerful science is, and thus the more capable of uncovering mechanisms that owe part of their efficacy to the fact that

152. In the conclusion to his inaugural lecture at the Collège de France, Bourdieu (1982a: 56) stresses that a science of institutions, and of the beliefs that underpin their functioning, "presupposes a belief in science." The sociologist could not "have faith in the possibility and the necessity to universalize the freedom from the institution that sociology offers if he did not believe in the liberating virtues of what is no doubt *the least illegitimate of all symbolic powers, that of science*" (my translation and emphasis).

they are misrecognized, and thus of reaching into the foundations of symbolic violence.[153]

Thus reflexivity is not at all a form of "art for art's sake." A reflexive sociology can help free intellectuals from their illusions—and first of all from the illusion that they do not have any, especially about themselves—and can at least have the negative virtue of making it more difficult for them to bring a passive and unconscious contribution to symbolic domination.

You remind me here of Durkheim's aphorism (1921: 267) which says that sociology "increases the range of our action by the mere fact that it increases the range of our science." But I must come back to my question: doesn't the disillusionment reflexivity produces also carry the risk of condemning us to this "passively conservative attitude" from which the founder of the *Année sociologique* was already defending himself? [154]

There is a first level of answer to this question which is the following: if the risk is only to disenchant and undermine adolescent rebellion, which oftentimes does not last beyond intellectual adolescence, then it is not that great of a loss.

This is your antiprophetic side[155] and perhaps one of the traits that distinguish your work from that of Foucault.

There is, it is true, a side of Foucault's work (there is, of course, considerably more to his work than that) which theorizes the revolt of the adolescent in trouble with his family and with the institutions that relay family pedagogy and impose "disciplines" (the school, the clinic, the asylum, the hospital, and so on), that is, forms of social constraint that are very external. Adolescent revolts often represent symbolic denegations, utopian responses to general social controls that allow you to avoid carrying out a full analysis of the specific historical forms,

---

153. "If 'there is no science but of the hidden,' it is clear why sociology is allied with the historical forces which, in every epoch, oblige the truth of power relations to come into the open, if only by forcing them to veil themselves yet further" (Bourdieu and Passeron 1979: xxi).

154. The Durkheim quote (1921: 267) begins thus: "Sociology in no way imposes upon man a passively conservative attitude. On the contrary."

155. "If, as Bachelard says, 'every chemist must fight the alchemist within,' every sociologist must fight the social prophet within that his public asks him to incarnate" (Bourdieu, Chamboredon, and Passeron 1973: 42).

and especially of the *differential* forms, assumed by the constraints that bear on agents of different milieux, and also of forms of social constraint much more subtle than those that operate through the drilling *(dressage)* of bodies.[156]

Naturally, it is not pleasurable to disenchant adolescents, especially since there are quite sincere and profound things in their revolts: an inclination to go against the established order, against the resignation of submissive adults, against academic hypocrisy, and a whole range of things that they grasp very well because they are not disenchanted, cynical, they have not made the kind of about-face that most of the people of my generation, at least in France, have made. Perhaps it is necessary, to be a good sociologist, to combine some dispositions associated with youth, such as a certain force of rupture, of revolt, of social "innocence," and others more commonly associated with old age, such as realism, and the capacity to confront the rough and disappointing realities of the social world.

I believe that sociology does exert a disenchanting effect, but this, in my eyes, marks a progress toward a form of scientific and political realism that is the absolute antithesis of naive utopianism. Scientific knowledge allows us to locate real points of application for responsible action; it enables us to avoid struggling where there is no freedom—which is often an alibi of bad faith—in such a manner as to dodge sites of genuine responsibility.[157] While it is true that a certain kind of sociology, and perhaps particularly the one I practice, can encourage sociologism as submission to the "inexorable laws" of society

156. Bourdieu refers here to Foucault's (1977a) analysis of the "training" of the body in *Discipline and Punish*.

157. "Against those who would want to find in the enunciation of social laws, converted into destiny, an alibi for fatalistic or cynical surrender, we must recall that scientific explanation, which gives us the means to understand, even to exonerate, is also what may allow us to transform. Increased knowledge of the mechanisms which govern the intellectual world should not (I use such ambiguous language on purpose) have the effect of 'releasing the individual from the embarrassing burden of moral responsibility,' as Jacques Bouveresse fears. It should on the contrary teach her to situate her responsibilities where her liberties are really situated and resolutely to refuse the infinitesimal cowardice and laxnesss which leave social necessity with all its force, to fight within oneself and in others the opportunistic indifferentism or disabused conformism which grants the social world what it asks for, all the little concessions of resigned complacency and submissive complicity" (Bourdieu 1988a: 4–5, translation modified).

(and this even though its intention is exactly the opposite), I think that Marx's alternative between utopianism and sociologism is somewhat misleading: there is room, between sociologistic resignation and utopian voluntarism, for what I would call a reasoned utopianism, that is, a rational and politically conscious use of the limits of freedom afforded by a true knowledge of social laws and especially of their *historical* conditions of validity.[158] The political task of social science is to stand up both against irresponsible voluntarism and fatalistic scientism, to help define a rational utopianism by using the knowledge of the probable to make the possible come true. Such a sociological, that is, realistic, utopianism is very unlikely among intellectuals. First because it looks petty bourgeois, it does not look radical enough. Extremes are always more chic, and the aesthetic dimension of political conduct matters a lot to intellectuals.

This argument is also a way of disavowing an image of politics that is very dear to intellectuals, that is, the idea of a rational *zoon politicon* who constitutes him- or herself through the exercise of free will and through political self-proclamation.

I would not quite put it that way. Rather, I argue that this image itself is part of a historical project. Those who take up this position should know that they are the historical heirs of a long line of men and women who have been placed in historical conditions such that they had an opportunity to help freedom advance a little (Bourdieu 1989d). They must first come to grips with the fact that, to carry this project forward, there must be chairs of philosophy or departments of sociology (which implies specific forms of alienation), that philosophy or social science as official disciplines, sanctioned by the state, have to have been invented, etc. To make existence as an efficacious myth pos-

---

158. "A social law is a historical law that perpetuates itself only as long as we let it operate, that is, as long as those whom it serves (sometimes unbeknownst to them) are in a position to perpetuate the conditions of its efficacy. . . . One can claim to posit eternal laws, as conservative sociologists do about the so-called tendency of power toward concentration. In reality, science must know that it does nothing more than record, in the form of tendential laws, the logic which characterizes *u certain game, at a certain moment in time*, and which functions in favor of those who dominate the game and have the means to set the rules of the game in fact and in law. As soon as a law is stated, it can become the stake of struggles. . . . The uncovering of tendential laws is the condition of success of actions aimed at proving them wrong" (Bourdieu 1980b: 45–46, my translation).

sible for the intellectual who feels compelled to speak up on apartheid in South Africa, repression in Central America and Romania, or gender inequality at home, it took the Paris Commune, it took the Dreyfus trial, it took Zola and many others.[159] We must never forget that institutions of cultural freedom are social conquests, no less so than Social Security or the minimum wage (Bourdieu and Schwibs 1985).

Could one say that your method of analysis and the sociology you practice comprise both a theory of the social world and an ethic? Can one derive from your sociology a sort of ideal for personal conduct?

I would be tempted to answer both yes and no. I would say no if one abides by the old antinomy between the positive and the normative; I would say yes if we agree to think beyond this opposition. In point of fact, it contains an ethic because it is a science. If what I say is correct, if it is true that it is through knowledge of determinations that only science can uncover that a form of freedom which is the condition and correlate of an ethic is possible, then it is also true that a reflexive science of society implies, or comprises, an ethic—which does not mean that it is a scientistic ethic. (It goes without saying that this is not the only way to ground an ethic.) Morality is, in this instance, made possible by an awakening of consciousness that science can trigger under definite circumstances.

I believe that when sociology remains at a highly abstract and formal level, it contributes nothing. When it gets down to the nitty gritty of real life, however, it is an instrument that people can apply to themselves for quasi-clinical purposes. The true freedom that sociology offers is to give us a small chance of knowing what game we play and of minimizing the ways in which we are manipulated by the forces of the field in which we evolve, as well as by the embodied social forces that operate from within us.[160] I am not suggesting that so-

159. See Charle 1990 and Pinto 1984b for analyses of the "historical invention" of the figure of the modern intellectual as an "efficacious myth" progressively inscribed in mental and social structures. Consult Kauppi and Sulkunen 1992 for further illustrations.

160. Bourdieu (1982a: 29) writes: "Through the sociologist, a historical and historically situated agent, a socially determined subject, history, that is, the society in which it survives itself, reflects upon itself; and all social agents may, through him or her, know a little better what they are and what they do. But this task is precisely the last one that those who have a vested interest in misrecognition, denegation, and the refusal of knowledge would like to entrust the sociologist with" (my translation).

ciology solves all the problems in the world, far from it, but that it allows us to discern the sites where we do indeed enjoy a degree of freedom and those where we do not. So that we do not waste our energy struggling over terrains that offer us no leeway.[161]

Therefore I think that there is indeed a philosophical or an ethical usage of reflexive sociology. Its purpose is not to "pick" on others, to reduce them, to accuse them, to castigate them for, say, being "the son of a mere so-and-so." Quite the contrary. Reflexive sociology allows us to understand, to account for the world, or, to use an expression of Francis Ponge that I like a lot, to *necessitate the world* (Bourdieu 1986f). To understand fully the conduct of an individual acting in a space is tantamount to understanding the necessity behind what he or she does, to render necessary what might at first appear contingent. It is a way, not of justifying the world, but of learning to accept a lot of things that might otherwise be unacceptable.[162] (Of course, we must at all times keep in mind that the social conditions of access to this form of social tolerance are not universally granted, and that we should not require it of those who cannot accede to it. It is all well and good to be an antiracist, for instance, but it amounts to mere pharisaism when you are not simultaneously pushing for equal access to the social conditions—in housing, education, employment, etc.— that make antiracism possible.)

When you apply reflexive sociology to yourself, you open up the possibility of identifying true sites of freedom, and thus of building small-scale, modest, practical morals in keeping with the scope of human freedom which, in my opinion, is not that large. Social fields are universes where things continually move and are never completely predetermined. However, they are much more so than I believed

161. For Bourdieu, freedom and necessity are not antinomic terms that grow in inverse proportions; rather, they stand in a mutually reinforcing relation: "I doubt that there is any other freedom than that which is made possible by knowledge of necessity. . . . Contrary to appearances, it is by elevating the degree of perceived necessity and by providing a better knowledge of the laws of the social world that social science gives us more freedom. . . . All progress in the knowledge of necessity is a progress in *possible* freedom" (Bourdieu 1980b: 77, 44, my translation).

162. "What needs to be divulged, disseminated, is this scientific gaze, this gaze at once objectivizing and comprehensive, which, turned back upon ourselves, enables us to assume ourselves and even, if I may say so, to claim ourselves. . . . It is not a matter of locking up social agents in an 'originary social being' treated as a fate, a nature, but to offer them the *possibility* of assuming their habitus without guilt or suffering" (Bourdieu 1980b: 42, my translation).

when I first set out to do sociology. I am often stunned by the degree to which things are determined: sometimes I think to myself, "This is impossible, people are going to think that you exaggerate." And, believe me, I do not rejoice over this. Indeed, I think that if I perceive necessity so acutely, it is because I find it particularly unbearable. As an individual, I personally suffer when I see somebody trapped by necessity, whether it be the necessity of the poor or that of the rich.

The study that you have recently launched on the experience of "social suffering" seems to me to proceed from such an ethical conception of sociology understood as a sort of *social maieutics*. It is particularly interesting because it falls at the intersection of social science, politics, and civic ethics. And it illustrates what could be a possible Socratic function of sociology: to short-circuit the censorship built into established forms of social and political representation.

Over the past decade, the political world has grown more and more closed unto itself, on its internal rivalries, its idiosyncratic squabbles and its specific stakes. Leaders of government are prisoners of a reassuring entourage of benign technocrats who ignore just about everything of the ordinary lives of their citizenry, including the extent of their own ignorance. They are happy to rule via the magic of public opinion polls, that pseudoscientific technology of rational demagogy which can give them little more than extorted answers to imposed questions that the individuals surveyed often did not raise, in those terms, until they were raised for them. It is in reaction to this that I proposed to do an exploratory study of the social suffering, misery, malaise, or ressentiment that lay *underneath* the recent demands of noninstitutionalized forms of protest (by high-school and university students, nurses, teachers, motormen, etc.), and behind the tensions that erupted around the question of "Arab scarfs" and the degradation of public housing, and that drive the "private politics" of daily discriminations and recriminations.[163]

Emmanuel Terray (1990) showed that, in the Hippocratic tradition,

163. Bourdieu's analysis of the housing market deals with "one of the major foundations of petty-bourgeois misery or, more precisely, of all petty miseries, all the limitations placed on freedom, on wishes, on desires, which encumber life with worries, disappointments, restraints, failures, and also, almost inevitably, with melancholia and ressentiment" ("Un signe des temps," introduction to the issue of *Actes de la recherche en sciences sociales* on "The Economy of Housing", nos. 81/82, March 1990, p. 2, my translation).

genuine medicine begins with the treatment of invisible diseases, i.e., with the knowledge of facts of which the sick person says nothing because she is not aware of them or because she omits to reveal them. This research endeavors to convert social malaise into readable symptoms that can then be treated politically. For this, it is necessary to break through the screen of projections, sometimes absurd, often odious, behind which suffering hides and to help the very people who nourish the most unjustifiable social fantasies and hatreds (such as racism) in their effort, necessarily painful, to evoke the social operations of demoralization and degradation, themselves just as unjustifiable, which feed their revolt, anguish or desperation.

This study is premised on the idea that *the most personal is the most impersonal*, that many of the most intimate dramas, the deepest malaises, the most singular suffering that women and men can experience find their roots in the objective contradictions, constraints and double binds inscribed in the structures of the labor and housing markets, in the merciless sanctions of the school system, or in mechanisms of economic and social inheritance. The goal, then, is to make an unformulated, repressed discourse emerge by talking with people who are likely to be good "historians" of their own disease because they are situated in sensitive areas of social space, and with "practical experts," that is, official practitioners of "social problems" (police officers, social workers, union activists, judges, etc.) who occupy strategic locations in the social world, and who are living thesauri of spontaneous knowledge about its functioning. Armed with full knowledge of the individual's social trajectory and life-context, we proceed by means of very lengthy, highly interactive, in-depth interviews aimed at helping interviewees discover and state the hidden principle of their extreme tragedies or ordinary misfortunes; and at allowing them to rid themselves of this external reality that inhabits and haunts them, possesses them from the inside, and dispossesses them of initiative in their own existence in the manner of the monster in *Alien*. *Alien* may be seen as a sort of modern myth which offers a good image of what we call *alienation*, that is, this presence of otherness at the very heart of subjectivity.

I should give concrete examples of how we proceed but it would be too long. Let me say simply that conducting these interviews can be a harrowing and very painful process—for the informant but also, often, for the researchers as well. I will never forget that young woman employed as a mail sorter on Alleray Street in Paris whom we interviewed one night, and the roomy and gloomy, dusty hall where she works, two nights out of three, from nine till five the next morning, standing upright in front of the sixty-six slots into which she allocates the incoming mail, and the poor, sorrowful, grey words, in spite of her Southern accent, with which she described her topsy-turvy life, her commute in the morning cold, after the night shift, back to her small apartment in a distant suburb, her nostalgic yearning for a return to a home country that now seems beyond reach . . . One of the pulsions that led me to launch this study is the naively ethical feeling that we cannot let state technocrats continue like that, in a state of total civic irresponsibility, and that it would be intolerable and unconscionable for social scientists *not* to intervene, with all due awareness of the limitations of their discipline.

What else to say of this study except that it transgresses nearly all the precepts of official methodology and that it is for this very reason that it has some chance of capturing what all bureaucratic surveys overlook *by definition*. I think—or at least I hope—that it can fulfill a double function, scientific and political. It will remind researchers of that which the routine of ordinary surveys (not to mention formal and formalistic methodological or theoretical exercises) blocks from their view. And it will remind the technocrats who rule our society of everything that the formally democratic procedures of official political life (and in particular the rituals of party life, with its caucuses, platforms, motions, etc.), the well-rehearsed intercourse with the media, and the apparently scientific assurances of economic forecasting cause them to ignore: new species of suffering and a growing sense of injustice deprived of means of public expression.

7   The Personal is Social

In your inaugural lecture at the Collège de France, you stated that "every proposition set forth by the [science of society] can and ought to apply to the sociologist himself" (Bourdieu 1982a: 7). Can we do a Bourdieuan sociology of Bourdieu? Can you explain yourself? If so, why this unwavering reticence to speak about the private person Pierre Bourdieu?

It is true that I have a sort of professional vigilance which forbids me to adopt the kind of egomaniacal postures that are approved of and even rewarded by the intellectual institution, especially in France.

But this reluctance to talk about myself has another reason. By revealing certain private information, by making bovaristic confessions about myself, my lifestyle, my preferences, I may give ammunition to people who utilize against sociology the most elementary weapon there is—relativism. It is easy to destroy scientific work, both on the object and on the subject of analysis, which is the condition of scientific discourse, with one stroke of simplistic relativization ("after all, this is only the opinion of a so-and-so, of the daughter of a teacher, etc., inspired by resentment, jealousy, etc.").[164] The personal questions that are put to me are often inspired by what Kant would call "pathological motives": people are interested in my background or in my tastes insofar as it may give them weapons against what worries them in what I write about class and taste.

My sociological discourse is separated from my personal experience by my sociological practice, which is itself in part the product of a sociology of my social experience. And I have never ceased taking myself as an object, not in a narcissistic sense but as one representative of a category. One of the things that often irritates people is that when I analyze myself—*Homo Academicus* contains pages and pages on me to the extent that I belonged to the category I call the "oblates"—I say aloud the truth of others by speaking about myself.

It is not a matter of defending myself, my identity, my privacy, but of protecting the autonomy of my discourse and of my discoveries—if we may call them that—in relation to the singular person I am. Which does not mean that I, the concrete individual Pierre Bourdieu, can escape objectivation: I can be objectivized *like anybody else* and, like anybody else, I have the taste and preferences, the likes and the dislikes that correspond roughly to my position in social space. I am socially classified and I know precisely what position I occupy in social classifications. If you understand my work, you can very easily deduce a

164. Stanley Hoffman (1986: 47) offers an exemplary instance of this dismissive individualizing reduction that makes short shrift of the existence of the scientific field in his review of *Distinction* when he asks: "If each of us is the product of class habitus, moreover, is scientific observation of habitus possible? Could [Bourdieu's] system account for his own peculiar habitus . . . ? But what happens, then, to the *pretense of being scientific*? Indeed, this enormous book, overtly a schematic, debatable interpretation of French society, is, *more deeply, a revelation of—and a catharsis by—Pierre Bourdieu*" (emphasis added). For a discussion of "particularizing reduction," see Bourdieu's (1991d) "Introduction to a Japanese Reading of 'Distinction'."

great many things about me from knowledge of this position and of what I write. I have given you all the tools necessary for that; as for the rest, leave it to me . . .

Could we say that, while it is not reducible to that, your sociology is, in part, an attempt to cope with the "social conversion" entailed by your trajectory and training, and to fully master the vision of the social world they have enabled you to gain?

Everything that I have done in sociology and anthropology I have done as much against what I was taught as thanks to it. I would not want this formula to be understood as the claim, so frequent among artists and writers, to be a great initiator, an "uncreated creator" who owes nothing to anybody.[165] By this I simply mean that I had to break with the pretension to theoretical *hauteur* that came as a part of my academic trajectory as a student of philosophy at the Ecole normale supérieure, while at the same time constantly calling upon my training, and particularly my theoretical and philosophical training, to put it to use. In my student days, those who distinguished themselves by a "brilliant cursus," as we say in French, could not, without derogating, engage in practical tasks as vulgarly commonplace as those which make up the trade of the sociologist. We see again that the social sciences are difficult for social reasons: the sociologist is the one who goes out in the street to interview Mr. or Mrs. Anybody, listens to her, and tries to learn from her. This is what Socrates used to do, but the same who celebrate Socrates today are the last to understand and to accept this sort of renunciation of the role of the philosopher-king in the face of the "vulgar" that sociology demands.

It goes without saying that the conversion I had to effect to come to sociology was not unrelated to my own social trajectory. I spent most of my youth in a tiny and remote village of Southwestern France, a very "backward" place as city people like to say. And I could meet the demands of schooling only by renouncing many of my primary experiences and acquisitions, and not only a certain accent. . . . Anthropology and sociology have allowed me to reconcile myself with my primary experiences and to take them upon myself, to assume them without losing anything I subsequently acquired. It is something that is not common among class "defectors" (*transfuges*) who

165. For a critique of this ideology, read, for instance, "But Who Created the Creators?" (Bourdieu 1980b: 207–21) and Bourdieu's (1988d) analysis of Flaubert.

often feel great unhappiness and shame about their origins and originary experiences.[166] The research I did, around 1960, in this village
helped me discover a lot of things about myself and about my object of study.

Reading Flaubert, I found out that I had also been profoundly
marked by another social experience, that of life as a boarder in a public school (internat). Flaubert writes somewhere that "anyone who has
not known boarding school by age ten knows nothing about society."
My late friend Erving Goffman showed in Asylum (Goffman 1961) how
inmates develop extraordinarily creative strategies to survive the oftentimes terrifying constraints that "total institutions" can impose on
them. Sometimes I wonder where I acquired this ability to understand or even to anticipate the experience of situations that I have not
known firsthand, such as work on an assembly line or the dull routine
of unskilled office work. I believe that I have, in my youth and
throughout my social trajectory which caused me, as always in the
case of upwardly mobile people, to cross through very varied social
milieus, taken a whole series of mental photographs that my sociological work tries to process.

And you continue to snap such mental photographs in your daily life?

Flaubert said something like "I would like to live all lives." This is
something that I can relate to very well, to experience all human experiences. I find that one of the most extraordinary rewards of the craft
of sociology is the possibility it affords one to enter into the life of
others. People who might bore others to death, for instance, at parties
where bourgeois conventions forbid you to speak of "serious" topics, that is, of yourself, your work, etc., can become fascinating as
soon as they talk about what they do on their job. It goes without saying that, in daily life, I do not constantly do sociology but, unwittingly, I take something like social "snapshots" that I will develop and
use later. I believe that part of what is called "intuition," which under-

---

166. See, for example, the narratives collected in *Strangers in Academia: Academics
from the Working Class* (Ryan and Sackrey 1984) and the candid autobiographies of
Nancy Rosenblum and Donald Cressey (in Bennett Berger 1990) for moving personal
testimonies of the "hidden injuries of class" suffered by academics of popular background. For a related effort to assume this contradiction via social analysis, see Hoggart
1967. Annie Ernaux's *La place* (1984) offers an exceptionally penetrating literary account
of this experience.

girds many research hypotheses or analyses, originates in those snapshots, often in very old ones.

From this angle, the work of the sociologist is akin to that of the writer or the novelist (I think in particular of Proust): like the latter, our task is to provide access to and to explicate experiences, generic or specific, that are ordinarily overlooked or unformulated.

You suggest that sociologists could find inspiration and learn from writers like Faulkner, Joyce, Simon, or Proust (whom you are fond of quoting, for example, in *Distinction*). You do not perceive a necessary opposition between literature and sociology.[167]

There are, of course, significant differences between sociology and literature, but we should be careful not to turn them into an irreconcilable antagonism. It goes without saying that sociologists must not and cannot claim to compete with writers on their own turf. This would expose them to being "naive writers" (in the sense in which we speak of naive painters) by virtue of their ignorance of the accumulated exigencies and potentialities inscribed in the very logic of the literary field. But they can find in literary works research clues and orientations that the censorship specific to the scientific field tend to forbid to them or to hide from them.[168] And they can also bring into view, through their work of recording and analysis, discourses which, though they are not inspired by a properly "literary" intent, can produce literary effects, and put to writers questions analogous to those that photography raised for painters at the end of the nineteenth century.

I want to use this opportunity to say that writers teach us much more than that. Let me give you an example of how they have helped

---

167. Bourdieu has written extensively on literature and writers, whether it be on Flaubert, Faulkner, Virginia Woolf, Belgian literature, readers and readings, comic books, or on the literary field as a whole (see Bourdieu 1987j, 1988d, 1987a: 132–43, 1985g, 1971c, 1983d respectively). In the 1970s, he directed a research seminar on literature at the Ecole normale supérieure out of which came a large number of theses and publications, some of which have appeared in *Actes de la recherche en sciences sociales* (articles by Boltanski, Chamboredon, Charle, Ponton, de Saint Martin, and Thiesse). Those who are quick to recoil at the idea of a kinship between literature and social science should consult Robert Nisbet's (1976) brief but illuminating survey of the commonalities of classical sociology and literature in terms of their psychological impulse, history, techniques of representation, and cognitive purpose, in *Sociology as an Art Form*. Read also Mäzlisch (1989: chap. 4) on the novelistic "tradition of lament" which provided the background for the birth of both revolutionary and academic sociology.

me escape the censorships and presuppositions implied in the scientistic or positivist representation of scientific work. A few months ago, a childhood friend from Béarn came to see me to seek my advice about personal problems he was going through and experiencing in a most dramatic fashion. He gave me an account that I would qualify as Faulknerian and of which, at first, I could not make sense, although I had nearly all the relevant factual information at my disposal. After several hours of discussion, I began to understand: what he was telling me, at one and the same time, was three or four homologous and intertwined stories, his own life-story, that of his relation to his wife, who had died a few years before and whom he suspected of having cheated on him with his elder brother; the life-story of his son and of the latter's relation to his fiancée, whom he considered not to be a "good" girl; the life-story of his mother, silent and mysterious witness to these two stories, plus a couple of additional peripheral life-stories. I could not tell which main life-story was the most painful to him, his own or that of his son (in which what was at stake was the future of the relation between the father and the son through the question of the future of the farm and its land), and which one served to mask the other or allowed the other to be told in a veiled form, by dint of homology. What is sure is that the logic of this account rested on the permanent ambiguity of anaphors, of the "him," "his," or "her" and "hers" in particular: I could not tell whether they referred to himself, to his son, to his son's fiancée, or to his mother, who functioned as interchangeable subjects whose very substitutability was the spring of the drama he was living. I realized right there, very clearly, the full extent to which the linear life-stories with which ethnographers and sociologists are content are artificial and how the apparently exceedingly formal researches of Virginia Woolf, Faulkner, or Claude Simon would appear today to me to be more "realistic" (if the word has any meaning), anthropologically more truthful, closer to the truth of temporal experience, than the linear narratives to which traditional novels have accustomed us.

Thus I was led to bring back to the fore of my thinking a whole set of questions that had been repressed concerning biography[169] and,

168. See Bourdieu's (1990i) use of Virginia Woolf's novels to elucidate the male experience of gender domination.

169. For a critical programmatic discussion of these issues, including an attack on the linear conception of life-stories, see "The Biographical Illusion." In this paper, Bourdieu (1987c: 71) proposes to substitute for the "socially irreproachable artifact" of

more generally, on the logic of the interview as a process, i.e., on the relations between the temporal structure of lived experience and the structure of discourse and, at the same time, to raise to the status of legitimate scientific discourse, worthy of scientific publication and debate, a whole range of so-called "raw" documents that I tended to exclude, more unconsciously than consciously. In the same fashion, in my work on Flaubert, I stumbled upon many problems—and solutions—that he had himself encountered, such as that of the combined use of direct style, indirect style, and free indirect style which lies at the heart of the problem of transcription and publication of interviews.

In short, I believe that literature, against which a good many sociologists have, from the origins to this day, thought necessary to define themselves in order to assert the scientificity of their discipline (as Wolf Lepenies [1988] demonstrates in *Die drei Kulturen*), is on many points more advanced than social science, and contains a whole trove of fundamental problems—those concerning the theory of narrative for instance—that sociologists should make their own and subject to critical examination instead of ostentatiously distancing themselves from forms of expression and thinking that they deem compromising.

Like many illustrious French scholars, such as Durkheim, Sartre, Aron, Lévi-Strauss, Foucault, and Derrida, you are an alumnus of the Ecole normale supérieure of the Rue d'Ulm in Paris, the traditional breeding ground of the French intelligentsia. At the same time, as *La noblesse d'Etat* (Bourdieu 1989a) abundantly attests, you are one of the sharpest critics of elite schools, of their products and of their privileges. You write that you "never feel fully justified as an intellectual," that you do not feel "at home" in the academic universe.[170]

---

the "life-story" the constructed "notion of *trajectory* understood as a series of *positions* successively occupied by the same agent (or the same group) in a space which itself is constantly evolving and subject to ongoing transformations. To try to understand a life as a unique and self-sufficient series of successive events with no links other than the association with a 'subject' whose constancy is no doubt merely that of a proper name, is nearly as absurd as to try to make sense of a route in the metro without taking into account the structure of the subway network, that is, the matrix of objective relations between the different train stations. Biographical events may be properly defined as so many *locations* and *moves (placements et déplacements)* in social space, that is, to be more precise, in the different successive states of the structure of the different species of capital at stake in the field under consideration" (translation modified).

170. "Most of the questions that I address to intellectuals, who have so many answers and, at bottom, so few questions, are no doubt rooted in the feeling of being a

This is something that I feel very strongly and that I have experienced most acutely at two moments of my life: when I entered the Ecole normale and when I was nominated to the Collège de France. Throughout my studies at the Ecole normale, I felt formidably ill-at-ease. I have vivid memories of Groethuysen's[171] description of the arrival of Rousseau in Paris which, for me, was like an illumination. I can also refer you to a text of Sartre (1987) on Nizan, a foreword to Nizan's *Aden d'Arabie*, which describes word for word, emotion for emotion, what I felt when I joined the Ecole normale. This is another proof that none of this was singular: it was the product of a social trajectory.

In France, to come from a distant province, to be born South of the Loire, endows you with a number of properties that are not without parallel in the colonial situation. It gives you a sort of objective and subjective externality and puts you in a particular relation to the central institutions of French society and therefore to the intellectual institution. There are subtle (and not so subtle) forms of social racism that cannot but make you perceptive; being constantly reminded of your otherness stimulates a sort of permanent sociological vigilance. It helps you perceive things that others cannot see or feel. Now, it is true that I am a product of the Ecole normale who has betrayed the Ecole normale. But you had to be from the Ecole normale to write such things about the Ecole normale without appearing motivated by ressentiment . . .

One could also describe your election to the chair of Sociology at the Collège de France, the single most prestigious scientific institution in France, in your own language, i.e., as a process of "social consecration." How has this nomination affected your scientific practice? More generally, what use do you make of your knowledge of the functioning of the academic universe?

It is no happenstance if the time when I was nominated to the Collège de France coincided with extended work on what I call the social

---

stranger in the intellectual universe. I question this world because it questions me, and in a very profound manner, which goes well beyond the mere sentiment of social exclusion: I never feel fully justified as an intellectual, I do not feel 'at home'; I feel like I have to be answerable—to whom, I do not know—for what appears to me to be an unjustifiable privilege" (Bourdieu 1980b: 76, my translation).

171. Modern historian Bernard Groethuysen is the author of a study of the origins of the "Bourgeois Spirit" in France, a book on *Jean-Jacques Rousseau* (Groethusen 1977 and 1983), and other works in philosophical anthropology.

magic of consecration and "rites of institution" (Bourdieu 1981b, 1982b: 121–34; Bourdieu and de Saint Martin 1982; Bourdieu 1989a). Having given a lot of thought to what an institution, and particularly an academic institution, is and does, it was impossible for me not to know what was implied in agreeing to be thus consecrated.[172]

By undertaking a reflection on what I was experiencing, I sought a degree of freedom from what was happening. My work is often read—misread in my eyes—as deterministic and fatalistic. But to do a sociology of intellectuals, to do a sociology of the Collège de France, of what it means to deliver an inaugural lecture at the Collège de France, at the very moment when you are being taken in and by the game, is to assert that you are trying to be free from it.[173] For me, sociology has played the role of a socioanalysis that has helped me to understand and to tolerate things (beginning with myself) that I found unbearable before. So, to come back to your question on the Collège de France, since this is where we started, I believe that, whatever slight chance I may have of not being finished off by consecration, I owe to the fact of having worked to analyze consecration. I even think that I might be able to use the authority that this consecration has given me to give more authority to my analysis of the logic and effects of consecration.

Unfortunately, whether we like it or not, scientific analyses of the social world, and of the intellectual world in particular, are liable to two different readings and uses. On the one hand, uses that may be called *clinical*, such as those I just evoked with the idea of socio-

172. "Cultural consecration does indeed confer on the objects, persons, and situations it touches a sort of ontological promotion akin to a transubstantiation" (Bourdieu 1984a: 6). In *La noblesse d'Etat*, Bourdieu argues that the power to consecrate, that is, to produce sacred social divides and orders (as in the institution—in the active sense—of a consecrated elite, i.e., a category not only superior and separate, but also "recognized and which recognizes itself as worthy of being recognized," is what specifically defines the "magic of the State" as a symbolic power (Bourdieu 1989a: 140–62, 533–39 and passim, citation page 6, my translation; see also Bourdieu and Wacquant 1991).

173. Bourdieu's (1982a) inaugural lecture was what its title indicates: a "Lecture on the Lecture." Before a standing-room-only audience comprising his peers, distinguished foreign guests, and official scientific authorities, Bourdieu proceeded to analyze, with disenchanting acumen, the ceremonial mechanisms "which effect the act of delegation whereby the new master is authorized to speak with authority and which institute his word as legitimate discourse, delivered from the proper quarter" (Bourdieu 1982a: 7, my translation).

analysis, in that they treat the products of science as instruments for a self-understanding shorn of self-complacency; and, on the other hand, uses that may be called *cynical*, because they consist in seeking in the analysis of social mechanisms tools for adjusting one's behavior in the social world (this is what some readers of *Distinction* do when they treat it as a manual of etiquette) or to guide one's strategies in the academic field. I need not say that I continually strive to discourage cynical readings and to encourage clinical ones. But there is little doubt that the logic of intellectual or political struggles inclines us towards the cynical use, and especially towards a polemical usage of sociology taken as a particularly powerful weapon of symbolic battle, rather than to the clinical usage which offers a means of knowing and understanding oneself and others.

Did you embrace sociology and not philosophy or psychoanalysis because you thought that you would find in social science more powerful tools for demystification and self-appropriation?

To give a full answer to this question would require a long intellectual socioanalysis.[174] Let me just say that I think that, given what I was socially, given what we may call my social conditions of production, sociology was the best thing for me to do, if not to feel in agreement with life, then at least to find the world more or less acceptable. In this limited sense, I believe that I succeeded in my work: I effected a sort of self-therapy which, I hope, has at the same time produced tools that may be of use to others.

I continually use sociology to try to cleanse my work of the social determinants that necessarily bear on sociologists. Now, of course, I do not for one minute believe or claim that I am fully liberated from them. At every moment, I would like to be able to see what I do not see and I am endlessly, obsessively wondering: "Now, what is the next black box that you have not opened? What have you forgotten in

174. Bourdieu (1987a: 13–71; 1990a: 1–29) offers an adumbration of such a socio-analysis. A critical factor to take into account in Bourdieu's transition from philosophy to the social sciences is the sociopolitical and military conjuncture in which it was initiated: everything indicates that sociology and anthropology offered him a politically more efficacious and ethically more relevant intellectual vocation in the gruesome context of the war of Algerian independence than the abstract and ethereal debates of philosophy could.

your parameters that is still manipulating you?" One of my intellectual heroes is Karl Kraus.[175] In his unique manner, he is one of the few
intellectuals who has produced a genuine critique of intellectuals, inspired by a genuine faith in intellectual values (and not by an anti-
intellectualist ressentiment), and a critique with real effects.

I believe that sociology, when it is reflexive, enables us to track
down and to destroy the last germs of ressentiment. Ressentiment is
not, as with Scheler ([1963] who wrote truly awful things about the
ressentiment of women), synonymous with the hatred of the dominant experienced by the dominated. It is rather, as Nietzsche, who
coined the term, suggested, the sentiment of the person who transforms a sociologically mutilated being—I am poor, I am black, I am a
woman, I am powerless—into a model of human excellence, an elective accomplishment of freedom and a *devoir-être,* an ought-to-be, a
fatum, built upon an unconscious fascination with the dominant. Sociology frees you from this kind of sickly strategy of symbolic inversion because it compels you to ask: Do I not write this because . . .
Isn't the root of my revolt, my irony, my sarcasm, of the rhetorical
vibration of my adjectives when I describe Giscard d'Estaing playing
tennis (Bourdieu 1984a: 210) the fact that, deep down, I envy what he
is? Ressentiment is for me the form par excellence of human misery; it
is the worst thing that the dominant impose on the dominated (perhaps the major privilege of the dominant, in any social universe, is to
be structurally freed from ressentiment). Thus, for me, sociology is an
instrument of liberation and therefore of *generosity.*

**To conclude, *Homo Academicus* reads in more ways than one as your autobiography:
as a sublimated effort at scientifically mastering your relation to the University,**

175. The charismatic Austrian playwright, poet, essayist and satirist Kraus
(1874–1936) spent his life uncovering and denouncing the compromises of intellectuals
(especially journalists) with established political and economic authorities. He was the
founder and, for the better part of forty years, sole writer of the authoritative Viennese
review *Die Fackel* ("The Torch") in which he continually unmasked the mechanisms of
control and censorship entailed in the emerging professionalization of cultural production. He was unique in his unrelenting use of techniques of provocation (trials, faked
petitions, *ad personam* attacks, etc.) to disclose and condemn intellectual opportunism
and what he called "journalistic banditry" (Pollak's [1981] sociological analysis of his
"Sociology-in-action of Intellectuals" suggests several parallels between Kraus's and
Bourdieu's stance in the intellectual world). A lively biographical-cum-intellectual por-

which contains in capsule form your entire trajectory, it stands as an exemplification of an antinarcissistic reflexivity or self-appropriation. You seem to suggest as much in the preface to the English translation when you write that the book "comprises a considerable proportion of self-analysis by proxy" (Bourdieu 1988a: xxvi).[176]

I would rather say that it is an *anti-biography*, insofar as to do an autobiography is oftentimes a manner of erecting oneself a mausoleum which is also a cenotaph. This book is indeed both an attempt to test the outer boundaries of reflexivity in social science and an enterprise in self-knowledge. Contrary to what the ordinary representation of self-knowledge as the exploration of singular depths would lead us to believe, the most intimate truth of what we are, the most unthinkable unthought (*l'impensé le plus impensable*), is also inscribed in the objectivity and in the history of the social positions that we have held in the past and that we presently occupy.[177]

This is why, in my view, the history of sociology, understood as an exploration of the *scientific unconscious of the sociologist* through the explication of the genesis of problems, categories of thought, and instru-

---

trait of Kraus in Habsburg Vienna can be found in Timms 1986; for a selection of his texts and aphorisms, see Kraus 1976a and 1976b.

176. Bourdieu (1988a: xxvi) closes this preface by confessing that "the special place held in my work by a somewhat peculiar sociology of the university institution is no doubt explained by the particular force with which I felt the need to gain rational mastery over the disappointment felt by an 'oblate' faced with the annihilation of the truths and the values to which he was destined and dedicated, rather than take refuge in feelings of self-destructive ressentiment" (translation modified). I have argued elsewhere (Wacquant 1990a) that *Homo Academicus* is, at bottom, an invitation to a *collective* sociological self-accounting by intellectuals.

177. The long, socioanalytic preface which opens *The Logic of Practice* (Bourdieu 1990a: 20–21, translation modified) concludes with those words: "By opposition to personalist denegation which, refusing scientific objectivation, can construct but a fantasized person, sociological analysis, particularly when it it places itself in the properly anthropological tradition of the exploration of forms of classification, makes a genuine self-reappropriation possible through the objectivation of the objectivity which haunts the supposed site of subjectivity, such as these social categories of thought, perception, and appreciation which are the unthought principle of all representation of the so-called objective world. By forcing us to discover externality at the heart of internality, banality behind the illusion of rarity, the common in the search for the unique, sociology not only has the effect of denouncing all the impostures of narcissistic egotism; it also offers us what may be the only means to contribute, if only through the awareness of determinations, to the construction, otherwise abandoned to the forces of the world, of something like a subject."

ments of analysis, constitutes an absolute prerequisite for scientific practice. And the same is true of the sociology of sociology. I believe that if the sociology I propose differs in any significant way from the other sociologies of the past and of the present, it is above all in that it *continually turns back onto itself the scientific weapons it produces.* It uses the knowledge it gains of the social determinations that may bear upon it, and particularly the scientific analysis of all the constraints and all the limitations associated with the fact of occupying a definite position in a definite field at a particular moment and with a certain trajectory, in an attempt to locate and neutralize their effects.

To adopt the point of view of reflexivity is not to renounce objectivity but, on the contrary, to give it its full generality by questioning the privilege of the knowing subject, arbitrarily freed, as purely noetic, from the work of objectivation. It is to work to account for the empirical "subject" in the very terms of the objectivity constructed by the scientific "subject"—in particular by situating him or her at a determinate place in social space—and, thereby, to acquire the awareness and (possible) mastery of all the constraints that may impinge on the scientific subject through the ties that bind him to the empirical objects, those interests, pulsions, presuppositions, with which he must break in order fully to constitute himself as such.

Classical philosophy has for a long time taught us that we must look in the "subject" for the conditions of objectivity and thus the limits of the objectivity he or she institutes. Reflexive sociology teaches us that that we must look in the object constructed by science for the *social conditions of possibility of the "subject"* (with, for instance, the situation of *scholē* and the whole inherited baggage of concepts, problems, methods, etc., which make his activity possible) and for the possible limits of his acts of objectivation. This compels us to repudiate the absolutist claims of classical objectivity, but without for all that being forced into the arms of relativism; for the conditions of possibility of the scientific "subject" and of the scientific object are one and the same. And to each advance in the knowledge of the social conditions of production of scientific "subjects" corresponds an advance in the knowledge of the scientific object, and conversely. This can be seen most clearly when research takes as its object the scientific field itself, that is, the true *subject* of scientific knowledge.

Far from undermining the foundations of social science, then, the sociology of the social determinants of sociological practice is the only possible ground for a possible freedom from these determinations. And it is only on condition that he avail himself of the full use of this freedom by continually subjecting himself to this analysis that the sociologist can produce a rigorous science of the social world which, far from sentencing agents to the iron cage of a rigid determinism, offers them the means of a potentially liberating awakening of consciousness.

III

**The Practice of Reflexive Sociology
(The Paris Workshop)**

Pierre Bourdieu

I am more than half-inclined to liken Descartes' rules to this precept of I-don't-remember-what chemist: take what you must and proceed as you must, you will then get what you wish to get. Do not admit of anything that is not truly obvious (that is, admit only that which you have to admit); divide the topic into the required parts (that is, do what you have to do); proceed according to order (in the order according to which you have to proceed); provide complete enumerations (that is, the ones you have to provide): here is precisely the manner of people who say that you must seek the good and shun the bad. All of this is surely appropriate, except that you lack the criteria of good and bad.

Leibniz, *Philosophische Schriften*

1   Handing Down a Trade

Today, to make an exception, I would like to try and explicate a little the pedagogical purposes that I pursue in this seminar. Next time I will ask each of the participants briefly to introduce themselves and to present the topic of their research in a few sentences—this, I insist, in a very casual manner, without any special preparation. What I expect is not a formal presentation, that is, a defensive discourse closed unto itself whose first aim (as is readily understandable) is to exorcize your fear of criticism, but rather a simple, unpretentious, and candid exposition of the work done, of the difficulties encountered, of the problems uncovered, etc. Nothing is more universal and universalizable than difficulties. Each of us will find considerable comfort in discovering that a good number of the difficulties that we attribute to our own idiosyncratic awkwardness or incompetence are universally shared; and all will benefit more fully from the apparently highly particularized advice that I may give.

I would like to say in passing that, among all the dispositions that I would wish to be capable of inculcating, there is the ability to *apprehend research as a rational endeavor* rather than as a kind of mystical quest, talked about with bombast for the sake of self-reassurance but also with the effect of increasing one's fear or anguish. Such a realistic stance (which does not mean that it is cynical) aims at maximizing the yield of your investments and is geared toward an optimal allocation of your resources, beginning with the time you have at your disposal. I know that this manner of experiencing scientific work is somewhat disenchanted and disenchanting, and that I run the risk of damaging the image of themselves that many researchers like to keep. But it is perhaps the best and the only way of sheltering oneself from the much more serious disappointments that await the scholar who falls from on high after many a years of self-mystification during which he spent more energy trying to conform to the glorified image that he has of research, that is of himself as a researcher, than in simply doing his job.

A research presentation is in every respect the very opposite of an exhibition, of a *show*[1] in which you seek to show off and to impress others. It is a discourse in which you *expose yourself*, you take risks. (In order to be sure to defuse your defense mechanisms and to neutralize the strategies of presentation of self that you will likely use, I will not hesitate to give you the floor by surprise and to ask you to speak without forewarning and preparation.) The more you expose yourself, the greater your chances of benefiting from the discussion and the more constructive and good-willed, I am sure, the criticisms and advice you will receive. The most efficient way of wiping out errors, as well as the terrors that are oftentimes at their root, is to be able to laugh about them together, which, as you will soon discover, will happen quite often . . .

I will on occasion—I may do it next time—present the research work that I am presently conducting. You will then see in a state that one may call "becoming," that is muddled, cloudy, works that you usually see only in their *finished* state. Homo academicus relishes the finished. Like the *pompier* (academic) painters, he or she likes to make the strokes of the brush, the touching and retouching disappear from his works. I have at times felt a great anguish after I discovered that painters such as Couture, who was Manet's master, had left behind magnificent sketches, very close to impressionist painting—which constructed itself against *pompier* painting—and that they had often "spoiled," in a sense, these works by putting the finishing touches stipulated by the ethic of work well done and well polished whose expression can be found in the Academic aesthetic.[2] I will try to present this research work in progress in its fermenting confusion—

1. In English in the original.
2. See Bourdieu 1987i for a historical analysis of the symbolic revolution entailed in the emergence of impressionist painting in nineteenth-century France.

within limits, of course, for I am well aware that, for obvious social reasons, I am less entitled to confusion than you are, and that you will be less inclined to grant me that right than I would you, and in a sense rightly so (yet again, only in reference to an implicit pedagogical ideal which certainly deserves to be questioned, that which leads us for instance to assess the value of a course, its pedagogic yield, to the quantity and the clarity of the notes that one takes in it).

One of the functions of a seminar such as this one is to give you an opportunity to see *how research work is actually carried out.* You will not get a complete recording of all the mishaps and misfirings, of all the repetitions that proved necessary to produce the final transcript which annuls them. But the high-speed picture that will be shown to you should allow you to acquire an idea of what goes on in the privacy of the "laboratory" or, to speak more modestly, the workshop—in the sense of the workshop of the artisan or of the Quattrocento painter—i.e., it will include all the false starts, the wavering, the impasses, the renunciations, and so on. Researchers whose work is at various stages of advancement will present the objects they have tried to construct and will submit themselves to the questioning of all the others who, in the manner of old *compagnons,* fellow-workers of the trade, as they say in the traditional language of the *métiers,*[3] will contribute the collective experience they have accumulated over all the trials and errors of the past.

The *summum* of the art, in the social sciences, is, in my eyes, to be capable of engaging very high "theoretical" stakes by means of very precise and often apparently very mundane, if not derisory, empirical objects. Social scientists tend too easily to assume that the sociopolitical importance of an object is in itself sufficient warrant for the importance of the discourse that addresses it. This is perhaps what explains why those sociologists who are most prone to equate their standing with that of their object (as do some of those who, today, concern themselves with the state or with power) often pay the least attention to method. What counts, in reality, is the rigor of the *con-*

3. William H. Sewell (1980: 19–39) offers a detailed historical exegesis of the notion of *métier* under the Old Regime. His capsule characterization of the corporate idiom in eighteenth-century France is worth quoting since it captures two key dimensions of the *métier* of the sociologist as Bourdieu conceives it: "Gens de métier could be defined as the intersection of the domain of manual effort or labor with the domain of art or intelligence."

struction of the object. The power of a mode of thinking never manifests itself more clearly than in its capacity to constitute socially insignificant objects into scientific objects (as Goffman did of the minutiae of face-to-face interaction),[4] or, what amounts to the same thing, to approach a major socially significant object from an unexpected angle—something I am presently attempting by studying the effects of the monopoly of the state over the means of legitimate symbolic violence by way of a very down-to-earth analysis of what a certificate (of illness, invalidity, schooling, etc.) is and does. In this sense, the sociologist of today is, *mutatis mutandis*, in a position quite similar to that of Manet or Flaubert who, in order to realize fully the mode of construction of reality they were inventing, had to apply it to objects traditionally excluded from the realm of academic art, exclusively concerned with persons and things socially designated as important, which explains why they were accused of "realism." The sociologist could well make his or hers Flaubert's motto: "To write well about the mediocre."

We must learn how *to translate highly abstract problems into thoroughly practical scientific operations*, which presupposes, as we will see, a very peculiar relation to what is ordinarily called "theory" and "research" *(empirie)*. In such an enterprise, abstract precepts such as the ones enunciated in *Le métier de sociologue* (Bourdieu, Chamboredon, and Passeron 1973; English translation 1991), if they have the virtue of arousing attention and putting us on notice, are not of much help. No doubt because there is no manner of mastering the fundamental principles of a practice—the practice of scientific research is no exception here—than by practicing it alongside a kind of guide or coach who provides assurance and reassurance, who sets an example and who corrects you by putting forth, *in situation*, precepts applied directly to the *particular case* at hand.

Of course, it may very well happen that, after listening to a two-hour discussion on the teaching of music, the logic of combat sports, the emergence of subsidized housing markets or Greek theology, you will wonder whether you have not wasted your time and if you have learned anything at all. You will not come out of this seminar with neat summaries on communicative action, on systems theory or even

4. See the epitaph written by Bourdieu (1983e) for *Le Monde* upon Goffman's sudden death. See also Boltanski 1974.

on the notions of field and habitus. Instead of giving a formal exposition of the notion of structure in modern mathematics and physics and on the conditions of applicability of the structural mode of thinking to sociology, as I used to do twenty years ago[5] (this was undoubtedly more "impressive"), I will say much the same thing but in a practical form, that is, by means of very trivial remarks and elemental questions—so elemental indeed that we too often forget entirely to raise them—and by immersing myself, each time, into the detail of each particular study. One can really supervise a research, since this is what is involved here, only on condition of actually *doing it* along *with* the researcher who is in charge of it: this implies that you work on questionnaire construction, on reading statistical tables or interpreting documents, that you suggest hypotheses if necessary, and so on. It is clear that, under such conditions, one can supervise only a very small number of research projects and that those who pretend to supervise a large number of them do not really do what they claim they are doing.

Given that what is to be communicated consists essentially of a *modus operandi*, a mode of scientific production which presupposes a definite mode of perception, a set of principles of vision and di-vision, there is no way to acquire it other than to make people see it in practical operation or to observe how this *scientific habitus* (we might as well call it by its name) "reacts" in the face of practical choices—a type of sampling, a questionnaire, a coding dilemma, etc.—without necessarily explicating them in the form of formal precepts.

The teaching of a *métier*, a craft, a trade, or, to speak like Durkheim (1956: 101), a social "art" understood as "pure practice without theory," requires a pedagogy which is completely different from that suited to the teaching of knowledge (*savoirs*). As can be clearly seen in societies without writing and schools—but this remains true of what is transmitted within societies with formal schooling and even within schools themselves—a number of modes of thinking and action, and oftentimes the most vital ones, are transmitted from practice to practice, through total and practical modes of transmission founded upon direct and lasting contact between the one who teaches and the one

5. See Bourdieu's (1968b) discussion in "Structuralism and Theory of Sociological Knowledge," where he sets out his debt to, and differences with, structuralism as a social epistemology.

who learns ("Do as I do").[6] Historians and philosophers of science, and especially scientists themselves, have often observed that a good part of the craft of the scientist is acquired via modes of transmission that are thoroughly practical.[7] And the part played by the pedagogy of silence, which leaves little room for explication of both the schemata transmitted and the schemata at work in the process of transmission itself, is surely all the greater in those sciences where the contents of knowledge and the modes of thinking and of action are themselves less explicit and less codified.

Sociology is a more advanced science than is ordinarily believed, even among sociologists. Perhaps a good criterion of the position of a social scientist in his or her discipline might be how high his idea is of what he must master in order to be abreast of the achievements of his science. The propensity to evolve an unpretentious grasp of your scientific capabilities cannot but increase as your knowledge of the most recent achievements in matters of method, techniques, concepts or theories, grows. But sociology is yet little codified and little formalized. Therefore one cannot, as much as is done elsewhere, rely on automatisms of thinking or on the automatisms that take the place of thinking (on the *evidentia ex terminis*, the "blinding evidence" of symbols that Leibniz used to oppose to Cartesian *évidence*,) or yet on all these codes of proper scientific conduct—methods, protocols of observation, etc.—that constitute the law of the most codified scientific fields. Thus, in order to obtain adequate practices, one must count principally upon the embodied schemata of habitus.

The scientific habitus is a rule "made man," an embodied rule or, better, a scientific *modus operandi* that functions in a practical state according to the norms of science without having these norms as its explicit principle:[8] it is this sort of scientific "feel for the game" *(sens du*

6. See Bourdieu 1990a. Connerton 1989 provides an effective and terse defense of this argument; also Jackson 1989: chap. 8.

7. See Kuhn 1970 and Latour and Woolgar 1979. This point is also supported by Rouse 1987 and Traweek 1989. Donald Schon (1983) shows in *The Reflective Practitioner* that professionals (in management and engineering, architecture, town planning and psychotherapy) know more than they can put into words; as competent practitioners, they "exhibit a kind of knowing-in-practice, most of which is tacit," and rely on improvization learned in action rather than on formulas learned in graduate school.

8. See Bourdieu 1990g and Brubaker 1989a for an analysis of Bourdieu's theory as a working scientific habitus.

jeu) that causes us to do what we do at the right moment without needing to thematize what had to be done and still less the knowledge of the explicit rule that allows us to generate this conformable practice. Thus the sociologist who seeks to transmit a scientific habitus has more in common with a high-level sports coach than with a Professeur at the Sorbonne. He or she says very little by way of first principles and general precepts. Of course, she may set those forth as I did in *Le métier de sociologue,* but only if she knows that she cannot stop at that point: there is nothing worse, in a sense, than epistemology when it becomes a topic for society conversation and essays[9] and a *substitute for research.* She proceeds by way of practical suggestions, and in this she looks very much like a coach who mimicks a move ("if I were you I would do this . . . ") or by "correcting" practices as they are executed, in the spirit of practice itself ("I would not ask this question, at least not in this form").

2 Thinking Relationally

None of this could be truer than when it comes to the construction of the object, no doubt the most crucial research operation and yet the most completely ignored, especially by the dominant tradition, organized as it is around the opposition between "theory" and "methodology." The paradigm (in the sense of exemplary instantiation) of theoreticist "theory" is offered by the work of Parsons, that conceptual *melting pot*[10] produced by purely theoretical compilation (that is, entirely foreign to any application) of a select few grand *oeuvres* (Durkheim, Pareto, Weber, and Marshall—and, curiously, not Marx) reduced to their "theoretical" or, better, professorial dimension, or yet, closer to us, by the "neo-functionalism" of Jeffrey Alexander.[11] Born of the necessities of teaching, such eclectic and classificatory compilations are good for teaching, but for no other purpose. On the other side, we find "methodology," that catalogue of precepts that properly pertain neither to epistemology, understood as reflection aimed at uncovering the schemata of scientific practice apprehended

9. "Essay" does not capture the slightly pejorative connotation of the French *dissertation* as an empty and gratuitous discourse.

10. In English in the original.

11. See Parsons 1937, Alexander 1980–82, 1985, and Alexander's (1987b) *Twenty Lectures,* which originated in a series of course lectures to undergraduates.

in its failures as well as in its successes, nor to scientific theory. I think here of Paul Lazarsfeld. The couple formed by Parsons and Lazarsfeld (with Merton and his theories of the "middle range" standing midway between the two) has formed a sort of socially very powerful "scientific" *holding* that reigned over world sociology for the better part of three decades after World War II.[12] The division between "theory" and "methodology" establishes as an epistemological opposition an opposition that is in fact constitutive of the social division of scientific labor at a certain time (expressed by the opposition between professors and the staff of bureaus of applied research).[13] I believe that this division into two separate instances must be completely rejected, as I am convinced that one cannot return to the concrete by combining two abstractions.

Indeed, the most "empirical" technical choices cannot be disentangled from the most "theoretical" choices in the construction of the object. It is only as a function of a definite construction of the object that such a sampling method, such a technique of data collection and analysis, etc., becomes imperative. More precisely, it is only as a function of a body of hypotheses derived from a set of theoretical presuppositions that any empirical datum can function as a proof or, as Anglo-American scholars put it, as *evidence*.[14] Now, we often proceed as if what counts as evidence was evident because we trust a *cultural routine*, most often imposed and inculcated through schooling (the famous "methodology" courses taught at American universities). The fetishism of "evidence" will sometimes lead one to reject empirical works that do not accept as self-evident the very definition of "evidence." Every researcher grants the status of data only to a small fraction of the given, yet not, as it should be, to the fraction called forth by his or her problematics, but to that fraction vouchsafed and guaranteed by the pedagogical tradition of which they are part and, too often, by that one tradition alone.

It is revealing that entire "schools" or research traditions should develop around *one* technique of data collection and analysis. For ex-

12. For further elaboration, see Bourdieu 1988e. Pollak (1979, 1980) sketches an analysis of Lazarsfeld's activities aimed at the methodical exportation of positivist social science—canons and institutions—outside of the United States.

13. Coleman (1990a) offers rich biographical reminiscences on these two "poles" of Columbia sociology and on their rapprochement and mutual legitimation in the 1950s.

14. In English in the original.

ample, today some ethnomethodologists want to acknowledge nothing but conversation analysis reduced to the exegesis of a text, completely ignoring the data on the immediate context that may be called ethnographic (what is traditionally labeled the "situation"), not to mention the data that would allow them to situate this situation within the social structure. These "data," which are (mis)taken for the *concrete* itself, are in fact the product of a formidable *abstraction*—it is always the case since all data are constructions—but in this case an abstraction which ignores itself as such.[15] Thus we will find monomaniacs of log-linear modeling, of discourse analysis, of participant observation, of open-ended or in-depth interviewing, or of ethnographic description. Rigid adherence to this or that one method of data collection will define membership in a "school," the symbolic interactionists being recognizable for instance by the cult of participant observation, ethnomethodologists by their passion for conversation analysis, status attainment researchers by their systematic use of path analysis, etc. And the fact of combining discourse analysis with ethnographic description will be hailed as a breakthrough and a daring challenge to methodological monotheism! We would need to carry out a similar critique in the case of techniques of statistical analysis, be they multiple regression, path analysis, network analysis, factor analysis, or event-history analysis. Here again, with a few exceptions, monotheism reigns supreme.[16] Yet the most rudimentary sociology of sociology teaches us that methodological indictments are too often no more than a disguised way of making a virtue out of necessity, of feigning to dismiss, to ignore in an active way, what one is ignorant of in fact.

And we would need also to analyze the rhetoric of data presentation which, when it turns into an ostentatious display of data, often serves to mask elementary mistakes in the construction of the object, while at the opposite end, a rigorous and economical exposition of the *pertinent* results will, measured by the yardstick of such an exhibitionism of the *datum brutum*, oftentimes incur the *a priori* suspicion of

15. See Bourdieu's (1990d) analysis of the discursive interaction between house buyers and house sellers and, for contrast, compare his structural constructivism with the straightforward interactional discourse–analytic framework of Schegloff 1987.

16. "Give a hammer to a child," warns Abraham Kaplan (1964:112) "and you will see that that everything will seem to him to deserve to be hit with it." Everett C. Hughes's (1984) discussion of "methodological ethnocentrism" is relevant here.

the fetishizers of the *protocol* (in the twofold sense of the term) of a form of "evidence." Poor science! How many scientific crimes are committed in thy name! . . . To try to convert all these criticisms into a positive precept, I will say only that we must beware of all sectarian dismissals which hide behind excessively exclusive professions of faith. We must try, in every case, to mobilize all the techniques that are relevant and practically usable, given the definition of the object and the practical conditions of data collection. One can, for instance, utilize correspondence analysis for carrying out a discourse analysis, as I recently did in the case of the advertisement strategies of various firms involved in the construction of single-family homes in France (Bourdieu 1990c), or combine the most standard statistical analysis with a set of in-depth interviews or ethnographic observations, as I tried to do in *Distinction* (Bourdieu 1984a). The long and the short of it is, social research is something much too serious and too difficult for us to allow ourselves to mistake scientific *rigidity*, which is the nemesis of intelligence and invention, for scientific *rigor*, and thus to deprive ourselves of this or that resource available in the full panoply of intellectual traditions of our discipline and of the sister disciplines of anthropology, economics, history, etc. In such matters, I would be tempted to say that only one rule applies: "it is forbidden to forbid,"[17] or, watch out for methodological watchdogs! Needless to say, the extreme liberty I advocate here (which seems to me to make obvious sense and which, let me hasten to add, has nothing to do with the sort of relativistic epistemological *laissez faire* which seems so much in vogue in some quarters) has its counterpart in the extreme vigilance that we must apply to the conditions of use of analytical techniques and to ensuring that they fit the question at hand. I often find myself thinking that our methodological "police" *(pères-la-rigueur)* prove to be rather unrigorous, even lax, in their use of the very methods of which they are zealots.

Perhaps what we will do here will appear to you insignificant. But, first, the construction of an object—at least in my personal research experience—is not something that is effected once and for all, with one stroke, through a sort of inaugural theoretical act. The program of observation and analysis through which it is effected is not a blue-

17. The reader will recognize here the famed May '68 French slogan, *il est interdit d'interdire*.

print that you draw up in advance, in the manner of the engineer. It is, rather, a protracted and exacting task that is accomplished little by little, through a whole series of small rectifications and amendments inspired by what is called *le métier*, the "know-how," that is, by the set of practical principles that orients choices at once minute and decisive. It is thus in reference to a somewhat glorified and rather unrealistic notion of research that some would express surprise at the fact that we should discuss at such length apparently negligible details such as whether the researcher ought to disclose his status as a sociologist or take the cover of a less threatening identity (say, that of ethnographer or historian) or hide it entirely, or whether it is better to include such questions in a survey instrument designed for statistical analysis or to reserve it for in-depth, face-to-face interviews with a select number of informants, and so on.

This constant attention to the details of the research procedure, whose properly social dimension (how to locate reliable and insightful informants, how to present yourself to them, how to describe the aims of your research and, more generally, how to "enter" the world under study, etc.) is not the least important, should have the effect of putting you on notice against the fetishism of concepts, and of "theory," born of the propensity to consider "theoretical" instruments—habitus, field, capital, etc.—in themselves and for themselves, rather than to put them in motion and to make them *work*. Thus the notion of field functions as a conceptual shorthand of a mode of construction of the object that will command, or orient, all the practical choices of research. It functions as a *pense-bête*, a memory-jogger: it tells me that I must, at every stage, make sure that the object I have given myself is not enmeshed in a network of relations that assign its most distinctive properties. The notion of field reminds us of the first precept of method, that which requires us to resist by all means available our primary inclination to think the social world in a substantialist manner. To speak like Cassirer (1923) in *Substance and Function*: one must *think relationally*. Now, it is easier to think in terms of realities that can be "touched with the finger," in a sense, such as groups or individuals, than in terms of relations. It is easier for instance to think of social differentiation in the form of groups defined as populations, as with the realist notion of class, or even in terms of antagonisms between these groups, than in the form of a space of relations.[18] The ordinary objects of research are realities which are pointed out to the researcher by the fact that they "stand out," in a sense, by "creating problems"—as, for instance, in the case of "teen-age welfare mothers in Chicago's black ghetto." Most of the time, researchers take as objects of research the problems of social order and domestication posed by more or less arbitrarily defined populations, produced through the successive partitioning of an initial category that is itself pre-constructed: the "elderly," the "young," "immigrants," "semi-professions," or the "poverty population," and so on. Take for instance "The youth of the western housing project of Villeurbanne."[19] The first and most pressing scientific priority, in all such cases, would be *to take as one's object the social work of construction of the pre-constructed object*. That is where the point of genuine rupture is situated.

To escape from the realist mode of thinking, however, it does not suffice to employ the grand words of Grand Theory. For instance, concerning power, some will raise subtantialist and realist questions of location (in the manner of those cultural anthropologists who wandered in an endless search for the "locus of culture"); others will ask where power comes from, from the top or from the bottom ("Who Governs?"), as did those sociolinguists who worried about where the locus of linguistic change lies, among the petty bourgeois or among the bourgeois, etc.[20] It is for the purpose of breaking with this substantialist mode of thinking, and not for the thrill of sticking a new label on old theoretical wineskins, that I speak of the "field of power" rather than of the dominant class, the latter being a realist concept designating an actual population of holders of this tangible reality that we call power. By field of power, I mean the relations of force that obtain between the social positions which guarantee their occupants a

18. See Bourdieu 1985a, 1987b, 1989e for elaborations. Bourdieu draws on the work of logician Peter F. Strawson (1959) to ground his relational conception of social space and of the epistemological status of individuals in it.

19. A structural equivalent for the United States would be something like the "gang members of Chicago's South Side housing projects."

20. On the search for the locus of power, see Robert Dahl's (1961) *Who Governs*, and the "community power structure" debate for the view "from above." The view "from below" is represented by the tradition of proctological historiography and recent anthropology (e.g., Scott 1985). On the locus of linguistic change, see Labov 1980.

quantum of social force, or of capital, such that they are able to enter into the struggles over the monopoly of power, of which struggles over the definition of the legitimate form of power are a crucial dimension (I think here in particular of the confrontation between "artists" and "bourgeois" in the late nineteenth century.)[21]

This being said, one of the main difficulties of relational analysis is that, most of the time, social spaces can be grasped only in the form of distributions of properties among individuals or concrete institutions, since the data available are attached to individuals or institutions. Thus, to grasp the subfield of economic power in France, and the social and economic conditions of its reproduction, you have little choice but to interview the top two hundred French CEOs (Bourdieu and de Saint Martin 1978; Bourdieu 1989a: 396–481). When you do so, however, you must beware at every moment of regression to the "reality" of preconstructed social units. To guard against it, I suggest that you use this very simple and convenient instrument of construction of the object: the *square-table of the pertinent properties of a set of agents or institutions*. If, for example, my task is to analyze various combat sports (wrestling, judo, aikido, boxing, etc.), or different institutions of higher learning, or different Parisian newspapers, I will enter each of these institutions on a line and I will create a new column each time I discover a property necessary to characterize one of them; this will oblige me to question all the other institutions on the presence or absence of this property. This may be done at the purely inductive stage of initial locating. Then I will pick out redundancies and eliminate columns devoted to structurally or functionally equivalent traits so as to retain all those traits—and only those traits—that are capable of discriminating between the different institutions and are thereby analytically relevant. This very simple instrument has the virtue of forcing you to think relationally both the social units under consideration and their properties, which can be characterized either in terms of presence and absence (yes/no) or gradationally (+, 0, −, or 1, 2, 3, 4, 5).

It is at the cost of such a work of construction, which is not done in one stroke but by trial and error, that one progressively constructs so-

21. On the field of power see Bourdieu 1989a and above, part 1, sec. 3; on the clash between "artists" and "bourgeois" at the close of the nineteenth century in France, see Bourdieu 1983d and 1988d, and Charle 1987.

cial spaces which, though they reveal themselves only in the form of highly abstract, objective relations, and although one can neither touch them nor "point to them," are what makes the whole reality of the social world. I will refer you here to the work I recently published (Bourdieu 1989a) on the *Grandes écoles*[22] and in which I recount, by means of a very condensed chronicle of a research project spread over the better part of two decades, how one moves from monography to a genuinely constructed scientific object, in this case the field of the academic institutions entrusted with the reproduction of the field of power in France. It becomes all the more difficult to avoid falling into the trap of the preconstructed object in that I am here dealing with an object in which I am by definition interested without clearly knowing what the veritable principle of that "interest" is. It could be, for example, the fact that I am an alumnus of the Ecole normale supérieure.[23] The first-hand knowledge I have of it, which is all the more pernicious when it is experienced as demystified and demystifying, generates a whole series of supremely naive questions that every *normalien* will find interesting because they immediately "come to the mind" of the *normalien* who wonders about his or her school, that is, about himself or herself: for example, does the ranking upon entry into the school contribute to determining the choice of disciplines, mathematics and physics or literature and "philo"? (The spontaneous problematic, in which a considerable measure of narcissistic complacency enters, is in fact ordinarily much more naive than this. I can refer you here to the myriad volumes claiming scientific status published over the last twenty years on this or that *Grande école*.) One can end up writing a voluminous book packed with facts that have every appearance of being perfectly scientific but which misses the root of the mat-

22. The French *Grandes écoles* are elite graduate schools that are separate from the regular university system. They include the Ecole nationale d'administration (ENA), which prepares higher civil servants, created in 1945; the Ecole des hautes études commerciales (HEC, est. 1881), which trains executives and business experts; the Ecole polytechnique and the Ecole Centrale (for engineers, 1794); and the Ecole normale supérieure (1794), which produces top teachers and university professors. Entrance to these schools is by highly selective national competitive examinations after one to four years of special post–high school preparatory education.

23. Pierre Bourdieu graduated from the Ecole normale supérieure (thereby becoming a *normalien*) in 1954, three years after Foucault, one year before Jacques Derrida, and along with historian Le Roy Ladurie and literary theorist Gérard Genette.

ter, if, as I believe, the Ecole normale supérieure, to which I may be tied by affective attachments, positive or negative, produced by my prior investments, is in reality but a point in a space of objective relations (a point whose "weight" in the structure will have to be determined); or if, to be more precise, the truth of this institution resides in the network of relations of opposition and competition which link it to the whole set of institutions of higher learning in France, and which link this network itself to the total set of positions in the field of power which these schools grant access to. If it is indeed true that the real is relational, then it is quite possible that I know nothing of an institution about which I think I know everything, since it is nothing outside of its relations to the whole.

Whence the problems of strategy that one cannot avoid, and which will crop up again and again in our discussions of research projects. The first of these may be posed as follows: is it better to conduct an extensive study of the totality of the relevant elements of the object thus constructed or to engage in an intensive study of a limited fragment of that theoretical ensemble devoid of theoretical justification? The choice most often approved of socially, in the name of a naively positivist idea of precision and "seriousness," is the second one, that which consists of "studying exhaustively a very precise and well-circumscribed object," as thesis advisors like to say. (It would be too easy to show how such typically petty bourgeois virtues as "prudence," "seriousness," "honesty," and so on, which would be as apposite in the management of a small business or in a mid-level bureaucratic position, are here transmuted into "scientific method"; and also how a socially approved nonentity—the "community study" or the organizational monograph—can accede to recognized scientific existence as a result of a classical effect of social magic.)

In practice, we shall see that the issue of the boundaries of the field, apparently a positivist question to which one can give a theoretical answer (an agent or an institution belongs to a field inasmuch as it produces and suffers effects in it), will come up time and again. Consequently you will almost always be confronted with this alternative between the intensive analysis of a practically graspable fragment of the object and the extensive analysis of the true object. The scientific profit to be gained from knowing the space from which you have isolated the object under study (for instance a particular elite school) and that you must try to map out even roughly, with secondary data for lack of better information, resides in that, by knowing what you do and what the reality from which the fragment has been *abstracted* consists of, you can at least adumbrate the main force lines that structure the space whose constraints bear upon the point under consideration (in a manner similar to those nineteenth-century architects who drew wonderful charcoal sketches of the totality of the building inside of which the part that they wanted to represent in detail was located). Thus you will not run the risk of searching (and "finding") in the fragment studied mechanisms or principles that are in reality external to it, residing in its relations to other objects.

To construct a scientific object also demands that you take up an active and systematic posture vis-à-vis "facts." To break with empiricist passivity, which does little more than ratify the preconstructions of common sense, without relapsing into the vacuous discourse of grand "theorizing," requires not that you put forth grand and empty theoretical constructs but that you tackle a very concrete empirical case with the purpose of *building a model* (which need not take a mathematical or abstract form in order to be rigorous). You must link the pertinent data in such a manner that they function as a self-propelling program of research capable of generating systematic questions liable to be given systematic answers, in short, to yield a coherent system of relations which can be put to the test *as such*. The challenge is *systematically* to interrogate the particular case by constituting it as a "particular instance of the possible," as Bachelard (1949) put it, in order to extract general or invariant properties that can be uncovered only by such interrogation. (If this intention is too often lacking in the work of historians, it is no doubt because the definition of their task inscribed in the social definition of their discipline is less ambitious, or pretentious, but also less demanding, on this count, than that thrust upon the sociologist.)

Analogical reasoning, based on the reasoned intuition of homologies (itself founded upon knowledge of the invariant laws of fields) is a powerful instrument of construction of the object. It is what allows you to immerse yourself completely in the particularity of the case at hand without drowning in it, as empiricist idiography does, and to realize the intention of *generalization*, which is science itself, not through the extraneous and artificial application of formal and empty conceptual constructions, but through this particular manner of thinking the particular case which consists of actually thinking it as such. This mode of thinking fully accomplishes itself logically in and through the *comparative method* that allows you to think relationally a particular case constituted as a "particular instance of the possible" by resting on the structural homologies that exist between different fields (e.g., between the field of academic power and the field of religious power via the homology between the relations professor/intellectual, bishop/theologian) or between different states of the same field (the religious field in the Middle Ages and today for instance).[24]

If this seminar functions as I want, it will offer a practical social realization of the method I am trying to advance. In it, you will listen to people who are working on very different objects and who will submit themselves to a questioning constantly guided by the same principles, so that the *modus operandi* of what I wish to transmit will be transmitted in a sense *practically*, through its repeated application to various cases, without need for explicit theoretical explication. While listening to others, each of us will think about his or her own research, and the situation of institutionalized comparison thereby created (as with ethics, this method functions only if it can be inscribed in the mechanisms of a social universe) will oblige each participant, at once and without contradiction, both to particularize her object, to perceive it as a particular case (this, against one of the most common fallacies of social science, namely the universalization of the particular case), and to generalize it, to discover, through the application of general questions, the invariant properties that it conceals under the appearance of singularity. (One of the most direct effects of this mode of thinking is to forbid the kind of semigeneralization that leads one to produce abstract-concrete concepts born of the smuggling, into the scientific universe, of unanalyzed native words or facts.) During the time when I was a more guiding supervisor, I strongly advised researchers to study at least *two* objects, for instance to take, in the case of historians, besides their principal object (say, a publisher under the Second Empire), the contemporary equivalent of this object (a Parisian publishing house). The study of the present has at least the virtue of forcing the historian to objectivize and to control the prenotions that he is likely to project onto the past, if only by the fact that he uses words of the present to name past practices, such as the

24. See Bourdieu 1971b and "Maxwell's Devil: The Structure and Genesis of the Religious Field" in Bourdieu forthcoming a.

word "artist" which often makes us forget that the corresponding notion is an extraordinarily recent invention (Bourdieu 1987d, 1987j, 1988d).[25]

3   A Radical Doubt

The construction of a scientific object requires first and foremost a break with common sense, that is, with the representations shared by all, whether they be the mere commonplaces of ordinary existence or official representations, often inscribed in institutions and thus present both in the objectivity of social organizations and in the minds of their participants. *The preconstructed is everywhere.* The sociologist is literally beleaguered by it, as everybody else is. The sociologist is thus saddled with the task of knowing an object—the social world—of which he is the product, in a way such that the problems that he raises about it and the concepts he uses have every chance of being the product of this object itself. (This is particularly true of the classificatory notions he employs in order to know it, common notions such as names of occupations or scholarly notions such as those handed down by the tradition of the discipline.) Their self-evident character arises from the fit between objective structures and subjective structures which shields them from questioning.

How can the sociologist effect in practice this radical doubting which is indispensable for bracketing all the presuppositions inherent in the fact that she is a social being, that she is therefore socialized and led to feel "like a fish in water" within that social world whose structures she has internalized? How can she prevent the social world itself from carrying out the construction of the object, in a sense, through her, through these unself-conscious operations or operations unaware of themselves of which she is the apparent subject? To not construct, as positivist hyperempiricism does when it accepts without critical examination the concepts that offer themselves to it ("achievement" and "ascription," "profession," "actor," "role," etc.)

25. Similarly, Charle (1990) has shown that "intellectuals," as a modern social group, schema of perception, and political category, are a recent "invention," which took place in France in the late nineteenth century and crystallized around the Dreyfus affair. For him, as for Bourdieu (1989d), to apply the notion indiscriminately to thinkers and writers of prior epochs results in either anachronism or presentist analyses that end up obfuscating the historical singularity of "intellectuals."

is still to construct, because it amounts to recording—and thus to ratifying—something already constructed. Ordinary sociology, which bypasses the radical questioning of its own operations and of its own instruments of thinking, and which would no doubt consider such a *reflexive intention* the relic of a philosophic mentality, and thus a survival from a prescientific age, is thoroughly suffused with the object it claims to know, and which it cannot really know, because it does not know itself. A scientific practice that fails to question itself does not, properly speaking, know what it does. Embedded in, or taken by, the object that it takes as its object, it reveals something of the object, but something which is not really objectivized since it consists of the very principles of apprehension of the object.

It would be easy to show that this half-scholarly science[26] *borrows its problems, its concepts, and its instruments of knowledge from the social world,* and that it often *records* as a datum, as an empirical given independent of the act of knowledge and of the science which performs it, facts, representations or institutions which are the *product of a prior stage of science.* In short, it records itself without recognizing itself . . .

Let me dwell on each of these points for a moment. Social science is always prone to receive from the social world it studies the *issues* that it poses about that world. Each society, at each moment, elaborates a body of *social problems* taken to be legitimate, worthy of being debated, of being made public and sometimes officialized and, in a sense, *guaranteed by the state.* These are for instance the problems assigned to the high-level commissions officially mandated to study them, or assigned also, more or less directly, to sociologists themselves via all the forms of bureaucratic demand, research and funding programs, contracts, grants, subsidies, etc.[27] A good number of ob-

26. In French *science demi-savante.*

27. A prime example would be the field of poverty research in the United States, whose creation is largely a by-product of the 1960s "War on Poverty" and of the subsequent demands of the state for knowledge on populations it had failed to domesticate. The official redefinition of the problem effected by the Office of Economic Opportunity in 1964 turned what was hitherto a sociopolitical issue into a legitimate area of "scientific" inquiry, thereby drawing scores of scholars—especially economists—to new research centers, journals, and conferences devoted to poverty and its public management, eventually leading to the institutionalization of the highly technical (and highly ideological) discipline of "public policy analysis." This entailed not only the uncritical adoption by social scientists of bureaucratic categories and government mea-

jects recognized by official social science and a good many titles of studies are nothing other than social problems that have been smuggled into sociology—poverty, delinquency, youth, high school dropouts, leisure, drunken driving, and so on—and which vary with the fluctuations of the social or scholarly consciousness of the time, as an analysis of the evolution over time of the main realist divisions of sociology would testify (these can be grasped through the subheadings used in mainstream journals or in the names of research groups or sections convening periodically at the World Congress of Sociology).[28] Here is one of the mediations through which the social world constructs its own representation, by using sociology and the sociologist

surements (such as the famed federal "poverty line" which continues to define the boundaries of discourse despite its oft-revealed and growing conceptual inadequacies) and concerns (Does welfare receipt make poor people work less? Do public aid recipients share a culture or engage in behaviors that violate "mainstream" norms? What are the most economical means to make them "self-sufficient"—i.e., socially and politically invisible?) which has reified the moralistic and individualistic perception of poverty by the dominant into "scientific facts" (Katz 1989: 112–23). Haveman (1987) makes a good case that, in the process, the federal government also reshaped the face of social science *in toto:* in 1980, poverty-related research absorbed fully 30 percent of all federal research expenditures compared to .6 percent in 1960. The recent spread of discourse on the "underclass" is a further illustration of how a major influx of funding triggered by foundations can redefine the terms of social scientific debate without critical discussion of the premises built into the new demand.

28. This can also readily be seen in the evolution of the categories used to sort out books in the journal of reviews *Contemporary Sociology,* or in changes in the chapter headings of handbooks (e.g., Smelser 1988) and in the entries of encyclopedias of social science. The taxonomy of topics used by the *Annual Review of Sociology* is a good example of a mix of commonsensical, bureaucratic, and plainly arbitrary divisions inherited from the (academic) history of the discipline: it is a rare mind who can retrospectively impart a degree of (socio)logical coherence to the way it parcels out its subject matter. Opening each volume is the category "Theory and Methods," as always made into a self-contained topic. Then come "Social Processes," a category so broad that it is hard to see what could possibly not fall under it, and "Institutions and Culture," which hypostatizes culture into a distinct object. Why "Formal Organizations" have been separated from "Political and Economic Sociology" is unclear; how they can in turn be distinguished from "Stratification and Differentiation" is also moot. "Historical Sociology" has the dubious privilege of being reified into a separate specialty (presumably on the basis of method, but then should it not be regrouped with "Theory and Methods," and why do other approaches not have "their" sections?). Just why "Sociology of World Religion" has a rubric all to itself is a mystery. "Policy" is a direct offshoot of bureaucratic state demand for social knowledge. And, crowning all the other categories in its sanctification of common sense, the rubric "Individual and Society."

for this purpose. For a sociologist more than any other thinker, to leave one's thought in a state of unthought *(impensé)* is to condemn oneself to be nothing more than the *instrument* of that which one claims to think.

How are we to effect this rupture? How can the sociologist escape the underhanded persuasion which is exercised on her every time she reads the newspapers or watches television or even when she reads the work of her colleagues? The mere fact of being on the alert is important but hardly suffices. One of the most powerful instruments of rupture lies in the social history of problems, objects, and instruments of thought, that is, with the history of the work of social construction of reality (enshrined in such common notions as role, culture, youth, etc., or in taxonomies) which is carried out within the social world itself as a whole or in this or that specialized field and, especially, in the field of the social sciences. (This would lead us to assign to the teaching of the social history of the social sciences—a history which, for the most part, remains to be written—a purpose entirely different from the one it presently serves.) A good part of the collective work that finds an outlet in *Actes de la recherche en sciences sociales* deals with the social history of the most ordinary objects of ordinary existence. I think for instance of all those things that have become so common, so taken for granted, that nobody pays any attention to them, such as the structure of a court of law, the space of a museum, a voting booth, the notion of "occupational injury" or of "cadre," a two-by-two table or, quite simply, the act of writing or taping.[29] History thus conceived is inspired not by an antiquarian interest but by a will to understand why and how one understands.

To avoid becoming the object of the problems that you take as your object, you must retrace the history of the *emergence* of these problems, of their progressive constitution, i.e., of the collective work, oftentimes accomplished though competition and struggle, that proved necessary to make such and such issues to be known and recognized *(faire connaître et reconnaître)* as *legitimate problems*, problems that are avowable, publishable, public, official. One thinks here of the problem of "work accidents" or occupational hazards studied by Rémi Lenoir (1980) or of the invention of the "elderly" *(troisième âge)* scru-

29. See, respectively, Lenoir 1980, Boltanski 1979, Garrigou 1988, Bourdieu 1977a: 36–38, 188, and Sayad 1985.

tinized by Patrick Champagne (1979) and, more generally, to such staples of the sociology of "social problems" as family, divorce, delinquency, drugs, and female labor force participation. In all these cases we will discover that the problem that ordinary positivism (which is the first inclination of every researcher) takes for granted has been *socially produced*, in and by a *collective work of construction of social reality*;[30] and that it took meetings and committees, associations and leagues, caucuses and movements, demonstrations and petition drives, demands and deliberations, votes and stands, projects, programs, and resolutions to cause what was and could have remained a *private*, particular, singular problem to turn into a *social problem*, a public issue that can be publicly addressed (think of the fate of abortion or homosexuality)[31] or even an official problem that becomes the object of official decisions and policies, of laws and decrees.

Here one would need to analyze the particular role of the political field (Bourdieu 1981a) and especially of the bureaucratic field. Through the very peculiar logic of the *administrative commission*, a logic that I am currently investigating in the case of the elaboration of the public policy of individual housing assistance in France around 1975,[32] the bureaucratic field contributes decisively to the constitution, and to the consecration, of "universal" social problems. The imposi-

30. While Bourdieu's position may appear akin to the "social constructionist" approach to social problems (e.g., Schneider 1985, Gusfield 1981, Spector and Kitsuse 1987), it differs substantially from the latter in that it grounds the social work of symbolic and organizational construction in the objective structure of the social spaces within which the latter takes place. This grounding operates at the level of the positions and the dispositions of claim makers and claim takers. Bourdieu advocates neither a "strict" nor a "contextual" constructionist position (as defined by Best 1989: 245–89) but a "structural constructivism" which causally relates claims-making and their products to objective conditions. See Champagne 1990 for an analysis of the social construction of "public opinion" along those lines.

31. Kristin Luker (1984) and Faye Ginsburg (1988) offer detailed historical and ethnographic accounts of the social construction of abortion as a public issue at the political and grass-roots level. Pollak (1988a) sketches an analysis of the public framing of the link between AIDS and homosexuality in recent French political discourse. Boltanski unravels the conditions of efficacy of strategies designed to transform personal incidents and outrage into socially accepted issues and injustices in his important article on "Denunciation" (Boltanski with Daré and Schiltz 1984, and Boltanski 1990).

32. See the entire March 1990 issue of *Actes de la recherche en sciences sociales* devoted to "The Economics of Housing" (Bourdieu 1990b, 1990c, 1990d; Bourdieu and de Saint Martin 1990; Bourdieu and Christin 1990).

tion of *problématique* that the sociologist—as every other social agent—suffers and of which he becomes a relay and support every time he takes up on his own account questions which are an expression of the sociopolitical mood of the times (for instance by including them in his survey questionnaires or, worse, by designing his survey around them) is all the more likely when the problems that are *taken for granted* in a given social universe are those that have the greatest chances of being allocated *grants*,[33] material or symbolic, of being, as we say in French, *bien vus*, in high favor with the managers of scientific bureaucracies and with bureaucratic authorities such as research foundations, private firms, or governmental agencies. (This explains why public opinion polls, the "science without scientist," always beget the approval of those who have the means of commissioning them and who otherwise prove so critical of sociology whenever the latter breaks with their demands and commands.)[34]

I will only add, to complicate things still a bit more, and to make you see how difficult, indeed well-nigh desperate, the predicament of the sociologist is, that the work of production of official problems, that is, those problems endowed with the sort of universality that is granted by the fact of being guaranteed by the state, almost always leaves room for what are today called *experts*. Among those so-called experts are sociologists who use the authority of science to endorse the universality, the objectivity, and the disinterestedness of the bureaucratic representation of problems. This is to say that any sociologist worthy of the name, i.e., who does what, according to me, is required to have some chance of being the *subject* of the problems she can pose about the social world, must include in her object the contribution that sociology and sociologists (that is, her own peers) make, in all candor, to the production of official problems—even if this is very likely to appear as an unbearable mark of arrogance or as a betrayal of professional solidarity and corporatist interests.

33. In English in the text: here Bourdieu plays on the words "grants" and "for granted" to emphasize the organic link between the material and the cognitive imposition of problematics.

34. Ever since the introduction of public opinion polls in French political life in the 1960s, Bourdieu has been a persistent and often caustic critic of their social uses. His 1971 paper provocatively entitled "Public Opinion Does Not Exist" (Bourdieu 1979e) has been reprinted in numerous collections and journals and translated into six languages. This issue is broached again in "A Science Without Scientist" (Bourdieu 1987a: 217–24).

In the social sciences, as we well know, epistemological breaks are often social breaks, breaks with the fundamental beliefs of a group and, sometimes, with the core beliefs of the body of professionals, with the body of shared certainties that found the *communis doctorum opinio*. To practice radical doubt, in sociology, is akin to becoming an outlaw. This was no doubt acutely felt by Descartes, who, to the dismay of his commentators, never extended the mode of thinking that he so intrepidly inaugurated in the realm of knowledge to politics (see the prudence with which he talks of Machiavelli).

I now come to the concepts, the words, and the methods that the "profession"[35] employs to speak about, and to think, the social world. Language poses a particularly dramatic problem for the sociologist: it is in effect an immense repository of naturalized preconstructions,[36] and thus of preconstructions that are ignored as such and which can function as unconscious instruments of construction. I could take here the example of *occupational taxonomies*, whether it be the names of occupations that are in currency in daily life or the socioeconomic categories of INSEE (the French National Institute of Economic and Statistical Research), an exemplary instance of *bureaucratic conceptualization*,[37] of the bureaucratic universal, and, more generally, the example of all the taxonomies (age groups, young and old, gender categories, which we know are not free from social arbitrary) that sociologists use without thinking about them too much because they are the social categories of understanding shared by a whole society.[38] Or,

35. In English in the original, as Bourdieu prepares to critique the Anglo-American sociological concept of "profession."

36. Or, in Wittgenstein's (1977: 18) words, "Language sets everyone the same traps; it is an immense network of easily accessible wrong turnings." This view is shared by Elias (1978a: 111) who counts "inherited structures of speech and thought" among the most serious obstacles to a science of society: "The means of speaking and thinking available to sociologists at present are for the most part unequal to the task we ask them to perform." He points out in particular, following Benjamin Lee Whorf, that Western languages tend to foreground substantives and objects at at the expense of relations and to reduce processes to static conditions.

37. Another example would be the bureaucratic invention, and subsequent reification, of the "poverty line" in U.S. social "science" (Beeghley 1984; Katz 1989: 115–17).

38. Maurice Halbwachs (1972: 329–48) showed long ago that there is nothing "natural" about the category of age. Pialoux (1978), Thévenot (1979), Mauger and Fossé-Polliak (1983), and Bourdieu's (1980b: 143–54) "Youth is Nothing But a Word" carry that argument further in the case of youth. Champagne (1979) and Lenoir (1978) apply it to

as in the case of what I called the "categories of professorial judgment" (the system of paired adjectives used to evaluate the papers of students or the virtues of colleagues [Bourdieu 1988a: 194–225]), they belong to their professional corporation (which does not exclude their being founded, in the final analysis, upon homologies between structures, i.e., upon the fundamental oppositions of social space, such as rare/banal, unique/common, etc.).

But I believe that one must go further and call into question not only classifications of occupations and the concepts used to designate classes of jobs, but the very concept of occupation itself, or of *profession,* which has provided the basis for a whole tradition of research and which, for some, stands as a kind of methodological motto. I am well aware that the concept of "profession" and its derivatives (professionalism, professionalization, etc.) has been severely and fruitfully questioned in the works of Magali Sarfatti Larson (1977), Randall Collins (1979), Elliott Friedson (1986), and Andrew Abbott (1988) in particular, who have highlighted, among other things, the conflicts endemic to the world of professions. But I believe that we must go beyond this critique, however radical, and try, as I do, to *replace* this concept with that of field.

The notion of profession is all the more dangerous because it has, as always in such cases, all appearance of neutrality in its favor and because its use has been an improvement over the theoretical jumble *(bouillie)* of Parsons. To speak of "profession" is to fasten on a true reality, onto a set of people who bear the same name (they are all "lawyers" for instance); they are endowed with a roughly equivalent economic status and, more importantly, they are organized into "professional associations" endowed with a code of ethics, collective bodies that define rules for admission, etc. "Profession" is a folk concept which has been uncritically smuggled into scientific language and which imports into it a whole social unconscious. It is the *social product* of a historical work of construction of a group and of a

the sociopolitical construction of the "elderly." Countless historical studies of gender relations have, in recent years, demonstrated the arbitrariness of the categories of male and female; perhaps the most incisive of these is Joan Scott's (1988); see also several of the articles published in the two issues of *Actes de la recherche en sciences sociales* on "Male/Female" (June and September 1990). For an extended discussion of the struggles over the definition of "natural" categories, see Lenoir (in Champagne et al. 1989: 61–77).

representation of groups that has surreptitiously slipped into the science of this very group. This is why this "concept" works so well, or too well in a way: if you accept it to construct your object, you will find directories on hand, lists and biographies drawn up, bibliographies compiled, centers of information and data bases already constituted by "professional" bodies, and, provided that you be a bit shrewd, funds to study it (as is very frequent in the case of lawyers for instance). The category of profession refers to realities that are, in a sense, "too real" to be true, since it grasps at once a mental category and a social category, socially produced only by superseding or obliterating all kinds of economic, social, and ethnic differences and contradictions which make the "profession" of "lawyer," for instance, a space of competition and struggle.[39]

Everything becomes different, and much more difficult if, instead of taking the notion of "profession" at face value, I take seriously the work of *aggregation* and symbolic imposition that was necessary to produce it, and if I treat it as a field, that is, as a structured space of social forces and struggles.[40] How do you draw a sample in a field? If, following the canon dictated by orthodox methodology, you take a random sample, you mutilate the very object you have set out to construct. If, in a study of the juridical field, for instance, you do not draw the chief justice of the Supreme Court, or if, in an inquiry into the French intellectual field of the 1950s, you leave out Jean-Paul Sartre, or Princeton University in a study of American academia, your field is destroyed, insofar as these personas or institutions alone mark a crucial position. There are positions in a field that admit only one occupant but command the whole structure.[41] With a random or representative sample of artists or intellectuals conceived as a "profession," however, *no problem.*[42]

39. See the two issues of *Actes de la recherche en sciences sociales* on law and legal experts, no. 64 (September 1986), and no. 76/77 (March 1989, particularly the articles by Yves Dezalay, Alain Bancaud, and Anne Boigeol).

40. The concept of field is explained at length in part 2, sec. 3, above. See Boltanski 1984a and 1987 for an in-depth examination of the organizational and symbolic invention of the category of "cadres" in French society, and Charle 1990 on that of "intellectuals" proceeding along the same analytical lines.

41. For example, Sartre both dominated, and was in turn dominated by his own domination in, the French intellectual field of the 1950s (see Boschetti 1988 and Bourdieu 1980e, 1984b).

42. In English in the original.

If you accept the notion of profession as an instrument, rather than an object, of analysis, none of this creates any difficulty. As long as you take it as it presents itself, the given (the hallowed *data* of positivist sociologists) gives itself to you without difficulty. Everything goes smoothly, everything is taken for granted. Doors and mouths open wide. What group would turn down the sacralizing and naturalizing recording of the social scientist? Studies of bishops or corporate leaders that (tacitly) accept the church or business problematic will enroll the support of the Episcopate and of the Business Council, and the cardinals and corporate leaders who zealously come to comment on their results never fail to grant a certificate of objectivity to the sociologist who succeeds in giving objective, i.e., public, reality to the subjective representation they have of their own social being. In short, as long as you remain within the realm of socially constituted and socially sanctioned appearances—and this is the order to which the notion of "profession" belongs—you will have all appearances with you and for you, even the appearance of scientificity. On the contrary, as soon as you undertake to work on a genuine constructed object, everything becomes difficult: "theoretical" progress generates added "methodological" difficulties. "Methodologists," for their part, will have no difficulty finding plenty to nit-pick about in the operations that have to be carried out in order to grasp the constructed object as best one can. (Methodology is like spelling of which we say in French: *c'est la science des ânes,* "it is the science of the jackasses." It consists of a compendium of errors of which one can say that you must be dumb to commit most of them.) Among those difficulties, there is the question I touched upon earlier, of the boundaries of the field. The most daring of positivists solve that question—when they do not purely and simply neglect to pose it by using preexisting lists—by what they call an "operational definition" ("In this study, I shall call 'writer' . . . "; "I will consider as a 'semiprofession' . . . "), without seeing that the question of the definition ("So and so is not a *true* writer!") is at stake within the object itself.[43] There is a struggle

43. Peter Rossi's (1989: 11–13) strenuous effort to pass off a socially arbitrary definition of "homelessness" as grounded in "scientific" considerations is exemplary in its degree of positivist ingenuousness and notable for its blindness to its own presuppositions (including that of the existence of a sort of Platonic essence of homelessness). Instead of (at minimum) showing how different definitions produce populations of different sizes, compositions and trajectories and of analyzing the political and scientific inter-

within the object over who is part of the game, who in fact deserves the title of writer. The very notion of writer, but also the notion of lawyer, doctor, or sociologist, despite all efforts at codification and homogenization through certification, is at stake in the field of writers (or lawyers, etc.): the struggle over the legitimate definition, whose stake—the word definition says it—is the boundary, the frontiers, the *right of admission,* sometimes the *numerus clausus,* is a universal property of fields.[44]

---

ests involved in the contention opposing their various advocates, Rossi is content to assert *ex cathedra* his definition tailored to existing data and preconceptions. In his struggle to "operationalize" a notion borrowed from everyday discourse in a way that will not challenge but reinforce the latter, Rossi seeks to cumulate congruity with ordinary common sense, with scholarly common sense and with the practical constraints of bureaucratic survey research. Noting that "it is easy to get bogged down in academic exercises in definition," he explains: "I will use a definition of homelessness that covers the *essence of that term* and is also *practical to use in actual research.* Although my ultimate conception is that homelessness is a matter of degree, I am *constrained to use the definition most common in the social science studies* of homelessness that I rely on. . . . There are some very *persuasive logistical reasons* why most studies of the homeless have adopted this definition in practice" (emphasis added). The construction—in this case, it might be more appropriate to talk of destruction—of his object follows neither the main observable articulations of the phenomenon nor a theoretically guided problematic of its causes and variations. It ends up yielding a "fairly narrow definition" which basically borrows and ratifies that of state bureaucracies whose interest in normalizing and minimizing the phenomenon is amply documented: it centers "mainly on the most accessible of the homeless, clients of agencies that provide services, such as shelters, food kitchens, and medical clinics set up to serve the homeless." It excludes all those that the state does not want to recognize as bona fide homeless (inhabitants of hospitals, jails, prisons, nursing homes, and all the "precariously housed," including people forced to rent or occupy rooms in the dwelling of parents or friends, etc.).

This positivist tour de force climaxes when Rossi replaces the ordinary, commonsensical category of "homelessness" by another category of the current "sociological vernacular" (Merton), that of "extreme poverty," defined here, with the same sense of self-evidence (and the same self-assured arbitrariness), as having income below 75 percent of the "official poverty line," another bureaucratic construct. Homelessness and poverty are thus transmogrified from a sociopolitical condition—a set of *historical relations* and *categories* resulting from struggles over the production and allocation of social wealth—to a *state* measured by neat, clear-cut atomistic variables that allow one to count, divide, and discipline individuals.

44. On recent changes in the social definition and functions of legal experts, see Dezalay 1989; on the struggle to define what a writer is in seventeenth-century France, Viala 1985; on the dilemmas of women writers to be recognized as such, de Saint Martin 1990b.

Empiricist resignation has all appearances going for it and receives all approvals because, by avoiding self-conscious construction, it leaves the crucial operations of scientific construction—the choice of the problem, the elaboration of concepts and analytical categories—to the social world *as it is,* to the established order, and thus it fulfills, if only by default, a quintessentially conservative function of ratification of the *doxa.* Among all the obstacles that stand in the way of the development of a scientific sociology, one of the most formidable is the fact that genuine scientific discoveries come at the highest *costs* and with the lowest profits, not only in the ordinary markets of social existence but also, too often, in the academic market, from which greater autonomy could be expected. As I tried to argue concerning the differential social and scientific costs and benefits of the notions of *profession* and *field,* it is often necessary, in order to produce science, to forego the appearances of scientificity, even to contradict the norms in currency and to challenge ordinary criteria of scientific rigor. Appearances are always in favor of the apparent. True science, very frequently, isn't much to look at, and, to move science forward, it is often necessary to take the risk of not displaying all the outward signs of scientificity (we often forget how easy it is to simulate them). Among other reasons because the half-wits or *demi-habiles,* as Pascal calls them, who dwell on superficial violations of the canons of elementary "methodology," are led by their positivist confidence to perceive as so many "mistakes" and as effects of incompetence or ignorance what are methodological choices founded upon a deliberate refusal to use the escape hatches of "methodology."

I need not say that the obsessive reflexivity which is the condition of a rigorous scientific practice has nothing in common with the false radicalism of the questioning of science that is now proliferating. (I am thinking here of those who introduce the age-old philosophical critique of science, more or less updated to fall in line with the reigning fashion in American social science, whose immune system has paradoxically been destroyed by several generations of positivist "methodology.") Among these critiques, one must grant a special place to those of ethnomethodologists, even though, in some of their formulations, they converge with the conclusions of those who reduce scientific discourse to rhetorical strategies about a world itself reduced to the state of a text. The analysis of the logic of practice, and of the spontaneous theories with which it arms itself in order to make sense of the world, is not an end in itself—no more so than the critique of the presuppositions of ordinary (i.e., unreflexive) sociology, especially in its uses of statistical methods. It is an absolutely decisive moment, but only a moment, of the rupture with the presuppositions of lay and scholarly common sense. If one must objectivize the schemata of practical sense, it is not for the purpose of proving that sociology can offer only one point of view on the world among many, neither more nor less scientific than any other, but to *wrench scientific reason from the embrace of practical reason,* to prevent the latter from contaminating the former, to avoid treating as an instrument of knowledge what ought to be the object of knowledge, that is, everything that constitutes the practical sense of the social world, the presuppositions, the schemata of perception and understanding that give the lived world its structure. To take as one's object commonsense understanding and the primary experience of the social world as a nonthetic acceptance of a world which is not constituted as an *object* facing a subject is precisely the means of avoiding being *"trapped" within the object.* It is the means of submitting to scientific scrutiny *everything that makes the doxic experience of the world possible,* that is, not only the preconstructed representation of this world but also the cognitive schemata that underlie the construction of this image. And those among the ethnomethodologists who rest content with the mere description of this experience without questioning the social conditions which make it possible—that is, the correspondence between social structures and mental structures, the objective structures of the world and the cognitive structures through which the latter is apprehended—do nothing more than repeat the most traditional questionings of the most traditional philosophy on the reality of reality. To assess the limitations of this semblance of radicalism that their epistemic populism imparts to them (due to their rehabilititation of ordinary thinking), we need only observe that ethnomethodologists have never seen the *political implications* of the doxic experience of the world which, as fundamental acceptance of the established order situated outside the reach of critique, is the most secure foundation of a conservatism more radical than that which labors to establish a political orthodoxy.[45]

45. See above, part 2, sec. 1, for further discussion. It is easy to understand how such conservatism can, under definite historical circumstances, turn into its opposite: as Calhoun (1979) has shown in his revisionist critique of Thompson's analysis of the

4 Double Bind and Conversion

The example I just gave with the notion of profession is but a particular instance of a more general difficulty. In point of fact, it is the whole scholarly tradition of sociology that we must constantly question and methodically distrust. Whence the sort of *double bind* in which every sociologist worthy of the name is inescapably caught: without the intellectual instruments bequeathed by her scholarly tradition, she or he is little more than an amateur, an autodidactic, self-taught, spontaneous sociologist (and certainly not the best equipped of all lay sociologists, given the evidently limited span of the social experiences of most academics); but at the same time these instruments constantly put one in danger of simply substituting for the naive doxa of lay common sense the no less naive doxa of scholarly common sense *(sens commun savant)* which parrots, in technical jargon and under the official trappings of scientific discourse, the discourse of common sense (this is what I call the "Diafoirus effect").[46]

It is not easy to escape the horns of this dilemma, this alternative between the disarmed ignorance of the autodidact deprived of instruments of scientific construction and the half-science of the half-scientist who unknowingly and uncritically accepts categories of perception tied to a definite state of social relations, semi-constructed concepts more or less directly borrowed from the social world. This contradiction is never felt more strongly than in the case of ethnology where, owing to the difference in cultural traditions and to the resulting estrangement, one cannot live, as in sociology, under the illusion of immediate understanding. In this case, either you see nothing or you are left with the categories of perception and the mode of thinking (the legalism of anthropologists) received from your predecessors, who oftentimes themselves received them from another scholarly tradition (that of Roman law, for instance). All this inclines us toward a sort of *structural conservatism* leading to the reproduction of the scholarly *doxa*.[47]

---

formation of the English working class, a doxic worldview, that is, an unquestioned and unified cultural "tradition," can, when challenged, provide the cognitive mechanism necessary for radical collective action.

46. After the name of Molière's physician, who speaks a pretentious and falsely scholarly Latin in *Le Bourgeois gentilhomme*.

47. This point is argued more fully in Bourdieu 1986a and 1986c.

Thence the peculiar antinomy of the pedagogy of research: it must transmit both tested instruments of construction of reality (problematics, concepts, techniques, methods) *and* a formidable critical disposition, an inclination to question ruthlessly those instruments—for instance the occupational taxonomies of INSEE or others, which are neither given as a godsend nor issued ready for use out of reality. It goes without saying that, as with every message, the chances that this pedagogy will be successful vary substantially with the socially constituted dispositions of its recipients. The most favorable situation for its transmission is with people who combine an advanced mastery of scientific culture and a certain revolt against, or distance from, that culture (most often rooted in an estranged experience of the academic universe) that pushes them not to "buy it" at its face value or, quite simply, a form of resistance to the asepticized and derealized representation of the social world offered by the socially dominant discourse in sociology. Aaron Cicourel is a good illustration of this: he had hung around with "deliquents" in the slums of Los Angeles long enough in his youth to be spontaneously inclined to question the official representation of "delinquency." It is no doubt this intimate familiarity with that universe, joined with a solid knowledge of statistics and of statistical practices, that prompted him to ask of "delinquency" statistics questions that all the methodological precepts in the world would have been incapable of generating (Cicourel 1968).

At the risk of seeming to push radical doubt to its breaking point, I would like to evoke again the most pernicious forms that lazy thinking can take in sociology. I have in mind that very paradoxical case where a critical thought such as Marx's functions in a state of unthought *(impensé)*, not only in the minds of researchers (and this applies to both the advocates and the critics of Marx), but also within the reality that they record as a matter of pure observation. To conduct surveys on social classes without any further reflection on their existence or their nonexistence, on their size, and on whether they are antagonistic or not, as has often been done, especially with the aim of discrediting Marxist theory, is unknowingly to take as one's object the traces, within reality, of the effects wielded by Marx's theory, in particular via the activities of parties and unions who worked to "raise class consciousness."

What I am saying about the "theory effect" that the theory of class may have exerted, and of which "class consciousness" as we measure it empirically is in part the product, is but a particular illustration of a more general phenomenon. Due to the existence of a social science, and of social practices that claim kinship with this science, such as opinion polls, media advising, publicity, etc.,[48] but also pedagogy and even, more and more often, the conduct of politicians or government officials, businessmen, and journalists, there are, within the social world itself, more and more agents who engage scholarly, if not scientific, knowledge in their practices and more importantly in their work of production of representations of the social world and of manipulation of these representations. So that science increasingly runs the risk of inadvertently recording the outcome of practices that claim to derive from science.

Finally, and more subtly, surrendering to habits of thought, even those that can exert a powerful effect of rupture under other circumstances, can also lead to unexpected forms of naiveté. I will not hesitate to say that Marxism, in its most common social uses, often constitutes the form *par excellence* of the *scholarly preconstructed* because it stands above all suspicion. Let us suppose that we set out to study "legal," "religious," or "professorial" ideology. The word ideology itself purports to mark a break with the representations that agents claim to give of their own practice; it signifies that we should not take their statements to the letter, that they have interests, and so on. But, in its iconoclastic violence, the word leads us to forget that the domination from which one must tear away in order to objectivize it is exercised in large part because it is misrecognized as such. Therefore it makes us forget that we need to bring back into the scientific model the fact that the objective representation of practice had to be constructed against the primary experience of practice, or, if you prefer, that the "objective truth" of this experience is inaccessible to experience itself. Marx allows us to smash open the doors of *doxa*, of the doxic adherence to primary experience. But behind this door lies a trap and the *demi-habile* who trusts scholarly common sense forgets to return to the primary experience that scholarly construction had to bracket and to set aside. "Ideology" (really, by now, we would be better off calling it something else) does not appear as such, to us and to itself, and it is this misrecognition that gives it its symbolic efficacy.

48. See Champagne 1988 and 1990, on the uses of social science and pseudo–social science in the "new political space" of France.

In sum, it does not suffice to break with ordinary common sense, or with scholarly common sense in its ordinary form. *We must also break with the instruments of rupture which negate the very experience against which they have been constructed.* This must be done to build more complete models, models which encompass both the primary naiveté and the objective truth that this naiveté conceals and at which the *demi-habiles,* those who think they are smarter than everybody else, stop by falling for another form of naiveté. (I cannot refrain from saying here that the thrill of feeling smart, demystifying and demystified, of playing the role of the disenchanted disenchanter, is a crucial ingredient in a good number of sociological vocations . . . And the sacrifice that rigorous method demands is all the more costly for that.)

There is no risk of overestimating difficulty and dangers when it comes to thinking the social world. The force of the preconstructed resides in the fact that, being inscribed both in things and in minds, it presents itself under the cloak of the self-evident which goes unnoticed because it is by definition taken for granted. Rupture in fact demands a *conversion of one's gaze* and one can say of the teaching of sociology that it must first "give new eyes," as initiatory philosophers sometimes phrased it. The task is to produce, if not a "new person," then at least a "new gaze," *a sociological eye.* And this cannot be done without a genuine conversion, a *metanoia,* a mental revolution, a transformation of one's whole vision of the social world.

What is called "epistemological rupture,"[49] that is, the bracketing of ordinary preconstructions and of the principles ordinarily at work in the elaboration of these constructions, often presupposes a rupture with modes of thinking, concepts, and methods that have every appearance of *common sense,* of ordinary sense, and of good scientific sense (everything that the dominant positivist tradition honors and hallows) going for them. You will certainly understand that, when one is convinced, as I am, that the most vital task of social science and thus of the teaching of research in the social sciences is to establish as a fundamental norm of scientific practice the conversion of thought,

49. The notion of "epistemological rupture" (like that of "epistemological profile"), which many Anglo-American readers associate with Althusser (or with Foucault), originates with Gaston Bachelard and was used quite extensively by Bourdieu well before the heyday of structuralist Marxism (note the pivotal status it is given in Bourdieu, Chamboredon, and Passeron 1973, originally published in 1968).

the revolution of the gaze, the rupture with the preconstructed and with everything that buttresses it in the social order—and in the scientific order—one is doomed to be forever suspected of wielding a prophetic *magisterium* and of demanding personal conversion.

Being acutely aware of the specifically social contradictions of the scientific enterprise as I have tried to describe it, when I consider a piece of research submitted for my judgment, I am often compelled to ask myself whether I should try to impose the critical vision which seems to me to be the necessary condition of the construction of a genuine scientific object by launching into a critique of the preconstructed object that is always likely to appear as a *coup de force*, as a kind of intellectual *Anschluss*. This difficulty is all the more serious because in the social sciences the principle of mistakes is almost always rooted, at least in my experience, in socially constituted dispositions as well as in social fears and social fantasies. So that it is often difficult to state publicly a critical judgment which, beyond scientific practices, touches on the deepest dispositions of habitus, those intimately linked to social and ethnic origins, gender, and also to the degree of prior academic consecration. I have in mind here the exaggerated humility of some researchers (more frequent among women than among men, or among people of "modest" social background, as we sometimes say) which is no less fatal than arrogance. In my view, the right posture consists of a highly unlikely combination of definite ambition, which leads one to take a broad view (*à voir grand*), and the great modesty indispensable in burying oneself in the fullest detail of the object. Thus the research director who truly wants to fulfill his function would sometimes have to take up the role of the confessor or guru (in French, we say "director of consciousness"), a role that is quite dangerous and has no justification, by bringing back to reality the one who "sees too big" and by instilling more ambition in those who let themselves be trapped in the security of humble and easy undertakings.

In fact, the most decisive help that the novice researcher can expect from experience is that which encourages him or her to take into account, in the definition of her project, the real conditions of its realization, that is, the means she has at her disposal (especially in terms of time and of specific competence, given the nature of her social experiences and her training) and the possibilities of access to informants and to information, documents and sources, etc. Oftentimes, it is only at the conclusion of a protracted work of socioanalysis, through a whole sequence of phases of overinvestments and divestments, that the ideal match between a researcher and "her" object can be made.

The sociology of sociology, when it takes the very concrete form of the sociology of the sociologist, of his scientific project, of his ambitions and his failures, of his audacities and his fears, is not a *supplément d'âme* or a kind of narcissistic luxury: the bringing to awareness *(prise de conscience)* of the dispositions, favorable or unfavorable, associated with your social origins, academic background, and gender offers you a chance, if a limited one, to get a grip on those dispositions. Yet the ruses of social pulsions are countless, and to do a sociology of one's own universe can sometimes be yet another, most perverse, way of satisfying such repressed impulses in a subtly roundabout way. For instance, a former theologian turned sociologist who undertakes to study theologians may undergo a sort of regression and start talking like a theologian or, still worse, use sociology as a weapon to settle his past theologian's accounts. The same may be true of an ex-philosopher: she will also risk finding in the sociology of philosophy a covert way of waging philosophical wars by other means.

5   Participant Objectivation

What I have called *participant objectivation* (and which is not to be mistaken for participant observation)[50] is no doubt the most difficult exercise of all because it requires a break with the deepest and most unconscious adherences and adhesions, those that quite often give the object its very "interest" for those who study it—i.e., everything about their relation to the object they try to know that they least want to know. It is the most difficult but also the most necessary exercise because, as I tried to do in *Homo Academicus* (Bourdieu 1988a), the work of objectivation in this case touches on a very peculiar object within which some of the most powerful social determinants of the very principles of apprehension of any possible object are implicitly inscribed: on the one hand, the specific interests associated with

50. On this notion, see *The Logic of Practice* (Bourdieu 1990a), *Homo Academicus* (Bourdieu 1988a), Bourdieu 1978a, and part 2, sec. 1, above.

being a member of the academic field and with occupying a specific position in that field; on the other hand, the socially constituted categories of perception of the academic world and of the social world, those categories of professorial understanding which, as I said earlier, can furnish the underpinnings of an aesthetics (e.g., the *art pompier*, academic art) or of an epistemology (as with the epistemology of ressentiment which, by making a virtue out of necessity, always values the petty prudences of positivist rigor as against all forms of scientific audacity).

Without trying to explicate here all the teachings that a reflexive sociology can draw from such an analysis, I would like to suggest only one of the best concealed presuppositions of the scientific enterprise that work on such an object forced me to uncover and whose immediate consequence—proof that the sociology of sociology is a necessity, not a luxury—is a better knowledge of the object itself. In a first phase of my work, I had built a model of the academic space as a space of positions linked by specific relations of force, as a field of forces and a field of struggles to preserve or transform this field of forces. I could have stopped there but observations I had made in the past, in the course of my ethnographic work in Algeria, had sensitized me to the "epistemocentrism" associated with the scholarly viewpoint. Moreover, I was forced to look back upon my enterprise by the uneasiness that filled me, upon publication, by the feeling I had of having committed a kind of disloyalty by setting myself up as observer of a game I was still playing. I thus experienced in a particularly acute manner what was implicated in the claim to adopt the stance of the impartial observer, at once ubiquitous and invisible because dissimulated behind the absolute impersonality of research procedures, and thus capable of taking up a quasi-divine viewpoint on colleagues who are also competitors. By objectivizing the pretension to the regal position that turns sociology into a weapon *in* the struggles internal to the field instead of an instrument of knowledge *of* these struggles, and thus of the knowing subject himself who, no matter what he does, never ceases to wage them, I gave myself the means of reintroducing into the analysis the consciousness of the presuppositions and prejudices associated with the local and localized point of view of someone who constructs the space of points of view.

Awareness of the limits of objectivist objectivation made me discover that there exists, within the social world, and particularly within the academic world, a whole nexus of institutions whose effect is to render acceptable the gap between the objective truth of the world and the lived truth of what we are and what we do in it—everything that objectivized subjects bring up when they oppose objectivist analysis with the idea that "things are not that way." In this case, there exists for instance collective systems of defense which, in universes where everyone struggles for the monopoly over a market in which all of one's customers are also one's competitors and where life is therefore very hard,[51] enable us to accept ourselves by accepting the subterfuges or compensatory gratifications offered by the milieu. It is this *double truth*, objective and subjective, which constitutes the whole truth of the social world.

Although I hesitate a bit to do it, I would like to evoke as a final illustration a presentation made here some time ago on a post-election television debate,[52] an object which, due to its apparent easiness (everything about it is immediately given to immediate intuition), presents many of the difficulties that a sociologist can encounter. How are we to move beyond intelligent description, of the kind always exposed to "being redundant with the world" *(faire pléonasme avec le monde)*, as Mallarmé used to say? The danger is great, indeed, to restate in a different language what agents involved have already said or done and to bring out meanings of the first degree (there is a dramatization of the wait for the results, there is a struggle between the participants over the meaning of the result, etc.), or simply (or pompously) to identify meanings that are the product of conscious intentions and which agents themselves could state, if they had the time, and if they did not fear giving the show away. For the latter know very well—at least in practice and, more and more often today, in a conscious mode—that, in a situation whose stake is to impose the most favorable representation of one's own position, public admis-

51. This is what Bourdieu (1985d) calls the "market of restricted production," in opposition to the "generalized market" in which cultural producers submit their works to the public at large.

52. On the night of each national election, the main television channels in France organize special programs where prominent politicians, political scientists, journalists, and political commentators interpret and debate the estimated results of the vote and their significance for the political evolution of the country. Such programs are nearly universally identifiable by French television spectators and constitute an increasingly influential means of political action.

sion of failure, as an act of re-cognition, is *de facto* impossible. They also know that, to speak properly, figures and their meanings are no universal "facts," and that the strategy which consists in "denying the obvious" (54 percent is greater than 46 percent), although apparently doomed to fail, retains a degree of validity (party X won but party Y didn't really lose: X won but not as cleanly as in previous elections or by a smaller margin than predicted, etc.).

But is this what really matters? The problem of the break is raised with a special salience here because the analyst is contained within the object of his or her competitors in the interpretation of the object, and these competitors may also call upon the authority of science. It is raised in a particularly acute form because, in contradistinction to what happens in other sciences, a mere description, even a constructed description—i.e., one bent on capturing the relevant traits and only those—does not have the intrinsic value that it assumes in the case of the description of a secret ritual ceremony among the Hopis or of the coronation of a king in the Middle Ages: the scene has been seen and *understood* (at a certain level and up to a certain point) by twenty million television spectators and the recording gives a readout of it that no positivist transcription could match.

In fact, we cannot escape the indefinite series of mutually refutable interpretations—the hermeneuticist is involved in a struggle among hermeneuticists who compete to have the last word about a phenomenon or an outcome—unless we actually construct the space of objective relations *(structure)* of which the communicative exchanges we directly observe *(interaction)* are but the expression. The task consists in grasping a hidden reality which veils itself by unveiling itself, which offers itself to observers only in the anecdotal form of the interaction that conceals it. What does this all mean? Under our eyes we have a set of individuals, designated by surnames, Mr. Amar, journalist, Mr. Rémond, historian, Mr. X, political scientist, and so on, who exchange, as we say, utterances that apparently are liable to a "discourse analysis" and where all visible "interactions" apparently provide all the necessary tools for their own analysis. But in fact the scene that unravels on the television set, the strategies that agents deploy to win the symbolic struggle over the monopoly of the imposition of the verdict, for the recognized ability to tell the truth about the stake of the debate, are the expression of objective relations of force between the agents involved or, to be more precise, between the different fields in which they are implicated and in which they occupy positions of various standing. In other words, *the interaction is the visible and purely phenomenal resultant of the intersection of hierarchized fields.*

The space of interaction functions as a situation of linguistic market and we can uncover the principles that underlie its conjunctural properties.[53] First, it consists of a preconstructed space: the social composition of the group of participants is determined in advance. To understand what can be said and especially *what cannot be said* on the set, one must know the laws of formation of the group of speakers— who is excluded and who exclude themselves. The most radical censorship is absence. We must thus consider the ratios of representation (in both the statistical and the social sense) of the various categories (gender, age, occupation, education, etc.), and thus the chances of access to speech, measured by how much time is used up by each. A second characteristic is the following: the journalist wields a form of domination (conjunctural, not structural) over a space of play that he has constructed and in which he finds himself in the role of referee imposing norms of "objectivity" and "neutrality."

We cannot, however, stop here. The space of interaction is the locus where the intersection between several different fields is realized. In their struggle to impose the "impartial" interpretation, that is, to make the viewers recognize their vision as objective, agents have at their command resources that depend on their membership in objectively hierarchized fields and on their position within their respective fields. First we have the political field (Bourdieu 1981a): because they are directly implicated in the game and thus directly interested and seen as such, politicians are immediately perceived as judges and judged *(juges et parties)* and therefore are always suspected of putting forth interested, biased, and hence discredited interpretations. They occupy different positions in the political field: they are situated in this space by their membership in a party but also by their status in the party, their notoriety, local or national, their public appeal, etc. Then we have the journalistic field: journalists can and must adopt a rhetoric of objectivity and neutrality, with the assistance of "politologists" when needed. Then we have the field of "political

53. The concept of linguistic market is explicated in Bourdieu 1990f and part 2, sec. 5, above.

science" within which "media politologists" occupy a rather un-glamorous position, even if they enjoy considerable prestige on the outside, especially among journalists whom they structurally domi-nate. Next is the field of political marketing, represented by adver-tisers and media advisors who dress up their evaluations of politicians with "scientific" justifications. Last is the university field proper, represented by specialists in electoral history who have devel-oped a specialty in the commentary of electoral results. We thus have a progression from the most "engaged" to the most detached, struc-turally or statutorily: the academic is the one who has the most "hindsight," "detachment." When it comes to producing a *rhetoric of objectivity* which is as efficacious as possible, as is the case in such post-election news programs, the academic enjoys a structural advan-tage over all the others.

The discursive strategies of the various agents, and in particular rhetorical effects aimed at producing a front of objectivity, will de-pend on the balance of symbolic forces between the fields and on the specific resources that membership in these fields grants to the vari-ous participants. In other words, they will hinge upon the specific in-terests and the differential assets that the participants possess, in this particular symbolic struggle over the "neutral" verdict, by virtue of their position in the system of invisible relations that obtain between the different fields in which they operate. For instance, the pol-itologist will have an edge, as such, over the politician and the jour-nalist, due to the fact that he is more readily credited with objectivity, and because he has the option of calling upon his specific compe-tence, i.e., his command of electoral history to make comparisons. He can ally himself with the journalist, whose claims to objectivity he will thereby reinforce and legitimize. The resultant of all these objec-tive relations are relations of symbolic power which express them-selves in the interaction in the form of rhetorical strategies. It is these objective relations that determine for the most part who can cut some-body off, ask questions, speak at length without being interrupted, or disregard interruptions, etc., who is condemned to strategies of de-negation (of interests and interested strategies) or to ritual refusals to answer, or to stereotypical formulas, etc. We would need to push fur-ther by showing how bringing objective structures into the analysis allows us to account for the particulars of discourse and of rhetorical strategies, complicities, and antagonisms, and for the moves attempted and effected—in short, for everything that discourse analysis believes it can understand on the basis of discourse alone.

But why is the analysis especially difficult in this case? No doubt this is because those whom the sociologist claims to objectivize are competitors for the monopoloy over objective objectivation. In fact, depending on what object she studies, the sociologist herself is more or less distant from the agents and the stakes she observes, more or less directly involved in rivalries with them, and consequently more or less tempted to enter the game of metadiscourse under the cloak of objectivity. When the game under analysis consists, as is the case here, in delivering a metadiscourse about all other discourses—those of the politician who cheerfully proclaims electoral victory, of the journalist who claims to provide an objective report on the spread between the candidates, of the "politologist" and the specialist in electoral history who claim to offer us an objective explanation of the result by drawing on comparison of the margins and trends with past or present statistics—where it consists, in a word, in placing oneself *meta*, above the game, through the sole force of discourse, it is tempting to use the science of the strategies that the different agents develop to assure victory to their "truth" in order to tell the truth of the game, and thus to secure victory in the game for yourself. It is still the objective relation between political sociology and "media-oriented politology" or, to be more precise, between the positions that the observers and the observed occupy in their respective, objectively hierarchized, fields that determines the perception of the observer, especially by imposing on him blind spots indicative of his own vested interests.

Objectivation of the relation of the sociologist to his or her object is, as we can clearly see in this case, the necessary condition of the break with the propensity to invest in her object which is no doubt at the root of her "interest" in the object. One must in a sense renounce the use of science to intervene in the object in order to be in a position to carry out an objectivation which is not merely the partial and reductionist view that one can acquire, from within the game, of the other player(s), but rather the all-encompassing view that one acquires of a game that can be grasped as such because one has retired from it. Only the sociology of sociology—and of the sociologist—can give us a definite mastery of the social aims that can be pursued via the scientific goals we immediately seek. Participant objectivation, arguably the highest form of the sociological art, is realizable only to the extent that it is predicated on as complete as possible an objectivation of the interest to objectivize inscribed in the fact of participating, as well as on a bracketing of this interest and of the representations it sustains.

Appendix 1 How to Read Bourdieu

For the novice, finding an entry into Bourdieu's sprawling work poses the thorny problem of where to start. The following strategy reflects my personal preferences and what the participants in the Workshop on Pierre Bourdieu I organized found effective (only English-language writings are included and short pieces are given preference over longer ones). The order of listings, from the more (meta-) theoretical and conceptual to the more empirical, is somewhat arbitrary, since Bourdieu rarely separates epistemology, theory, and empirical work, but it is useful as a rough indication of the emphases of the papers. In general, readers are advised to read across empirical domains, to alternate more theoretical and more empirically oriented pieces, and, most of all, to understand Bourdieu in his own terms before "translating" him into more friendly lexicons because the style and the substance of his arguments are intimately conjoined.

Begin with Bourdieu's (1989e) "Social Space and Symbolic Power" (along with Brubaker's [1985] excellent overview; DiMaggio 1979 and Garnham and Williams 1980 are also useful), then move on to the article "On Symbolic Power" (Bourdieu 1979b, reprinted in *Language and Symbolic Power*) for a dense statement of Bourdieu's project in relation to various strands of classical sociology and philosophy (Hegel, Kant, Durkheim, Marx, Weber, Cassirer, Saussure, Lévi-Strauss, etc.), and to the 1986 interviews (Honneth, Kocyba, and Schwibs 1986; Bourdieu 1986a, both of which are reprinted in Bourdieu 1990h) which help situate it more fully in the context of the French and international intellectual scene. Although somewhat dated, "The Three Forms of Theoretical Knowledge" (Bourdieu 1973c) is a useful summary of what Bourdieu sees as the respective strengths and weaknesses of three fundamental forms of theorizing: subjectivist, objectivist, and praxeological (the transcendence of the first two). This article also serves as a useful introduction to *Outline of a Theory of Practice* (Bourdieu 1977a).

Next, read "Men and Machines," a terse piece wherein Bourdieu (1981c) outlines his conceptualization of the dialectic, or "ontological complicity," between social action incarnate in bodies (habitus, dispositions) and in institutions (fields, or spaces of positions), by which he proposes to overcome the dichotomies of action and structure and micro- and macroanalysis. "The Forms of Capital" (Bourdieu 1986b) presents Bourdieu's conception of the main species of capital or power: economic, cultural, social, and symbolic, and the specific effects and properties of each, as well as typical strategies and dilemmas of conversion. "Social Space and the Genesis of Groups" (Bourdieu 1985a) is a major statement of Bourdieu's concept of social space and of his theory of group formation, including the role of symbolic power and politics in the constitution of social collectives. "The Economy of Linguistic Exchanges" (Bourdieu 1977c) extends this model to the analysis of language and leads into *Language and Symbolic Power* (1991e). Thompson (1991) effectively discusses how Bourdieu's sociology of language and politics fits into his broader theory of practice.

Bourdieu's view on the classification struggles through which correspondences between cultural and economic power are established, and which constitutes the link between *Reproduction* and *Distinction*, is expressed succinctly in Bourdieu and Boltanski 1981. "Changes in Social Structure and Changes in the Demand for Education" (Bourdieu and Boltanski 1977) analyzes the structure and functioning of the system of class strategies of reproduction and reconversion. "Marriage Strategies as Strategies of Social Reproduction" (Bourdieu 1977b) takes this analysis into the realm of kinship, and offers a paradigm for the study of group formation. Bourdieu and de Saint Martin's (in Bourdieu 1988a: 194–225) exploration of the "categories of professorial judgment" provides a forceful empirical illustration of the operation and mutual reinforcement of social and academic classifications that brings together many of these themes.

An early empirical elaboration of the central concept of field is found in "The Specificity of the Scientific Field" (Bourdieu 1975d), wherein Bourdieu also provides the basis for a sociological theory of scientific progress and adumbrates his sociological epistemology, both of which are further developed in Bourdieu 1991f. "The Field of Cultural Production" (1983d) exemplifies his approach to culture and power and his use of the concepts of field, habitus, interest, structural homology, etc., in the context of a detailed inquiry into the formation and functioning of the French literary scene of the late nineteenth century. "The Force of Law: Toward a Sociology of the Juridical Field" (Bourdieu 1987g) is an application of Bourdieu's framework to the legal domain, and outlines a sociological theory of the significance of formal codification in society. "The Historical Genesis of A Pure Aesthetics" (Bourdieu 1987d) is a succinct overview of the "invention" of the artistic gaze—of its institutionalization in the artistic field and embodiment in the aesthetic habitus. Bourdieu's conception of the historic emergence and role of intellectuals is similarly put forth in the article on "The Corporatism of the Universal" (Bourdieu 1989d).

Readers of a more empirical bent might want to begin with "The Categories of Professorial Judgment" before working their way backwards to the more conceptual pieces, then take up Bourdieu's case studies of fields. "The Invention of the Artist's Life" (Bourdieu 1987j) provides a good test for the potency of Bourdieu's theory because it can be measured against traditional literary or philosophical analyses of Flaubert, such as Sartre's (see Sartre's mammoth 4-volume study *The Family Idiot* [1981–91]). Its restricted title notwithstanding, "Program for a Sociology of Sport" (Bourdieu 1988f) is an exceptionally lucid illustration of Bourdieu's relational mode of thinking which is valuable also for highlighting his ability to shuttle constantly between theoretical abstraction and empirical concreteness and to connect phenomenal realms and analytical concerns that apparently have little or nothing in common (in this case, Vivaldi, the sociology of sociology, rugby, videos, neo-Kantian philosophy, petty-bourgeois cultural goodwill, classification struggles, and professionalization). It also provides a terse statement of the pivotal place of the body and of belief in Bourdieu's sociology. "The Disenchantment of the World," the long essay on the mutually constituting relation between "Economic Structures and Temporal Structures" which opens *Algeria 1960* (Bourdieu 1979c), is an alternate candidate for a first reading: written for the most part in the mid-1960s, it does not deploy Bourdieu's full conceptual arsenal, which makes it somewhat easier to comprehend, yet it instances very clearly his characteristic mode of sociological reasoning. For two lucid and powerful exemplifications of what Bourdieu means by "constructing the object," see his analyses of two polls, one on the spontaneous classification of political figures ("The Parlour Game," Bourdieu 1984a: 546–59), the second a "Hit Parade of French Intellectuals" (Bourdieu 1988a: 256–70).

Once all or part of this is digested, one must read together *Distinction* (Bourdieu 1984a, especially chapters 2, 3, 5–7, the conclusion, and postcript, beginning with the postcript) and *The Logic of Practice* (Bourdieu 1990a, arguably Bourdieu's best and most important book), into which the paper entitled "The Scholastic Fallacy" (Bourdieu 1990e) offers an opening, before tackling *Homo Academicus* (1988a). The single most easily accessible book in English is the collection of essays and talks entitled *In Other Words* (Bourdieu 1990h, though the translation has its weaknesses), which provides a number of leads, avenues, and windows into Bourdieu's intellectual enterprise.

Appendix 2 A Selection of Articles from
Actes de la recherche en sciences sociales

This selection is designed to give an indication of the range, diversity, and depth of the empirical investigations conducted within or at the frontiers of Bourdieu's theoretical framework (titles are given in translation; complete bibliographic data is found in the References). The papers selected express my own preferences, but all the major past and present contributors from the Center for European Sociology are represented. Many more pieces could be added; the interested reader is referred to the journal itself for further exploration (an index of articles published from 1975 to 1988 can be found in the November 1988 issue). For a synoptic presentation of the main research projects in progress as of the early 1990s see Centre de sociologie de l'éducation et de la culture, *Rapport d'activité* (Paris, EHESS, June 1990, 56 pp., mimeo).

Alvim and Lopes 1990. "Working-Class Families or Families of Working Women?"

Balazs 1983. "Factors and Forms of the Experience of Unemployment."

Balazs and Faguer 1991. "'What Will They Become?' The Social Effects of Television."

Bancaud 1989. "A 'shifting constancy': A Sociology of Judges."

Boltanski 1975. "The Constitution of the Field of Comic Strips."

Boltanski 1979. "Social Taxonomies and Class Struggle: The Mobilization of the 'Middle Class' and the Invention of 'cadres.'"

Boltanski 1980. "The University, Business, and the Growth of Bourgeois Wage Earners."

Boltanski with Daré and Schiltz 1984. "Denunciation."

Bonvin 1982. "A Surrogate Family: A Private Parochial High School."

Chamboredon 1975. "Sociology of Sociology and the Social Interests of Sociologists."

Chamboredon and Fabiani 1977. "Children's Books: The Field of Publishing and the Social Definitions of Childhood."

Champagne 1979. "Young Farmers and Old Peasants: The Crisis of Succession and the Invention of the 'Elderly.'"

Champagne 1984. "The Demonstration: The Production of A Political Event."

Champagne 1988. "The Political Circle: The Social Uses of Public Opinion Polls and the New French Political Space."

Chapoulie 1979. "The Pedagogical Competence of Teachers as a Stake of Conflicts."

Charle 1978. "Business in the Structure of the Dominant Class in France around 1900."

Charle 1983. "The Parisian Academic Field at the Close of the Nineteenth Century."

Delsaut 1976. "The Twofold Wedding of Jean Célisse."

Delsaut 1988a. "Notes Toward a Socioanalysis, 1: L'*inforjetable*."

Delsaut 1988b. "Notes Toward a Socioanalysis, 2: A Class Picture."

Desrosières 1978. "The Matrimonial Market and the Structure of Social Classes."

Dezalay 1989. "Family Law: From the Notable to the Expert, or The Restructuring of the Field of Specialists in Business Bankruptcy."

Dezalay, Sarat, and Silbey 1989. "From Protest to Meritocratic Knowledge: Outline of a Social History of Legal Sociology in the United States."

Dumont 1984. "The Worldly Success of A Fake Science: The Physiognomy of Johann Kaspar Lavater."

Encrevé and Fornel 1983. "Sense in Practice: The Construction of Reference and the Social Structure of Interaction in the Question/Answer Couplet."

Fabiani 1983. "The Programs, the Men, the Works: Philosophy Professors in the Classroom and in the City at the Turn of the Century."

Faguer 1991. "The Effects of a 'Total Education': A Jesuit High School, 1960."

Fornel 1983. "Legitimacy and Speech Acts."

Gamboni 1983. "Scorn and Misunderstanding: Elements for a Theory of Contemporary Iconoclasm."

Garcia 1986. "The Social Construction of A Perfect Market: The Strawberry Market of Fontaines-en-Sologne."

Garrigou 1988. "The Secret of the Voting Booth."

Gaxie 1990. "Beyond Surface Appearances . . . On How to Measure Public Opinion."

Grignon 1977. "The Relations between the Transformations of the Religious Field and the Transformation of Political Space."

Guillemin 1982. "Aristocrats, Property Owners, and School Credentials: The Struggle for Local Power in the 'Départment' of Manche, 1830–1875."

Heinich 1987. "The Arts and Sciences in the Classical Age: Cultural Professions and Institutions."

Karady 1983. "The Professors of the Republic: Academic Market, University Reform, and the Transformation of the Professorial Function at the End of the Nineteenth Century."

Karady 1985. "Hungarian Jews Under Anti-Semitic Legislation: A Study of a Sociological Conjuncture, 1938–1943."

Karady 1988. "Durkheim and the Beginnings of Academic Ethnology."

Lagrave 1990. "Feminist Research or Research on Women? The Field of Women's Studies and Feminism in France."

Laks 1983. "Langage and Social Practice: A Sociolinguistic Study of a Group of Teenagers in Suburban Paris."

Lardinois 1985. "How To Classify the Hindu Family."

Latour and Fabbri 1977. "The Rhetoric of Science: Power and Duty in a Natural Science Article."

Lenoir 1978. "The Invention of the 'Elderly' and the Constitution of the Field of Management of Old Age."

Lenoir 1980. "The Notion of 'Work Injury' as a Stake of Struggle."

Lenoir 1985. "The Crumbling of the Social Basis of Familialism."

Loirand 1989. "From Falling to Jumping: The Genesis and Transformation of Competitive Parachuting."

Maresca 1981. "The Representation of the Peasantry: Ethnographic Notes on the Work of Representation of Peasant Leaders."

Mauger and Fossé-Poliak 1983. "'Loubards': The Culture of Male Working-Class Youth."

Merllié 1983. "A Nomenclature and Its Applications: The Case of Statistics on the Social Origins of Students."

Merllié 1990. "The Gender of Writing: Remarks on the Social Perception of Femininity."

Muel-Dreyfus 1977. "Primary School Teachers, Peasants, and the Republican Order at the Turn of the Century."

Offerlé 1988. " How Many Votes? Voters, Parties and the Socialist Electorate in France at the End of the Nineteenth Century."

Pialoux 1978. "Youth With No Future and Temporary Work."

Pinell 1987. "A Modern-Day Plague and Tomorrow's Medicine: French Cancerology in the Interwar Years."

Pinçon 1985. "A Paternalistic Boss."

Pinto 1975. "The Military, Army Recruits, and Social Classes."

Pinto 1984. "The Vocation of the Universal: The Formation of the 'Intellectual' around 1900."

Pollak 1979. "Paul Lazarsfeld, Founder of A Multinational Scientific Concern."

Pollak 1981. "A Sociology-in-Action of Intellectuals: The Struggles of Karl Kraus."

Pollak with Schiltz 1987. "Social Identity and the Management of A Public Health Risk: How Homosexuals Face AIDS."

Ponton 1977. "Images of the Peasantry in Rural Novels at the End of the Nineteenth Century."

Pudal 1988. "Communist Leaders: From 'Son of the People' to 'Teacher of the Masses.'"

de Saint Martin 1980. "A Prominent Family."

de Saint Martin 1985. "Matrimonial Strategies among the Aristocracy: Notes Toward an Investigation."

de Saint Martin 1989. "The Nobility and 'Noble' Sports."

de Saint Martin 1990. "'Women Writers' in the Literary Field."

Sayad 1977. "The Three 'Ages' of Algerian Emigration in France."

Sayad 1979. "Illegitimate Children."

Sayad 1985. "From Oral Messages to Taped Letters: Techniques and Forms of Communication between Algerian Migrant Workers and their Families."

Scherrer 1990. "The Erosion of Lenin's Image."

Suaud 1982. "Religious Conversions and Economic Reconversions."

Suaud 1989. "The Space of Sports, Social Space, and Effects of Age: The Diffusion of Tennis, Squash, and Golf in the Greater Nantes Area."

Thèvenot 1979. "Difficult Youth: The Social Functions of Fuzziness and Rigor in Classifications."

Verdès-Leroux 1976. "Power and Social Assistance: Fifty Years of Social Work."

Verdès-Leroux 1981. "A Self-Perpetuating Total Institution: The French Communist Party."

Verger 1982. "The Artist Seen Through the School's Lens: Academic Taxonomies and the Artistic 'Vocation.'"

Verger 1987. "The Art of Estimating Art, or, How to Compare the Incomparable."

Vernier 1985. "Matrimonial Strategies and Choice of Incestuous Object: Dowry, Degree, Sexual Liberty, and Given Names."

Vernier 1989. "Fetishism of the Name, Intrafamily Emotional Exchanges, and Elective Affinities."

Villette 1976. "Social Psychology and Moral Retraining in Industrial Firms."

Wacquant 1989a. "Body and Soul: Ethnographic Notes of an Apprentice Boxer."

Winkin 1990. "Goffman and Women."

Zarca 1979. "The Social Trajectories of Shopkeepers."

Appendix 3 Selected Recent Writings on Pierre Bourdieu

This list of writings on Bourdieu, compiled from the References, makes no attempt at comprehensiveness. The secondary literature that has appeared in French alone, or in the sole field of education, exceeds the space available here. What I propose is, again, a selection, limited (with a few exceptions) to post-1980 pieces and tailored to represent a broad array of views on Bourdieu by sociologists, anthropologists, philosophers, cultural critics and educationalists. Only book reviews of special interest are cited, and the large and growing number of dissertations that make intensive use of Bourdieu's theories are excluded from mention.

Accardo 1983
Accardo and Corcuff 1986
Acciaiolo 1981
Adair 1984
Ansart 1990
Archer 1983
Arliaux 1985
Aronowitz and Giroux 1985
Barnard 1990
Bentley 1987
Berger 1986
Bidet 1979
Blasius and Winkler 1989
Bohn 1991
Bon and Schemeil 1980
Boschetti 1985
Bredo and Feinberg 1979

Broady 1990
Broady and Persson 1989
Brubaker 1985, 1989a, 1989b
Bürger 1990
Caillé 1981, 1987a, 1987b
Calhoun 1990, 1992
Calhoun, LiPuma, and Postone 1992
Caro 1980, 1982
Casanova 1990
de Certeau 1984
Cicourel in press
Coenen 1989
Collectif 'Révoltes Logiques' 1984
J. Collins 1992
R. Collins 1981a, 1989
Connell 1983
Corson 1991

Dal Lago 1985
Dennis 1986
DiMaggio 1979
Douglas 1981
Eagleton 1991
Earle 1988
Eder 1989
Ferry and Renault 1990
Foster 1986
Fournier and Lamont 1989
Frank 1980
Frow 1987
Garnham 1986
Garnham and Williams 1980
Gartman 1991
Gebauer and Wolff in press
Gerhards and Anheier 1989
Giddens 1986b
Giroux 1982
Gorder 1980
Grossetti 1986
Hanks 1987
Harker 1984
Harker, Mahar, and Wilkes 1990
Héran 1987
Hoffman 1986
Honneth 1986
Honneth, Kocyba, and Schwibs 1986
Ingram 1982
F. Inglis 1988
R. Inglis 1979
Jenkins 1982, 1986, 1989
Joppke 1986
Kot and Lautier 1984
Lakomski 1984
Lamont 1989
Lamont and Lareau 1988
Lash 1990
Lee 1988
Lemert 1986
Lichterman 1989
Lienard and Servais 1979
MacAloon 1988
McCleary 1989
Martin and Szelenyi 1987
Mary 1988

D. Miller and Branson 1987
M. Miller 1989
Miyajima et al. 1987
Miyajima 1990
Mortier 1989
Müller 1986
Murphy 1982, 1983
Nash 1986
Ortiz 1983
Ortner 1984
Österberg 1988
Ostrow 1981, 1990
Paradeise 1981
Passeron 1986
Pels 1989
Perrot and de la Soudrière 1988
Rancière 1984
Rasmussen 1981
Rittner 1984
Robinson and Garnier 1985
Robbins 1988, 1991
Rupp and de Lange 1989
Sack 1988
Sanchez de Horcájo 1979
Schatzki 1987
Schiltz 1982
Schwenk 1989
Sewell 1992
Snook 1990
Snyders 1976
Stamm 1983
Staub-Bernasconi 1989
Steinrücke 1989
Sulkunen 1982
Swartz 1977, 1981
Thapan 1988
J. B. Thompson 1984, 1991
Turner 1990
Verboven 1989
Vervaëck 1989
Wacquant 1987, 1989b, 1990a, 1992
Willis 1983
Wilson 1988
Winckler 1989
Yamamoto 1988
Zolberg 1986

Acknowledgments

Portions of part 2 of this book have appeared previously in a different form. We are grateful to the editorial collective of the *Berkeley Journal of Sociology* for permission to reprint passages from Pierre Bourdieu and Loïc J. D. Wacquant, "For A Socio-Analysis of Intellectuals: On 'Homo Academicus'" (*Berkeley Journal of Sociology*, 34 [1989]: 1–29) and to the American Sociological Association and Basil Blackwell, Publishers, for permission to reprint revised sections of Loïc J. D. Wacquant, "Toward a Reflexive Sociology: A Workshop with Pierre Bourdieu" (*Sociological Theory* 7 [Spring 1989]: 26–63).

While working on this volume, I have enjoyed the intellectual and material support of a number of institutions and individuals: the Department of Sociology at the University of Chicago, where Bill Wilson proved a source of constant personal and intellectual encouragement that nicely counterbalanced the friendly but ferocious criticism of James Coleman; the Urban Poverty Project, and the Center for the Study of Politics, Culture and History at Wilder House, where much of the manuscript was physically produced; Clemens Heller, director of the Maison des sciences de l'homme, who facilitated needed travel at a critical juncture of this enterprise; and the Society of Fellows at Harvard University, where I found the sheltered environment necessary to write part 1 and complete the penultimate revisions of the manuscript.

Numerous friends and colleagues have been kind or foolish enough to take time away from their own work to scrutinize successive versions of this text, which no doubt became the better for it. Among them, I would like to single out Craig Calhoun, William Rogers Brubaker, David Stark, and Daniel Breslau. I am particularly indebted to Rogers for his unfailingly perspicacious suggestions and for pushing me to bring this project to a belated close. I have also benefited from the comments and reactions of Bennett Berger, Philippe Bourgois, Lynn Sharon Chancer, Randall Collins, Charles Crothers, Paul DiMaggio, David Laitin, Don Levine, Raymond T. Smith, George Steinmetz, John Thompson, Erik Olin Wright, and Norbert Wiley (who, unbeknownst to him, planted the seeds for this volume when he invited me to put together the original "Chicago Workshop" for *Sociological Theory*, a rather bold move for the editor of an established journal). Doug Mitchell brought to this undertaking his unique combination of enthusiasm, efficiency, and tactful sense of urgency; I wish every young sociologist the chance to work with an editor such as he. Claudia Rex provided superb copy editing under unusually strenuous conditions.

Members of the Center for European Sociology in Paris welcomed me in their midst for several short visits during which they offered valuable insights into their individual and collective research, the workings of *Actes de la recherche en sciences sociales*, and an accelerated socialization by proxy into the workaday world of Bourdieu's team. I want to thank them very sincerely (especially Yvette Delsaut, Monique de Saint Martin, Monique Armand, Abdelmalek Sayad and Patrick Champagne, as well Marie-Christine Rivière and Rosine Christin) for making me feel at home among them and for sharing with me the intellectual excitement of the Center.

Finally, I would like to thank Pierre Bourdieu, not only for his invariably patient and careful answers to the seemingly endless stream of questions, queries, and objections I kept throwing at him via various media (face-to-face discussions and transatlantic phone conversations, letters and packages, mailgrams and faxes) over the past three years, but also for giving me complete editorial freedom to shape the final product. It is little to say that, for me, the process of co-producing this book with him has been an education in itself, a lesson in intellectual integrity of the kind that no graduate school can offer.

To DeeDee and my friends from 63rd Street, my thanks for making sure that I kept my feet on the ground—or on the ring mat, to be precise—while immersed in the heady enterprise of social theory. "Hey, Louie, man, what you be talkin' 'bout: reflexive sociology, *what's that?*"

Loïc J. D. Wacquant
Chicago and Cambridge, October 1991

References and Bibliography

For convenience, I have listed separately Bourdieu's work (ordered by date of publication in the language cited—English whenever an English translation is available). This section contains only those works cited or quoted in this volume; it is not a complete bibliography of his publications, which by itself would take up the space of a booklet. Indeed, such a booklet exists, painstakingly compiled and edited by Yvette Delsaut (*Bibliographie des travaux de Pierre Bourdieu, 1958–1988,* Paris, Centre de Sociologie Européenne du Collège de France, 1988, 39 pp., mimeo), a shortened version of which appears as an appendix to Bourdieu's *In Other Words* (Cambridge: Polity Press, 1990, pp. 199–218); see also the bibliography compiled by Broady (1990).

Writings by Pierre Bourdieu

1961
"Révolution dans la révolution." *Esprit* 1 (January): 27–40.

1962
a. [1958] *The Algerians.* Boston: Beacon Press.
b. "Célibat et condition paysanne." *Etudes rurales* 5/6 (April): 32–136.
c. "Les relations entre les sexes dans la société paysanne." *Les temps modernes* 195 (August): 307–31.
d. "La hantise du chômage chez l'ouvrier algérien. Prolétariat et système colonial." *Sociologie du travail* 4: 313–31.

1963
with Jean-Claude Passeron. "Sociologues des mythologies et mythologies de sociologues." *Les temps modernes* 211 (December): 998–1021.

with Alain Darbel, Jean-Pierre Rivet and Claude Seibel. *Travail et travailleurs en Algérie*. Paris and The Hague: Mouton.

1964

"The Attitude of the Algerian Peasant Toward Time." Pp. 55–72 in *Mediterranean Countrymen*. Edited by Jesse Pitt-Rivers. Paris and The Hague: Mouton.

with Abdelmalek Sayad. *Le déracinement. La crise de l'agriculture traditionnelle en Algérie*. Paris: Editions de Minuit.

1965

"The Sentiment of Honour in Kabyle Society." Pp. 191–241 in *Honour and Shame: The Values of Mediterranean Society*. Edited by J. G. Peristiany. London: Weidenfeld and Nicholson.

with Luc Boltanski, Robert Castel, and Jean-Claude Chamboredon. *Un art moyen. Essai sur les usages sociaux de la photographie*. Paris: Editions de Minuit. Translated as *Photography: A Middle-Brow Art*. Cambridge: Polity Press; Stanford: Stanford University Press, 1990.

with Jean-Claude Passeron and Monique de Saint Martin. *Rapport pédagogique et communication*. Paris and the Hague: Mouton. Translated as *Academic Discourse: Linguistic Misunderstanding and Professorial Power*. Cambridge: Polity Press, forthcoming.

1966

"Condition de classe et position de classe." *European Journal of Sociology* 7, no. 2: 201–23.

with Alain Darbel. "La fin d'un malthusianisme." Pp. 135–54 in *Le partage des bénéfices, expansion et inégalités en France*. Edited by Darras. Paris: Editions de Minuit.

with Alain Darbel and Dominique Schnapper. *L'amour de l'art. Les musées d'art européens et leur public*. Paris: Editions de Minuit. Translated as *The Love of Art*. Cambridge: Polity Press; Stanford: Stanford University Press, 1990.

1967

a. "Systems of Education and Systems of Thought." *Social Science Information* 14, no. 3: 338–58.

b. Postface. Pp. 136–67 in Erwin Panofsky, *Architecture gothique et pensée scolastique*. Translated by Pierre Bourdieu. Paris: Editions de Minuit.

with Jean-Claude Passeron. "Sociology and Philosophy in France Since 1945: Death and Resurrection of a Philosophy Without Subject." *Social Research* 34, no. 1 (Spring): 162–212.

1968

a. 1968a. "Outline of a Sociological Theory of Art Perception." *International Social Science Journal* 10 (Winter): 589–612.

b. 1968b. "Structuralism and Theory of Sociological Knowledge." *Social Research* 35, no. 4 (Winter): 681–706.

1970

with O. Hahn. 1970. "La théorie." *VH 101* 2 (Summer): 12–21.

1971

a. [1966] "Intellectual Field and Creative Project." Pp. 161–88 in *Knowledge and Control: New Directions for the Sociology of Education.* Edited by Michael F. D. Young. London: Collier-Macmillan.
b. "Genèse et structure du champ religieux." *Revue française de sociologie* 12, no. 3 (July–September): 294–334.
c. "Disposition esthétique et compétence artistique." *Les temps modernes* 295 (February): 1345–78.
d. "Champ du pouvoir, champ intellectuel et habitus de classe." *Scolies* 1: 7–26.
e. "Une interprétation de la théorie de la religion selon Max Weber." *European Journal of Sociology* 12: 3–21.

1972

Esquisse d'une théorie de la pratique. Précédée de trois études d'ethnologie kabyle. Geneva: Droz.

1973

a. [1962] "The Algerian Subproletariate." Pp. 83–89 in *Man, State, and Society in the Contemporary Maghrib.* Edited by I. W. Zartman. London: Pall Mall Press.
b. [1971] "Cultural Reproduction and Social Reproduction." Pp. 71–112 in *Knowledge, Education, and Cultural Change.* Edited by Richard Brown. London: Tavistock.
c. "The Three Forms of Theoretical Knowledge." *Social Science Information* 12: 53–80.
d. [1970] "The Berber House." Pp. 98–110 in *Rules and Meanings.* Edited by Mary Douglas. Harmondsworth: Penguin.
with Jean-Claude Chamboredon, and Jean-Claude Passeron. [1968]. *Le métier de sociologue. Préalables épistémologiques.* 2d ed. Paris and the Hague: Mouton. Translated as *The Craft of Sociology: Epistemological Preliminaries.* Berlin and New York: Walter de Gruyter, 1991.

1974

a. "Avenir de classe et causalité du probable." *Revue française de sociologie* 15, no. 1 (January–March): 3–42.
b. [1966] "The School as a Conservative Force: Scholastic and Cultural Inequalities." Pp. 32–46 in *Contemporary Research in the Sociology of Education.* Edited by John Eggleston. London: Methuen.

c. "Les fractions de la classe dominante et les modes d'appropriation de l'oeuvre d'art." *Social Science Information* 13, no. 3: 7–32.
with Monique de Saint Martin. [1970]. "Scholastic Excellence and the Values of the Educational System." Pp. 338–71 in *Contemporary Research in the Sociology of Education.* Edited by John Eggleston. London: Methuen.

1975
a. "La critique du discours lettré." *Actes de la recherche en sciences sociales* 5/6: 4–8.
b. "La lecture de Marx: quelques remarques critiques à propos de 'Quelques remarques critiques à propos de "Lire le Capital".'" *Actes de la recherche en sciences sociales* 5/6: 65–79.
c. "L'ontologie politique de Martin Heidegger." *Actes de la recherche en sciences sociales* 5/6: 109–56.
d. "The Specificity of the Scientific Field and the Social Conditions of the Progress of Reason." *Social Science Information* 14, no. 6 (December): 19–47.
with Luc Boltanski. "Le fétichisme de la langue." *Actes de la recherche en sciences sociales* 2: 95–107.
with Yvette Delsaut. "Le couturier et sa griffe. Contribution à une théorie de la magie," *Actes de la recherche en sciences sociales* 1: 7–36.
with A. Casanova, and M. Simon. "Les intellectuels dans le champ de la lutte des classes." *La nouvelle critique* 87 (October): 20–26.

1977
a. *Outline of A Theory of Practice.* Cambridge: Cambridge University Press.
b. [1972] "Marriage Strategies as Strategies of Social Reproduction." Pp. 117–44 in *Family and Society: Selections from the Annales.* Edited by R. Foster and O. Ranum. Baltimore: The Johns Hopkins University Press.
c. "The Economy of Linguistic Exchanges." *Social Science Information* 16, no. 6: 645–668.
d. "Remarques provisoires sur la perception sociale du corps." *Actes de la recherche en sciences sociales* 14: 51–54.
with Luc Boltanski. [1973] "Changes in Social Structure and Changes in the Demand for Education." Pp. 197–227 in *Contemporary Europe: Social Structures and Cultural Patterns.* Edited by Scott Giner and Margaret Scotford-Archer. London: Routledge and Kegan Paul.
with Jean-Claude Passeron. [1970] *Reproduction in Education, Society and Culture.* London: Sage. Paperback edition with a new preface published 1990.

1978
a. "Sur l'objectivation participante. Réponses à quelques objections." *Actes de la recherche en sciences sociales* 20/21: 67–69.
b. "Classement, déclassement, reclassement." *Actes de la recherche en sciences sociales* 24: 2–22. Translated as the epilogue to Bourdieu and Passeron 1979.
c. "Sport and Social Class." *Social Science Information* 17, no. 6: 819–840.

d. "Capital symbolique et classes sociales." *L'arc* 72: 13–19. Translated in Bourdieu forthcoming a.

with Monique de Saint Martin. "Le patronat." *Actes de la recherche en sciences sociales* 20/21: 3–82.

1979

a. "Les trois états du capital culturel." *Actes de la recherche en sciences sociales* 30: 3–6.

b. [1977] "Symbolic Power," *Critique of Anthropology* 13/14 (Summer): 77–85.

c. *Algeria 1960*. Cambridge: Cambridge University Press.

d. "The Sense of Honor." Pp. 95–132 in *Algeria 1960*. Cambridge: Cambridge University Press.

e. [1971] "Public Opinion Does Not Exist." Pp. 124–30 in *Communication and Class Struggle*, vol. 1. Edited by A. Matelart and S. Siegelaub. New York: International General/IMMRC.

with Jean-Claude Passeron. [1964] *The Inheritors: French Students and their Relation to Culture*. Chicago: The University of Chicago Press.

1980

a. [1977] "The Production of Belief: Contribution to an Economy of Symbolic Goods." *Media, Culture and Society* 2 (July): 261–93.

b. *Questions de sociologie*. Paris: Editions de Minuit.

c. "Le capital social." *Actes de la recherche en sciences sociales* 31: 2–3.

d. "Le mort saisit le vif. Les relations entre l'histoire incorporée et l'histoire réifiée." *Actes de la recherche en sciences sociales* 32/33: 3–14.

e. "Sartre." *London Review of Books* 2, no. 20 (October 20): 11–12.

f. "Le Nord et le Midi: contribution à une analyse de l'effet Montesquieu." *Actes de la recherche en sciences sociales* 35: 21–25.

g. "L'identité et la représentation. Eléments pour une reflexion critique sur l'idée de région." *Actes de la recherche en sciences sociales* 35: 63–72.

h. "Les intellectuels sont-ils hors-jeu?" Pp. 61–66 in *Questions de sociologie*. Paris: Editions de Minuit.

i. "Comment libérer les intellectuels libres?" Pp. 67–78 in *Questions de sociologie*. Paris: Editions de Minuit.

1981

a. "La représentation politique. Eléments pour une théorie du champ politique." *Actes de la recherche en sciences sociales* 37 (February–March): 3–24. Reprinted in translation in Bourdieu 1991e.

b. "Epreuve scolaire et consécration sociale. Les classes préparatoires aux Grandes écoles." *Actes de la recherche en sciences sociales* 39: 3–70.

c. "Men and Machines." Pp. 304–17 in *Advances in Social Theory and Methodology: Toward an Integration of Micro- and Macro-Sociologies*. Edited by Karen Knorr-Cetina and Aaron V. Cicourel. London and Boston: Routledge and Kegan Paul.

d. "Retrouver la tradition libertaire de la gauche." *Libération* (December 23): 8–9.

e. Preface. Pp. 7–12 in Paul F. Lazarsfeld, Marie Jahoda, and Hans Zeisel, *Les chômeurs de Marienthal*. Paris: Editions de Minuit.

with Luc Boltanski. [1975] "The Educational System and the Economy: Titles and Jobs." Pp. 141–51 in *French Sociology: Rupture and Renewal Since 1968*. Edited by Charles C. Lemert. New York: Columbia University Press.

1982

a. *Leçon sur la leçon*. Paris: Editions de Minuit. Translated as "Lecture on the Lecture" in Bourdieu 1990h.

b. *Ce que parler veut dire. L'économie des échanges linguistiques*. Paris: Arthème Fayard.

with Monique de Saint Martin. "La sainte famille. L'épiscopat français dans le champ du pouvoir." *Actes de la recherche en sciences sociales* 44/45: 2–53.

1983

a. "The Philosophical Establishment." Pp. 1–8 in *Philosophy in France Today*. Edited by Alan Montefiore. Cambridge: Cambridge University Press.

b. "Vous avez dit 'populaire'?" *Actes de la recherche en sciences sociales* 46: 98–105. Reprinted in translation in Bourdieu 1991e.

c. "Les sciences sociales et la philosophie." *Actes de la recherche en sciences sociales* 47/48: 45–52.

d. "The Field of Cultural Production, or the Economic World Reversed." *Poetics* 12 (November): 311–56.

e. [1982] "Erving Goffman, Discoverer of the Infinitely Small." *Theory, Culture, and Society* 2, no. 1: 112–13.

1984

a. [1979] *Distinction: A Social Critique of the Judgement of Taste*. Cambridge, Mass: Harvard University Press; London: Routledge and Kegan Paul.

b. Prefazione. Pp. 5–6 in Anna Boschetti, *L'impresa intellettuale. Sartre e "Les Temps Modernes"*. Bari: Edizioni Dedalo.

with Didier Eribon. "Université: Les rois sont nus." *Le nouvel observateur* (November 2–8): 86–90.

1985

a. [1984] "Social Space and the Genesis of Groups." *Theory and Society* 14, no. 6 (November): 723–44. Reprinted in Bourdieu 1991e.

b. [1984] "Delegation and Political Fetishism." *Thesis Eleven* 10/11 (November): 56–70. Reprinted in Bourdieu 1991e.

c. "The Genesis of the concepts of 'Habitus' and 'Field.'" *Sociocriticism* 2, no. 2: 11–24.

d. [1971] "The Market of Symbolic Goods." *Poetics* 14 (April): 13–44.

e. "Les intellectuels et les pouvoirs." Pp. 93–94 in *Michel Foucault, une histoire de la vérité*. Paris: Syros.

f. "A Free Thinker: 'Do Not Ask Me Who I Am.'" *Paragraph* 5 (March): 80–87.
g. "Existe-t-il une littérature belge? Limites d'un champ et frontières politiques." *Etudes de lettres* (Lausanne) 4: 3–6.
h. "Les professeurs de l'Université de Paris à la veille de Mai 68." Pp. 177–84 in *Le personnel de l'enseignement supérieur en France au 19ème et 20ème siècle.* Edited by Christophe Charle and Régine Ferré. Paris: Editions du CNRS.
with Bernd Schwibs. "Vernunft ist eine historische Errungenschaft, wie die Sozialversicherung." *Neue Sammlung* 3: 376–94.
with Roger Chartier and Robert Darnton. "Dialogue à propos de l'histoire culturelle." *Actes de la recherche en sciences sociales* 59: 86–93.

1986
a. [1985] "From Rules to Strategies." *Cultural Anthropology* 1, no. 1 (February): 110–20.
b. [1983] "The Forms of Capital." Pp. 241–58 in *Handbook of Theory and Research for the Sociology of Education.* Edited by John G. Richardson. New York: Greenwood Press.
c. "Habitus, code et codification." *Actes de la recherche en sciences sociales* 64: 40–44. Reprinted in Bourdieu 1990h.
d. "La science et l'actualité." *Actes de la recherche en science sociales* 61: 2–3.
e. "D'abord défendre les intellectuels." *Le Nouvel Observateur* (September 12–18): 82.
f. "Nécessiter." *L'Herne* (June, special issue on Francis Ponge): 434–37.

1987
a. *Choses dites.* Paris: Editions de Minuit.
b. "What Makes a Social Class? On the Theoretical and Practical Existence of Groups." *Berkeley Journal of Sociology* 32: 1–18.
c. [1986] "The Biographical Illusion." *Working Papers and Proceedings of the Center for Psychosocial Studies*, no. 14. Chicago: Center for Psychosocial Studies.
d. "The Historical Genesis of a Pure Aesthetics." *The Journal of Aesthetics and Art Criticism.* Special issue on "Analytic Aesthetics," ed. Richard Schusterman, 201–10. Reprinted in Bourdieu forthcoming c.
e. "Scientific Field and Scientific Thought." Comparative Study of Social Transformation, CSST Working Paper. Ann Arbor: The University of Michigan.
f. "Variations et invariants. Eléments pour une histoire structurale du champ des Grandes écoles." *Actes de la recherche en sciences sociales* 70: 3–30.
g. [1986] "The Force of Law: Toward a Sociology of the Juridical Field." *Hastings Journal of Law* 38: 209–48.
h. "Legitimation and Structured Interests in Weber's Sociology of Religion." Pp. 119–36 in *Max Weber, Rationality, and Modernity.* Edited by Sam Whimster and Scott Lash. London: Allen and Unwin.
i. "L'institutionalisation de l'anomie." *Cahiers du Musée national d'art moderne* 19/20 (June): 6–19.
j. [1975] "The Invention of the Artist's Life." *Yale French Studies* 73: 75–103.

k. "Für eine Realpolitik der Vernunft." Pp. 229–34 in *Das Bildungswesen der Zukunft*. Edited by S. Muller-Rolli. Stuttgart: Ernst Klett.

l. "Revolt of the Spirit." *New Socialist* 46 (February): 9–11.

m. "L'assassinat de Maurice Halbwachs." *La Liberté de l'esprit, Visages de la Resistance* 16 (Fall): 161–68.

with Monique de Saint Martin. "Agrégation et ségrégation. Le champ des Grandes écoles et le champ du pouvoir." *Actes de la recherche en sciences sociales* 69: 2–50.

et al. *Eléments d'une analyse du marché de la maison individuelle*. Paris: Centre de Sociologie Européenne. Mimeo, 104pp.

1988

a. [1984] *Homo Academicus*. Cambridge: Polity Press; Stanford: Stanford University Press.

b. *L'ontologie politique de Martin Heidegger*. Paris: Editions de Minuit. Translated as *The Political Ontology of Martin Heidegger*. Cambridge: Polity Press; Stanford: Stanford University Press, 1991.

c. "On Interest and the Relative Autonomy of Symbolic Power." *Working Papers and Proceedings of the Center for Psychosocial Studies*, no. 20. Chicago: Center for Psychosocial Studies. Reprinted as "A Reply to Some Objections" in Bourdieu 1990h.

d. "Flaubert's Point of View." *Critical Inquiry* 14 (Spring): 539–62.

e. "Vive la crise! For Heterodoxy in Social Science." *Theory and Society* 17, no. 5 (September): 773–88.

f. "Program for a Sociology of Sport." *Sociology of Sport Journal* 5, no. 2 (June): 153–61.

g. "Penser la politique." *Actes de la recherche en sciences sociales* 71/72: 2–3.

h. "La vertu civile." *Le Monde*, September 16, pp. 1–2.

i. "A Long Trend of Change." Review of M. Lewin's *The Gorbatchev Phenomenon*. *The Times Literary Supplement*, August 12–18, 875–76.

j. Preface. Pp. i-v in Brigitte Mazon, *Aux Origines de l'Ecole des hautes études en sciences sociales. Le rôle du mécénat americain (1920–1960)*. Paris: Les Editions du Cerf.

1989

a. *La noblesse d'Etat. Grands corps et Grandes écoles*. Paris: Editions de Minuit.

b. "Reproduction interdite. La dimension symbolique de la domination économique." *Etudes rurales* 113/114 (January–June): 15–36.

c. "How Schools Help Reproduce the Social Order." *Current Contents/Social and Behavioral Science* 21, no. 8 (February 20): 16.

d. "The Corporatism of the Universal: The Role of Intellectuals in the Modern World." *Telos* 81 (Fall): 99–110.

e. [1988] "Social Space and Symbolic Power." *Sociological Theory* 7, no. 1 (June): 18–26.

f. "On the Possibility of a Field of World Sociology." Keynote address to the

Russell Sage Conference on "Social Theory in a Changing Society," the University of Chicago, April. Reprinted in Bourdieu and Coleman 1991.

with Patrick Champagne. "L'opinion publique." Pp. 204–6 in *50 idées qui ébranlèrent le monde. Dictionnaire de la glasnost.* Edited by Youri Afanassiev and Marc Ferro. Paris: Payot.

with Roger Chartier. "Gens à histoire, gens sans histoires." *Politix* 6 (Spring): 53–60.

with Loïc J. D. Wacquant. "For a Socioanalysis of Intellectuals: On 'Homo Academicus.'" *Berkeley Journal of Sociology* 34: 1–29.

1990

a. [1980] *The Logic of Practice.* Cambridge: Polity Press; Stanford: Stanford University Press.

b. "Droit et passe-droit. Le champ des pouvoirs territoriaux et la mise en oeuvre des règlements." *Actes de la recherche en sciences sociales* 81/82: 86–96.

c. with the collaboration of Salah Bouhedja, Rosine Christin, and Claire Givry."Un placement de père de famille. La maison individuelle: spécificité du produit et logique du champ de production." *Actes de la recherche en sciences sociales* 81/82: 6–35.

d. with the collaboration of Salah Bouhedja and Claire Givry. "Un contrat sous contrainte." *Actes de la recherche en sciences sociales* 81/82: 34–51.

e. "The Scholastic Point of View." *Cultural Anthropology* 5, no. 4 (November): 380–91.

f. "Principles for Reflecting on the Curriculum." *The Curriculum Journal* 1, no. 3 (December): 307–14.

g. "Animadversiones in Mertonem." Pp. 297–301 in *Robert K. Merton: Consensus and Controversy.* Edited by Jon Clark, Celia Modgil, and Sohan Modgil. London: The Falmer Press.

h. *In Other Words: Essays Toward a Reflexive Sociology.* Cambridge: Polity Press; Stanford: Stanford University Press.

i. "La domination masculine." *Actes de la recherche en sciences sociales* 84: 2–31.

j. "Les conditions sociales de la circulation des idées." *Romanistische Zeitschrift für Literaturgeschichte* 14, no. 1/2: 1–10.

with Rosine Christin. "La construction du marché. Le champ administratif et la production de la 'politique du logement.'" *Actes de la recherche en sciences sociales* 81/82: 65–85.

with Monique de Saint Martin. "Le sens de la propriété. La genèse sociale des systèmes de préférence." *Actes de la recherche en sciences sociales* 81/82: 52–64.

1991

a. "Aspirant philosophe. Un point de vue sur le champ universitaire dans les années 50." Pp. 15–24 in *Les enjeux philosophiques des années 50.* Paris: Centre Georges Pompidou.

b. "Un analyseur de l'inconscient." Preface to Abdelmalek Sayad, *L'immigration, ou les paradoxes de l'altérité*. Brussels: Editions De Boeck.

c. "Que faire de la sociologie? Entretien avec Pierre Bourdieu." *CFDT Aujourd'hui* 100: 134–57.

d. "Espace social et espace symbolique: introduction à une lecture japonaise de 'La distinction.'" *Nichifutsu Bunka* 54 (March): 43–54.

e. *Language and Symbolic Power*. Edited and with an introduction by John B. Thompson. Cambridge: Polity Press; Cambridge, Mass.: Harvard University Press.

f. "The Peculiar History of Scientific Reason." *Sociological Forum* 5, no. 2 (Spring): 3–26.

ed., with James S. Coleman. *Social Theory for a Changing Society*. Boulder, Colo.: Westview Press.

with E. Balibar, T. Ben Jelloun, S. Breton, M. Harbi, A. Laabi, E. Terray, and K. Titous. "Contre la guerre." *Libération* (February 21): 13.

with W. Hiromatsu, and H. Imamura. "Pour une *Realpolitik* de la raison." *Gendai Shiso* (March): 182–203.

with Loïc J. D. Wacquant. "Das Feld des Machts und die technokratische Herrschaft." Pp. 67–100 in Pierre Bourdieu, *Intellektuellen und die Macht*. Edited by Irene Dölling. Hamburg: VSA Verlag.

Forthcoming

a. *Practice, Class, and Culture: Selected Essays*. Edited and with an introduction, notes, and glossary by Loïc J. D. Wacquant. Cambridge: Polity Press.

b. "For a Politics of Morals in Politics." In *Practice, Class, and Culture: Selected Essays*. Cambridge: Polity Press.

c. *Essays on Art and Literature*. Edited by Randal Johnson. Cambridge: Polity Press.

d. *Academic Discourse: Linguistic Misunderstanding and Professorial Power*. Cambridge: Polity Press

General References

Abbott, Andrew. 1988. *The System of Professions: An Essay on the Division of Expert Labor*. Chicago: The University of Chicago Press.

Abrams, Philip. 1982. *Historical Sociology*. Ithaca, N.Y.: Cornell University Press.

Accardo, Alain. 1983. *Initiation à la sociologie de l'illusionnisme social. Lire Bourdieu*. Bordeaux: Editions Le Mascaret.

Accardo, Alain, and Philippe Corcuff, eds. 1986. *La sociologie de Pierre Bourdieu. Textes choisis et commentés*. Bordeaux: Editions Le Mascaret.

Acciaiolo, Gregory L. 1981. "Knowing What You Are Doing: Pierre Bourdieu's 'Outline of a Theory of Practice.'" *Canberra Anthropology* 4, no. 1 (April): 23–51.

Adair, Philippe. 1984. "La sociologie phagocytée par l'économique. Remarques critiques à propos de 'Ce que parler veut dire.'" *Sociologie du travail* 26, no. 1: 105–14.

Addelson, Katharine Pyne. 1990. "Why Philosophers Should Become Sociologists (and Vice Versa)." Pp. 119–47 in *Symbolic Interaction and Cultural Studies*. Edited by Howard S. Becker and Michael M. McCall. Chicago: The University of Chicago Press.

Alexander, Jeffrey C. 1980–82. *Theoretical Logic in Sociology*. 4 vols. Berkeley and Los Angeles: University of California Press.

———. 1987a. "The Centrality of the Classics." Pp. 11–57 in *Social Theory Today*. Edited by Anthony Giddens and Jonathan Turner. Cambridge: Polity Press.

———. 1987b. *Twenty Lectures: Sociological Theory Since World War II*. New York: Columbia University Press.

———. 1988. "The New Theoretical Movement." Pp. 77–101 in *Handbook of Sociology*. Edited by Neil J. Smelser. Newbury Park: Sage Publications.

———, ed. 1985. *Neo-Functionalism*. Newbury Park: Sage Publications.

Alexander, Jeffrey C., Bernhard Giesen, Richard Münch, and Neil J. Smelser, eds. 1987. *The Micro-Macro Link*. Berkeley and Los Angeles: University of California Press.

Alvim, Rosilène and José Sergio Leite Lopes. 1990. "Familles ouvrières, familles d'ouvrières." *Actes de la recherche en sciences sociales* 84: 78–84.

Ansart, Pierre. 1990. "Le structuralisme génétique," "Classements et distinction," "Les champs symboliques," "Reproduction et stratégies." Chapters 1, 5, 9, and 13 in *Les sociologies contemporaines*. Paris: Editions du Seuil.

Archer, Margaret. 1983. "Process Without System." *Archives européennes de sociologie* 24, no. 1: 196–221.

Arliaux, Michel. 1985. "Review of *Homo Academicus*." *Revue française de sociologie* 26, no. 4: 713–19.

Aron, Raymond. 1981. *Le spectateur engagé*. Paris: Gallimard.

Aronowitz, Stanley, and Henri Giroux. 1985. *Education Under Siege: The Conversative, Liberal, and Radical Debate Over Schooling*. London: Routledge and Kegan Paul.

Ashmore, Malcom. 1989. *The Reflexive Thesis: Wrighting Sociology of Scientific Knowledge.* Chicago: The University of Chicago Press.

Atkinson, Paul. 1990. *The Ethnographic Imagination: Textual Constructions of Reality.* London and New York: Routledge.

Auerbach, Erich. 1953. *Mimesis: The Representation of Reality in Western Literature.* Princeton: Princeton University Press.

Austin, J. L. 1962. *How to Do Things with Words.* New York: Oxford University Press.

Bachelard, Gaston. 1938. *La formation de l'esprit scientifique. Contribution à une psychanalyse de la connaissance objective.* Paris: Libraire Philosophique J. Vrin (4th ed. 1965).

———. 1949. *Le rationalisme appliqué.* Paris: Presses Universitaires de France (3rd ed. 1966).

———. 1984 [1934]. *The New Scientific Spirit.* New York: W. W. Norton.

Balazs, Gabrielle. 1983. "Les facteurs et les formes de l'expérience du chômage." *Actes de la recherche en sciences sociales* 50: 69–83.

Balazs, Gabrielle, and Jean-Pierre Faguer. 1991. "'Que deviendront-ils?' Les effets sociaux de la caméra." *Actes de la recherche en sciences sociales* 86/87: 92–98.

Baldwin, John B. 1988. "Habit, Emotion, and Self-Conscious Action." *Sociological Perspectives* 31, no. 1 (January): 35–58.

Bancaud, Alain. 1989. "Une 'constance mobile': la haute magistrature." *Actes de la recherche en sciences sociales* 76/77: 30–48.

Barnard, Henri. 1990. "Bourdieu and Ethnography: Reflexivity, Politics and Praxis." Pp. 58–85 in *An Introduction to the Work of Pierre Bourdieu: The Practice of Theory.* Edited by R. Harker et al. London: Macmillan.

Becker, Gary. 1976. *The Economic Approach to Human Behavior.* Chicago: The University of Chicago Press.

Becker, Howard S., and John Walton. 1986 [1975]. "Social Science and the Work of Hans Haacke." Pp. 103–19 in Howard S. Becker, *Doing Things Together: Selected Papers.* Evanston: Northwestern University Press.

Beeghley, Leonard. 1984. "Illusion and Reality in the Measurement of Poverty." *Social Problems* 31 (February): 322–33.

Beisel, Nicola. 1990. "Class, Culture, and Campaigns against Vice in Three American Cities, 1872–1892." *American Sociological Review* 55, no. 1 (February): 44–62.

Bellah, Robert N. 1973. "Introduction." Pp. ix–lv in Emile Durkheim. *On Morality and Society.* Chicago: The University of Chicago Press.

Bentley, G. Carter. 1987. "Ethnicity and Practice." *Comparative Studies in Society and History* 29, no. 1: 24–55.

Benveniste, Emile. 1969. *Le vocabulaire des institutions indo-européennes.* Paris: Editions de Minuit.

Berelson, Bernard, and G. A. Steiner. 1964. *Human Behavior.* New York: Harcourt Brace Jovanovich.

Berger, Bennett. 1981. *The Survival of a Counterculture: Ideological Work and Daily*

Life Among Rural Communards. Berkeley and Los Angeles: University of California Press.

———. 1986. "Taste and Domination." *American Journal of Sociology* 91, no. 6 (May): 1445–53.

———. 1989. "Structuralisme et volontarisme dans la sociologie de la culture." *Sociologie et sociétés* 21, no. 2 (October): 177–94.

———. 1991. "Structure and Choice in the Sociology of Culture." *Theory and Society* 20, no. 1: 1–20.

———, ed. 1990. *Authors of their Own Lives: Intellectual Autobiographies by Twenty American Sociologists.* Berkeley and Los Angeles: University of California Press.

Berger, Peter. 1966. *Invitation to Sociology: A Humanistic Perspective.* Harmondsworth: Pelican.

Berger, Peter, and Thomas Luckmann. 1966. *The Social Construction of Reality: A Treatise in the Sociology of Knowledge.* Harmondsworth: Penguin.

Best, Joel, ed. 1989. *Images of Issues: Typifying Contemporary Social Problems.* New York: Aldine de Gruyter.

Bidet, Jacques. 1979. "Questions to Pierre Bourdieu." *Critique of Anthropology* 13-14 (Summer): 203–8.

Blasius, Jorg, and Joachim Winkler. 1989. "Gibt es die 'Feinen Unterschiede'? Eine Empirische Überprüfung der Bourdieuschen Theorie." *Kölner Zeitschrift für Soziologie und Socialpsychologie* 41, no. 1 (March): 72–94.

Bloor, David. 1976. *Knowledge and Social Imagery.* London: Routledge and Kegan Paul.

Blumer, Herbert. 1969. *Symbolic Interactionism.* Englewood Cliffs, N.J.: Prentice-Hall.

Bohn, Cornelia. 1991. *Habitus und Kontext: Ein kritischer Beitrag zur Socialtheorie Bourdieus.* Darmstadt: Westdeutscher Verlag.

Boltanski, Luc. 1974. "Erving Goffman et le temps du soupçon." *Social Science Information* 12, no. 3: 127–47.

———. 1975. "La constitution du champ de la bande dessinée." *Actes de la recherche en sciences sociales* 1: 37–59.

———. 1979. "Taxinomies sociales et luttes de classes. La mobilisation de 'la classe moyenne' et l'invention des 'cadres.'" *Actes de la recherche en sciences sociales* 29: 75–105.

———. 1980. "L'université les entreprises et la multiplication des salariés bourgeois (1960–1975)." *Actes de la recherche en sciences sociales* 34: 17–44.

———. 1984. "How a Social Group Objectified Itself: 'Cadres' in France, 1936–45." *Social Science Information* 23, no. 3: 469–92.

———. 1987 [1982]. *The Making of a Class: "Cadres" in French Society.* Cambridge: Cambridge University Press.

Boltanski, Luc, with Yann Daré and Marie-Ange Schiltz. 1984. "La dénonciation." *Actes de la recherche en sciences sociales* 51: 3–40.

Bon, François, and Yves Schemeil. 1980. "La rationalisation de l'inconduite: Comprendre le statut du politique chez Pierre Bourdieu." *Revue française de sociologie* 30, no. 6: 1198–1230.

Bonvin, François. 1982. "Une seconde famille. Un collège d'enseignement privé." *Actes de la recherche en sciences sociales* 30: 47–64.

Boschetti, Anna. 1985. "Classi reali e classi costruite." *Rassegna Italiana di Sociologia* 26, no. 1 (January–March): 89–99.

———. 1988 [1985]. *The Intellectual Enterprise: Sartre and 'Les temps modernes.'* Evanston: Northwestern University Press.

Bourgois, Philippe. 1989. "In Search of Horatio Alger: Culture and Ideology in the Crack Economy." *Contemporary Drug Problems* (Winter): 619–49.

Bredo, E., and W. Feinberg. 1979. "Meaning, Power, and Pedagogy." *Journal of Curriculum Studies* 11, no. 4: 315–32.

Brint, Steven, and Jerome Karabel. 1989. *The Diverted Dream: Community Colleges and the Promise of Educational Opportunity in America, 1950–1985.* New York: Oxford University Press.

Broady, Donald. 1990. *Sociologi och epistemology. Om Pierre Bourdieus forfattarskap och den historiska epistemologin.* Stockholm: HLS Forlag.

Broady, Donald, and Mikäel Palme. 1990. "The Field of Institutions of Higher Learning in Sweden." Paper presented to the Colloque sur la comparaison des institutions de formation des dirigeants en Europe, Paris, Maison des sciences de l'homme, November 8–9 (forthcoming in the conference proceedings).

Broady, Donald, and Olle Persson. 1989. "Bourdieu i USA. Bibliometriska noteringar." *Sociologisk Forskning* (Stockholm) 26, no. 4: 54–73.

Brown, Richard Harvey. 1990. *Social Science as Civic Discourse: Essays on the Invention, Legitimation, and Uses of Social Theory.* Chicago: The University of Chicago Press.

Brubaker, Rogers. 1985. "Rethinking Classical Sociology: The Sociological Vision of Pierre Bourdieu." *Theory and Society* 14, no. 6 (November): 745–75.

———. 1989a. "Social Theory as Habitus." Paper presented at the Conference on "The Social Theory of Pierre Bourdieu," Center for Psychosocial Studies, Chicago, March. (Forthcoming in Calhoun, LiPuma, and Postone 1992).

———. 1989b. "Review of Pierre Bourdieu, 'Choses dites.'" *Contemporary Sociology* 18, no. 5 (September): 783–84.

Brubaker, Rogers, and Loïc J. D. Wacquant. Forthcoming. "Rethinking the Puzzle of Structure and Agency." *Annual Review of Sociology* 20.

Bryant, C. G. A. 1985. *Positivism in Social Theory and Research.* New York: Saint Martin's Press.

Bürger, Peter. 1990. "The Problem of Aesthetic Value. Pp. 23–34 in *Literary Theory Today.* Edited by Peter Collier and Helga Geyer-Ryan. Ithaca, N.Y.: Cornell University Press.

Burke, Kenneth. 1989. *On Symbols and Society.* Edited and with an introduction by Joseph R. Gusfield. Chicago: The University of Chicago Press.

Caillé, Alain. 1981. "La sociologie de l'intérêt est-elle interessante?" *Sociologie du travail* 23, no. 3: 257–74.

———. 1987a. *Critique de Bourdieu.* Cours, séminaires et travaux, no. 8. Lausanne: Université de Lausanne, Institut d'anthropologie et de sociologie.

———. 1987b. "Valeurs des biens et valeur des personnes: champs, marché et légitimité." *Bulletin du M.A.U.S.S.* 24 (December): 129–44.

Calhoun, Craig J. 1979. "The Radicalism of Tradition: Community Strength or 'Venerable Disguise and Borrowed Language'?" *American Journal of Sociology* 88, no. 5: 886–914.

———. 1982. *The Question of Class Struggle.* Chicago: The University of Chicago Press.

———. 1990. "Putting the Sociologist in the Sociology of Culture: The Self-Reflexive Scholarship of Pierre Bourdieu and Raymond Williams." *Contemporary Sociology* 19, no. 4 (July): 500–505.

———. 1992. "Habitus, Field of Power and Capital: The Question of Historical Specificity." Forthcoming in Calhoun, LiPuma, and Postone 1992.

Calhoun, Craig, Edward LiPuma, and Moishe Postone, eds. 1992. *Exploring the Social Theories of Pierre Bourdieu.* Cambridge: Polity Press. (Forthcoming)

Camic, Charles. 1986. "The Matter of Habit." *American Journal of Sociology* 91, no. 5: 1039–87.

Caro, Jean-Yves. 1980. "La sociologie de Pierre Bourdieu: éléments pour une théorie du champ politique." *Revue française de science politique* 6 (December).

———. 1982. *Les économistes distingués.* Paris: Presses de la Fondation Nationale des Sciences Politiques.

Casanova, Pascale. 1990. "Au bon plaisir de Pierre Bourdieu." Radio program broadcast on France Culture, 23 June 1990.

Cassirer, Ernst. 1923 [1910]. *Substance and Function: Einstein's Theory of Relativity.* Chicago: Open Court.

———. 1936. "The Influence of Language upon the Development of Scientific Thought." *The Journal of Philosophy* 33: 309–27.

Certeau, Michel de. 1984. "Foucault and Bourdieu." Pp. 45–60 in *The Practice of Everyday Life.* Berkeley and Los Angeles: University of California Press.

Chamboredon, Jean-Claude. 1975. "Sociologie de la sociologie et intérêts sociaux des sociologues." *Actes de la recherche en sciences sociales* 2: 2–20.

Chamboredon, Jean-Claude, and Jean-Louis Fabiani. 1977. "Les albums pour enfants. Le champ de l'édition et les définitions sociales de l'enfance." *Actes de la recherche en sciences sociales* 13: 60–79; 14: 55–74.

Champagne, Patrick. 1979. "Jeunes agriculteurs et vieux paysans. Crise de la succession et apparition du troisième age." *Actes de la recherche en sciences sociales* 26/27: 83–107.

———. 1984. "La manifestation. La production de l'évènement politique." *Actes de la recherche en sciences sociales* 52/53: 18–41.

———. 1988. "Le cercle politique. Usages sociaux des sondages et nouvel espace politique." *Actes de la recherche en sciences sociales* 71/72: 71–97.

———. 1990. *Faire l'opinion. Le nouvel espace politique.* Paris: Editions de Minuit ("Le sens commun").

Champagne, Patrick, Rémi Lenoir, Dominique Merllié, and Louis Pinto. 1989. *Introduction à la pratique sociologique.* Paris: Dunod.

Chancer, Lynn S. 1987. "New Bedford, Massachusetts, March 6, 1983–March

22, 1984: The 'Before' and 'After' of a Group Rape." *Gender and Society* 1, no. 3 (September): 239–60.

Chapoulie, Jean-Michel. 1979. "La compétence pédagogique des professeurs comme enjeu de conflits." *Actes de la recherche en sciences sociales* 30: 65–85.

Charle, Christophe. 1978. "Les milieux d'affaires dans la structure de la classe dominante vers 1900." *Actes de la recherche en sciences sociales* 20/21: 83–96.

———. 1983. "Le champ universitaire parisien à la fin du 19ème siècle." *Actes de la recherche en sciences sociales* 47/48: 77–89.

———. 1987. *Les élites de la République, 1880–1900.* Paris: Fayard.

———. 1990. *Naissance des "intellectuels," 1880–1900.* Paris: Editions de Minuit ("Le sens commun").

———. 1991. *Histoire sociale de la France au XIXème siècle.* Paris: Editions du Seuil.

Chartier, Roger. 1988a. *Cultural History: Between Practices and Representations.* Cambridge: Polity Press; Ithaca, N.Y.: Cornell University Press.

———. 1988b. "L'histoire culturelle." Pp. 90–94 in *L'histoire en France.* Paris: Editions La Découverte.

Chomsky, Noam. 1967. "General Properties of Language." Pp. 73–88 in *Brain Mechanisms Underlying Speech and Language.* Edited by I. L. Darley. New York and London: Grune and Straton.

Cicourel, Aaron V. 1968. *The Social Organization of Juvenile Justice.* Chicago: Wiley.

———. 1974. *Cognitive Sociology.* New York: Free Press.

———. 1985. "Raisonnement et diagnostic: le rôle du discours et de la compréhension clinique en médecine." *Actes de la recherche en sciences sociales* 60: 79–88.

———. In press. "Habitus and the Developmental Emergence of Practical Reasoning." In *Sozialer Sinn und Geschmack,* edited by Gunther Gerbauer and Christoph Wulff. Berlin.

Clark, Terry N. 1973. *Prophets and Patrons.* Cambridge, Mass.: Harvard University Press.

Clifford, James, and George E. Marcus, eds. 1986. *Writing Culture: The Poetics and Politics of Ethnography.* Berkeley and Los Angeles: University of California Press.

Coenen, Harry. 1989. "Praxeologie en strukturatietheorie: preliminaire opmerkingen bij een vergelijking." *Antropologische Verkenningen* 8, no. 2 (Summer): 8–17.

Coleman, James S. 1986. "Social Theory, Social Research and a Theory of Action." *American Journal of Sociology* 91, no. 6 (May): 1309–35.

———. 1990a. "Columbia in the Fifties." Pp. 75–103 in *Authors of Their Own Lives: Intellectual Autobiographies by Twenty American Sociologists.* Edited by Bennett Berger. Berkeley and Los Angeles: University of California Press.

———. 1990b. *Foundations of Social Theory.* Cambridge, Mass.: Belknap Press of Harvard University Press.

Collectif 'Révoltes Logiques.' 1984. *L'empire du sociologue.* Paris: Editions La Découverte.

Collins, Jim. 1992. "Determination and Contradiction: An Appreciation and Critique of the Work of Pierre Bourdieu on Language and Education." Forthcoming in Calhoun, LiPuma, and Postone 1992.

Collins, Randall. 1979. *The Credential Society.* New York: Academic Press.

———. 1981a. "Cultural Capitalism and Symbolic Violence." Pp. 173–182 in *Sociology Since Mid-Century: Essays in Theory Cumulation.* New York: Academic Press.

———. 1981b. "On the Microfoundations of Macrosociology." *American Journal of Sociology* 86: 984–1014.

———. 1985. *Three Sociological Traditions.* New York: Oxford University Press.

———. 1987. "Interaction Ritual Chains, Power, and Property." Pp. 193–206 in *The Micro-Macro Link,* edited by Jeffrey C. Alexander et al. Berkeley and Los Angeles: University of California Press.

———. 1988. *Theoretical Sociology.* San Diego: Harcourt Brace Jovanovich.

———. 1988–89. "For a Sociological Philosophy." *Theory and Society* 17, no. 5: 669–702.

———. 1989. "Review of *Homo Academicus.*" *American Journal of Sociology* 95, no. 2 (September): 460–63.

Connell, R. W. 1983. "The Black Box of Habit on the Wings of History: Reflections on the Theory of Reproduction." Pp. 140–61 in *Which Way is Up? Essays on Sex, Class, and Culture.* London: George Allen and Unwin.

Connerton, Paul. 1989. *How Societies Remember.* Cambridge: Cambridge University Press.

Cookson, Peter W., Jr., and Carolyn Hoges Persell. 1985a. *Preparing for Power: America's Elite Boarding Schools.* New York: Basic Books.

———. 1985b. "English and American Residential Secondary Schools: A Comparative Study of the Reproduction of Social Elites." *Comparative Education Review* 29, no. 3 (August): 283–98.

Corbin, Alain. 1986 [1982]. *The Foul and The Fragrant.* Cambridge: Harvard University Press.

———. 1990. *Le village des cannibales.* Paris: Aubier.

Corson, David. 1991. "Language, Power, and Minority Education." *Language and Education* 5: in press.

Coser, Lewis A. 1990. "Sociological Theories in Disarray." *Contemporary Sociology* 18, no. 4 (July): 477–79.

Coulon, Alain. 1991. "Le métier d'étudiant. Approches ethnométhodologique et institutionnelle de l'entrée dans la vie universitaire." University of Paris VIII, Department of Education, Thèse de doctorat d'Etat.

Cournot, A. 1912 [1851]. *Essai sur les fondements de nos connaissances et sur les caractères de la critique philosophique.* Paris: Hachette.

Crow, G. 1989. "The Use of the Concept of Strategy in Recent Sociological Literature." *Sociology* 23, no. 1 (February): 1–24.

Dahl, Robert. 1961. *Who Governs? Democracy and Power in an American City.* New Haven: Yale University Press.

Dal Lago, Alessandro. 1985. "Il sociologo non temperato." *Rassegna Italiana di Sociologia* 26, no. 1 (January–March): 79–89.

Darnton, Robert. 1984. *The Great Cat Massacre and Other Episodes in French Cultural History.* New York: Vintage.

Davidson, Arnold I., ed. 1989. "Symposium on Heidegger and Nazism." *Critical Theory* 15, no. 2 (Winter): 407–88.

Davis, Nathalie Zemon. 1975. *Society and Culture in Early Modern France.* Stanford: Stanford University Press.

DeGeorge, Richard, and Fernande DeGeorge, eds. 1972. *The Structuralists from Marx to Lévi-Strauss.* New York: Doubleday.

Delsaut, Yvette. 1976. "Le double mariage de Jean Célisse." *Actes de la recherche en sciences sociales* 4: 3–20.

———. 1988a. "Carnets de socioanalyse, 1: L'*inforjetable.*" *Actes de la recherche en sciences sociales* 74: 83–88.

———. 1988b. "Carnets de socioanalyse, 2: Une photo de classe." *Actes de la recherche en sciences sociales* 75: 83–96.

Dennis, Shirley. 1986. "A Critical Review and Appropriation of Pierre Bourdieu's Analysis of Social and Cultural Reproduction." *Journal of Education* 16, no. 2 (Spring): 96–112.

Derrida, Jacques. 1990. *L'institution philosophique.* Paris: Galilée.

de Saint Martin, Monique. *See* Saint Martin, Monique de

Desrosières, Alain. 1978. "Marché matrimonial et structure des classes sociales." *Actes de la recherche en sciences sociales* 20/21: 97–107.

Detleff, Müller, Fritz Ringer, and Brian Simon, eds. 1987. *The Rise of Modern Educational Systems.* Cambridge: Cambridge University Press.

Dewey, John. 1958. *Art as Experience.* New York: Capricorn.

Dezalay, Yves. 1989. "Le droit des familles: du notable à l'expert. La restructuration du champ des professionnels de la restructuration des entreprises." *Actes de la recherche en sciences sociales* 76/77: 2–28.

Dezalay, Yves, Austin Sarat, and Susan Silbey. 1989. "D'une demarché contestataire à un savoir méritocratique. Esquisse d'une histoire sociale de la sociologie juridique américaine." *Actes de la recherche en sciences sociales* 78: 79–93.

DiMaggio, Paul. 1979. "Review Essay on Pierre Bourdieu." *American Journal of Sociology* 84, no. 6 (May): 1460–74.

———. 1982. "Cultural Capital and School Success: The Impact of Status Culture Participation on the Grades of U.S. High School Students." *American Sociological Review* 47: 189–201.

———. 1990. "Cultural Aspects of Economic Action and Organization." Pp. 113–36 in *Beyond the Marketplace: Rethinking Economy and Society.* Edited by Roger Friedland and A. F. Robertson. New York: Aldine de Gruyter.

———. 1991a. "Social Structure, Institutions, and Cultural Goods: The Case of the United States." Pp. 133–55 in *Social Theory for a Changing Society.* Edited by Pierre Bourdieu and James S. Coleman. Boulder, Colo.: Westview Press.

———. 1991b. "Cultural Entrepreneurship in Nineteenth-Century Boston:

The Creation of an Organizational Base for Higher Culture in America." Pp. 374–97 in *Rethinking Popular Culture: Contemporary Perspectives in Cultural Studies*. Edited by Chandra Mukerji and Michael Schudson. Berkeley and Los Angeles: University of California Press.

DiMaggio, Paul, and Walter W. Powell. 1991. Introduction. Pp. 1–38 in *The New Institutionalism in Organizational Analysis*. Edited by Walter W. Powell and Paul J. DiMaggio. Chicago: The University of Chicago Press.

DiMaggio, Paul, and Michael Useem. 1978. "Social Class and Arts Consumption: The Origins and Consequences of Class Differences in Exposure to the Arts in the Americas." *Theory and Society* 5, no. 2 (March): 141–61.

Dobry, Michel. 1986. *Sociologie des crises politiques*. Paris: Presses de la Fondation nationale des Sciences Politiques.

Don, Yehuda, and Victor Karady, eds. 1989. *Social and Economic History of Central European Jewry*. New Brunswick: Transaction Publishers.

Douglas, Mary. 1981. "Good Taste: Review of Pierre Bourdieu, 'La distinction.'" *Times Literary Supplement* (London), February 13: 163–69.

Dreyfus, Hubert L. 1991. *Being-in-the-World: A Commentary on Heidegger's Being and Time, Division I*. Cambridge, Mass: MIT Press.

Dreyfus, Hubert L., and Paul Rabinow. 1983. *Michel Foucault: Beyond Structuralism and Hermeneutics*. 2d ed. Chicago: The University of Chicago Press.

Dumézil, Georges. 1987. *Entretiens avec Didier Eribon*. Paris: Gallimard.

Dumont, Martine. 1984. "Le succès mondain d'une fausse science: la physiognomonie de Johann Kaspar Lavater." *Actes de la recherche en sciences sociales* 54: 2–30.

Dupréel, Eugène. 1978. *Les Sophistes: Protagoras, Gorgias, Prodicus, Hippias*. Paris: Editions Griffon (Bibliothèque Scientifique).

Durkheim, Emile. 1921. *De la méthode dans les sciences sociales*. Paris: Librairie F. Alcan.

———. 1956 [1938]. *Education and Sociology*. Glencoe, Ill.: The Free Press.

———. 1965 [1912]. *The Elementary Forms of the Religious Life*. New York: The Free Press.

———. 1966 [1895]. *The Rules of the Sociological Method*. New York: Free Press.

Durkheim, Emile, and Marcel Mauss. 1963 [1903]. *Primitive Classification*. Edited by Rodney Needham. Chicago: The University of Chicago Press.

Eagleton, Terry. 1991. "From Adorno to Bourdieu." Pp. 125–58 in *An Introduction to Ideology*. London: Verso.

Earle, William James. 1988. "Bourdieu's 'Habitus.'" Unpublished paper, Department of Philosophy, Baruch College, City University of New York.

Eder, Klaus. 1989. *Klassenlage, Lebensstil und kulturelle Praxis: Beiträge zur Auseinandersetzung mit Pierre Bourdieus Klassentheorie*. Frankfurt: Suhrkamp Verlag.

Eldridge, John. 1990. "Sociology in Britain: A Going Concern." Pp. 157–78 in *What Has Sociology Achieved*. Edited by Christopher G. A. Bryant and Henk A. Becker. New York: Saint Martin's Press.

Elias, Norbert. 1978a. *What is Sociology?* New York: Columbia University Press.

———. 1978b. *The Civilizing Process*. Oxford: Oxford University Press.

———. 1983. *The Court Society*. Oxford: Oxford University Press.

———. 1987a [1983]. *Involvement and Detachment*. Oxford and New York: Basil Blackwell.

———. 1987b. *Die Gesellshaft der Individuen*. Frankfurt: Surkamp Verlag.

Elias, Norbert, and Eric Dunning. 1986. *Quest for Excitement: Sport and Leisure in the Civilizing Process*. Oxford: Basil Blackwell.

Elster, Jon. 1984a. *Sour Grapes*. Cambridge: Cambridge University Press.

———. 1984b. *Ulysses and the Sirens*. Cambridge: Cambridge University Press.

———. 1986. *Rational Choice*. New York: New York University Press.

———. 1990. "Marxism, Functionalism and Game Theory." Pp. 97–118 in *Structures of Capital: The Social Organization of the Economy*. Edited by Sharon Zukin and Paul DiMaggio. Cambridge: Cambridge University Press.

Empson, W. 1935. *Some Versions of the Pastorals*. London: Chatto and Windus.

Encrevé, Pierre, and Michel de Fornel. 1983. "Le sens en pratique. Construction de la référence et structure sociale de l'interaction dans le couple question/réponse." *Actes de la recherche en sciences sociales* 46: 3–30.

Eribon, Didier. 1989. *Michel Foucault*. Paris: Flammarion. English Translation published by Harvard University Press, 1990.

Ernaux, Annie. 1984. *La place*. Paris: Gallimard.

Eyerman, R., T. Svensson, and T. Soderqvist, eds. 1987. *Intellectuals, Universities, and the State*. Berkeley and Los Angeles: University of California Press.

Fabiani, Jean-Louis. 1983. "Les programmes, les hommes et les oeuvres. Professeur de philosophie en classe et en ville au tournant du siècle." *Actes de la recherche en sciences sociales* 47/48: 3–20.

———. 1989. *Les philosophes de la République*. Paris: Editions de Minuit ("Le sens commun").

Faguer, Jean-Pierre. 1991. "Les effets d'une 'éducation totale.' Un collège jésuite, 1960." *Actes de la recherche en sciences sociales* 86/87: 25–43.

Farias, Victor. 1989 [1987]. *Heidegger and Nazism*. Edited and with a foreword by Joseph Margolis and Paul Bunell. Philadelphia: Temple University Press.

Farkas, George, Robert P. Grobe, Daniel Sheehan, and Yuan Shuan. 1990. "Cognitive and Noncognitive Determinants of School Achievement: Gender, Ethnicity, and Poverty in an Urban School District." *American Sociological Review* 55: 127–42.

Featherstone, Mike. 1987a. "Leisure, Symbolic Power and the Life Course." Pp. 113–38 in *Leisure, Sport and Social Relations*. Edited by J. Home et al. London: Routledge and Kegan Paul.

———. 1987b. "Consumer Culture, Symbolic Power and Universalism." Pp. 17–46 in *Mass Culture, Popular Culture and Social Life in the Middle East*. Edited by G. Stauth and S. Zubaida. Boulder, Colo.: Westview Press.

Ferry, Luc, and Alain Renault. 1990 [1986]. "French Marxism (Pierre Bourdieu)." Pp. 153–84 in *French Philosophy of the Sixties: An Essay on Anti-Humanism*. Amherst: University of Massachussetts Press.

Filloux, Jean-Claude. 1970. Introduction. Pp. 5–68 in Emile Durkheim, *La science sociale et l'action*. Paris: Presses Universitaires de France.

Fine, Michelle. 1991. *Framing Dropouts*. Albany: State University of New York Press.

Fiske, Alan Page. 1991. *Structure of Social Life: The Four Elementary Forms of Human Relations*. New York: The Free Press.

Flaubert, Gustave. 1987 [1870]. *A Sentimental Education*. Oxford: Oxford University Press.

Foley, Douglas E. 1989. "Does the Working Class Have a Culture in the Anthropological Sense of the Term?" *Cultural Anthropology* 4, no. 2 (May): 137–62.

Fornel, Michel de. 1983. "Légitimité et actes de langage." *Actes de la recherche en sciences sociales* 46: 31–38.

Foster, Steven W. 1986. "Reading Pierre Bourdieu." *Cultural Anthropology* 1, no. 1: 103–10.

Foucault, Michel. 1977a [1975]. *Discipline and Punish*. New York: Pantheon.

———. 1977b. *Language, Counter-memory, Practice; Selected Essays and Interviews*. Ithaca, N.Y.: Cornell University Press.

———. 1980. *Power/Knowledge: Selected Interviews and Other Writings, 1972–1977*. New York: Pantheon.

———. 1988. *Michel Foucault: Politics, Philosophy, Culture: Interviews and Other Writings*. Edited by Lawrence D. Kritzman. London: Routledge.

Fournier, Marcel, and Michèle Lamont, eds. 1989. "La culture comme capital." Special issue of *Sociologie et sociétés* 21, no. 2 (October).

Fox, Robin. 1985. *Lions of the Punjab: Culture in the Making*. Berkeley: University of California Press.

Frank, Arthur. 1980. "Review of *Outline of A Theory of Practice*." *Contemporary Sociology* 9, no. 2 (March): 256–57.

Friedrichs, Robert. 1970. *A Sociology of Sociology*. New York: The Free Press.

Friedson, Elliott. 1986. *Professional Powers: A Study of the Institutionalization of Formal Knowledge*. Chicago: The University of Chicago Press.

Frow, J. 1987. "Accounting for Tastes: Some Problems in Bourdieu's Sociology of Culture." *Cultural Studies* 1, no. 1: 59–73.

Gal, S. 1988. "Language and Political Economy." *Annual Review of Anthropology* 18: 345–67.

Gamboni, Dario. 1983a. *Un iconoclasme moderne. Théorie et pratiques contemporaines du vandalisme artistique*. Lausanne: Editions d'En bas.

———. 1983b. "Mépris et méprises. Eléments pour une étude de l'iconoclasme contemporain." *Actes de la recherche en sciences sociales* 49: 2–28.

———. 1989. *La plume et le pinceau. Odilon Redon et la littérature*. Paris: Editions de Minuit.

Gans, Herbert. 1975. *High Culture and Low Culture: An Analysis and Evaluation of Taste*. New York: Harper.

———. 1989. "Sociology in America: The Discipline and the Public." *American Sociological Review* 54, no. 1 (February): 1–16.

Garcia, Marie-France. 1986. "La construction sociale d'un marché parfait: le marché au cadran de Fontaines-en-Sologne." *Actes de la recherche en sciences sociales* 65: 2–13.

Garfinkel, Harold. 1967. *Studies in Ethnomethodology*. Englewood Cliffs, N.J.: Prentice-Hall.

Garnham, Nicholas. 1986. "Extended Review: Bourdieu's 'Distinction.'" *The Sociological Review* 34, no. 2 (May): 423–33.

Garnham, Nicholas, and Raymond Williams. 1980. "Pierre Bourdieu and the Sociology of Culture." *Media, Culture, and Society* 2, no. 3 (Summer): 297–312.

Garrigou, Alain. 1988. "Le secret de l'isoloir." *Actes de la recherche en sciences sociales* 71/72: 22–45.

Gartman, David. 1991. "Culture as Class Symbolization or Mass Reification: A Critique of Bourdieu's *Distinction*. *American Journal of Sociology* 97, no. 2 (September): 421–47.

Gaxie, Daniel. 1990. "Au-dela des apparences. . . . Sur quelques problèmes de mesure des opinions." *Actes de la recherche en sciences sociales* 81/82: 97–113.

Gaxie, Daniel, and P. Lehinge. 1984. *Enjeux municipaux*. Paris: Presses Universitaires de France.

Gebauer, Gunther, and Christoph Wulff. In press. *Sozialer Sinn und Geschmack*. Berlin.

Geertz, Clifford. 1974. *The Interpretation of Cultures*. New York: Basic Books.

———. 1987. *Works and Lives: The Anthropologist as Author*. Stanford: Stanford University Press.

Gerhards, Jürgen, and Helmut K. Anheier. 1989. "The Literary Field: An Empirical Investigation of Bourdieu's Sociology of Art." *International Sociology* 4, no. 2: 131–46.

Gerth, Hans, and C. Wright Mills, eds. 1946. *From Max Weber: Essays in Sociology*. New York: Oxford University Press.

Giddens, Anthony. 1977. "Positivism and Its Critics." Pp. 28–89 in *Studies in Social and Political Theory*. New York: Basic Books.

———. 1979. *Central Problems in Social Theory: Action, Structure, and Contradiction in Social Analysis*. Berkeley and Los Angeles: University of California Press.

———. 1984. *The Constitution of Society: Outline of the Theory of Structuration*. Cambridge: Polity Press.

———. 1986a. "Action, Subjectivity, and the Constitution of Meaning." *Social Research* 53, no. 3 (Fall): 529–545.

———. 1986b. "The Politics of Taste." *Partisan Review* 53, no. 2: 300–305.

———. 1987. "A Reply to My Critics." Pp. 249–301 in *Social Theory and Modern Societies: Anthony Giddens and His Critics*. Edited by David Held and John B. Thompson. Cambridge: Cambridge University Press.

———. 1990a. "Structuration Theory and Sociological Analysis." Pp. 297–315 in *Anthony Giddens: Consensus and Controversy*. Edited by Jon Clark, Celia Modgil, and Sohan Modgil. London: Farmer Press.

————. 1990b. *The Consequences of Modernity.* Cambridge: Polity Press; Stanford: Stanford University Press.

Giddens, Anthony, and Jonathan Turner, eds. 1987. *Social Theory Today.* Cambridge: Polity Press; Stanford: Stanford University Press.

Ginsburg, Faye. 1988. *Contested Lives: The Abortion Debate in an American Community.* Berkeley and Los Angeles: University of California Press.

Giroux, Henri. 1982. "Power and Resistance in the New Sociology of Education: Beyond Theories of Social and Cultural Reproduction." *Curriculum Perspectives* 2, no. 3: 1–13.

————. 1983. *Theory and Resistance in Education: A Pedagogy for the Opposition.* New York: Bergin and Garvey.

Goffman, Erving. 1961. *Asylum: Essays on the Social Situation of Mental Patients and Other Inmates.* Harmondsworth: Penguin Books.

————. 1981. *Forms of Talk.* Philadelphia: University of Pennsylvania Press.

Goldmann, Lucien. 1975 [1964]. *Towards a Sociology of the Novel.* London: Tavistock.

Goodwin, Marjorie Harness. 1990. *He-Said-She-Said: Talk as Social Organization Among Black Children.* Bloomington: Indiana University Press.

Gorder, K. L. 1980. "Understanding School Knowledge: A Critical Appraisal of Basil Bernstein and Pierre Bourdieu." *Educational Theory* 30, no. 4: 335–46.

Gouldner, Alvin W. 1970. *The Coming Crisis of Western Sociology.* New York: Basic Books.

————. 1979. *The Future of Intellectuals and the Rise of the New Class.* Oxford: Oxford University Press.

Gramsci, Antonio. 1971. *Selections from the Prison Notebooks.* New York: International Publishers.

Granovetter, Mark. 1985. "Economic Action and Social Structure: The Problem of Embeddedness." *American Journal of Sociology* 91: 481–510.

————. 1990. "The Old and New Economic Sociology." Pp. 89–112 in *Beyond the Marketplace: Rethinking Economy and Society.* Edited by Roger Friedland and A. F. Robertson. New York: Aldine de Gruyter.

Greenacre, M. J. 1984. *Theory and Application of Correspondence Analysis.* New York: Academic Press.

Grignon, Claude. 1977. "Sur les relations entre les transformations du champ religieux et les transformations de l'espace politique." *Actes de la recherche en sciences sociales* 16: 3–34.

Grignon, Claude, and Jean-Claude Passeron. 1989. *Le savant et le populaire.* Paris: Editions du Seuil.

Groethusen, Bernard. 1977. *Origines de l'esprit bourgeois en France.* Paris: Gallimard.

————. 1983. *Jean-Jacques Rousseau.* Paris: Gallimard.

Grossetti, Michel. 1986. "Métaphore économique et économie des pratiques." *Recherches sociologiques* 17, no. 2: 233–46.

Guillemin, Alain. 1982. "Aristocrates, propriétaires et diplômés. La lutte pour le pouvoir local dans le département de la Manche, 1830–1875." *Actes de la recherche en sciences sociales* 42: 33–60.

Guiraud, Pierre. 1965. *Le français populaire.* Paris: Presses Universitaires de France.

Gusfield, Joseph. 1981. *The Culture of Public Problems: Drinking-Driving and the Symbolic Order.* Chicago: The University of Chicago Press.

Habermas, Jürgen. 1986. *Autonomy and Solidarity: Interview with Jürgen Habermas.* Edited by Peter Dews. London: Verso.

Halbwachs, Maurice. 1972. *Classes sociales et morphologie.* Paris: Editions de Minuit.

Hall, Stuart. 1977. "The Hinterland of Science: Ideology and the 'Sociology of Knowledge.'" Pp. 9–32 in *On Ideology.* Edited by the Center for Contemporary Cultural Studies. London: Hutchinson.

Hanks, William F. 1987. "Discourse Genres in a Theory of Practice." *American Ethnologist* 14, no. 4 (November): 668–92.

———. 1990. *Referential Practice: Language and Lived Space Among the Maya.* Chicago: The University of Chicago Press.

Hareven, Tamara K. 1990. "A Complex Relationship: Family Strategies and the Processes of Economic Change." Pp. 215–44 in *Beyond the Marketplace: Rethinking Economy and Society.* Edited by Roger Friedland and A. F. Robertson. New York: Aldine de Gruyter.

Harker, Richard K. 1984. "On Reproduction, Habitus and Education." *British Journal of Sociology of Education* 5, no. 2 (June): 117–27.

Harker, Richard, Cheleen Mahar, and Chris Wilkes, eds. 1990. *An Introduction to the Work of Pierre Bourdieu: The Practice of Theory.* New York: Saint Martin's Press.

Haveman, Robert. 1987. *Poverty Policy and Poverty Research: The Great Society and the Social Sciences.* Madison: University of Wisconsin Press.

Heinich, Nathalie. 1987. "Arts et sciences à l'âge classique: professions et institutions culturelles." *Actes de la recherche en sciences sociales* 66/67: 47–78.

Henley, Nancy. 1977. *Body Politics.* Englewood Cliffs, N.J.: Prentice-Hall.

Héran, François. 1987. "La seconde nature de l'habitus. Tradition philosophique et sens commun dans le langage sociologique." *Revue française de sociologie* 28, no. 3 (July–September): 385–416.

Hirschman, Albert. 1987. "Interests." Pp. 882–87 in *The New Palgrave: Dictionary of Economics.* Edited by John Eatwell et al. London: Macmillan.

———. 1991. *The Rhetoric of Reaction: Perversity, Futility, Jeopardy.* Cambridge, Mass.: Belknap Press of Harvard University Press.

Hoffman, Stanley. 1986. "Monsieur Taste." *New York Review of Books* 33, no. 6 (April): 45–48.

Hoggart, Richard. 1967. *The Uses of Literacy: Aspects of Working-Class Life.* London: Chatto and Windus.

Honneth, Axel. 1986. "The Fragmented World of Symbolic Forms: Reflections on Pierre Bourdieu's Sociology of Culture." *Theory, Culture, and Society* 3: 55–66.

Honneth, Axel, Hermann Kocyba, and Bernd Schwibs. 1986. "The Struggle for Symbolic Order: An Interview with Pierre Bourdieu." *Theory, Culture, and Society* 3: 35–51.

Hughes, Everett C. 1984 [1961]. "Ethnocentric Sociology." Pp. 473–77 in *The Sociological Eye: Selected Papers*. New Brunswick: Transaction Books.

Hunt, Lynn. 1984. *Politics, Culture, and Class in the French Revolution*. Berkeley and Los Angeles: University of California Press.

Hunt, Lynn, ed. 1989. *The New Cultural History*. Berkeley and Los Angeles: University of California Press.

Husserl, Edmund. 1982 [1913]. *Ideas Pertaining to a Pure Phenomenology and to a Phenomenological Philosophy. First Book: General Introduction to a Pure Phenomenology*. The Hague: Martinus Nijhoff.

Les idées de mai. 1970. Paris: Gallimard ("Idées").

Ingram, D. 1982. "The Possibility of Communication Ethic Reconsidered: Habermas, Gadamer and Bourdieu on Discourse." *Man and World* 15: 149–61.

Inglis, Fred. 1988. "The Conflict of the Faculties." *The Times Higher Education Supplement*, October 30, 18–19.

Inglis, R. 1979. "Good and Bad Habitus: Bourdieu, Habermas and the Condition of England." *The Sociological Review* 27, no. 2: 353–69.

Jackson, Michael. 1983. "Knowledge and the Body." *Man* 18, no. 2: 327–45.

———. 1989. *Paths Toward a Clearing: Radical Empiricism and Ethnographic Inquiry*. Bloomington: Indiana University Press.

Jacoby, Russell. 1987. *The Last Intellectuals: American Culture in the Age of Academe*. New York: Noonday Press.

Jameson, Fredric. 1990. *Postmodernism or, The Cultural Logic of Capitalism*. Durham: Duke University Press.

Jauss, Hans Robert. 1982. *Toward an Aesthetic of Reception*. Minneapolis: University of Minnesota Press.

Jay, Martin. 1990. "Fieldwork and Theorizing in Intellectual History: A Reply to Fritz Ringer." *Theory and Society* 19, no. 3 (June): 311–22.

Jenkins, Richard. 1982. "Pierre Bourdieu and the Reproduction of Determinism." *Sociology* 16, no. 2 (May): 270–81.

———. 1986. "Review of 'Distinction.'" *Sociology* 20, no. 1 (February): 103–5.

———. 1989. "Language, Symbolic Power and Communication: Bourdieu's 'Homo Academicus.'" *Sociology* 23, no. 4 (November): 639–45.

Joppke, Christian. 1986. "The Cultural Dimension of Class Formation and Class Struggle: On the Social Theory of Pierre Bourdieu." *Berkeley Journal of Sociology* 31: 53–78.

Kaplan, Abraham. 1964. *The Conduct of Inquiry: Methodology for Behavioral Science*. San Francisco: Chandler.

Karabel, Jerry. 1984. "Status Group Struggle, Organizational Interests, and the Limits of Institutional Autonomy: The Transformation of Harvard, Yale, and Princeton, 1918–1940." *Theory and Society* 13: 1–40.

———. 1986. "Community Colleges and Social Stratification in the 1980s." Pp. 13–30 in *The Community College and Its Critics*. Edited by L. S. Zwerling. San Francisco: Jossey-Bass.

Karabel, Jerry, and A. H. Halsey, eds. 1977. *Power and Ideology in Education*. New York: Oxford University Press.

Karady, Victor. 1983. "Les professeurs de la République. Le marché scolaire, les réformes universitaires et les transformations de la fonction professorale à la fin du 19ème siècle." *Actes de la recherche en sciences sociales* 47/48: 90–112.

———. 1985. "Les Juifs de Hongrie sous les lois antisémites. Etude d'une conjoncture sociologique, 1938–1943." *Actes de la recherche en sciences sociales* 56: 3–30.

———. 1988. "Durkheim et les débuts de l'ethnologie universitaire." *Actes de la recherche en sciences sociales* 74: 23–32.

Karady, Victor, and Wolfgang Mitter, eds. 1990. *Bildungswesen und Sozialstruktur in Mitteleuropa im 19. und 20. Jahrhundert.* Cologne: Bohlau Verlag.

Karp, Ivan. 1986. "Agency and Social Theory: A Review of Anthony Giddens." *American Ethnologist* 13, no. 1 (February): 131–37.

Katsilis, John, and Richard Rubinson. 1990. "Cultural Capital, Student Achievement, and Educational Reproduction in Greece." *American Sociological Review* 55: 270–79.

Katz, Michael B. 1989. *The Undeserving Poor: From the War on Poverty to the War on Welfare.* New York: Pantheon.

Kauppi, Niilo. 1991. *Tel Quel: La constitution sociale d'une avant-garde.* Helsinki: The Finnish Society of Sciences and Letters.

———. Forthcoming. "Textual Strategies or Strategies with Texts? 'Tel Quel' or the Social Conditions of Possibility of an Avant Garde." In *Tracing the Semiotic Boundaries of Politics.* Edited by Pertti Ahonen. Berlin: Mouton de Gruyter.

Kauppi, Niilo, and Pekka Sulkunen, eds. 1992. *Vanguards of Modernity: Society, Intellectuals, and the University.* Publications of the Research Unit for Contemporary Culture 32. Jyväskylä, Finland: University of Jyväskylä.

Kestenbaum, Victor. 1977. *The Phenomenological Sense of John Dewey: Habit and Meaning.* Atlantic Highlands, N.J.: Humanities Press.

Knorr-Cetina, Karin. 1981. "The Micro-Sociological Challenge of Macro-Sociology: Towards a Reconstruction of Social Theory and Methodology." Pp. 1–47 in *Advances in Social Theory and Methodology: Toward an Integration of Micro- and Macro-Sociologies.* Edited by Karen Knorr-Cetina and Aaron V. Cicourel. London and Boston: Routledge and Kegan Paul.

Kot, A., and B. Lautier. 1984. "Métaphore économique et magie sociale chez Pierre Bourdieu." Pp. 70–86 in *L'empire du sociologue.* Paris: Editions La Découverte.

Koyré, Alexandre. 1966. *Etudes d'histoire de la pensée scientifique.* Paris: Presses Universitaires de France.

Kraus, Karl. 1976a. *In These Great Times: A Karl Kraus Reader.* Edited and translated by Harry Zohn. Chicago: The University of Chicago Press.

———. 1976b. *Half Truths and One-and-a-Half Truths. Selected Aphorisms.* Edited and translated by Harry Zohn. Chicago: The University of Chicago Press.

Kuhn, Thomas. 1970. *The Structure of Scientific Revolutions.* 2d ed. Chicago: The University of Chicago Press.

Labov, William. 1973. *Language in the Inner City: Studies in the Black English Vernacular.* Philadelphia: University of Pennsylvania Press.

————, ed. 1980. *Locating Language in Time and Space*. New York: Academic Press.

Lacroix, Bernard. 1981. *Durkheim et le politique*. Paris: Presses de la Fondation nationale des sciences politiques.

Lagrave, Rose-Marie. 1990. "Recherches féministes ou recherches sur les femmes?" *Actes de la recherche en sciences sociales* 83: 27–39.

Lakomski, G. 1984. "On Agency and Structure: Pierre Bourdieu and J. C. Passeron's theory of Symbolic Violence." *Curriculum Inquiry* 14, no. 2: 151–163.

Laks, Bernard. 1983. "Langage et pratiques sociales. Etude sociolinguistique d'un groupe d'adolescents." *Actes de la recherche en sciences sociales* 46: 73–97.

Lamb, Stephen. 1989. "Cultural Consumption and the Secondary School Plans of Australian Students." *Sociology of Education* 62: 95–108.

Lamont, Michèle. 1989. "Slipping the World Back In: Bourdieu on Heidegger." *Contemporary Sociology* 18, no. 5 (September): 781–83.

Lamont, Michèle, and Annette P. Lareau. 1988. "Cultural Capital: Allusions, Gaps, and Glissandos in Recent Theoretical Developments." *Sociological Theory* 6, no. 2 (Fall): 153–68.

Lardinois, Roland. 1985. "Peut-on classer la famille hindoue." *Actes de la recherche en sciences sociales* 57/58: 29–46.

Lareau, Annette. 1987. "Social Class and Family-School Relationships: The Importance of Cultural Capital." *Sociology of Education* 56: 73–85.

Larson, Magali Sarfatti. 1977. *The Rise of Professionalism: A Sociological Analysis*. Berkeley and Los Angeles: University of California Press.

Lash, Scott. 1990. "Modernization and Postmodernization in the Work of Pierre Bourdieu." Pp. 237–65 in *Sociology of Postmodernism*. London: Routledge.

Lash, Scott, and John Urry. 1987. *The End of Organized Capitalism*. Cambridge: Polity Press.

Latour, Bruno, and Paolo Fabbri. 1977. "La rhétorique de la science. Pouvoir et devoir dans un article de science exacte." *Actes de la recherche en sciences sociales* 13: 81–95.

Latour, Bruno, and Steve Woolgar. 1979. *Laboratory Life: The Social Construction of Scientific Facts*. London: Sage.

Laumann, Edward O., and David Knoke. 1988. *The Organizational State*. Madison: University of Wisconsin Press.

Lave, Jean. 1989. *Cognition in Practice: Mind, Mathematics and Culture in Everyday Life*. Cambridge: Cambridge University Press.

Lebart, Ludovic, Alain Morineau, and Kenneth M. Warwick. 1984. *Multivariate Descriptive Statistical Analysis: Correspondence Analysis and Related Techniques for Large Matrices*. New York: John Wiley and Sons.

Lee, Orville III. 1988. "Observations on Anthropological Thinking about the Culture Concept: Clifford Geertz and Pierre Bourdieu." *Berkeley Journal of Sociology* 33: 115–30.

Lemert, Charles C. 1986. "French Sociology: After the 'Patrons,' What?" *Contemporary Sociology* 15, no. 5 (September): 689–92.

―――――. 1990. "The Habits of Intellectuals: Response to Ringer." *Theory and Society* 19, no. 3 (June): 295–310.

―――――, ed. 1982. *French Sociology Since 1968: Rupture and Renewal.* New York: Columbia University Press.

Lenoir, Rémi. 1978. "L'invention du 'troisième âge' et la constitution du champ des agents de gestion de la vieillesse." *Actes de la recherche en sciences sociales* 26/27: 57–82.

―――――. 1980. "La notion d'accident du travail: un enjeu de luttes." *Actes de la recherche en sciences sociales* 32/33: 77–88.

―――――. 1985. "L'effondrement des bases sociales du familialisme." *Actes de la recherche en sciences sociales* 57/58: 69–88.

Lepenies, Wolf. 1988. *Between Literature and Science: The Rise of Sociology.* Cambridge: Cambridge University Press; Paris: Editions de la Maison des sciences de l'homme.

Levi, Giovanni. 1989. "Les usages de la biographie." *Annales: économies, sociétés, civilisations*, no. 6 (November–December): 1325–36.

Levine, Donald N. 1985. *The Flight from Ambiguity: Essays in Social and Cultural Theory.* Chicago: The University of Chicago Press.

Levine, Lawrence W. 1988. *High-Brow/Low-Brow: The Emergence of Cultural Hierarchy in America.* Cambridge: Harvard University Press.

Lévi-Strauss, Claude. 1970 [1955]. *Tristes tropiques.* New York: Atheneum.

Lévi-Strauss, Claude, and Didier Eribon. 1988. *De près et de loin.* Paris: Odile Jacob. Translated as *Conversations with Claude Lévi-Strauss.* Chicago: The University of Chicago Press, 1991.

Lewin, Moishe. 1985. *The Making of the Soviet System: Essays in the Social History of Interwar Russia.* New York: Pantheon.

Lichterman, Paul. 1989. "Revisiting a Gramscian Dilemma: Problems and Possibilities in Bourdieu's Analysis of Culture and Politics." Paper presented at the Annual Meeting of the American Sociological Association, San Francisco.

Lieberson, Stanley. 1984. *Making It Count: The Improvement of Social Research and Theory.* Berkeley and Los Angeles: University of California Press.

Lienard, Georges, and Emile Servais. 1979. "Practical Sense: On Bourdieu." *Critique of Anthropology* 13-14 (Summer): 209–19.

Loirand, Gildas. 1989. "De la chute au vol. Genèse et transformations du parachutisme sportif." *Actes de la recherche en sciences sociales* 79: 37–49.

Lord, Albert B. 1960. *The Singer of the Tales.* Cambridge: Cambridge University Press.

Luhmann, Niklas. 1982. "The Economy as a Social System." In *The Differentiation of Society.* New York: Columbia University Press.

Luker, Kristin. 1984. *Abortion and the Politics of Motherhood.* Berkeley and Los Angeles: University of California Press.

McAllester Jones, Mary. 1991. *Gaston Bachelard, Subversive Humanist: Texts and Readings.* Madison: University of Wisconsin Press.

MacAloon, John J. 1988. "A Prefatory Note to Pierre Bourdieu's 'Program for a Sociology of Sport.'" *Sociology of Sport Journal* 5, no. 2 (June): 150–52.

McCleary, Dick. 1989. "Extended Review: Bourdieu's 'Choses dites.'" *The Sociological Review* 37, no. 2 (May): 373–83.

Maccoby, Eleanor E. 1988. "Gender as a Social Category." *Developmental Psychology* 24, no. 6 (November): 755–65.

McLeod. Jay. 1987. *Ain't No Makin' It: Leveled Aspirations in a Low-Income Neighborhood.* Boulder, Colo.: Westview Press.

Mallin, S. 1979. *Merleau-Ponty's Philosophy.* New Haven: Yale University Press.

March, James G. 1978. "Bounded Rationality, Ambiguity, and the Engineering of Choice." *Bell Journal of Economics* 9: 587–608.

Marcus, George E., and Dick Cushman. 1982. "Ethnographies as Texts." *Annual Review of Anthropology* 11: 25–69.

Marcus, George E., and Michael M. J. Fisher. 1986. *Anthropology as Cultural Critique: An Experimental Moment in the Human Sciences.* Chicago: The University of Chicago Press.

Maresca, Sylvain. 1981. "La représentation de la paysannerie. Remarques ethnographiques sur le travail de représentation des dirigeants agricoles." *Actes de la recherche en sciences sociales* 38: 3–18.

———. 1983. *Les dirigeants paysans.* Paris: Editions de Minuit ("Le sens commun").

Marin, Louis. 1988 [1981]. *Portrait of the King.* Minneapolis: University of Minnesota Press.

Margolis, Joseph, and Paul Bunell, eds. 1990. *Heidegger and Nazism.* Philadelphia: Temple University Press.

Martin, Bill, and Ivan Szelenyi. 1987. "Beyond Cultural Capital: Toward a Theory of Symbolic Domination." Pp. 16–49 in *Intellectuals, Universities and the State,* edited by R. Eyerman, T. Svensson, and T. Soderqvist. Berkeley and Los Angeles: University of California Press.

Marx, Karl. 1971. *Die Grundrisse.* Edited by David McLelland. New York: Harper and Row.

Mary, André. 1988. "Métaphores et paradigmes dans le bricolage de la notion d'habitus." *Cahiers du LASA* 8–9.

Mauger, Gérard, and Claude Fossé-Polliak. 1983. "Les loubards." *Actes de la recherche en sciences sociales* 50: 49–67.

Mauss, Marcel. 1950a [1902–3]. "Esquisse d'une théorie générale de la magie." Pp. 1–141 in *Sociologie et anthropologie.* Paris: Presses Universitaires de France. Translated as *A General Theory of Magic.* New York: Norton 1975.

———. 1950b [1936]. "Les techniques du corps." Pp. 365–86 in *Sociologie et anthropologie.* Paris: Presses Universitaires de France. Translated as "Techniques of the Body." *Economy and Society* 2: 70–88.

———. 1950c. *Sociologie et anthropologie.* Paris: Presses Universitaires de France.

Mäzlish, Bruce. 1989. *A New Science: The Breakdown of Connections and the Birth of Sociology.* New York: Oxford University Press.

Mazon, Brigitte. 1988. *Aux origines de l'Ecole des hautes études en sciences sociales. Le rôle du mécenat américain (1920–1960).* Paris: Les Editions du Cerf.

Medick, Hans, and David Warren, eds. 1984. *Interest and Emotion: Essays on the Study of Family and Kinship.* Cambridge: Cambridge University Press; Paris: Editions de la Maison des sciences de l'homme.

Mehan, Hugh, and Houston Wood. 1975. *The Reality of Ethnomethodology.* New York: Wiley.

Merleau-Ponty, Maurice. 1962 [1945]. *Phenomenology of Perception.* Atlantic Highlands, N.J.: Humanities Press.

———. 1963 [1949]. *The Structure of Behaviour.* Boston: Beacon Press.

Merllié, Dominique. 1983. "Une nomenclature et sa mise en oeuvre: les statistiques sur l'origine sociale des étudiants." *Actes de la recherche en sciences sociales* 50: 3–47.

———. 1990. "Le sexe de l'écriture. Note sur la perception sociale de la féminité." *Actes de la recherche en sciences sociales* 83: 40–51.

Merton, Robert K. 1968. *Social Theory and Social Structure.* New York: Free Press.

———. 1975. "Structural Analysis in Sociology." Pp. 21–52 in *Approaches to the Study of Social Structure.* Edited by Peter M. Blau. New York: The Free Press.

———. 1980. "On the Oral Transmission of Knowledge." Pp. 1–35 in *Sociological Traditions from Generation to Generation.* Edited by R. K. Merton and Mathilda White Riley. Norwood: Ablex.

———. 1987. "Three Fragments from a Sociologist's Notebooks: Establishing the Phenomenon, Specified Ignorance, and Strategic Research Materials." *Annual Review of Sociology* 13: 1–28.

Miller, Max. 1989. "Die kulturelle Dressur des Leviathans und ihre epistemologischen Reflexe." *Soziologische Revue* 12, no. 1 (January): 19–24.

Miller, Don, and Jan Branson. 1987. "Pierre Bourdieu: Culture and Praxis." Pp. 210–25 in *Creating Culture: Profiles in the Study of Culture.* Edited by Diane J. Austin-Broos. Sydney: Allen and Unwin.

Mills, C. Wright. 1959. *The Sociological Imagination.* New York: Oxford University Press.

Miyajima, Takashi. 1990. "The Logic of Bourdieu's Sociology: On Social Determinism, Autonomy, and the Body" (in Japanese). *Gendai Shisso* 18, no. 3: 220–29.

Miyajima, Takashi, Hidenori Fujita, Yuichi Akinaga, Kenji Haschimoto, and Kokichi Shimizu. 1987. "Cultural Stratification and Cultural Reproduction" (in Japanese). *Tokyo Daigaku Kyoiku Gakubu Kiyo* (Annals of the Faculty of Education of Tokyo): 51–89.

Monnerot, Jules. 1945. *Les faits sociaux ne sont pas des choses.* Paris: Gallimard.

Morgan, David H. 1989. "Strategies and Sociologists: A Comment on Crow." *Sociology* 23, no. 1 (February): 25–29.

Mortier, Freddy. 1989. "Actietheoretische analyse van rituelen volgens de praxeologie van Pierre Bourdieu." *Antropologische Verkenningen* 8, no. 2 (Summer): 40–48.

Muel-Dreyfus, Francine. 1977. "Les Instituteurs, les paysans et l'ordre républicain." *Actes de la recherche en sciences sociales* 17/18: 37–64.

Müller, Hans Peter. 1986. "Kultur, Geschmack und Distinktion. Grundzüge der Kultursoziologie Pierre Bourdieus." *Kölner Zeitschrift für Soziologie und Sozialforschung*, supplement, 162–70.

Münch, Richard. 1989. "Code, Structure, and Action: Building a Theory of Structuration from a Parsonian Point of View." Pp. 101–17 in *Theory Building in Sociology: Assessing Theory Cumulation*. Edited by Jonathan H. Turner. Newbury Park: Sage Publications.

Murphy, R. 1982. "Power and Autonomy in the Sociology of Education." *Theory and Society* 11: 179–203.

Murphy, Raymond. 1983. "The Struggle for Scholarly Recognition: The Development of the Closure Problematic in Sociology." *Theory and Society* 12: 631–58.

Nash, Roy. 1986. "Educational and Social Inequality: The Theories of Bourdieu and Boudon with Reference to Class and Ethnic Differences in New Zealand." *New Zealand Sociology* 1, no. 2 (November): 121–37.

Needham, Rodney. 1963. Introduction. Pp. vii–xlviii in Emile Durkheim and Marcel Mauss, *Primitive Classification*. Chicago: The University of Chicago Press.

Nisbet, Robert. 1976. *Sociology as an Art Form*. New York: Oxford University Press.

Oakes, Jeannie. 1985. *Keeping Track: How Schools Structure Inequality*. New Haven: Yale University Press.

O'Brien, Mary. 1981. *The Politics of Reproduction*. London: Routledge and Kegan Paul.

Offerlé, Michel. 1988. "Le nombre de voix: électeurs, partis et électorat socialistes à la fin du 19ème siècle en France." *Actes de la recherche en sciences sociales* 71/72: 5–21.

Ollman, Bertell. 1976. *Alienation: Marx's Conception of Man in Capitalist Society*. Cambridge: Cambridge University Press.

Olson, Mancur. 1965. *The Logic of Collective Action*. Cambridge, Mass.: Harvard University Press.

O'Neill, John. 1972. *Sociology as a Skin Trade: Essays Towards a Reflexive Sociology*. New York: Harper and Row.

Ortiz, Renato. 1983. "A procura de uma sociologia da pratica." Pp. 7–36 in Pierre Bourdieu. *Sociologia*. Sao Paulo: Atica.

Ortner, Sherry. 1984. "Theory in Anthropology Since the 1960s." *Comparative Studies in Society and History* 26: 126–66.

Ory, Pascal, and Jean-François Sirinelli. 1986. *Les intellectuels en France, de l'Affaire Dreyfus à nos jours*. Paris: Armand Colin.

Österberg, Dag. 1988. "Bourdieu's Doctrine of Habitus and the Socio-Cultural Fields." Pp. 173–80 in *Metasociology: An Inquiry into the Origins and Validity of Social Thought*. Oslo: Norwegian University Press.

Ostrow, James M. 1981. "Culture as a Fundamental Dimension of Experience: A Discussion of Pierre Bourdieu's Theory of the Human Habitus." *Human Studies* 4, no. 3 (July–September): 279–97.

———. 1990. *Social Sensitivity: An Analysis of Experience and Habit*. Stony Brook: State University of New York Press.

Paradeise, Catherine. 1981. "Sociabilité et culture de classe." *Revue française de sociologie* 21, no. 4 (October–December).

Parsons, Talcott. 1937. *The Structure of Social Action*. Glencoe, Ill: The Free Press.

Parsons, Talcott, and Neil J. Smelser. 1956. *Economy and Society: A Study in the Integration of Economic and Social Theory*. London: Routledge and Kegan Paul.

Passeron, Jean-Claude. 1986. "La signification des théories de la reproduction socio-culturelle." *International Social Science Journal* 38, no. 4 (December): 619–29.

Pels, Dick. 1989. "Inleiding." Pp. 7–21 in Pierre Bourdieu, *Opstellen over smaak, habitus en het veldbegrip*. Amsterdam: Van Gennep.

Peneff, Jean. 1988. "The Observers Observed: French Survey Researchers at Work." *Social Problems* 35, no. 5 (December): 520–35.

Pepper, Stephen C. 1942. *World Hypotheses*. Berkeley and Los Angeles: University of California Press.

Perinbanayagam, R. S. 1985. *Signifying Acts: Structure and Meaning in Everyday Life*. Carbondale: Southern Illinois University Press.

Perrot, Martyne, and Martin de la Soudrière. 1988. "Le masque ou la plume? Les enjeux de l'écriture en sciences sociales." *Informations sur les sciences sociales* 27, no. 3 (September): 439–60.

Phillips, Bernard S. 1988. "Toward a Reflexive Sociology." *The American Sociologist* 19, no. 2: 138–51.

Pialoux, Michel. 1978. "Jeunes sans avenir et marché du travail temporaire." *Actes de la recherche en sciences sociales* 26/27: 19–47.

Pinell, Patrice. 1987. "Fléau moderne et médecine d'avenir: la cancérologie française entre les deux guerres." *Actes de la recherche en sciences sociales* 68: 45–76.

Pinçon, Michel. 1985. "Un patronat paternel." *Actes de la recherche en sciences sociales* 57/58: 95–102.

———. 1987. *Désarrois ouvriers*. Paris: L'Harmattan.

Pinçon, Michel, and Monique Pinçon-Rendu. 1989. *Dans les beaux quartiers*. Paris: Editions du Seuil.

Pinto, Louis. 1975. "L'armée, le contingent et les classes." *Actes de la recherche en sciences sociales* 3: 18–41.

———. 1984a. *L'intelligence en action: Le Nouvel Observateur*. Paris: Anne-Marie Métailié.

———. 1984b. "La vocation de l'universel. La formation de l'intellectuel vers 1900." *Actes de la recherche en sciences sociales* 55: 23–32.

———. 1987. *Les philosophes entre le lycée et l'avant-garde. Les métamorphoses de la philosophie dans la France d'aujourd'hui*. Paris: L'Harmattan.

Platt, Robert. 1989. "Reflexivity, Recursion and Social Life: Elements for a Postmodern Sociology." *The Sociological Review* 37, no. 4 (November): 636–67.

Pociello, Christian. 1981. *Le Rugby ou la guerre des styles*. Paris: Anne-Marie Métailié.

Pollak, Michael. 1979. "Paul Lazarsfeld, fondateur d'une multinationale scientifique." *Actes de la recherche en sciences sociales* 25: 45–59.

———. 1980. "Paul Lazarsfeld: A Sociointellectual Portrait." *Knowledge* 2, no. 2 (December): 157–77.

————. 1981. "Une sociologie en actes des intellectuels: les combats de Karl Kraus." *Actes de la recherche en sciences sociales* 36/37: 87–103.

————. 1988. *Les homosexuels et le SIDA: sociologie d'une épidémie.* Paris: Anne-Marie Métailié.

Pollak, Michael, with Marie-Ange Schiltz. 1987. "Identité sociale et gestion d'un risque de santé. Les homosexuels face au SIDA." *Actes de la recherche en sciences sociales* 68: 77–102.

Pollner, Melvin. 1991. "Left of Ethnomethodology: The Rise and Decline of Radical Reflexivity." *American Sociological Review* 56, no. 3 (June): 370–80.

Ponton, Rémi. 1977. "Les images de la paysannerie dans le roman rural à la fin du 19ème siècle." *Actes de la recherche en sciences sociales* 17/18: 62–71.

Poulantzas, Nicos. 1973 [1968]. *Political Power and Social Classes.* London: New Left Books.

Powell, Walter W., and Paul DiMaggio, eds. 1991. *The New Institutionalism in Organizational Analysis.* Chicago: The University of Chicago Press.

Pudal, Bernard. 1988. "Les dirigeants communistes. Du 'fils du peuple' à 'l'instituteur des masses.'" *Actes de la recherche en sciences sociales* 71/72: 46–70.

————. 1989. *Prendre parti. Pour une sociologie historique du PCF.* Paris: Presses de la Fondation nationale des sciences politiques.

Quine, Willard Van Orman. 1969. *Ontological Relativity and Other Essays.* New York: Columbia University Press.

Rabinow, Paul. 1977. *Reflections on Fieldwork.* Berkeley and Los Angeles: University of California Press.

————. 1982. "Masked I Go Forward: Reflections on the Modern Subject." Pp. 173–85 in *A Crack in the Mirror: Reflexive Perspectives in Anthropology.* Edited by Jay Ruby. Philadelphia: University of Pennsylvania Press.

Rabinow, Paul, and William H. Sullivan, eds. 1979. *Interpretive Social Science: A Reader.* Berkeley and Los Angeles: University of California Press.

Rancière, Jacques. 1984. "L'éthique de la sociologie." Pp. 13–36 in *L'empire du sociologue.* Edited by Collectif 'Révoltes Logiques.' Paris: Editions La Découverte.

Rasmussen, David. 1981. "Praxis and Social Theory." *Human Studies* 4, no. 3 (July–September): 273–78.

Rébérioux, Madeleine. 1988. "L'histoire sociale." Pp. 95–99 in *L'histoire en France.* Paris: Editions La Découverte.

Récanati, R. 1982. *Les énoncés performatifs.* Paris: Editions de Minuit.

Richer, Laurent, ed. 1983. *L'activité désintéressée: fiction ou réalité juridique.* Paris: Economica.

Ricoeur, Paul. 1977. "Phenomenology and the Social Sciences." *The Annals of the Phenomenological Society* 2: 145–59.

Riemer, Jeffrey M. 1977. "Varieties of Opportunistic Research." *Urban Life* 5, no. 4 (January): 467–77.

Ringer, Fritz. 1990. "The Intellectual Field, Intellectual History, and the Sociology of Knowledge." *Theory and Society* 19, no. 3 (June): 269–94.

————. 1991. *Fields of Knowledge: French Academic Culture in Comparative Perspective, 1890–1920.* Cambridge: Cambridge University Press.

Rioux, Jean-Pierre, and Jean-François Sirinelli, eds. 1991. *La guerre d'Algérie et les intellectuels français.* Brussels: Editions Complexe.

Rittner, Volker. 1984. "Geschmack und Natürlichkeit." *Kölner Zeitschrift für Soziologie und Sozialforschung* 36, no. 2: 372–78.

Ritzer, George. 1990a. "Metatheory in Sociology." *Sociological Forum* 5, no. 1 (March): 3–17.

———, ed. 1990b. *Frontiers of Social Theory: The New Syntheses.* New York: Columbia University Press.

Robinson, Robert V., and Maurice A. Garnier. 1985. "Class Reproduction among Men and Women in France: Reproduction Theory on its Home Ground." *American Journal of Sociology* 91, no. 2 (September): 250–80.

Robbins, Derek. 1988. "Bourdieu in England." Typescript. School for Independent Study, North-East London Polytechnic.

———. 1991. *The Work of Pierre Bourdieu: Recognizing Society.* Milton Keynes: Open University Press.

Rogers, Susan Carol. 1991. *Shaping Modern Times in Rural France: The Transformation and Reproduction of an Averyronnais Community.* Princeton: Princeton University Press.

Rosaldo, Renato. 1989. *Culture and Truth: The Remaking of Social Analysis.* Boston: Beacon Press.

Ross, George. 1991. "Where Have All the Sartres Gone? The French Intelligentsia Born Again." Pp. 221–49 in *Searching for the New France.* Edited by James F. Hollifield and George Ross. London and New York: Routledge.

Rossi, Peter H. 1989. *Down and Out in America: The Origins of Homelessness.* Chicago: The University of Chicago Press.

Rouse, Joseph. 1987. *Knowledge and Power: Toward a Political Philosophy of Science.* Ithaca, N.Y.: Cornell University Press.

Rupp, Jan C. C., and Rob de Lange. 1989. "Social Order, Cultural Capital and Citizenship. An Essay Concerning Educational Status and Educational Power Versus Comprehensiveness of Elementary Schools." *The Sociological Review* 37, no. 4 (November): 668–705.

Ryan, Jake, and Charles Sackrey, eds. 1984. *Strangers in Paradise: Academics from the Working Class.* Boston: South End Press.

Sack, Hans-Gerhard. 1988. "The Relationship Between Sport Involvement and Life-Style in Youth Culture." *International Review for the Sociology of Sport* 23, no. 3: 213–32.

Sacks, Harvey, and Emmanuel A. Schegloff. 1979. "Two Preferences in the Organization of Reference to Persons in Conversation and their Interaction." Pp. 15–21 in *Everyday Language: Studies in Ethnomethodology.* Edited by George Psathas. New York: Irvington Press.

Sahlins, Marshall. 1985. *Islands of History.* Chicago: The University of Chicago Press.

———. 1989. "Post-structuralisme, anthropologie et histoire." *L'ethnographie* 105 (Spring): 9–34.

Saint Martin, Monique de. 1971. *Les fonctions sociales de l'enseignement scientifique.* Paris and The Hague: Mouton and De Gruyter.

———. 1980. "Une grande famille." *Actes de la recherche en sciences sociales* 31: 4–21.

———. 1985. "Les stratégies matrimoniales dans l'aristocratie. Notes provisoires." *Actes de la recherche en sciences sociales* 59: 74–77.

———. 1989a. "La noblesse et les 'sports' nobles." *Actes de la recherche en sciences sociales* 80: 22–31.

———. 1989b. "Structure du capital, différenciation selon les sexes et 'vocation' intellectuelle." *Sociologie et sociétés* 21, no. 2 (October): 9–25.

———. 1990a. "Une 'bonne' éducation: Notre Dame des Oiseaux." *Ethnologie française* 20, no. 1: 62–70.

———. 1990b. "Les 'femmes écrivains' et le champ littéraire." *Actes de la recherche en sciences sociales* 83: 52–56.

Sanchez de Horcájo, J. J. 1979. *La cultura, reproducio o cambia: el analysis sociologico de P. Bourdieu*. Monograph 23. Madrid: Centro de Investigaciones Sociologicas.

Sanjek, Roger, ed. 1990. *Fieldnotes: The Makings of Anthropology*. Ithaca, N.Y.: Cornell University Press.

Sartre, Jean-Paul. 1981–91. *The Family Idiot: Gustave Flaubert, 1821–1857*. 4 vols. Chicago: The University of Chicago Press.

———. 1987. Preface. Pp. 7–64 in Paul Nizan, *Aden, Arabie*. New York: Columbia University Press.

Saussure, Ferdinand de. 1974 [1960]. *Course in General Linguistics*. London: Fontana.

Sayad, Abdelmalek. 1977. "Les trois 'âges' de l'émigration algérienne en France." *Actes de la recherche en sciences sociales* 15: 59–79.

———. 1979. "Les enfants illégitimes." *Actes de la recherche en sciences sociales* 25: 61–81; 26/27: 117–132.

———. 1985. "Du message oral au message sur cassette: la communication avec l'absent." *Actes de la recherche en sciences sociales* 59: 61–72.

———. 1991. *L'immigration, ou les paradoxes de l'altérité*. Brussels: Editions De Boeck.

Schatzki, Theodore Richard. 1987. "Overdue Analysis of Bourdieu's Theory of Practice." *Inquiry* 30, nos. 1-2 (March): 113–36.

Schegloff, Emmanuel. 1987. "Between Macro and Micro: Contexts and Other Connections." Pp. 207–34 in the *Micro-Macro Link*. Edited by Jeffrey C. Alexander et al. Berkeley and Los Angeles: University of California Press.

Scheler, Max. 1963. *Ressentiment*. Introduction by Lewis A. Coser. New York: The Free Press.

Scherrer, Jutta. 1990. "L'érosion de l'image de Lénine." *Actes de la recherche en sciences sociales* 85: 54–69.

Schiltz, M. 1982. "Habitus and Peasantisation in Nigeria: A Yoruba Case Study." *Man* 17, no. 4: 728–46.

Schmidt, James. 1985. *Maurice Merleau-Ponty: Between Phenomenology and Structuralism*. New York: Saint Martin's Press.

Schneider, Joseph W. 1985. "Social Problems Theory: The Constructionist View." *Annual Review of Sociology* 11: 209–29.

Schon, Donald. 1983. *The Reflective Practicioner: How Professionals Think in Action*. New York: Basic Books.

Schorske, Carl E. 1981 [1961]. *Fin-de-Siècle Vienna: Politics and Culture*. New York: Vintage.

Schudson, Michael. 1978. *Discovering the News*. New York: Basic Books.

Schutz, Alfred. 1970. *On Phenomenology and Social Relations*. Edited and with an introduction by Helmut R. Wagner. Chicago: The University of Chicago Press.

Schwenk, Otto G. 1989. "Wohlfahrsstaat, Klasse und Kultur. Eine Prüfung der Argumente Pierre Bourdieus im Lichte empirischer Befünde zum Wirken des Wohlfahrtsstaat." *Soziologenkorrespondenz* 13: 155–79.

Scott, James C. 1985. *Weapons of the Weak: Everyday Forms of Peasant Resistance*. New Haven: Yale University Press.

———. 1990. *Domination and the Arts of Resistance: Hidden Transcripts*. New Haven: Yale University Press.

Scott, Joan. 1988. *Gender and the Politics of History*. New York: Columbia University Press.

Searle, John R. 1983. *Intentionality: An Essay in the Philosophy of Mind*. Cambridge: Cambridge University Press.

Sewell, William H., Jr. 1980. *Work and Revolution in France: The Language of Labor from the Old Regime to 1848*. Cambridge: Cambridge University Press.

———. 1987. "Theory of Action, Dialectic and History: Comment on Coleman." *American Journal of Sociology* 93, no. 1 (July): 166–72.

———. 1992. "A Theory of Structure: Duality, Agency, and Transformation." *American Journal of Sociology* 98, no. 1 (Forthcoming)

Sharrock, Wes, and Bob Anderson. 1986. *The Ethnomethodologists*. London: Tavistock.

Shusterman, Richard, ed. 1989. *Analytic Aesthetics*. Oxford and New York: Basil Blackwell.

Sica, Alan. 1989. "Social Theory's 'Constituency.'" *The American Sociologist* 20, no. 3 (Fall): 227–41.

Simon, Herbert. 1957. *Models of Man*. New York: Wiley.

Skocpol, Theda R. 1979. *States and Social Revolutions: A Comparative Analysis of France, Russia, and China*. Cambridge: Cambridge University Press.

Smelser, Neil J., ed. 1988. *Handbook of Sociology*. Newbury Park, Calif.: Sage Publications.

Snook, Ivan. 1990. "Language, Truth and Power: Bourdieu's 'Ministerium.'" Pp. 160–80 in *An Introduction to the Work of Pierre Bourdieu*, edited by Richard Harker, Cheleen Mahar, and Chris Wilkes. New York: Saint Martin's Press, 1990.

Snyders, George. 1976. *Ecole, classe et culture de classe. Une relecture critique de Baudelot-Establet, Bourdieu-Passeron et Illich*. Paris: Presses Universitaires de France.

Spector, Malcom, and John I. Kitsuse. 1987. *Constructing Social Problems*. New York: Aldine de Gruyter.

Spencer, J. 1989. "Anthropology as a Kind of Writing." *Man* 24, no. 1: 145–64.

Staub-Bernasconi, Silvia. 1989. "Theoretiker und Praktikerinnen sozialer Arbeit: Essay über symbolische Macht und die Bewegungsgesetze des Bildungscapitals." *Schweizerische Zeitschrift für Sociologie* 14, no. 3 (December): 445–68.

Steinrücke, Margareta. 1989. "Notiz zum Begriff der Habitus bei Bourdieu." *Das Argument* 30, no. 1 (January–February): 92–95.

Stinchcombe, Arthur. 1986. "The Development of Scholasticism." Pp. 45–52 in *Approaches to Social Theory*. Edited by Siegwart Lidenberg, James S. Coleman, and Stefan Nowak. New York: Russell Sage Foundation.

Strawson, Peter F. 1959. *Individuals: An Essay in Metaphysics*. London: Methuen.

Suaud, Charles. 1978. *La vocation. Conversion et reconversion des prêtres ruraux*. Paris: Editions de Minuit ("Le sens commun").

———. 1982. "Conversions religieuses et reconversions économiques." *Actes de la recherche en sciences sociales* 44/45: 72–94.

———. 1989. "Espace des sports, espace social et effets d'âge. La diffusion du tennis, du squash et du golf dans l'agglomération nantaise." *Actes de la recherche en sciences sociales* 79: 2–20.

Sudnow, David. 1978. *Ways of the Hand: The Organization of Improvised Conduct*. Cambridge: Harvard University Press.

Sulkunen, Pekka. 1982. "Society Made Visible: On the Cultural Sociology of Pierre Bourdieu." *Acta Sociologica* 25, no. 2: 103–15.

Swartz, David. 1977. "Pierre Bourdieu: The Cultural Transmission of Social Inequality." *Harvard Educational Review* 47 (November): 545–54.

———. 1981. "Classes, Educational Systems and Labor Markets." *European Journal of Sociology* 22, no. 2: 325–53.

Swedberg, Richard. 1990. *Economics and Sociology: Redefining Their Boundaries*. Princeton: Princeton University Press.

Swedberg, Richard, Ulf Himmelstrand, and Göran Brulin. 1987. "The Paradigm of Economic Sociology: Premises and Promises." *Theory and Society* 16, no. 2: 169–214.

Szelenyi, Ivan. 1988. *Socialist Entrepreneurs: Enbourgeoisement in Rural Hungary*. Cambridge: Polity Press; Madison: University of Wisconsin Press.

Sztompka, Piotr. 1986. *Robert K. Merton: An Intellectual Profile*. New York: Saint Martin's Press.

———. 1991. *Society in Action: The Theory of Social Becoming*. Chicago: The University of Chicago Press; Cambridge: Polity Press.

Terdiman, Richard. 1985. *Discourse/Counterdiscourse: The Theory and Practice of Symbolic Resistance*. Ithaca, N.Y.: Cornell University Press.

Terray, Emmanuel. 1990. *La politique dans la caverne*. Paris: Editions du Seuil.

Thapan, Meenakshi. 1988. "Some Aspects of Cultural Reproduction and Pedagogic Communication." *Economic and Political Weekly*, March 19, 592–96.

Thévenot, Laurent. 1979. "Une jeunesse difficile. Les fonctions sociales du flou et de la rigueur dans les classements." *Actes de la recherche en sciences sociales* 26/27: 3–18.

Thompson, E. P. 1963. *The Making of the English Working Class*. Harmondsworth: Penguin.

Thompson, John B. 1984. "Symbolic Violence: Language and Power in the Sociology of Pierre Bourdieu." Pp. 42–72 in *Studies in the Theory of Ideology*. Cambridge: Polity Press.

———. 1991. Editor's introduction. In Pierre Bourdieu, *Language and Symbolic Power*. Cambridge: Polity Press; Cambridge: Harvard University Press.

Tiles, Mary. 1984. *Bachelard: Science, and Objectivity*. Cambridge: Cambridge University Press.

Tilly, Charles. 1986. *The Contentious French: Four Centuries of Popular Struggles*. Cambridge: Harvard University Press.

———. 1990. *Coercion, Capital, and European States, A.D. 990–1990*. New York: Basil Blackwell.

Timms, Edward. 1986. *Karl Kraus—Apocalyptic Satirist: Culture and Catastrophe in Habsburg Vienna*. New Haven: Yale University Press.

Traweek, Susan. 1989. *Beamtimes and Lifetimes: The World of High-Energy Physicists*. Cambridge: Harvard University Press.

Turner, Jenny. 1990. "Academicus Unchained." *City Limits*, January 4–11.

Turner, Jonathan. 1987. "Analytic Theorizing." Pp. 156–94 in *Social Theory Today*. Edited by Anthony Giddens and Jonathan Turner. Cambridge: Polity Press.

Tyler, Stephen A. 1987. *The Unspeakable: Discourse, Dialogue, and Rhetoric in the Postmodern World*. Madison: University of Wisconsin Press.

Urry, John. 1990. *The Tourist Gaze: Leisure and Travel in Contemporary Society*. Newbury Park, Calif.: Sage Publications.

Van Maanen, John. 1988. *Tales of the Field: On Writing Ethnography*. Chicago: The University of Chicago Press.

Van Parijs, Philippe. 1981. "Sociology as General Economics." *European Journal of Sociology* 22, no. 2: 299–324.

Verboven, Dick. 1989. "Bourdieu in breder perspectief: parallellen en divergenties tussen de praxeologische benaderingen van Leuven en Gent." *Antropologische Verkenningen* 8, no. 2 (Summer): 1–7.

Verdès-Leroux, Jeannine. 1976. "Pouvoir et assistance: cinquante ans de service social." *Actes de la recherche en sciences sociales* 2/3: 152–72.

———. 1978. *Le travail social*. Paris: Editions de Minuit ("Le sens commun").

———. 1981. "Une institution totale auto-perpétuée: le Parti Communiste Français." *Actes de la recherche en sciences sociales* 36/37: 33–63.

Verger, Annie. 1982. "L'artiste saisi par l'école. Classements scolaires et 'vocation' artistique." *Actes de la recherche en sciences sociales* 42: 19–32.

———. 1987. "L'art d'estimer l'art. Comment classer l'incomparable." *Actes de la recherche en sciences sociales* 66/67: 105–21.

Vernier, Bernard. 1985. "Stratégies matrimoniales et choix d'objet incestueux. Dôt, diplôme, liberté sexuelle, prénom." *Actes de la recherche en sciences sociales* 57/58: 3–27.

———. 1989. "Fétichisme du nom, échanges affectifs intra-familiaux et affinités électives." *Actes de la recherche en sciences sociales* 78: 2–17.

Vervaëck, Bart. 1989. "Over lijnen, cirkels en spiralen: een kritiek op Pierre Bourdieu." *Antropologische Verkenningen* 8, no. 2 (Summer): 8–17.

Viala, Alain. 1985. *Naissance de l'écrivain. Sociologie de la littérature à l'âge classique.* Paris: Editions de Minuit ("Le sens commun").

———. 1988. "Prismatic Effects." *Critical Inquiry* 14, no. 3 (Spring): 563–73.

Villette, Michel. 1976. "Psychosociologie d'entreprise et rééducation morale." *Actes de la recherche en sciences sociales* 4: 47–65.

Wacquant, Loïc J. D. 1987. "Symbolic Violence and the Making of the French Agriculturalist: An Inquiry Into Pierre Bourdieu's Sociology." *Australian and New Zealand Journal of Sociology* 23, no. 1 (March): 65–88.

———. 1989a. "Corps et âme: notes ethnographiques d'un apprenti-boxeur." *Actes de la recherche en sciences sociales* 80: 36–67.

———. 1989b. "Toward a Reflexive Sociology: A Workshop with Pierre Bourdieu." *Sociological Theory* 7, no. 1 (Spring): 26–63.

———. 1989c. "Portraits académiques. Autobiographie et censure scientifique dans la sociologie américaine." *Revue de l'Institut de Sociologie* 1/2: 143–54.

———. 1990a. "Sociology as Socio-Analysis: Tales of 'Homo Academicus.'" *Sociological Forum* 5, no. 4 (Winter): 677–89.

———. 1990b. "Exiting Roles or Exiting Role Theory? Critical Notes on Ebaugh's 'Becoming An Ex.'" *Acta Sociologica* 33, no. 4 (Winter): 397–404.

———. 1992. "Bourdieu in America: Notes on the Transatlantic Importation of Social Theory." Forthcoming in Calhoun, LiPuma, and Postone 1992.

Wacquant, Loïc J. D., and Craig Jackson Calhoun. 1989. "Intérêt, rationalité et culture. A propos d'un récent débat sur la théorie de l'action." *Actes de la recherche en sciences sociales* 78: 41–60.

Wallace, Walter L. 1988. "Toward a Disciplinary Matrix in Sociology." Pp. 23–76 in *Handbook of Sociology.* Edited by Neil J. Smelser. Newbury Park: Sage Publications.

Weber, Max. 1949. *The Methodology of the Social Sciences.* Edited by Edward A. Shils and Henry A. Finch. Glencoe, Ill.: The Free Press.

Weber, Max. 1978 [1918–20]. *Economy and Society.* Berkeley and Los Angeles: University of California Press.

Weis, Lois, ed. 1988. *Class, Race, and Gender in American Education.* Albany: State University of New York Press.

Wexler, Philip. 1987. *The New Sociology of Education.* London: Routledge.

Wiley, Norbert. 1990. "The History and Politics of Recent Sociological Theory." Pp. 392–415 in *Frontiers of Social Theory: The New Syntheses.* Edited by George Ritzer. New York: Columbia University Press.

Willis, Paul. 1977. *Learning to Labour: How Working-Class Kids Get Working-Class Jobs.* New York: Columbia University Press.

———. 1983. "Cultural Production and Theories of Reproduction." In *Race, Class, and Education.* Edited by L. Barton and S. Walker. London: Croom-Helm.

Wilson, Elizabeth. 1988. "Picasso and pâté de foie gras. Pierre Bourdieu's Sociology of Culture." *Diacritics* 18, no. 2 (Summer): 47–60.

Winckler, Joachim. 1989. "'Monsieur le Professeur!' Anmerkungen zur Soziologie Pierre Bourdieus." *Sociologia Internationalis* 27, no. 1: 5–18.

Winkin, Yves. 1990. "Goffman et les femmes." *Actes de la recherche en sciences sociales* 83: 57–61.

Wippler, Reinhard. 1990. "Cultural Resources and Participation in High Culture." Pp. 187–204 in *Social Institutions: Their Emergence, Maintenance, and Effects*. Edited by Michael Hechter, Karl-Dieter Opp, and Reinhard Wippler. New York: Aldine Publishing Company.

Wittgenstein, Ludwig. 1977. *Vermischte Bemerkungen*. Frankfurt: Suhrkamp Verlag.

———. 1980. *Remarks on the Philosophy of Psychology*. Oxford: Basil Blackwell.

Wolfe, Alan. 1989a. *Whose Keeper? Social Science and Moral Obligation*. Berkeley and Los Angeles: University of California Press.

———. 1989b. "Market, State, and Society as Codes of Moral Obligation." *Acta Sociologica* 32, no. 3: 221–36.

Woolard, K. 1985. "Language Variation and Cultural Hegemony: Towards an Integration of Sociolinguistics and Social Theory." *American Ethnologist* 12: 738–48.

Woolf, Stuart, ed. 1991. *Domestic Strategies: Work and Family in France and Italy, 1600–1800*. Cambridge: Cambridge University Press; Paris: Editions de la Maison des sciences de l'homme.

Woolf, Virginia. 1987 [1927]. *To the Lighthouse*. New York: Harvest/HBJ Books.

Woolgar, Steve, ed. 1988. *Knowledge and Reflexivity: New Frontiers in the Sociology of Knowledge*. London: Sage.

Wrong, Dennis. 1961. "The Oversocialized Conception of Man." *American Sociological Review* 26: 183–93.

Yamamoto, Tetsuji. 1988. *Power/Practices/Discourse: Foucault, Bourdieu, Illich*. Tokyo: Discours.

Zarca, Bernard. 1979. "Artisanat et trajectoires sociales." *Actes de la recherche en sciences sociales* 29: 3–26.

Zelizer, Viviana. 1988. "Beyond the Polemics on the Market: Establishing a Theoretical and Empirical Agenda." *Sociological Forum* 3, no. 4 (Fall): 614–34.

Zolberg, Vera. 1986. "Taste as a Social Weapon." *Contemporary Sociology* 15, no. 4 (July): 511–15.

———. 1990. *Constructing a Sociology of the Arts*. Cambridge: Cambridge University Press.

Zukin, Sharon, and Paul DiMaggio, eds. 1990. *Structures of Capital: The Social Organization of the Economy*. Cambridge: Cambridge University Press.

Zukerman, Harriet. 1988. "The Sociology of Science." Pp. 511–74 in *Handbook of Sociology*. Edited by Neil J. Smesler. Newbury Park, Calif.: Sage.

Name Index

Abbott, Andrew, 242
Abrams, Philip, 16, 91n.35
Accardo, Alain, 2n.1
Adair, Philippe, 115n.67
Addelson, Katharine Pyne, 157
Alexander, Jeffrey C., 3n.3, 31, 31n.53, 32, 162, 224, 224n.11
Althusser, Louis, 8, 19, 155n.111, 156, 164, 251n.49
Anderson, Bob, 40, 144
Ansart, Pierre, 2n.1, 11n.21, 132n.85
Apel, Otto, 139
Arendt, Hannah, 102n.55
Aristotle, 128, 183
Aron, Raymond, 46, 46n.83
Aronowitz, Stanley, 79
Ashmore, Malcolm, 36n.63, 43n.77
Atkinson, Paul, 41n.72
Auerbach, Erich, 124
Augstein, Rudof, 154n.109
Austin, J. L., 147–48, 148n.100, 169

Bachelard, Gaston, 5n.7, 35, 35n.60, 45n.82, 73, 74, 95n.43, 161n.115, 174, 177n.132, 181, 194, 195n.155, 233, 251n.49
Bakhtin, Mikhail, 141
Baldwin, John B., 122n.77
Bancaud, Alain, 243n.39
Barnard, Henri, 41, 41n.73, 42n.75, 66n.8

Barthes, Roland, 154, 156
Baudrillard, Jean, 154
Becker, Gary S., 25n.45, 115n.67, 118
Becker, Howard, 110n.63
Beeghley, Leonard, 241n.37
Beisel, Nicola, 4n.4
Bell, Daniel, 77n.17
Bellah, Robert, 49, 50n.90
Benveniste, Emile, 147
Benzécri, Jean-Pierre, 96n.47
Berelson, Bernard, 96
Berger, Bennett, 36n.63, 37, 38, 38n.68, 43n.77, 63n.2, 80n.24, 205n.166
Berger, Peter, 9n.17
Best, Joel, 239n.30
Bidet, Jacques, 79, 135–36
Blanchot, Maurice, 154n.109
Blau, Peter, 23
Bloch, Maurice, 10n.19
Bloor, David, 36n.63, 37, 43n.77, 71
Blumer, Herbert, 9n.17, 23
Bohn, Cornelia, 2n.1, 104n.56
Boigeol, Anne, 243n.39
Boltanski, Luc, 14, 26, 94n.42, 142n.95, 145, 160, 206n.167, 221n.4, 238n.29, 239n.31, 243n.40, 262
Bon, François, 2n.1
Boschetti, Anna, 155n.111, 243n.41
Bourgois, Philippe, 82n.26
Bouveresse, Jacques, 196n.157

313

Subject Index

Academia, 254–55; and split between theory and research, 34

Academic field, 78n.19, 100–101, 102, 105; barriers to entry in, 75; bias in, 39; contradictions in, 89–90; distance from, 45

Academic space: as site of struggle, 70–71, 254

Actes de la recherche en sciences sociales, 57, 57n.105, 65, 65n.7, 238

Aden d'Arabie (Nizan), 209

Aesthetics, 5, 87–88, 88n.33, 263; and philosophy, 153–55; and *scholē,* 88

"Against War" (Bourdieu et al.), 56n.102

Agency, 3, 3n.3; in rational action theory, 123; in social phenomenology, 9

Agent, 7, 8–9, 19, 49, 70, 97, 129–30, 130n.84; as bearers of capital, 108–9; complicity with symbolic violence, 167–68, 168n.122; determinations of, 105, 168; and determinism, 136–37; as different from subject, 20–22, 107, 121–22, 137, 140; as different from the individual, 19, 107; domination and, 52; and economy, 124, 124n.78; in a field, 100–102, 101n.52, 102n.55, 105, 107, 232, 257; habitus and, 18, 105, 120–21, 123–24; and history, 123–24, 139; ideology and, 250–51; and lines of action, 129, 129n.83; in praxeology, 11; and rules, 115; and schemata, 12,

13; and social reality, 10, 127–28, 128n.82; and social reproduction, 139–40; and social space, 214–15; strategy and, 256, 258; struggle of, 48, 69. *See also* Biography

Algeria 1960 (Bourdieu), 124n.78, 263–64

The Algerians (Bourdieu), 46n.83, 54n.99

"The Algerian Subproletariate" (Bourdieu), 137n.91

Algerian war of liberation, 45, 45n.81

Alienation, 201

Alien (Scott), 201

Analogy, homology and, 233–34

Annual Review of Sociology, 237n.28

Anthropology, 4, 70, 117, 159, 229, 248; and reflexivity, 41–42, 41n.72, 42n.74

Anticipation, 152

Antinomies, 3, 13, 15, 15n.27, 23, 75, 188–89; rejection of, 10–11, 10n.19; resilience of, 178–79, 181–82; scientific, 181

Antinomy, 172; of historicity, 156n.112; of pedagogy of research, 249

Apparatus, 102, 102n.53

Arbitrariness: of capital, 119; cultural, 170, 172–73

Art, 85, 87; analogy with sociology, 219–21, 220n.3; as an object, 85–86; and class, 87–88; social conditions of possibility, 86–87. *See also* Gaze: artistic

321